Collecting in the Icon Age

Paul Wilson · Peter Tolmie

Collecting in the Icon Age

IT's Impact on Collecting Practices

Springer

Paul Wilson
Lavendon, Olney, UK

Peter Tolmie
Department of Information Systems
University of Siegen
Siegen, Germany

ISBN 978-3-031-86469-8 ISBN 978-3-031-86470-4 (eBook)
https://doi.org/10.1007/978-3-031-86470-4

This Springer imprint is published by the registered company Springer Nature Switzerland AG
The registered company address is: Gewerbestrasse 11, 6330 Cham, Switzerland

Competing Interests The authors have no competing interests to declare that are relevant to the content of this manuscript.

Contents

Abbreviations

2D	Two Dimensional
3D	Three Dimensional
AD	Anno Domini
AI	Artificial Intelligence
AIP	Archival Information Package
AR	Augmented Reality
BBC	British Broadcasting Corporation
BCE	Before Common Era
CAVE	Cave Automatic Virtual Environment
CD	Compact Disc
CD-ROM	Compact Disc Read Only Memory
CE	Common Era
CSCW	Computer-Supported Cooperative Work
CT	Computerized tomography
DCC	Digital Curation Centre
DIP	Dissemination Information Package
DMS	Document Management System
DNA	Deoxyribonucleic acid
DPLA	Digital Public Library of America
DT	Digital Technology
DVD	Digital Video Disc
GB	Gigabyte
GUI	Graphical User Interface
HD	Hard Disc Drive
ICA	International Council on Archives
ICO	Information Carrier Object
IETF	Internet Engineering Task Force
iOS	iPhone Operating System
IoT	Internet of Things
ISO	International Organisation for Standardization
IT	Information Technology

IWM	Imperial War Museum
JSTOR	Journal Storage
LLM	Large Language Model
LODLAM	Linked Open Data for Libraries, Archives, and Museums
LP	Long Playing Record
MA	Metaverse AI
MARC	Machine Readable Cataloguing Record
MO	Magneto-Optical Disc
MODS	Metadata Object Description Schema
MR	Mixed Reality
MS	Microsoft
MSF	Metaverse Standards Forum
NARA	US National Archives and Records Administration
NAS	Networked Attached Storage
NASA	US National Aeronautics and Space Administration
NFT	Non-Fungible Token
OA	Office Automation
OAI	Open Archive Initiative
OAIS	Open Archival Information System
OCR	Optical Character Recognition
OFC	Order From Chaos
OMI	Open Metaverse Interoperability Group
ORA	Orientation, Reasoning, and Assumptions
P&C	Process and Challenges
PC	Personal Computer
PMH	Protocol for Metadata Harvesting
RFID	Radio Frequency Identification
RM	Research Material
SIP	Submission Information Package
SSD	Solid-State Drive
TV	Television
URI	Uniform Resource Identifier
VR	Virtual Reality
WWW	World Wide Web
XR	Extended Reality

Chapter 1
The Icon Age and Collecting Practices—A Primer

Abstract This book is focused on how people in different settings go about creating and maintaining collections. Collecting has featured in human practice for aeons but is now being reshaped by technology. We term this new era 'The Icon Age' because objects in computer systems are largely represented by icons on screens. We define collecting and describe some of the principal ways in which it has been considered, including: what motivates collectors; the types of objects collected; the types of collectors; the academic study of collecting; and the collecting sciences. We provide a more detailed description of what is meant by the Icon Age and how it came about through the introduction of the graphical user interface in the 1980s. Inspired by ethnomethodology, our own findings are derived from investigations into a variety of different types of collections. Ethnomethodology involves looking at what people in particular settings are actually doing to get things done and how they organise manage, use, and reason about their activities. Finally, we outline how the book is organised and the content of its chapters.

This book is about collecting and collecting practices and, more specifically, about how collecting practices have been reshaped by the use of computing technology by a large percentage of the world's population. The new era associated with this change in technology we have named 'the Icon Age' because it is one in which objects in computer systems are largely represented to their users by icons displayed on a screen. This is of central concern in collecting because it is objects upon which collecting activities are focused. A more detailed explanation of 'the Icon Age' is given below.

However, collecting is an age-old human activity and much has been written about it, so it seems appropriate to reflect first of all on its status prior to the emergence of the Icon Age, as this will help with assessing the impact of the new technology. Please bear in mind that it is not our intention to provide a detailed exposition of all of the prior work on this topic. Instead, we aim to provide more of a backdrop against which those aspects of collecting which have been impacted by the Icon Age can be discussed later in the book.

P. Wilson and P. Tolmie, *Collecting in the Icon Age*,
https://doi.org/10.1007/978-3-031-86470-4_1

1.1 Collecting

Like many people, the authors of this book have a wide variety of collecting experiences. We have record collections, we file documents, we have kitchens full of crockery and pans and food stuffs, we collect items such as stamps, books and sheet music, and we visit museums and libraries. So, what is it about all of these things that connects them to something we might describe as collecting? What appears to have motivated people to collect things down the ages? What kind of impact does collecting have on people's lives? What sorts of things get collected? Who are the people who do collecting? How is collecting understood as an activity, culturally and scientifically? And are there identifiable patterns in how collecting is pursued? We explore all of these questions a little further below.

1.1.1 Definitions

There are many definitions of collecting to be found in the literature. For example, Belk in *Collecting in a Consumer Society* suggests that:

> Collecting is the process of actively, selectively, and passionately acquiring and possessing things removed from ordinary use and perceived as part of a set of non-identical objects or experiences (Belk 1995).

This would seem to exclude things like files and kitchen stuff. However, he does qualify the definition by saying that.

> Accumulating does not preclude a consumer from imposing or finding a unifying principle for items accumulated and then proceeding to add to the resulting collection according to this principle; by so doing an accumulation can become a collection (Belk 1995).

In contrast to this, Macdonald offers a rather broader view:

> ... it is analytically useful to distinguish "collecting" as a self-aware process of creating a set of objects conceived to be meaningful as a group. Exactly how "groupness" is perceived is not the defining matter: collecting is as much about creating a rationale as filling it (Macdonald 2006).

Even broader definitions are provided by Aristides, Alsop and Pearce:

> An obsession organized (Aristides 1988).
>
> To collect is to gather objects belonging to a particular category the collector happens to fancy…and a collection is what has been gathered (Alsop 1982).
>
> For Pearce, … the best definition of a collection is simply that a collection exists if its owner thinks it does (Pearce 1998).

However, perhaps it is Andrew Dillon who best summarises the position we have taken in this book:

> Collecting may best be considered on a continuum stretching from consumer to hoarder, covering all humankind, with most of us situated somewhere between the extremes and shifting on this continuum depending on the material objects we are considering at any moment in our lives. (Dillon 2019).

1.1.2 Motivations

One of the prime questions researchers have concerned themselves with is 'Why do people collect?'. A very early text on collecting—*Lock, Stock & Barrel: The story of Collecting* (Rigby and Rigby 1944)—gives four key motivations: physical security (collecting food and materials for shelter); distinction (providing recognition of achievement); immortality (being passed on after death, perhaps bearing the owners name); and knowledge/aesthetic satisfaction (*op. cit*). Another way of expressing aesthetic motivations is that people like the things they collect—even have a passion for them (Formanek 1991). They enjoy being with their objects, looking at them, caring for them and handling them (Belk 1995; Danet and Katriel 1989). People also become very attached to their collections and somehow see them as an extension of themselves (Belk 1995; Pearce 1995b). Beyond this, people often associate memories with objects in their collections—particularly collections of items associated with their own past (Belk 1995; Pearce 1995b).

The ability to set their own rules for their collections and to be able to seek out and obtain desired, missing, or rare objects can provide collectors with feelings of control, mastery, success, completion and closure (Belk 1995; Pearce 1995a, 1995b; Muensterberger 1994; Danet and Katriel 1989). People also like the way collecting enables them to mix with like-minded people, to have the kudos of being known as a collector, and to receive the interest, admiration and praise given them by other people (Belk 1995; Pearce 1995b; Muensterberger 1994). Perhaps the ultimate motivation is that a collection to some people may act as a monument to them after their death, enabling them to live on and endowing them with a kind of immortality (Belk 1995; Pearce 1995b; Rigby and Rigby 1944).

There has also been an extensive literature investigating psychoanalytical motivations for collecting, many of which have been based on Freud's biological drive model (Formanek 1991), for example, Baudrillard's *The System of Objects* (1968); and Muensterberger's *Collecting: An unruly passion* (1994). Some of this material explores the notion that collecting is motivated by childhood experiences and sexual experience or repression (Macdonald 2006). However, Pearce, while not entirely discounting such views, prefers to consider collecting to be just an integral part of human personality and more likely to be associated with a passion for possession (Pearce 1995b). Elsewhere, Pearce writes

> As a serious attempt to explain the social phenomenon of collecting as a whole, the notion of anal retention is best taken with a dose of salts (Pearce 1995b).

Pearce also discusses the literature on the fetishist nature of collecting objects, whereby the collector's focus is on the object itself rather than any associated social relationships. Here, she points out that:

> Psychologists use the word to describe a particular form of sexual orientation, unfortunately in many ways, because it is this that has given a useful idea an uncomfortable feel (Pearce 1994b).

More recently, Dillon notes that contemporary psychoanalytic work has reduced the emphasis on childhood trauma as a driving force for collecting and instead concentrates more on the sense of control and knowledge of the world that it provides (Dillon 2019).

Another particularly influential work which attempts to explain mankind's desire to '*collect, organise and conserve the human record*' is Derrida's *Archive Fever: A Freudian Impression.* This posits two conflicting forces. One is a death drive, and the other is a conservation or archive drive that is linked to the pleasure principle (Manof 2004; Derrida 1995). However, Formanek records that an alternative to the Freudian view of collecting has emerged which focuses more on the relationship with other people and with the '*development of a healthy, cohesive, stable sense of self*' (Formanek 1991).

1.1.3 Positive and Negative Effects

Given that collecting seems to be a widespread activity among humans, some have been concerned with whether it is a force for good or ill. A good overview of the research on this question is provided by Belk (1995). He and others note the positive effects to be:

- Success in competition with other collectors further enhances prestige and feelings of self-esteem.
- Collectors may develop a sense of fellowship with other collectors.
- Collectors have saved innumerable works of art, books, and historical treasures that would otherwise have been lost.
- After a lifetime of collecting, the objects of a collection may serve as memory cues for a lifetime of experiences.

Possible negative effects include:

- Obsessive, compulsive, or addictive collecting behaviours.
- Rechannelling a collector's attention away from their family because of the individual and private nature of most collecting with, in extreme cases, the collector becoming a virtual recluse.
- When the collector can be seen as being driven or controlled by the collection rather than controlling it, we are likely to judge the boundary into fetishism to have been crossed.

- Some collectors may be labelled manic hoarders or Accumulators rather than collectors.

On this last point, in the next chapter it will be found that we use the term 'Accumulators' to cover a particular set of collecting practices. We should make it clear here that our use of the word does not include manic or compulsive hoarding activities, which are a distinct psychological condition referred to as Hoarding Disorder (HD) (Edwards et al. 2023). We do not address HD collecting in this book.

1.1.4 Types of Objects Collected

Objects are fundamental to collecting. If there are no objects, there is no collecting. This is an obvious point—but a very significant one with respect to the subject of this book. That is not just because digital technology provides new tools to support collecting practices; but crucially, *it introduces new types of objects that can be collected.*

There is a variety of literature describing the types of things that people collect, and much of it makes no reference to IT. For example, Danet and Katriel distinguish between ephemeral experiences that are collected, such as jokes and proverbs, and Material Objects. The latter may be animate (perhaps collections of chickens or fish), or inanimate; and the inanimate objects might be either objects from the natural world such as shells or rocks; or be manufactured artefacts such as sculptures or helmets (Danet and Katriel 1989).

Danet and Katriel also note that collected objects are experienced aesthetically, and they distinguish between aesthetic objects by destination (such as tapestries, paintings, and jewellery) and those that become aesthetic objects by metamorphosis (such as chocolate wrappers and postage stamps) (*op. cit.*).

Another way of categorising objects is in terms of transients, rubbish and durables. According to Thompson (2017), *durables* have increasing value and infinite expected lifetimes; whereas *transients* have decreasing value and finite expected lifespans, at which point they become *rubbish*. Then, sometimes, they are retrieved and turned into *durables* (such as vintage glass bottles).

The choices that collectors make when deciding what to collect depend on a complicated mix of factors including the social culture they move in, their own personal interests, and the characteristics of the objects concerned (Pearce 1995b). Sometimes, the perceived value and/or rarity of objects enters the calculations—but sometimes not. Imperfections may be desirable (as in a stamp misprint) but sometimes not (as in a book with a price-clipped dustjacket) (Danet and Katriel 1989). As collectors specialise and narrow the overall scope of their collections, they often focus on more detailed features of the category of objects concerned. At the end of the day, however, it is the collector who decides (Pearce 1995b); and it is clear that, overall, they choose to collect a huge range of different things. Indeed, Pomian goes so far as to say that:

> …every natural object known to man and every artefact, however strange, will show up somewhere in the world as part of a museum or private collection (Pomian 1990).

1.1.5 *Types of Collectors*

Collecting related to accumulating the essentials of life such as food, clothing, shelter, and farming activities, has been carried out by most humans from time immemorial. However, the collecting of more aesthetic treasures, such as jewellery, sculptures, pottery and books, was originally strictly in the domain of the ruling classes and the wealthy. There are good indications that large quantities of such items were assembled by early civilisations in China, India, Sumeria, Egypt, Crete, Assyria, Babylonia, and Persia—particularly in their temples (Rigby and Rigby1944). In contemporary society, however, with a wider distribution of wealth and leisure time, more people have started to be able to collect such items (Belk 1995); though, of course, the more valuable pieces are still only accessible to wealthier individuals. The same appears to be true of institutions—the wealthier they are, the more likely they are to collect luxury goods. Belk notes that:

> Prominent types of institutional collections have included religious, royal, commercial, governmental, and non-commercial business collections, in approximately that sequence of historical emergence (Belk 1995).

Regarding the scale of collecting across populations, twentieth-century American studies seem to suggest that, by the end of the century, at least a third of Americans had at least one active collection, with this affecting over 60% of households and there being an overall average of 2.6 collections per household (Belk 1995). A British 1993 survey of contemporary collecting, which had about 900 respondents, established a similar figure of about one third of people having one or more collections. Here, about 42% of the collectors were men and 58% women. The split by age group was: 18–25, 23%; 26–35, 22%; 36–45, 22%; 46–55, 13%; 56–65, 15%; and 65+, 8% (Pearce 1998). Belk notes that:

> Nearly all Western children collect, and boys and girls are equally likely to be avid collectors before their teenage years. During adolescence collecting declines for both sexes, but especially for girls (Belk 1995).

Regardless of whether they collected when they were young, many men start collecting in middle age when their finances and family have been firmly established and they are looking for new challenges (Ackerman 1990).

1.1.6 *Collecting's Cultural Landscape*

A vast infrastructure of clubs, societies, magazines, media programmes, dealers, fairs, and auctions supports the collecting public. Large numbers of books have been, and continue to be, published about different types of collecting, about specific collections and collectors, and about the history of collecting institutions (Pearce 1995b; Danet and Katriel 1989). Dealers and auction houses play an important role for the more conventional types of collected objects such as art works, jewellery and books. Indeed, some collectors may rely on a particular dealer to acquire the objects they desire (Muensterberger 1994).

Alongside of this, there is an infrastructure to underpin the protection of collectors. Demand has always encouraged fakery and exploitation; from the Egyptians to middle age religious relic forgers, to contemporary forgers of paintings (Jones 1990). To combat forgery, collectors are able to draw on the knowledge of a wide range of experts, some with professional qualifications (as in the art world) and some simply acknowledged as such within their fields.

Pearce alerts us to one other phenomenon signifying how embedded collecting has become in modern life, namely the increasing presence of collections, collecting, and collecting institutions in works of fiction. She provides several examples, including Fowles' *The Collector* (1963), Moore's *The Great Victorian Collection* (1975), Eco's *Foucault's Pendulum* (1989), and Byatt's *Possession* (1990) (Pearce 1995b). This is equally the case in cinema and television and spanning multiple genres, ranging from horror (e.g., The Collector (2009)), to documentary (for instance, Koleksiyoncu: The Collector (2002); Herb and Dorothy (2008); and Rewind This! (2013), to comedy (such as the recent British TV series, Detectorists (2014).

1.1.7 The Cycle of Collecting

In a world with so many collectors of such a diverse range of things, it would be unlikely for there to be a standard collecting lifecycle. Nevertheless, there are some practices which almost all collectors undertake. To begin with, the collection has to be started. This may occur in a whole variety of ways, including an individual inheriting family heirlooms, by putting souvenirs in a drawer (Pearce 1995a), by being given gifts (Pearce 1995b), or even by looting—a practice that was perhaps more common in ancient times (Casson 2001), but that still occurs today.

Having started a collection, the collector is likely to establish some sort of routine for including new items (Belk 1995). This may involve the ordering or classification of the items concerned—even if only reflected in their placement in their storage location (Pearce 1995b). This activity can become very sophisticated involving comprehensive numbering, labelling, and indexing of both the objects concerned and the storage or display facilities (Kohler 2007). These practices may be developed over time as new items are acquired. The collector is likely to become more attached to the collection as it expands and, at some point may decide to specialise (Pearce 1995b).

Eventually, there will be an end to the collection. This may occur for a variety of reasons. In the case of individual collectors, they may just lose interest and let the collection gather dust in a cupboard or box. This often occurs among younger people (Belk 1995). A more catastrophic reason for collections to come to an end is if their contents are stolen or destroyed through some natural catastrophe. For individuals, this can cause an intense sense of loss and feelings of agony and anger (Pearce 1995b). However, assuming that theft does not occur, and the collection is not destroyed by fire or flood, collections may be disposed of through lack of interest, organisational change, economic necessity, or, in the case of individuals, old age. In the latter circumstance, many collectors endeavour to pass their collection to younger members of their family, either directly or as a stipulation in a will. More ambitious collectors may try to get a museum or other institution to take it on (Pearce 1995b).

1.1.8 The Academic Study of Collecting

Danet and Katriel (1989) note that there was very little academic research into collecting until the mid-1980s. Up until then any related research had been mainly undertaken under the Material Culture label, which had emerged alongside the development of anthropology and archaeology in the mid-nineteenth century (Pearce 1994a). However, a sudden burst of interest in collecting in the mid-1980s followed by the establishment of the *Journal of the History of Collecting* in 1989 (Macdonald 2006), signified the emergence of the new field of Collection Studies which addresses three main topics: (a) collection policies; (b) the history of collections and of collecting; and (c) the nature of the collections themselves and the reasons why people collect (Pearce 1994b, 1998). The background to this development, and the research and papers which contributed to it, are described in some detail by Susan Pearce in her book *On Collecting* (1995b)—itself a manifestation of the new field. Indeed, the combination of Pearce's various publications between 1994 and 1998, and Belk's (1995) book, *Collecting in a Consumer Society*, both heavily referenced in this chapter, seem to provide a comprehensive manifesto for this new focus on collecting. It seems an interesting coincidence that this should emerge just shortly after the time we pinpoint for the start of the Icon Age.

Among the various approaches taken to studying the artefacts in collections, Pearce notes that a classic statement of the approach that the working material culturalist was using every day had emerged from the study of Gravestones in New England in the 1960s (Deetz and Dethlefsen 1967). Pearce summarises the technique as dating, seriation, diffusion, typology, and style classification (Pearce 1994d). Another approach to interpreting meaning from objects is to identify: (a) its function and the effect it has on the world; (b) its type and general classification within a particular set of objects; and (c) its history and past associations (Hodder 1994). An example of an historical interpretation could be of a tribal cultural object which might be seen variously as: commodity; artefact; specimen; art; someone else's heirloom; treasured cultural heritage; or sacred emblem (Ames 1991). In yet another analytical perspective, Pearce suggests investigating the material of the object (raw material, design, construction, and technology); its history (function and use); the environment it is located in (spatial relationships); and its significance (emotional or psychological messages) (Pearce 1994c). Beyond this, another perspective on the academic study of collecting is 'objectification'. The goal here is to examine how consumers recontextualise objects and their component parts, to give them meanings that fit in with their own identities and social environments. An illustration of how such notions provide insights into collecting is provided in an investigation of collectors of Melissa brand plastic shoes (Scaraboto et al. 2016).

1.1.9 The Collecting Sciences

Another important part of the overall landscape of collecting is the collecting sciences. These are sciences that typically collect specimens from the field and analyse, interpret and store them. Associated fields of study include palaeontology (the study of fossils), natural history (the study of plants, animals, rocks, etc.), ethnology (the study of different societies and cultures), and archaeology (the study of the buildings, graves, tools, and other objects that belonged to people who lived in the past) (Cambridge Dictionary 2023). All such sciences depend on collecting artefacts from the field and therefore have developed rigorous procedures for finding, selecting, extracting, recording, and transporting objects from field to storage. Typically, such collections grow increasingly large and consequently classification has become an important element in how these fields not only understand artefacts but also manage large volumes of items, keep them in order, and make them accessible to researchers and, in some cases, to the general public. These kinds of collections are typically retained for the long term, if not indefinitely, and therefore preservation techniques may have to be applied to prevent the deterioration of some types of specimens (Kohler 2007).

1.2 Collecting in the Icon Age

On 7th June 1983, Paul Wilson, one of the authors of this book, was attending the Office Automation show in the Barbican in London and he came across the Apple stand with lots of people crowding round it. He found a spot where he could see what was going on and stayed there quite a time, mesmerised, watching a demonstration of Apple's Lisa machine. What he was seeing was very, very different to the prevailing command line interfaces in the modern personal computer. LISA was an £8,500 desktop computer which used a MOUSE device to move the cursor round the screen, and which made heavy use of pictures (ICONS) on the screen to help users know what they were doing and to select commands. He wrote later:

> You will not be able to comprehend the potential of this machine until you have seen a demonstration by an experienced user. But then you will realise that the office systems we've been messing around with up to now have been crude (Wilson 2025).

The following year, 1984, Apple introduced the Macintosh with a similar graphical user interface (GUI) and a price tag some £6000 cheaper (Wilson 1984), and proceeded to sell over 250,000 during the next 12 months (Macro 2014). The Icon Age had taken off.

Apple hadn't invented the GUI. It had gradually emerged over the preceding 15 years or so, reputedly starting with Sutherland's 1962 sketchpad system with a CRT display and a light pen and control board (Greengard 2019); followed by Doug Engelbart's ARC system in the late 1960s, which included the first use of a mouse device for a computer (Thompson 2007). In the early 1970s, the Xerox Palo Alto Research Centre had built an experimental workstation—the Alto—and included many of the elements of a GUI. The experience gained in this development was used to produce its Xerox Star system in 1981, but with a price tag of $100,000 it was not a commercial success (Sirk 2020; Thompson 2007). Furthermore, a product that potentially reduced the use of paper in offices, was probably not what the management of Xerox—a business which largely revolved around the use of paper—was particularly excited by. Consequently, many of the Star project team members left the company—some of them joining Apple. In the meantime, Steve Jobs was interested in using GUIs in his line of Apple computers, and engineered a visit to Xerox PARC to see what they were doing (Sirk 2020). A few years later, first Lisa, and then the Macintosh, emerged, both with a GUI containing images, or icons, of objects that users would normally interact with in an office including documents, stationery pads, folders, and a wastebasket (Birss 1984), adopting, in other words, the so-called desktop metaphor (Johnson 1987).

So, although the GUI and icons had been around for a good few years, it wasn't until the early 1980s that they started to become widely known to the general public; and it is this emergence which we are deeming to be the start of the 'Icon Age' referred to in the title of this volume.

From then, it didn't take long for the manufacturers of personal computers and their customers to realise that the GUI was significantly easier to use than a command line interface. The major supplier of personal computer operating systems at that time—Microsoft—issued its first Windows GUI in 1985 and followed that up with a series of upgrades—Windows98, Windows 2000, Windows XP, and Vista, in which the GUI eventually became an integral part of the operating system (Thompson 2007). Both Microsoft and Apple continue to be the major suppliers of personal computer operating systems in 2025, and both continue to front their products with icon-based GUIs.

The embedding of the icon-based interface was further cemented in the worldwide human psyche with the arrival of the iPhone in 2007 with its app icons, touch screen, and multi-touch gestures such as swipe and pinch (Verstraete 2014). It was reported that in 2024 there were more than 1.2 billion active iPhones in use in the world (Wise 2024a). The Android phone operating system which also sports an icon-based interface had even more users—some 3 billion active devices in 2024 (Wise 2024b). So, it seems that more than half of mankind's 8 billion people in 2024 were familiar with and using an icon-based interface. This is the Icon Age in which the practice of collecting is being performed.

1.3 Our Interests and Their Pursuit

Fundamentally, this book is interested in examining how people in different types of settings and with different ends in mind go about creating and maintaining collections. More specifically, it is interested in how the everyday activities of collecting have been affected by the onset of the Icon Age.

In order to accomplish this investigation, we have adopted a certain research ethos, and this has given a particular flavour to its outcomes. This ethos is founded primarily upon the view that, to understand collecting and how it has been transformed by the Icon Age, it is necessary to understand: (a) how exactly it is done; (b) the situations in which it is done; and (c) the character of the things upon which it is exercised.

To realise this programme of research, a range of materials that capture people's collecting practices and their associated contexts and objects of interest were assembled under the auspices of what has come to be termed in certain quarters an 'ethnomethodologically informed' approach (Hughes et al. 1992). Ethnomethodology, as the word suggests, is focused upon identifying the ethno-methods adopted by people to do the things they do. To put this into context, the central premise of ethnomethodology is that the world is made orderly by the people who inhabit it; it is not the outcome of some theoretical grand narrative. Thus, to understand what is going on in any particular setting, you look first and foremost at what the people in the setting are doing themselves to make things proceed in an orderly and mutually intelligible fashion. This necessarily implies that researchers need to embed themselves in the setting and to acquire insight into how people in the setting reason about their affairs and account for them to one another. Harold Garfinkel, the founding father of ethnomethodology, insisted that an elaboration of the 'accountable' character of social interaction (i.e., accountable to members of the self-same setting) is the central pillar of an ethnomethodological approach:

> Elaborating the accountable character of social interaction is central to ethnomethodological studies (Garfinkel 1967). In place of generalised versions of social order, ethnomethodology seeks to elaborate the social order in lived details of the incarnate organisation of social interaction—i.e., in details of its situated, embodied, and material character as it is made observable and reportable in local circumstances by the particular parties to it for the practical purposes of the work they are collaboratively engaged in 'here and now' (Benford et al. 2012).

For the purposes of this particular book, a focus upon how social activities are brought about implies a certain orientation to the research data, with the constant aim being to uncover features of how collections are organised, managed, and used and, in particular, how the collections themselves, their contents, and the practices surrounding their constitution, are reasoned about. It should also be noted that this approach to the study of people's activities has now become mainstream in certain domains, such as Human–Computer Interaction and Computer-Supported Cooperative Work (CSCW) (Randall et al. 2021). More specific detail about just how this approach was applied in practice is given in Chap. 3.

1.4 How This Book Is Organised

As noted above, this book is focused upon people's practices in the very diverse field of collecting, the contexts in which they pursue those practices, and, by necessity, the objects to which those practices relate. By adopting the approach outlined above, our investigations came to recognise that people's practices may be manifested in different ways when engaged in different strands of collecting, so we have elected to identify those types of people and to refer to them throughout this text. They are Accumulators, Librarians, Filers, Archivists, Museum and Gallery Curators, Private Curators, and Amateur Collectors. We have labelled these diverse perspectives 'Collecting Contexts', and describe what they are, and provide short histories of each, in Chap. 2.

The authors have been steered towards their wide-ranging views of collecting by an examination of their own diverse range of collections and other collecting practices they have studied, so these are described in Chap. 3. It became clear along the way that the practices associated with each context had certain shared characteristics, so these were compiled into an overall collecting Practice Hierarchy. This is presented in Chap. 4. The impact that the Icon Age has so far had on each of these practices is then examined in Chap. 5.

With these foundations in place, Chap. 6 steps back to consider the nature of the objects that are central to collecting. The affordances and features of these objects are then identified, and the impact of the Icon Age on them is examined. Chapter 7 then re-examines the collecting contexts described in Chap. 2 and highlights the overall impact that the Icon Age has had on those broad domains. Chapter 8 explores the notion that IT has introduced a growing uniformity of IT practices across different collecting contexts and across time and space. Chapter 9 wraps up the volume by looking beyond the Icon Age to see what technology developments might emerge in the future and how they might affect collecting downstream. Finally, Chap. 10 provides a closing summary of the principal messages contained in the book.

References

Ackerman PH (1990) On collecting: a psychoanalytic view. Maine Antique Dig 1990:22A–24A

Alsop J (1982) The rare art traditions: a history of collecting and its linked phenomena. Harper and Row, New York

Ames M (1991) Cannibal tours, glass boxes and the politics of interpretation. In: Ames M (ed) Cannibal tours and glass boxes: the anthropology of Museums. University of British Columbia Press, Canada, pp 139–150

ARISTIDES (1988) Life and letters: calm and uncollected. Am Sch 53(3):327–336

Baudrillard J (1968) The system of objects. Verso, London

Belk RW (1995) Collecting in a consumer society. Routledge

Benford S, Tolmie P, Ahmed AY, Crabtree A, Rodden T (2012) Supporting traditional music-making: designing for situated discretion. In: Proceedings of the ACM 2012 conference on Computer Supported Cooperative Work, p 127–136

Birss EW (1984) The integrated software and user interface of Apple's Lisa. In: Fraily DJ (ed) Proceedings of the national computer conference AFIPS'84, July 9–12, 1984. Association for computing machinery, New York, pp 319–28
Byatt AS (1990) Possession. Chatto and Windus
Cambridge Dictionary (2023) Definitions of palaeontology, natural history, ethnology, archaeology. https://dictionary.cambridge.org/dictionary/english/. Accessed 26 March 2023
Casson L (2001) Libraries in the ancient world. Yale University Press
Danet B, Katriel T (1989) No two alike: play and aesthetics in collecting. Play Cult 2(3):255–71
Deetz J, Dethlefsen ES (1967) Death's head, cherub, urn and willow. Nat Hist 76(1967):29–37
Derrida J (1995) Archive fever: a freudian impression. Prenowitz E (transl). University of Chicago Press, Chicago and London
Detectorists (2014) [TV Series] Crook M (dir) Channel X(UK), Lola Entertainment
Dillon A (2019) Collecting as routine human behavior: personal identity and control in the material and digital world. Inf Cult 54(3):255–280
Eco U (1989) Foucault's pendulum. Secker and Warburg, London
Edwards V, Salkovskis PM, Bream V (2023) Do they really care? Specificity of social support issues in hoarding disorder and obsessive–compulsive disorder. Br J Clin Psychol 62(3):573–591
Formanek R (1991) Why they collect: collectors reveal their motivations. J Soc Behav Pers 6(6):275–286
Fowles J (1963) The collector. Jonathan Cape
Garfinkel H (1967) Studies in ethnomethodology. Prentice-Hall, Englewood Cliffs
Greengard S (2019) Virtual reality. The MIT Press
Herb and Dorothy (2008). [Film]. Sasaki M (dir) Fine line media
Hodder I (1994) The contextual analysis of symbolic meanings. In: Pearce SM (ed) Interpreting objects and collections. Routledge, Chapter 2
Hughes JA, Randall D, Shapiro D (1992) Faltering from ethnography to design. In: Proceedings of the 1992 ACM conference on computer-supported cooperative work, CSCW 1992, Toronto, Canada, 1–4 November 1992. ACM Press, pp 115–122
Johnson J (1987) How faithfully should the electronic office simulate the real one? ACM SIGCHI Bull 19(2):21
Jones M (1990) Why fakes? In: Jones M (ed) Fake? The art of deception. British Museum Publications Ltd, London, pp 11–16
Kohler RE (2007) Finders, keepers: collecting sciences and collecting practices. Hist Sci 45(4):428–454
Koleksiyoncu. The Collector (2002) [Film]. Beaudin J (dir) Christal Films
Macdonald S (2006) Collecting practices. In: Macdonald S (ed) A companion to museum studies. Blackwell Publishing Ltd, pp 81–97
Macro A (2014) The Mac in numbers: surprising apple stats. Macworld, 21st Feb 2023. https://www.macworld.com/article/670960/the-mac-in-numbers-surprising-apple-stats.html. Accessed 28 Feb 2023
Manof M (2004) Theories of the archive from across the disciplines. Portal Libr Acad 4(1):9–25
Moore B (1975) The Great Victorian collection. Jonathan Cape
Muensterberger W (1994) Collecting: an unruly passion. Princeton University Press
Pearce SM (1994a) Introduction. In: Pearce SM (ed) Interpreting objects and collections. Routledge, pp 1–6
Pearce SM (1994b) Collecting reconsidered. In: Pearce SM (ed) Interpreting objects and collections. Routledge, pp 193–204
Pearce SM (1994c) Thinking about things. In: Pearce SM (ed) Interpreting objects and collections. Routledge, pp 125–132
Pearce SM (1994d) Commentary at the start of Chapter 5 (Deetz J and Dethlefsen's paper on Death's head, cherub, urn and willow). In: Pearce SM (ed) Interpreting objects and collections. Routledge

Pearce SM (1995a) Collecting as medium and message. In: Hooper-Greenhill E (ed) Museum, media, message. Routledge, (reprinted 2001), pp 15–23
Pearce SM (1995b) On collecting. Routledge
Pearce SM (1998) Collecting in contemporary practice. Sage Publications
Pomian K (1990) The collection: between the visible and the invisible. Collectors and curiosities. Polity, Oxford, pp 6–25
Randall D, Rouncefield M, Tolmie P (2021) Ethnography, CSCW and ethnomethodology. Comput Support Coop Work (CSCW) 30:189–214
Rewind This! (2013) [Film] Johnson J (dir) Imperial PolyFarm productions
Rigby D, Rigby E (1944) Lock, stock and barrel: the story of collecting. Lippincott, Philadelphia, J.B
Scaraboto D, Ferreira MC, Chung E (2016) Materials matter: an exploration of the curatorial practices of consumers as collectors. Res Consum Cult Theory 18:217–243
Sirk C (2020) Xerox PARC and the origins of GUI. 12 June 2020, https://crm.org/articles/xerox-parc-and-the-origins-of-gui. Accessed 24 Nov 2022
The Collector (2009) [Film] Dunstan M (dir) LD entertainment, fortress features, imaginarium entertainment group
Thompson J (2007) Feel the depth. Personal computer world magazine, pp 63–69
Thompson M (2017) Rubbish theory—the creation and destruction of value, New. Pluto Press, London
Verstraete G (2014) Mapping the rise of the iPhone–between phones and mobile media. NECSUS. Eur J Media Stud 3(1):21–41
Wilson PA (1984) Information technology. The Ergonomist, The Ergonomics Society, March 1984, pp 3–4
Wilson PA (2025) Sorties into the IT Hurricane, 3rd edn. Self-published in Blurb, distributed by Ingram
Wise J (2024a) How many iPhones are there in 2024? (Models). https://earthweb.com/blog/how-many-iphones-are-there. Accessed 27 Nov 2024
Wise J (2024b) Android users: how many people use android phones in 2024? https://earthweb.com/blog/how-many-people-use-android. Accessed 27 Nov 2024

Chapter 2
Collecting Contexts

Abstract Collecting occurs in many different settings or contexts of use. Seven gross contexts are identified, according to their chief protagonists: Accumulators; Librarians; Filers; Archivists; Museum and Gallery Curators; Private Curators; and Amateur Collectors. The history of each context up to the start of the Icon Age is briefly described together with a working definition for each one. **Accumulators** started collecting food, cooking utensils and clothing thousands of years ago but have now become prolific collectors of consumer items. The first **libraries** emerged around 300O BCE. The arrival of the printing press in 1455 spurred the growth of the modern library. Factual information has been **filed** ever since writing started on clay tablets. However, the arrival of the vertical filing cabinet around 1900 formed the basis of modern ideas about filing. **Archives** provide long-term storage for files and other material for which there is no longer an immediate need. Churches and States have always amassed treasures; but the modern **museum/gallery** emerged from the culture of Wonder Cabinets displaying unusual and exotic items in the sixteenth and seventeenth centuries. Powerful people and organisations have also amassed **private** collections of treasures over the centuries. In contrast, the **Amateur** Collector is a more recent phenomenon—though in the twentyfirst century their numbers are huge and the range of objects they collect is vast.

Collecting is something that humans have been doing in all kinds of contexts since the early days of our evolution. As we are investigating collecting practices in this book, we have chosen to be open to a wide range of those contexts. There are two reasons for this: first, we believe that many practices may be manifested differently in different contexts; and, secondly, we believe Information Technology has had an impact on many, if not all, of those contexts—perhaps even bringing some of them closer together. We have labelled the contexts we will be incorporating in our investigations with the names of their chief protagonists: Accumulators; Librarians; Filers; Archivists; Museum and Gallery Curators; Private Curators; and Amateur Collectors. A brief description and history of each of them is provided in this chapter.

P. Wilson and P. Tolmie, *Collecting in the Icon Age*,
https://doi.org/10.1007/978-3-031-86470-4_2

2.1 Accumulators

Between 7 and 2 million years ago, our ancestors learned to walk on two legs which freed up their hands to carry food and tools (Heylighen 2023); and between one million and 300,000 years ago, we started using fire (Harari 2014). These two developments may have stimulated some of human's earliest collecting instincts by enabling them to accumulate food, hunting weapons, fire-making equipment, and cooking utensils. Here, we suggest that **Accumulators collect objects out of functional necessity and make use of the items in their collections**. Dillon takes a similar stance on Accumulators being collectors:

> Viewed this way, then, possessions, clothes, and consumption patterns render all of us collectors of some kind, with materials in our lives existing through phases of use and non-use, attended to periodically, with some garnering more or less of our attention as our lives unfold. Disposal is neither assured nor enacted for some objects, while others are used up, worn out, or discarded by active choice. (Dillon 2019).

Some of the earliest evidence of food accumulation practices has been found in archaeological sites dating from 13,000 to 9600 associated with the sedentary hunter-gatherer Natufian people in the Levant; and evidence of food storage pits from the period 9400–6600 BCE was found at a site in Shangshan in China in which the occupants appear to have systematically exploited nuts (acorns), wild cereals (rice), and water chestnuts. Remnants of pottery containers have been dated to 15,000–10,000 BCE for China, Japan, and Siberia, 9400 BCE for West Africa, and around 5500–5000 BCE for the Brazilian Amazon (de Saulieu and Testart 2015). These facts appear in a paper discussing the shift from hunter-gatherer to sedentary farmers. However, one extract from the paper also clearly illustrates the human propensity for accumulation:

> Inventing and diversifying pottery, increasing foraging with its ever more varied equipment (containers, stone mortars, baskets, fish nets and traps, drying racks, etc.), embarking on agriculture, starting to store food (in pits), all these remain, up to a point, compatible with a nomadic life. However, the multiplication of inventions and the accumulation of necessary equipment became increasingly burdensome. Mobility was thereby limited. People began to stay longer in one place. This increasing and almost enforced sedentarism of hunter-gatherers weighed down by their tools furthered their involvement in agriculture (op. cit.).

The extent of this multiplication of domestic objects in the period leading up to the end of pre-Christian era is illustrated by the contents of a book on household food storage in Ancient Israel and Judah from the Late Neolithic, through the Bronze Age to the Iron Age (approx. 3300 BCE to 500 BCE), where the foods, etc., stored included: dairy products; water; oil; wine; and grain. The associated artefacts that were also collected included: bowls; open kraters; closed kraters; jugs; decanters; juglets; flasks; cooking pots; cooking jugs; storage jars; ovoid jars; carinated jars; waisted jars; pithi; holemouth jars; small holemouth jars; spouted jars; pot stands; lamps; pounders; grindstones; querns; and clay loomweights (Frank 2018).

Clothes, too, are objects that most humans use and accumulate. It is thought that weaving and cord-making began as early as 40,000 BCE, and fabric has been found dating from 18,000 BCE in France. In those early days, evidence suggests that some people wore string skirts, elaborate caps and snoods for the head, and bandeaux for the chest (a series of straps that amounted to a cupless brassiere) (Angier 1999). In the Neolithic and Bronze ages, fabrics were probably produced on warp-weighted looms. One such loom, dating from 3100 BCE, was found in Austria. The loomweights were found in three rows parallel to the wall of a pit house (Grömer 2016). Estimates of how many clothes individuals in Europe would have had in the pre-Roman era, around 500 BCE, are based on the number of fibula (a brooch used for fastening garments) found in graves. The largest number was found in a Swiss cemetery indicating that the lady concerned had about 13 peploi (a tubular cloth garment) (op. cit.).

The Neolithic, Bronze, and Iron Ages were also the era in which metallurgy became more pervasive and in which large quantities of jewellery and weapons were produced and accumulated. The jewellery worn included very long dress pins, massive tiaras, wide metal belts, leg rings, and large sets of ornaments worn on the chest. The weapons included axes, daggers—subsequently replaced by swords for personal man-to-man combat, and protective armour and helmets. Such items were often included in grave sites or buried as separate hoards. For example, in the Unetice Culture in the Prague region, many bronze hoards have been found (perhaps indicating a need to keep one's accumulations safe), as well as large quantities of jewellery (Grömer 2016). The rationale for depositing such hoards has been the subject of much debate. What is of no doubt is that the items constituting a hoard had first to be accumulated and brought together (Joy 2016). Grave sites excavated around the world have produced some of the most spectacular accumulations of goods, including the numerous and diverse objects found in Tutankhamun's magnificent tomb dated around 1,350 BCE (Hoving 1979), and the huge accumulation of terracotta replicas of people, horses, and other artefacts in China's extraordinary Qin Shi Huang mausoleum from around 200 BCE (Portal 2007). It should be noted that we have classed all these types of activities as instances of accumulating simply because there is a lack of knowledge about the motivations and practices surrounding them. Many so-called hoards could equally be the result of many years of deliberate collecting by individuals, groups or organisations. Archaeologists continue to develop and apply methodologies to understand hoard-related behaviours better (Joy 2016).

Another type of metal object that first appeared in the Iron Age was metal coinage. King Alyattes in Western Anatolia struck the first coins around 640 BCE (Harari 2014) and people have been attempting to accumulate them ever since.

Food and food storage containers, clothes, jewellery, and money, all continued to be produced and accumulated throughout the subsequent millennia up to the present day. By the 1970s, most households in the western world were regularly accumulating cooled or frozen food in fridges with an integral or separate freezer compartment (van den Eijnde 2020), along with collections of tinned food, other foodstuffs such as herbs and spices, cooking pans, crockery, and cutlery, and the vast majority of people had collections of clothes and jewellery.

Money is interesting because, although by the 1970s people were undoubtedly keeping collections of coins and notes in their pockets and wallets and drawers (and some, reputedly, under their mattresses), many were also collecting non-physical money in banks. Another type of non-physical and widely accumulated material is academic and scientific data. Such material had been collected for many centuries but the quantity in the twentieth century was growing rapidly. In this context, we should also remember the libraries of commercial companies and corporations that accumulated books and fragments of information for the use of their employees (Robertson 2021). The computer database, too, is another way of accumulating a store of non-physical information and was well-established before the start of the Icon Age.

The latter half of the twentieth century saw a huge growth in new products, advertising, and consumption in general. This, combined with an increase in prosperity and leisure time, increased the amount of accumulation across a wide variety of objects, such as record collections, photos, gardening products, tools, half-used pots of paint, and toys, to name but a few. Accumulators had become prolific collectors and were everywhere by the start of the Icon Age.

2.2 Librarians

Language leaves no trace, so we don't really know when it first appeared (Heylighen 2023). However, its emergence stimulated a new way of thinking and communicating between 70,000 and 30,000 years ago—a way that enabled humans to talk not only about things they could see and touch, but also about things that don't physically exist—imagined objects and ideas (Harari 2014). Language also facilitated the passage of *copied* knowledge between many different people and across many generations. It did so via oral storytelling practices, which employed metre, rhyme, and plot to serve as mnemonics (Logan and McLuhan 2016). One of the most striking demonstrations of the power of the oral tradition is the transmission of the Indian Vedas, Upanishads, and other documents across many generations from about 1500 BCE onwards using mnemonic procedures that ensured the accurate transmission of even exceptionally long texts (Lerner 1998).

While oral storytelling was effective, there was always a risk of errors, and this limited the amount of material that could be passed on. The development of writing on portable objects (as opposed to cave walls), overcame such problems. The earliest evidence of this kind of writing is on clay tablets produced by the Sumerian people that were found in Nippur in Southern Mesopotamia (now southern Iraq). The tablets date to between 3400 and 3000 BCE and appear to be simple lists of commodities (Casson 2001; Harari 2014).

One of the earliest examples of a library was in the ancient Ebla site in Syria, where around 2000 clay tablets were found in the remains of the royal palace in a room roughly 3.5 × 4 m. The palace had been burned down by invaders around 2300 BCE and the tablets had evidently fallen off wooden shelves that had burned through (Casson 2001). In this volume, we suggest that **Librarians collect works recorded**

on portable media and provide access to them through institutions known as libraries.

An alternative writing surface to clay tablets had been developed by the Chinese. They used split bamboo strips tied in bundles. It is believed that it was this narrow surface that resulted in Chinese being written in vertical columns (Byers 2021), though some vertical writing has been found on pre-bamboo bronze artefacts (Kurlansky 2016). The Egyptians created another alternative writing surface, perhaps as early as 3000 BCE. This was a type of paper in 3–6 m rolls made from the papyrus plant, which grew in abundance along the Nile where there were optimum growing conditions. The Egyptians were exporting papyrus to the Levant by 1100 BCE and then to the Greek world a few centuries later. The Egyptians had a monopoly on papyrus production, making it a relatively expensive product, but despite this it became the writing surface of preference for the Greeks and Romans until at least 200 CE. The long pieces of papyrus were kept rolled up for ease of handling and storage and these came to be referred to as *Scrolls*. Unfortunately, because Papyrus requires particularly dry conditions to survive, the only papyrus scrolls ever found outside Egypt were those found in a cave near the Dead Sea (Casson 2001; Kurlansky 2016).

Papyrus texts were what was contained in the best-known example of an ancient library—the one set up in Alexandria around 280 BCE. It contained over 530,000 scrolls on all types of subjects and was open to anyone who had appropriate scholarly or literary qualifications. It also contributed alphabetical order to the world. Sadly, the library was probably badly damaged by fire during invasions around 48 BCE and destroyed completely in fighting around 270 CE (Casson 2001).

Many great libraries followed in Alexandria's footsteps. Pergamon's library around 160 BCE contained at least 200,000 rolls and consisted of 4 rooms, the largest of which was 16 m × 14 m (Casson 2001). By the end of the pre-Christian era, Rome had three public libraries. In 350 CE a catalogue of Rome's notable buildings recorded that there were now 29 libraries in the city (*op. cit.*). During this period, three other writing surfaces emerged: (a) A hollowed-out tablet probably filled with beeswax, on which marks could be scratched (two such *Wax Tablets* bound together with a raised edge between them was known as a *Diptych*); (b) *Parchment* made by scraping animal hide and drying it. *Vellum* is a particularly fine type of parchment) (Kurlansky 2016); and (c) *Paper*, which was first made in China and other central Asian countries by mixing cellulose-based materials like wood, bark and cotton, with water, then putting the liquid on a screen and allowing it to dry (*op. cit.*). Along with these developments, sometime during the first century CE the Romans were the first to make the transition from the scroll to the *Codex*—a collection of parchment pages held together between two flat pieces of wood secured by cord running through holes drilled along one edge (Casson 2001). As time went by paper gradually gained the ascendency, taking over from parchment until the modern book emerged.

During the fifth and sixth centuries CE, the western Roman Empire was subject to constant attack and most of the libraries that had been established did not survive. However, other great libraries were established in the seat of the eastern Holy Roman Empire in Constantinople, and these survived until the 1400s. It was also around the time of the demise of the western Roman empire that monasteries started to establish their own libraries and to engage in the practice of handwriting copies of existing works (in which, inevitably, errors were introduced) (Casson 2001).

Major libraries were also founded in other parts of the world between 200 BCE and 1000 CE. In China, the Imperial Library, established around 100 BCE, was said to contain about 33,000 volumes. In India, Buddhist monasteries in Nalanda and Vikramashila had very large libraries in the seventh century CE; and, in the Islamic world, a major library was established in the eighth century CE in Baghdad that was dedicated to collecting Greek writings. Other major libraries were in place around 1000 CE in Cairo and Cordova; the latter containing over 400,000 books (Kurlansky 2016; Byers 2021).

A major change occurred in 1455 when the printing press was invented. The Chinese had been the first to use carved wooden blocks for printing in the eighth century CE. The oldest printed book ever found is a Buddhist prayer book called the Diamond Sutra printed in 868 CE (Kurlansky 2016). However, it was the introduction of moveable type by Guttenberg in 1455 that revolutionised book production, removed the need for scribes to make copies, guaranteed the exact same text in each book printed, increased the availability of books, and reduced the number of texts lost for all time due to censorship, war, fires, and other disasters (Heylighen 2023; Kurzweil 2005; Logan and McLuhan 2016; Spinney 2022). This, combined with major developments in knowledge and discovery during and after the Age of Enlightenment, spurred the development of libraries into the well-established institutions to be found all around the world by the twentieth century.

Some of the primary functions of the modern library are selecting content (a bigger than ever challenge given the ever-increasing numbers of books, and the politics and ethics governing selection) (Saponaro and Evans 2019); categorising and indexing its stock (a discipline that has been honed ever since the Sumerians assembled their clay tablets in rooms) (Harari 2014); and lending to individuals either directly or via libraries elsewhere. This last function brings with it a set of problems that have been experienced through the ages: defacing of content; late return or non-return; and theft (Casson 2001).

The twentieth century presented librarians with a number of technology challenges even before the start of the Icon Age. One of these was a growing variety of media on which texts might be recorded and/or distributed, including: records; audiotape; photographs; and microfilm and microfiche (which many libraries used for storing newspapers, etc.) (Logan and McLuhan 2016; Stibic 1981). The other challenge was the early choppy swell of the approaching IT hurricane. One of the earliest impacts on libraries was the development of a standard format for Machine Readable Cataloguing information (MARC) by the Library of Congress in the 1960s. This could be widely shared between MARC-based systems nationally and internationally (Miller 2022). It was reported that, by 1975, over 4 million such records were being held in libraries. As a result, there was a growing trend for libraries to abandon their card-based catalogues (Logan and McLuhan 2016).

Perhaps the most visible impact of IT on Librarians was the transfer of information from traditional secondary sources such as abstracting and bibliographic services (which many libraries subscribed to) into databases which could be searched online. About 100 such online services were available in 1977 with the number growing steadily. Related to this were Selective Dissemination of Information (SDI) services, in which the user specified keywords and was then periodically sent relevant new abstracts (Logan and McLuhan 2016; Stibic 1981). These developments, together with the inevitable impact of IT on back-end administration systems, meant that, by the start of the Icon Age, Librarians were well aware that their futures would be full of change.

2.3 Filers

The 5000-year-old Sumerian clay tablets referred to in the above section on Librarians appear to have been a simple form of bookkeeping, recording details about commodities such as animals, jars, baskets, and foodstuffs, for example '29,086 measures barley 37 months Kushim' (Casson 2001; Harari 2014). This perhaps was the first example of a filing system. Other early examples are the use of documents as legal evidence around 2150 BCE in Egypt, and the Code of Hammurabi, King of Babylonia around 1800 BCE (Danet and Bogoch 1992). Another example, which also illustrates how vital such information can be, concerns the Romans who, having lost their access to supplies of Papyrus, had their ability to rapidly transmit written orders severely disrupted, with the collapse of the empire following on shortly after (Logan and McLuhan 2016). Such factual information about the status of goods, work activities, organisational arrangements, plans, the law, and suchlike has been increasingly needed, produced and stored ever since these early beginnings. Thus, for the purposes of this book, we will assume that **Filers collect factual information assembled on a specific media that they (or others) may wish to refer to and/or use later**. This understanding of filing as a form of collecting has a number of precedents, where it has been applied to the filing of papers and manuscripts, and to subsequent similar practices with digital objects (Williams et al. 2009).

Filed information is usually to be found in work premises, or in places where work is organised and managed. It may also be found in domestic houses where information relating to individuals, the family, and the dwelling may be kept. Generally speaking, the bigger and more successful a work activity becomes the more files it will generate, and the more organised such information will need to be. For individuals, it is usually how prosperous they are that will dictate the amount of written documentation they will have. Wealthy people from 2500 BCE onwards will have had files relating to their transactions, finances, and possessions. Peasants in Europe many centuries ago may have had no such information. However, by the late 1800s in Europe, even a poor person may have had a birth or wedding certificate and possibly even a few letters or postcards from relatives or friends stored away somewhere.

It was in the late 1800s when significant changes started to occur to the management of records and paperwork. The backdrop to these developments was the office desk with multiple different pigeonholes and different-sized drawers for paper storage

(Robertson 2021); and the notion of the well-established bookkeeping book which, due to its binding, represented a stable and relatively tamper-proof source of information acceptable in a court of law. Similar bound books were also used to collect correspondence in parts of the US government (*op. cit.*). However, in the last quarter of the century, looseleaf systems entered the US market including the Box File, the Flat File (or board file) with a compressor spring at one end, the Shannon Arch File with two upright posts onto which documents with punched holes could be placed, and Document Files–flat boxes cut in half along the diagonal (*op. cit.*). Then, towards the end of the century, the vertical filing cabinet with two or more drawers burst onto the scene in the USA. Within twenty years, it had become the paper storage container of choice (*op. cit.*).

The vertical cabinet had a huge impact on some companies. For example, in the late 1920s the Brooklyn Edison company combined many of its files into a centralised file bureau with over 450 filing cabinets and had a staff of 87 women who filed at least 3500 new items a day and responded to about 100 requests each day for information (Robertson 2021).

The prominence of the vertical cabinet also spurred demand for training and advice. For example, a company called Library Bureau was able to sell miniature filing cabinets to 250 US schools to enable them to teach the elements of filing without the students having to wait in line to practice on the full-size cabinets (Robertson 2021); and James McCord's (1920) book 'A Textbook of filing' was written to provide extremely comprehensive and well-illustrated guidance (McCord 1920). There was also a demand for skilled professionals to manage filing operations in businesses. These people established regional groups in the USA, joined institutions such as the Special Library Association, and prompted the publication of filing periodicals (Robertson 2021). By the 1950s, the scope and terminology of the topic had developed to become Records Management. A 1957 journal paper proclaimed Records Management to be a new profession and suggested that corporations were starting to place responsibility for all their files in a single executive (Shaw 1957).

Despite all these corporate and professional activities, vast numbers of departments and office-based individuals still had to undertake their own filing with little help or guidance. However, the simplicity of the vertical cabinet design with its inbuilt index on tabs on manila separators, made this perfectly feasible, either with tabs created as needed and put into alphabetical order, or by using a separately maintained subject index as preferred by the more sophisticated filer. Even people in non-commercial organisations such as educators and clergymen found a use for filing cabinets (Robertson 2021). There was less use in people's homes where cardboard folders, drawers and bureaus continued to be used for paper storage, though some people did see the possibilities described in a 1940 paper, which noted the potential of the vertical cabinet to store things like Christmas card lists, bills, letters, dog licence receipts, recipes, magazine clippings, income tax records, and birth certificates (*op. cit.*).

As suggested by that 1940 article, paper had become as integral to the home as it was to the office; and in both environments the steady increase in paper was relentless. By the 1970s, a new phenomenon of 'information overload' was being reported (Robertson 2021); and in 1986, Dorf started her book 'File...Don't Pile' with the following:

> Let's face it, this is a paper-oriented society. It was twenty-five years ago. Despite technology, it still is... Don't delude yourself into thinking your problem with paper is unique. You have company from all walks of life, all ages, in every money bracket and marital status, male or female, with or without children. The Ph.D (Piled-high-and-deep) desk can belong to anybody. (Dorff 1986).

As described in the previous section regarding Librarians, online information systems appeared in the 1970s (Stibic 1981) and these provided the public's first experience of how a computer could be used to support the search and retrieval aspect of filing practice. In the background, research was being done to understand how the power of the computer could be harnessed for the search process (for example, Jones 1974); and for the storage of the documents themselves (Hendley 1983). Could these technologies help to ease the paper proliferation problem? The stage was set for the filer's world to be invaded by computers.

2.4 Archivists

In 78 BC, the Tabularium was completed in Rome. Its purpose was to house the bronze tabulae containing the laws and the official deeds of the Roman State (Musei Capitolini 2023). It was an archive in the classical sense of the word—a place where government records were kept for the purpose of governing a territory and its population. Such archives, along with other institutions and monuments, often signify a nation's identity. This is a bit of a problem for countries that have had their archives shipped away. For example, at the start of the twenty-first century, the Cuban archive was in Madrid and the Haitian archive in France (Eliassen 2016; Featherstone 2006).

A more general view of what an Archivist does is provided on the website of the National Museum of American History, which says:

> In the course of daily life, individuals and organizations create and keep information about their personal and business activities. Archivists identify and preserve these documents of lasting value. These records—and the places they are kept—are called "archives." Archival records take many forms, including correspondence, diaries, financial and legal documents, photographs, and moving image and sound recordings. All state governments as well as many local governments, universities, businesses, libraries, and historical societies, maintain archives. (National Museum of American History 2023).

The International Council on Archives (ICA), which was founded in 1948 and had over 2000 members in 161 countries in 2023, provides a simpler definition: 'Archives are the documentary by-product of human activity retained for their long-term value' (International Council on Archives 2023).

Even this explanation, however, might be seen as a little narrow, since it limits what is archived to documents and, by implication, information. A more colloquial view of an archive might be anything that is pulled out and placed in a relatively inaccessible place in the expectation that it is unlikely to be accessed very often, if at all. The top of the Wikipedia article on 'Archive' seems to reflect this:

> An archive is an accumulation of historical records or materials—in any medium—or the physical facility in which they are located (Wikipedia 2023a).

This lack of clarity about what archives and archivists are, is extensively explored in a paper by Proctor (2010). In it, she notes that, while the earliest use of the word 'archive' first appears in the mid-seventeenth century, and 'Archivist' first appears in 1753, the officials appointed to look after British government records after the Public Record Office Act became law in 1838 were called Keepers of Records. In that case, perhaps it was intentional not to use the words archive or archivists (indeed, it wasn't until 2006 that The National Archive acquired its current name)—but it doesn't seem surprising given Procter's conclusion that:

> The lack of success of the nineteenth-century public in 'pinning down' the archivist was at much the same level as it remains today (op. cit.).

Interestingly, the writings of two widely read authors on the subject of archives have probably not made the concepts any clearer to the non-specialist. One is the philosopher Michel Foucault, and the other is Jacques Derrida. Foucault uses the word 'archive' in at least three different ways across his works in order to explore particular phenomena and different contexts. One sense is used in his 1969 work 'The Archaeology of knowledge' (Foucault 1969) in which the archive is the system of discursivity that establishes the possibility of what can be said (Manof 2004; Eliassen 2016). A second sense deals with it from the perspective of its function as a historically embedded institution in which the archive is both a collection of documents and an instrument of power, discipline and knowledge (Eliassen 2016). A third sense is that archives were Foucault's preferred place of work, which he perceived as a refuge and space for experiment and experience—places in which time and space are organised differently (op. cit.).

Jacques Derrida provides a completely different perspective in his work 'Archive Fever: A Freudian Impression' (Derrida 1995). He suggests that archives are subject to two conflicting forces: a death drive; and a conservation drive. The death drive, sometimes linked to aggression and destruction, promotes forgetting and the eradication of the archive. The conservation drive is linked to the pleasure principle and motivates the preservation of the archive and its use to affirm the past, present and future (Manof 2004). Manof says about this book that:

> Although this volume certainly has its detractors, it is probably the most ambitious attempt by a contemporary scholar to understand the drive to collect, organize, and conserve the human record (op. cit.).

Together, these scholars—Foucault and Derrida—have inspired a huge amount of discussion in several different fields of study about what an archive might be (Manof 2004). However, it is an evolving conversation, so, for the purpose of this book, we shall say that **Archivists look after collections of objects that have been moved from their original locations and placed into long-term storage**. In this sense of the word, an archive can be anything from the stuff we put in the loft, to the French National Archives, which were created in 1794 following the revolution by amalgamating various government, religious, and private archives (Berger 2013). Looking ahead, this also resonates with Kim's notion of 'personal digital archiving', i.e.,

> I regard personal digital archiving as part of everyday record keeping with the goal of long-term preservation of documents, possibly beyond an owner's lifetime and a lifelong practice of forming a personal documentary heritage collection with objects that are meaningful to the owner, either as evidential resources or as memory objects. (Kim 2013).

Whether or not an anthology can be classed as an archive is a moot point. Certainly Jeremy Braddock, the author of 'Collecting as a Modernist Practice' (Braddock 2012), believes it should. He writes about 'Negro: an anthology' (Cunyard 1934):

> With its encyclopaedic reach and wide diversity of documentary materials, the Negro anthology anticipates a new category of late modernist collection: the archive (Braddock 2012).

Elsewhere, he describes a poetry collection (Abbott 1948) as a 'near-contemporary archive' (*op. cit.*). Interestingly, 1934 was the same year that the US Congress created the American National Archives Establishment, and the Society of American Archivists was founded in 1936 (Society of American Archivists 2023).

Some more familiar example of archives in the period immediately before the start of the Icon Age, appeared in business where the practice of sending away old documentation that was taking up too much space had become well-established. Such facilities were offered by service companies, which would typically store the boxed materials in cheap and safe underground spaces. One of the pioneer companies in this field was Iron Mountain in the USA, which started out with a depleted iron ore mine in the 1950s (Wikipedia 2025).

An alternative approach to the problem of lack of space put forward by some writers before digital technology emerged was to simply destroy some of the contents of an archive, which would also make it easier to find things that remained. Of course, this involves selecting items that are not worth keeping—a task replete with just as much potential for error as that of selecting items for inclusion in the archive in the first place. The latter activity has been criticised as being open to bias and inconsistencies and, in some cases, a desire to influence the story told by the contents of an archive (Yeo 2018).

These, then, were some of the perceptions of archiving to be found at the start of the Icon Age. However, it also worth noting that, in the computing industry, office automation was beginning to emerge at the beginning of the 1980s. This brought with it systems to archive office documents on products as diverse as the mainframe computer and optical discs (Pritchard and Cole 1983). A further note of interest, here, is that, although the word archive is now used extensively in the back-end data processing industry, the earliest use we could find of it was in an IBM Computing Dictionary dated around 1990, which defines the verb 'to archive' as:

To save data (usually electronic) in long term storage (such as magnetic tape or optical disc). This differs from backup in that it is intended that the data be kept for a long time, perhaps indefinitely. Data are archived when no longer in constant use, and the space taken up by the data is needed for other purposes. (IBM 1990).

2.5 Museum and Gallery Curators

Around 200 BCE, the city of Pergamum, in the northwest of current day Turkey, possessed on imposing collection of paintings and sculptures—one of the earliest art collections on record in the western world (Casson 2001). Perhaps this was an inspiration to art lovers in Rome: by 200 CE, Rome had an extensive collection of art works housed in temples and buildings, with officials appointed to look after statues and pictures, art historians, and a flourishing art market (Pearce 1995b). However, all this was to disappear as the Roman empire disintegrated in the fifth century CE. Over the centuries, country and state rulers continued to amass private collections of treasures. However, it was the great churches that collected some of the best objects, which may have been on show for a wider population to see. For example, the Abbey of St. Denis near Paris around 1130 CE was embellished with a combination of splendid old and newly commissioned objects (*op. cit.*). Other treasures were included in the great cathedrals that were built from the eleventh century onwards and which became artistic and cultural centres due to the many craftsmen who were involved in their expansion and maintenance (Icher 1998). The Christian churches were also responsible for stimulating a huge demand for the collection of holy artefacts and relics (bones and other bits of dead saints) during the middle ages (Belk 1995).

This, then, was the backdrop to the creation of the first set of collected works to have been officially called a 'Museum'. The Medici Palace in Florence was built in 1444 CE, and by the fourth quarter of the century had a large collection of paintings, pottery, gems and other rarities. The Medici family and its court referred to the Palace as a Museum—a Greek word (mouseion) meaning 'home of the muses', which had been used around 200 BCE in Alexandria (the location of the great library) to refer to its incumbent philosophical and literary scholars (Pearce 1995b). After the Medici's use of the word, it took a few more centuries for 'museum' to come into common use, though it was clearly making ground in 1714 when a German book called 'Museum Museorum' (Museum of Museums) was published (Valentini 1714). This listed a total of some 658 known collections, many from their published catalogues (Pearce 1995b).

Valentini's book probably included many of the so-called Wunderkammern (Wonder Cabinets) that had become popular during the sixteenth and seventeenth centuries. During that period, many new discoveries were being made and people became fascinated with unusual, exotic and rare items and started to collect such objects and to display them (Belk 1995; Muensterberger 1994). The cabinets were also known as studio, galleria, and museo in Italy, and sometimes 'cabinets of curiosities' or 'rarities' in Britain (Pearce 1995b).

The excitement around Wonder Cabinets had died down by the end of the seventeenth century (though the collecting habits it had inspired continued). However, it had prompted people to consider the merits of individual pieces among many things of the same type, and this inspired the development of various classification systems (Belk 1995). This new understanding that objects are meaningful and that organising them in certain ways can enhance the population's understanding of the world, was a major contributor to the emergence of the major national institutions that we now understand to be museums and art galleries (Macdonald 2006). These included: The Ashmolean Museum, which opened in Oxford, Britain, in 1683; the Uffizi Gallery (owned by the Medici family in Florence), which was donated to the State in 1743; the British Museum, which opened to the public in 1759; the Viennese royal collection, which was moved to the Belvedere Palace in 1776 and opened to the public 5 years later; the Louvre in Paris, which opened in 1793; the Rijksmuseum in Amsterdam, which opened in 1808; and the Smithsonian Institute, which opened in Washington D.C. in 1835 (Pearce 1995b; Belk 1995). Taking all of these things into consideration, here we take it that **Museum and Art Gallery Curators are involved in the collection of objects and cultural phenomena and their display for public viewing**.

The Industrial Revolution (approx. 1760–1840) was gaining pace in this period and would result in an explosion of material goods and a culture of consumerism that museums would eventually have to decide whether to reflect in their collections (Pearce 1995b). It was also in the 1800s that archaeology started to develop more rigorous scientific methods to unearth and analyse material objects, and this would eventually contribute towards the emergence of a new academic field of study of significant relevance to museums (Kohler 2007).

In the early twentieth century, a number of events signified a change in attitudes towards museums. Institutional collecting lost its status, and some academics—particularly anthropologists—decided they didn't need objects and museums to do their work and left to join universities (Kohler 2007; Macdonald 2006); and in 1909 Marinetti produced his 'Futurist Manifesto', in which he declared that museums were cemeteries (Braddock 2012). This was at the start of the art and literature Modernist movement that spanned much of the first half of the twentieth century. Modernism was both a movement and a style of art. It rejected traditional or accepted ideas, for example, the Phillips Memorial Gallery rejected the grandeur of marble interiors and declined to place exhibits in chronological order. Modernism also suggested that a collected set of objects is actually an authored work in its own right with its own specific aesthetics (*op. cit.*). The art works produced during the period rejected traditional styles and were innovative and experimental, prompting the establishment of the Museum of Modern Art in New York in 1929 (op. cit.).

In the second half of the twentieth century, the number of museums continued to grow. In the 1960s, it was said that a new museum was constructed in the USA every 3.3 days. This had increased to 230 a year in the 1980s. It was reported that a new museum was being set up in Britain at the rate of one a fortnight around the 1980s. In Japan and the USA, the museum boom was on an even bigger scale (Lumley 1988).

Despite this apparent robustness in the sector, museums and art galleries were facing a number of challenges at the start of the Icon Age:

- The growing appreciation of material culture theory had resulted in an increased awareness that by wrenching objects out of their normal context they lose some of their meaning unless their different aspects are specifically represented (Macdonald 2006; Pearce 1995b; Ames 1991).
- The acquisition of new objects in museums and art galleries is inevitably subject to the inclinations and preferences of those making the selections and can result in a non-representative collection (Belk 1995).
- Museums tend to uncritically celebrate objects rather than explore the consumer-culture relationship between people and goods (Belk 1995).
- Questions were being asked about the legitimacy of classifications developed many years previously (Macdonald 2006).
- Museums and galleries were often acquiring new material despite not having sufficient space to exhibit it all. As a consequence, the amount of material in storage was increasing, signifying a need for clear policies about disposal (Knell 2004; Macdonald 2006).
- Studies in the 1980s and early 1990s of visitors to major museums and art galleries (including MOMA, the Royal Academy, The British Museum, and the Louvre), indicated that 30% of visitors never actually go in the galleries, but instead just use the gift shop and/or restaurant. If they do go in, some just check out the most well-known pieces such as the Mona Lisa (Belk 1995).

We should also mention an important museum-related initiative that took place in 1994. The Collections Trust introduced its Spectrum standard of 21 Procedures for Collections Management in UK museums. By 2024, this standard was in its 5th version and was used by all accredited UK museums, and by many other institutions around the world (Collections Trust 2024).

2.6 Private Curators

Since ancient times, the powerful and wealthy have collected vast amounts of art, books, gems, and other valuables from around the globe, including places such as China, India, Egypt, Samaria, Assyria, Persia and Babylonia (Belk 1995). In the fourth century BCE, the Greeks started collecting paintings and sculptures (*op. cit.*); and Aristotle (who died in 322 BCE) was said to have had a large private library of books (Casson 2001).

In first century BCE Rome, Sulla is credited with being the first great private collector (Belk 1995). At that time, well-known public figures such as Mummius and Verres were reported to have collected art; and others such as Atticus and Varro had extensive private libraries. Cicero apparently curated both art and books (Casson 2001; Pearce 1995b). The word curate is used here in the sense of selecting and caring for objects. Hence, for the purposes of this text, **Private Curators will be**

considered to be individuals and organisations that build valuable collections of original, fine, or rare objects for their own use.

In medieval times, many large private libraries are known to have existed, including that owned by the first Caliph of the Umayyad Caliphate (661–750 CE). In China, by the thirteenth century CE several private libraries had more than 10,000 volumes (Byers 2021). Also in the thirteenth century, Duke Jean de Berry collected a wide variety of treasures including precious stones, objects made of precious metals, illuminated manuscripts, cameos, coins, medals, games, perfumes, animals, vases, tapestries, wall hangings, embroideries, religious relics, crucifixes, and footwarmers (note that not all of these items would necessarily classify de Berry as a Private Curator: the games and footwarmers, for example, might be the sort of things that would appear in an Amateur Collection). However, it was the Medici family in Florence that assembled the finest private collections in Italy from the late thirteenth century to the end of the fourteenth century (Belk 1995).

In the following centuries, the pattern continued, with more paintings, books, sculptures, jewellery, and unearthed archaeological finds becoming available to satisfy the curating ambitions of an increasing number of people made wealthy by global economic activity. In the twentieth century, it became increasingly common for companies and corporations to invest in art and other cultural objects—for example the Hard Rock Café chain's collection of music memorabilia and musical instruments (Shuker 2010). Not only does such a practice enhance an organisation's public image, but it also improves staff morale and can be a good financial investment. A study in 1989 indicated that there were over 1000 corporate art collections in the USA (Belk 1995). However, commercial companies are not the only type of organisations that undertake private curation. The Guggenheim Foundation is an example of a privately owned institution with a mission to collect, preserve, and interpret modern and contemporary art and to engage both local and global audiences (Guggenheim 2023a). Solomon Guggenheim started to curate his collection of modern paintings in 1929, and the Guggenheim Foundation was established in 1937. By the start of the Icon Age in the early 1980s, major Guggenheim museums were in place in New York and Venice (Guggenheim 2023b).

The Guggenheim is an example of a private collection being used to establish a *private* organisation dedicated to curating art works. However, over the millennia, there has been a regular pattern of private collections being used to establish *publicly-owned* institutions. For example, the Kanazawa Bunko in Japan started out as the private library of the Hojo Clan in 1275, was maintained by a local temple when the Clan died out, and was finally taken into public ownership in 1930 and became a museum specialising in historical documents and artefacts in 1954 (Byers 2021; Wikipedia 2023b). The Ark collection of John Tradescant and his son (who died in 1662) became the Ashmolean Museum in Oxford; Dr. Hans Sloan's collection was used to establish the British Museum in 1753; and Thomas Jefferson's book collection was used to re-establish the US Library of Congress after a fire in 1814 (Belk 1995).

One other facet of Private Curation emerged in the early twentieth century—the modernist anthology, which curates according to an ideological position rather than on an historical basis (Braddock 2012). As already described in Sect. 2.4, some people believe these to be archives. However, their assembly can also be conceived as a practice of Private Curation by an author who then presents the final published work to the public and libraries. The 'valuable' nature of such anthologies may not stem from a monetary value but from the originality and insight of the contents. By the latter part of the twentieth century, the notion of the modernist anthology had become widely understood and exploited, as represented by titles such as 'Angels of fire: Anthology of Radical Poetry in the 80s' (Paskin 1986) and more populist endeavours such as the many science fiction anthologies curated by Silverberg (for example, Silverberg 1978). This and all the other forms of Private Curation described above were playing a full role in the collecting landscape at the start of the Icon Age.

2.7 Amateur Collectors

Throughout history, most of the collecting described above, with the exception of accumulating, has been practised by the wealthy and powerful. However, as economic activity grew and prosperity spread in the sixteenth and seventeenth centuries, there was a surge in collecting activity in Europe, and new types of collectors emerged, including professionals such as doctors, lawyers and scholars (Belk 1995). In the eighteenth century, the things being collected widened: in France, for example, people were collecting ancient medals, minerals and anatomical specimens (Belk 1995). Also in the eighteenth century, Natural History collecting became popular, especially in England, and large numbers of clubs and societies were founded to support those involved (Pearce 1995b).

In the nineteenth century, an even wider circle of people became involved in collecting. There was said to have been a mania for collecting at that time (Macdonald 2006). In Victorian England (1837–1901) the Amateur Collector came from the broad ranks of society and collected, among other things, postage stamps, matchboxes, Staffordshire figures, postcards, biscuit tins, and 'railroadiana' (Belk 1995).

In the twentieth century, there was a growing understanding that a hobby was now 'serious leisure'. This had gradually come about since the Industrial Revolution because of fewer work hours, greater alienation from work activities, and increased affluence. Anybody could decide to collect anything because the inherent value of the objects was much less important than for the individual to be able to select and obtain the objects (Belk 1995). In other words, what was collected mattered less than how and why it was collected (Pearce 1995a). This is reflected in surveys of what people were collecting in the USA and Great Britain around the start of the Icon Age. The bewildering array of items included pencils, Winston Churchill memorabilia, maps of Transylvania, farm machinery, canning jars, police batons, Hawaiian shirts, Uncle Scrooge comic books, toy soldiers, sewing machines, dolls, photographs of midgets, advertising posters, automobile licence plates, beer cans, lawnmowers, matchbooks, Snoopy merchandise, cigar bands, radios, and anvils (Belk 1995). Hence, in this volume, we will adopt a deliberately broad notion of Amateur Collectors: **Amateur**

Collectors decide what they want to collect as a hobby, and then seek out and assemble appropriate items at their leisure.

Not only has the range of items being collected become very broad, but the number of people doing the collecting has also grown enormously. A study in the late 1960s found that at least two-thirds of all British 4-year-old children collected, and another study indicated that around one in three Americans had at least one collection at the end of the 1970s (Belk 1995). It is clear that, at the start of the Icon Age, Amateur Collecting had become a massive cultural phenomenon in both the USA and Great Britain, and probably within most other prosperous families elsewhere in the world.

2.8 Collecting Contexts on the Cusp

Below is a reminder of the working definitions we will apply in this volume to the seven collecting contexts described above. We also provide some of our own observations about their status on the cusp of the Icon Age early in the 1980s.

Accumulators collect objects out of functional necessity and make use of the items in their collections: Most people in the western world had expanded the scope of their accumulations in the face of rampant consumerism, and the prospects were for there to be a continuing avalanche of new products in the coming years to fuel this collecting instinct.

Librarians collect works recorded on portable media and provide their clients with access to them: Libraries had already been alerted to the impact of Information Technology by catalogue computerisation, new types of media, and online databases. The rising popularity of Word Processing and Desk Top Publishing presaged changes to the paper-based world, and computerisation would almost certainly be applied to Library admin and back-end systems. A wind of change was in the air.

Filers collect factual information assembled on a specific media that they may wish to refer to and/or use later: Although Filers may have been aware that Word Processing was spreading rapidly into all kinds of offices and that something called Electronic Mail was being used by a few pioneering people, they didn't really foresee any major imminent changes. Paper was continuing to flow, and filing cabinets, ring binders, box files, and cardboard wallets kept getting stuffed to overflowing.

Archivists look after collections of objects that have been moved from their original locations and placed into long-term storage: Archivists may have had some experience of microfilm and were certainly aware of the need for effective mass storage and indexing. Hence, the Archivist community may well have been looking forward to the possibilities of new computing technologies without perhaps knowing exactly what form it would take or what impact it would have.

Museum and Gallery Curators collect objects and cultural phenomena and display them for public viewing: These institutions were undoubtedly aware of the impact of computing on their back-office systems. However, they were probably unaware of any other potential impacts of IT. Nor were they particularly motivated to investigate them in the face of a variety of more pressing issues such as how best to display objects, the selection of new objects in a changing world, the legitimacy of some classification schemes, and the lack of display and storage space.

Private Curators are individuals and organisations that build valuable collections of original, fine or rare objects for their own use: This group, most of them being very wealthy, would be keen to take advantage of the latest developments to manage their collections and make them look great, and would have had the staff to investigate the possibilities for them. However, besides cataloguing software and desktop publishing to produce nice notices, the technology in the early 1980s had probably little to offer them in the immediate future.

Amateur Collectors decide what they want to collect as a hobby and then seek out and assemble appropriate items at their leisure. Most Amateur Collectors in the early 1980s would not have foreseen any impact of IT on their collecting activities.

References

Abbot CD (1948) Poets at work. Harcourt Brace

Ames M (1991) Cannibal tours, glass boxes and the politics of interpretation. In: Ames M (ed) Cannibal tours and glass boxes: the anthropology of museums. University of British Columbia Press, Canada, pp 139–150

Angier N (1999) Furs for evening, but cloth was the stone age standby. The New York Times, 14th December 1999. https://www.nytimes.com/1999/12/14/science/furs-for-evening-but-cloth-was-the-stone-age-standby.html. Accessed 24 Nov 2024

Belk RW (1995) Collecting in a consumer society. Routledge

Berger S (2013) The role of national archives in constructing national master narratives in Europe. Arch Sci 13(1):1–22

Braddock J (2012) Collecting as modernist practice. The Johns Hopkins University Press

Byers R (2021) The private library. Oak Knoll Press

Casson L (2001) Libraries in the ancient world. Yale University Press

Collections Trust (2024) Spectrum. https://collectionstrust.org.uk/spectrum/. Accessed 04 Nov 2024

Cunyard N (ed) (1934) Negro: an anthology. Wishart, London

Danet B, Bogoch B (1992) From oral ceremony to written document: the transitional language of Anglo-Saxon Wills. Lang Commun 12(2):95–122

Derrida J (1995) Archive fever: a freudian impression, Prenowitz E (transl). University of Chicago Press, Chicago and London

de Saulieu G, Testart A (2015) Innovations, food storage and the origins of agriculture. Environ Archaeol 20(4)

Dillon A (2019) Collecting as routine human behavior: personal identity and control in the material and digital world. Inf Cult 54(3):255–280

Dorff P (1986) File…don't Pile. St. Martin's Press, New York

Eliassen KO (2016) The archives of Michel Foucault. https://www.academia.edu/5473534/Archives_of_Michel_Foucault. Accessed 01 Dec 2022

Featherstone M (2006) Archive. Theory Cult Soc 23(2–3):591–596

Foucault M (1969) The archaeology of knowledge. Smith AMS (transl). Routledge, London and New York (2002)
Frank T (2018) Household food storage in Ancient Israel and Judah. Archaeopress Publishing Ltd
Grömer K (2016) The art of prehistoric textile making. Natural History Museum, Vienna
Guggenheim (2023a) The Solomon R. Guggenheim foundation. https://www.guggenheim.org/about-us/ . Accessed 24 Nov 2024
Guggenheim (2023b) History. https://www.guggenheim.org/about-us/history. Accessed 24 Nov 2024
Harari YN (2014) Sapiens. Harvill Secker, London
Hendley T (1983) Future optical based document storage and retrieval systems. Reprographics Q 16(4)
Heylighen F (2023) Mind, brain and body: an evolutionary perspective on the human condition. Lecture Notes 2025, Vrije Universiteit, Brussel
Hoving T (1979) Tutankhamun: the untold story. Hamish Hamilton Ltd., London
IBM (1990) IBM Jargon and General Computing Dictionary, Tenth edition, May 1990. p1-62
Icher F (1998) Building the great cathedrals. Zielonka A (transl), Harry N. Abrams, New York
International Council on Archives (2023) Home screen and discover archives. https://www.ica.org/en/the-international-council-on-archives; https://www.ica.org/en/discover-archives. Accessed 05 June 2023
Jones KS (1974) Automatic indexing. J Documentation 30(4)
Joy J (2016) Hoards as collections: re-examining the Snettisham iron age hoards from the perspective of collecting practice. World Archaeol 48(2):239–253
Kim S (2013) Landscape of personal digital archiving activities and research. In: Hawkins DT (ed) Personal archiving: preserving our digital heritage. Information Today Inc
Knell S (2004) Altered values: searching for a new collecting. In: Knell SJ (ed) Museums and the future of collecting, 2nd edn. Ashgate, Farnham, UK
Kohler RE (2007) Finders, keepers: collecting sciences and collecting practices. Hist Sci 45(4):428–454
Kurlansky M (2016) Paper—paging through history. W.W. Norton and Company
Kurzweil R (2005) The singularity is near. Penguin Books
Lerner FA (1998) The story of libraries: from the invention of writing to the computer age. The continuum International Publishing Group Inc., New York
Logan R, McLuhan M (2016) The future of the library. Peter Lang
Lumley R (ed) (1988) The museum time-machine: putting cultures on display. Routledge, London
Macdonald S (2006) Collecting practices. In: Macdonald S (ed) A companion to museum studies. Blackwell Publishing Ltd, pp 81–97
Manof M (2004) Theories of the archive from across the disciplines. Portal Libraries and the Academy 4(1):9–25
McCord JN (1920) A textbook of filing. Appleton
Miller RJ (2022) Metadata for digital collections. Facet Publishing Limited, London
Muensterberger W (1994) Collecting: an unruly passion. Princeton University Press
Musei Capitolini (2023) Tabularium. https://museicapitolini.org/en/sede/campidoglio_antico/tabularium. Accessed 10 March 2023
National Museum of American History (2023) What are archives. https://americanhistory.si.edu/archives/about/what-are-archives. Accessed 10 March 2023
Paskin S (1986) Angels of fire: anthology of radical poetry in the 80s. Random House
Pearce SM (1995a) Collecting as medium and message. In: Hooper-Greenhill E (ed), Museum, media, message. Routledge (reprinted 2001), pp 15–23
Pearce SM (1995b) On collecting. Routledge
Portal J (2007) The first emperor: China's terracotta army. Harvard University Press
Pritchard JAT, Cole I (1983) Planning office automation: information management systems. NCC, Manchester, UK

Proctor M (2010) What's an archivist? Some nineteenth-century perspectives. J Soc Arch 31(1):15–27

Robertson C (2021) The filing cabinet—a vertical history of information. The University of Minnesota Press

Saponaro MZ, Evans GE (2019) Collection management basics. Libraries Unlimited, Santa Barbara, California

Shaw AC (1957) What business thinks and says: records management—a new profession. J Bus Educ 33(3):117–118

Shuker R (2010) Wax trash and vinyl treasures: record collecting as a social practice. Ashgate Publishing Limited, Farnham, UK

Silverberg R (1978) Alpha 8. Berkely Publishing Corporation

Society of American Archivists (2023) Biography/History. https://digicoll.library.wisc.edu/cgi/f/findaid/findaid-idx?c=wiarchives;view=reslist;subview=standard;didno=uw-mil-uwmmss0172;focusrgn=bioghist;cc=wiarchives;byte=90899477. Accessed 12 March 2023

Spinney L (2022) The big idea: could the greatest works of literature be undiscovered? The Guardian, Manchester, UK, 30 May 2022

Stibic V (1981) Personal documentation for professionals. North Holland Publishing Company, Amsterdam

Valentini (1714) Museum Museorum, oder Vollständige Schau Bühne aller Materialien und Specereyen, Nebst deren Natürlichen Beschreibung, Election, Nutzen und Gebrauch, Aus andern Material- Kunst- und Naturalien-Kammern, Oost- und West-Indischen Reiss- Beschreibungen. J.D. Zunner, Frankfurt am Main

van den Eijnde J (2020) The human touch in kitchen technology: how technology changes our relationship with food in the rational and ritual kitchen. APRIA J 2(1):68–84

Wikipedia (2023a) Archive. https://en.wikipedia.org/wiki/Archive#Etymology. Accessed 11 March 2023

Wikipedia (2023b) Kanazawa Bunko. https://en.wikipedia.org/wiki/Kanazawa_Bunko. Accessed 14 March 2023

Wikipedia (2025) Iron Mountain (company). https://en.wikipedia.org/wiki/Iron_Mountain_(company). Accessed 20 March 2025

Williams P, John JL, Rowland I (2009) The personal curation of digital objects: a lifecycle approach. Aslib Proceedings, 5th July 2009

Yeo G (2018) Can we keep everything? The future of appraisal in a world of digital profusion. In: Brown C (ed) Archival futures. Facet Publishing, pp 45–63

Chapter 3
Source Materials and Their Analysis

Abstract The collecting contexts described in the previous chapter and our later findings emerged from analysis of the research materials described in this chapter. These include: accumulations assembled by the authors (a loft experiment; two sets of mementos; a special correspondence of 1500 emails; and a collection of data from an academic study); the authors' files—one amassed and maintained for over 40 years and now wholly digitised; one author's lifetime collection of letters; the results of an investigation into one of the author's household files; consultancy studies by one of the authors looking at two large commercial archives and four major museums and galleries; one author's investigation into a major private collection of sporting memorabilia; the authors' amateur collections of chocolate wrappers, stamps, photos, recorded/sheet music, and books; and two experiments by one of the authors—one to assemble story boards from objects in the other collections, and the other to assemble certificates, trophies, significant work outputs, and publications into a digital trophy gallery. Many of these collections were analysed by closely examining the practices associated with their assembly. The outcomes of this were used to create the practice hierarchy described in the following chapter. An extensive literature search was also undertaken to verify the hierarchy.

This chapter presents the basic building blocks out of which the rest of this book was constructed. We begin by describing the research materials we used to examine the assembly and maintenance of collections both before and during the Icon Age. After that, we describe some additional resources that have provided us with useful extra material. We then wrap up by outlining both the general and the specific ways in which we have approached analysing all of these materials, so that the reader can better understand the disciplinary framing of our work.

P. Wilson and P. Tolmie, *Collecting in the Icon Age*,
https://doi.org/10.1007/978-3-031-86470-4_3

3.1 Research Materials

The following research materials are organised roughly in terms of the contexts described in Chap. 2. Two things need to be borne in mind: first, the gathering of the materials preceded any notion of there being distinct contexts, so the contexts are an *outcome* of our analysis; secondly, we have put things in certain contexts to facilitate their presentation, but some materials contain aspects one might associate with several different contexts. Where the latter is the case, we say so and freely acknowledge the organisation of this chapter is primarily to make it easier to read. We do not claim that collecting is cut up in such neat terms. Furthermore, while the chapter refers to numerous different studies and resources, the primary source of data was a large collection of mixed work and personal documents, PAWDOC (see Sect. 3.1.3.1), that was systematically built and maintained from 1981 to the present day. This provided the richest source of materials, which cover both the practices used to assemble collections and the move from paper to digital.

The title of each collection described in this chapter is followed by a short form in brackets. For example, 'Sheet Music Collection (Sheet)'. This short form will be used when referencing the research materials elsewhere in the book.

3.1.1 Research Materials in the Accumulating Context

In Chap. 2, we suggested that Accumulators collect objects primarily as a functional consequence of their activities rather than seeking to build collections *as collections* of some kind. This gives collections assembled by Accumulators a relatively heterogenous character. Specific kinds of accumulations we have looked at include, at a more personal level, the things people put in their lofts, mementos, and emails, and, in more professional contexts, audio-visual materials such as research data and production stems and rushes.

3.1.1.1 Loft Collection (Loft)

Lofts are often dumping grounds for a range of different objects that have no evident role to play in people's everyday lives, but that they are reluctant to throw away. The loft in Wilson's house is no different in this respect. However, unlike many people's lofts, he has used certain techniques to organise the materials in his loft into a more structured collection (see Fig. 3.1). In 2004, he sorted, organised, labelled, and indexed the contents of his loft in a Filemaker database. He continued to operate this until moving house in 2015. Once in his new house, he discovered a free downloadable smart phone app called uGrokit that could act as a database for an RFID tag and reader system. So, he applied the same sort of system as before but with the

Fig. 3.1 Position labelling in the Wilson loft

data stored in a uGrokit database (though without the RFID Tags or Reader) and has continued in the same way ever since (Wilson 2016d).

3.1.1.2 Mementos

Although mementos or memorabilia may seem to constitute an Amateur Collection at first sight, for many people they are just a body of bits and pieces kept after various events have taken place that slowly accumulate around their homes, without being organised in any particular way. In our own study, we found we had quite distinct orientations to mementos. For Tolmie, they are just an accumulation, while for Wilson they are perhaps closer to an Amateur Collection.

Tolmie's Memento Collection (MemTol)

Under Tolmie's bed, there are a number of plastic boxes containing mementos of various kinds, including paper documents, such as meaningful receipts and tickets, programmes, personal letters, and so on. There are also other items of memorabilia under the bed and dotted around the house that are not documents, but rather bits and pieces that stand as mementos of places visited and major events (stones and shells, films, stuff made by Tolmie's children, ceramics, lockets of hair, baby teeth, old toys, etc.). Other than being clustered in certain places, these mementos have no organisation.

Wilson's Memento Collection (MemWil)

Wilson has kept mementos for many years—originally just in drawers and envelopes, then in files, then in folders for each year into which anything of potential downstream use or interest without a dedicated folder could be placed. When Wilson retired, he used some of this material, together with his retirement cards and messages, to construct a photobook of all his work experiences. Then he sorted out the boxes of year folders, digitised them and created an index, while documenting his reasons for keeping the items and their potential interest for whoever inherited them (Wilson 2012).

3.1.1.3 Daily Email Collection (Email)

In September 2001, having changed workplace, to beat the traffic Wilson used to leave his house at 6.30 am while his wife was still sleeping. So, occasionally he would email her while later going through his email and she sometimes replied. In January 2003, he started including his Word-a-Day email to his wife and this gradually developed into a daily habit. He also started storing his wife's replies in a Word document as a useful history of what was preoccupying them at the time. As they slipped into this routine, his wife started sending him messages if something came up during the day. This continued until January 2012 when Wilson retired, regardless of whether he was working nearby or away from home. Over that period, he accumulated a collection of 1507 such emails in Word documents, but they have never been formally indexed.

3.1.1.4 Research Data Collection (Data)

There is a whole literature on the storage and management of research data that focuses especially on how it might be indexed and made available within organisations (Straf et al. 1985) and/or shared across distributed communities (Mosconi et al. 2019). However, at the level of individual researchers, concerns with its management are much more local, personal concerns. We give here an example of one of Tolmie's numerous studies—the 24-h study—to illustrate how, for a researcher, an accumulated body of research data may constitute a personal collection of sorts, for use both during and after the work has been completed.

In 2014, as part of a project looking at people's interactions with physical and digital 'objects' in their homes, Tolmie and one of his colleagues decided to document in fine detail all of the interactions they had with things in their homes over a 24-h period (see Crabtree and Tolmie 2016). The interest was to inform the then prevalent discourse about the Internet of Things, by exploring what people actually did with things in their everyday lives. For Tolmie, this entailed going about his everyday business in his home constantly accompanied by a video camera, filming everything he did, and storing the files away for later analysis. By undertaking this exercise, he amassed an amorphous collection of videos, photographs, audio recordings, and text documents. The analyses, in turn, generated a further collection of materials, and the collection continued to grow, self-referentially, until the completion of the project in 2015. These materials might now be considered an archive, but during their collection they were actively used. Just for Tolmie on his own, the collection contains: 35 mp4 video files occupying 51.62 GB of storage; 3 m4a audio recordings (spoken accounts of interactions not filmed); 67 photographs (jpg); 5 MS Word documents (3 relating to analysis and 2 draft versions of papers); 2 MS Excel spreadsheets (used for quantitative analysis and graph preparation); 2 MS PowerPoint presentations; and 2 pdfs (versions of the published paper relating to the study). These materials are also replicated across two other disc drives for backup purposes. The distinctiveness of these materials in terms of collecting relates to how accumulations can arise by having a very specific and active goal in mind, with the creation of the collection being temporally constrained in its construction and use.

3.1.1.5 Television Ingest Study (TVBC)

Another temporally focused accumulation is the body of audio-visual materials assembled during the production of various kinds of media. As part of a project addressed to improving workflows in the television and film production industry, several ethnographic studies were undertaken by Tolmie at a major broadcasting company. Here, the primary interest was in the workflows associated with the ingest of production collaterals associated with TV broadcasts to the company's shared digital repository. To that end, Tolmie spent a week at one of their production sites in London, following the workflow associated with the ingest process across various departments. Ingest involves creating a store of all the digital collaterals associated with a specific programme so that these can be accessed by editors. While the materials might be considered a digital archive, they are distinct from long-term archival materials because, at the point of ingest, they amount to an accumulation that is still open to being added to and modified. In addition, while the construction of archives may be subject to certain deadlines and expectations, the pressures of ingesting all the materials for a scheduled broadcast are entirely different and colour how the work proceeds. Typically, archival work is rather slow and lapidary (see Sect. 3.1.4.2 below), but, in this context, it is highly time sensitive and delays can cause serious issues, hence their interest in developing the most efficient digital workflow possible. An additional point of interest here is how, at the time of the study, the materials to be ingested, while in digital format, were acquired on physical media. As a result, there was a need to conjointly maintain both a digital and physical collection, with there being no question of disposing of the original media.

3.1.2 Research Materials in the Library Context

In the case of the Library context, we did not have our own data to turn to. Here, we have made use of detailed secondary sources, such as ethnographic studies undertaken by other researchers, blog posts by Librarians, and YouTube videos prepared by Librarians or capturing the work of Librarians. These materials cover a wide range of different library settings and activities and, in all cases, provide insight into the practices used by Librarians to get their job done and how these have changed over time.

3.1.3 Research Materials in the Filing Context

The most extensive source of data we drew upon when analysing the impact of digital technology upon collecting practices was a large collection of files amassed by Wilson over more than 40 years, which is described further below. By way of contrast, we also look at Tolmie's collection of documents and, in addition, how purely household-related documents are managed in both households.

3.1.3.1 PAWDOC Collection (PAWDOC)

This section gives background to how the PAWDOC collection came into being, its basic architecture, its scale, and the various ways in which it has been analysed.

Background

Wilson joined the Office Automation (OA) team at the UK's National Computing Centre in Manchester in 1980. His job was to seek out best practice in worldwide industry and research organisations and feed it back to UK industry via books, papers, workshops, and talks. His first task was investigating the planning of OA Electronic Message Systems along with a colleague, John Prichard. In December 1980, they conducted a one-week lightning fact-finding tour of five US organisations, including the Amoco Research Centre in Tulsa. Here, they were told that an OA filing system was in full operational use. Their visit report describes it as follows:

> Electronic filing is so successful that no filing cabinets have been bought for 3 years … There is a centralised filing system … and documents … are given a serial number by the computer and stored in chronological order. An AS [Administrative Secretary] creates an entry in the electronic filing system by specifying and keying in a subject heading, who from, whom to and date of the document to be filed. She chooses the subject title … although managers/professionals can specify this if they wish to …. All searching of the electronic filing system is performed from a screen terminal by professionals and managers themselves using subject, date, author, keywords etc. (Wilson 2019).

This and another 26 visits made Wilson and Prichard hungry to try out the technology for themselves. However, NCC's OA Division did not install its Zynar Local Area Network with Apple PCs, until September 1981. In the meantime, they decided to go electronic manually by digitising their diaries (Wilson 1984) and applying the Amoco approach to their paper files (using Index Cards) (Wilson 1990).

Initially their index had just three elements: Reference Number, Title, and Keywords. They particularly wanted to be able to refer to each-other's files and to the files of their colleagues; and they wanted to be able to keep documents together when necessary. So, they structured the Reference Number with three elements: an Owner Identifier; a Serial Number; and a Sub-Serial Number, for example, PW0142/01. A document owned by someone called John Arthur Smith might therefore have the Reference Number JAS3791/03, such that the index owner would know who to ask for it. The Reference Number was written in the top right corner of each document, and the documents were stored in Reference Number order. The index was created on two sets of cards held in a plastic box. The first set—the Title Index—recorded Reference Number, Title, and Keywords. The second set—the Keyword Index—recorded the Keywords in alphabetical order, and every Reference Number and Title that had been given that Keyword. Wilson initiated this new filing system in June 1981, and, despite the heavily manual approach, it was the beginning of the collection that ultimately came to be called PAWDOC.

PAWDOC Contents, Growth, and Size

From its inception, Wilson used PAWDOC to store most of his documents, and it soon became an integral part of his working life. It gave him immediate and absolute control over his paperwork.

All types of material were stored including letters, internal memos, circulars, reports, specifications, minutes, overhead slides, 35 mm slides, notes, training materials, brochures, manuals, maps, emails, computer magazines, journal articles, and conference proceedings. Prior to 1996, less-used documents were archived in boxes, and eventually there were 45 boxes in store. In 1996, he started to digitise newly acquired documents (disposing of most originals) and to store them together with Born Digital documents in a Document Management System (DMS). This enabled additional types of items to be stored including executable programs and videos.

The boxes in store were removed in 2001 and gradually digitised over the following 13 years.

During the first phase of the use of the system when Wilson was working as a consultant, between 1981 and 2000, an average of 696 index entries were created each year. From 2001 to 2011, when he was working on highly confidential bids, the average was 272 a year; and from when he retired in 2012, to 2023, 37 new entries on average were created each year. In July 2024, the digital footprint of the collection amounted to some 51Gb, consisting of 17,372 Index entries representing 32,090 electronic files, and 333 physical hardcopy documents in two archive boxes.

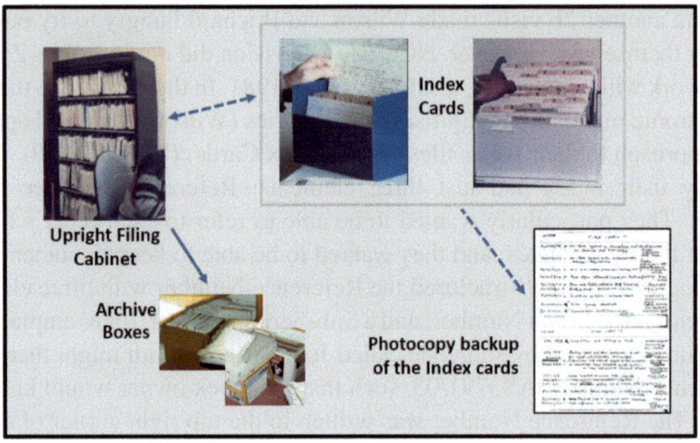

Fig. 3.2 Card index architecture

PAWDOC Architecture

PAWDOC evolved over the years using four types of prototype solutions: card index, electronic index, electronic index and document management system, and electronic Index and file storage in Windows 10 folders. The way these evolved and are related to each other is described below.

1. Card index system, June 1981–December 1987 (see Fig. 3.2)

This consisted of paper documents stored in an upright cabinet in serial number order, and an index on 6 × 4-inch cards.

In 1986, Wilson expanded the Reference Number to include a Set Identifier to enable various different journals, such as 'Ergonomics' and 'Creativity & Innovation Newsletter' to be included in the Index, for example, PAW/ERG/Aug84/833. This enabled a variety of other types of objects to also be stored in the Index, for example, Ring Binders and 35 mm slides.

By 1986, the amount of paper had overflowed the upright filing cabinet and Wilson had started to archive less frequently accessed documents to cardboard liquor boxes, which were stored around his office.

2. Electronic Index, January 1988–December 1994 (see Fig. 3.3)

After being provided with a Macintosh computer at work, the general-purpose database, Filemaker, was selected to hold the Index. This necessitated rigorous definition of the fields and the opportunity was taken to add a minimal number of additional fields to aid the search process (Publication Date and Creation Date); to manage the collection (Movement Status); and to enable items most eligible for archiving to be identified (Date Last Accessed).

3. Electronic Index and Document Management System, January 1995–February 2018 (see Fig. 3.4)

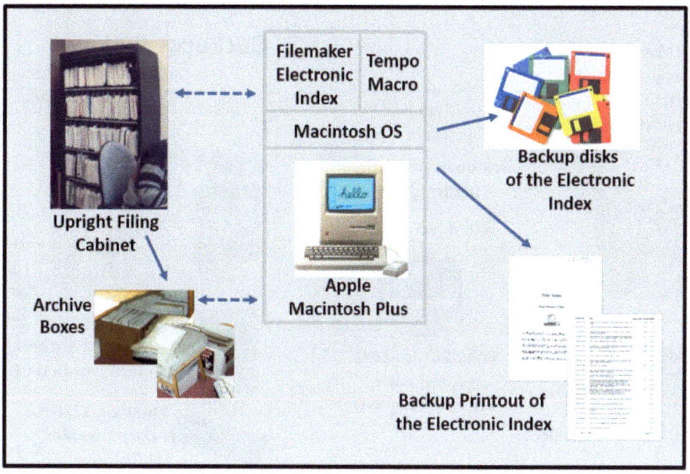

Fig. 3.3 Architecture of the electronic index system

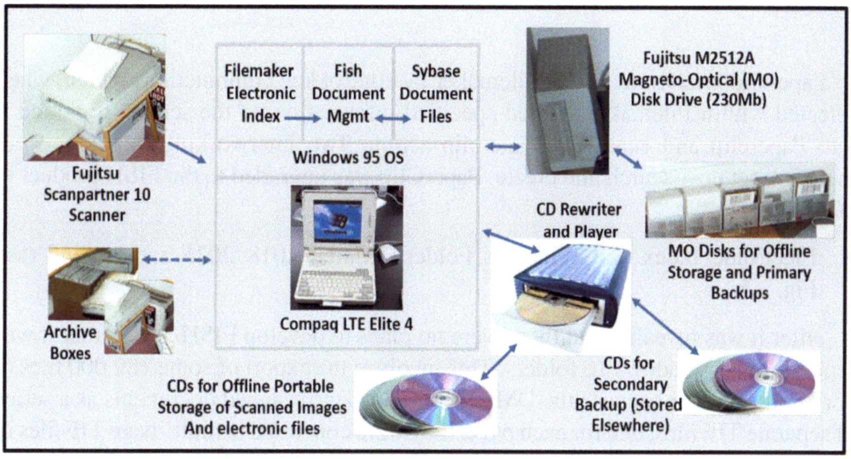

Fig. 3.4 Architecture of the combined index and document management system

In 1994, Fujitsu offered to support the work by providing a scanner and a magneto-optical storage system. In 1995 DDS, the European distributors of the PaperClip document management system (DMS), also provided PaperClip on long-term loan. By the beginning of 1996, these components were operational. Paperclip provided drawers, folders within drawers, and documents within folders. All the PAWDOC folders were contained in a single drawer; and a single folder was allocated to each PAWDOC Reference Number. Multiple documents could be contained within a folder.

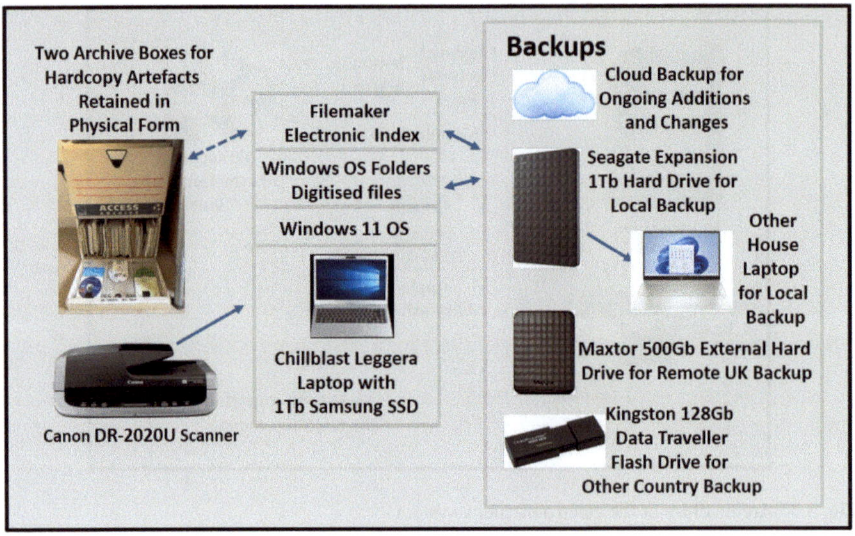

Fig. 3.5 Electronic index and windows folders architecture

Paperclip interworked with Filemaker by control key combinations which, when selected within Filemaker, copied specified information on the screen, imported it into Paperclip and enacted a Paperclip action. Two interworking functions were therefore set up—search and create. PaperClip was upgraded to the FISH product in 2000.

4. Electronic Index and Windows Folders, March 2018–2025 and beyond (see Fig. 3.5)

After it was revealed that there were no plans to develop FISH any further it was replaced with Windows 10 folders. This involved the export of some 189,000 files (a very large number because the DMS held multi-page scanned documents as a series of separate TIF files, one for each page; they were converted to multi-page TIF files in the export) and was undertaken successfully in 2018. An integral part of the change was replacing the slash in the Reference Number to a hyphen (for example, PAW/DOC/7592/01 to PAW-DOC-7592-01) because Windows does not permit slashes in file names.

PAWDOC as a Focus of Study

Throughout the operation of PAWDOC, one of the main aims was to provide practical feedback to product developers and system designers regarding the requirements of individuals using personal electronic filing systems (Wilson 1990). To this end, care was always taken to document as much as possible about the operation and usage of the system. Some analyses of this material have already been published (see Wilson

1990; 2001; 2016c; 2025) and this book is heavily premised upon both this prior body of work and a number of qualitative and quantitative analyses of the data that have been specifically conducted over the past five years (see Sect. 3.3.1).

3.1.3.2 Tolmie's Files (TolDoc)

Tolmie makes no real distinction between the organisation of his work and personal electronic documents. He has three primary places, and he keeps these: on the desktop of his laptop and on two more or less fully replicated external hard drives. The documents on the desktop fall into three broad categories: a loose group of documents relating to specific up-and-coming events or awaiting some kind of specific action; documents in a folder entitled 'Current' that are largely (though not entirely) work-related where the work is still in progress; and documents in a folder entitled 'Done' waiting to be copied to the two external hard drives. As well as documents relating to specific tasks, the Current folder contains: an admin folder to store things like task lists, contact information, and documents readily used for reference such as passports, etc.; a financial folder housing documents used to manage the household accounts; and an email archive that was created to store potentially useful emails when Google announced its capping of account storage in 2023.

Tolmie regularly copies documents over to the two external hard drives as a backup and long-term store. Files here date back to at least 2006. The folders on the hard drives are organised using a variety of terms, including employers, utilities, specific work projects, specific topics (such as food and drink, gardening, and holidays), official documents (e.g., tax), other service providers (e.g., banks, insurance), and types of documents (e.g., papers). There is no index supporting these, so referring to the contents requires either drilling down through potentially relevant folders or doing a global search using likely search terms. There are also older repositories of documents on a collection of 9 defunct disc drives that have failed for various reasons and that are awaiting the opportunity to run recovery software. This includes material that was never properly classified because, for a period of time when Tolmie was exceptionally busy, he simply periodically cleared all of the contents of his desktop to a single folder labelled 'Desktop [date]', for later filing. As this happened a number of times, these folders are nested across a number of generations.

Tolmie's paper documents can be very loosely categorised in terms of: currently active documents (i.e., ones that are awaiting some kind of action to be taken or response); historical documents awaiting filing; and historical documents that have already been filed in box files on a bookcase. Currently, active documents are mostly all placed together on top of a bookcase next to Tolmie's desk in his office. These elide between work-related documents and household documents, without much distinction. The historical documents awaiting filing are currently organised in multiple piles around Tolmie's office, on the floor, in boxes, and on shelves. These piles have a loose coherence. There are two piles of documents that are largely unordered that have just accumulated over time. As a result, they are vaguely stratified, such that older documents are at the bottom and more recent ones at the top. There is a box with more papers of a similar order, but that also contains some items of memorabilia. There is a third pile that has been staggered such that there is a separation between documents from different sources, making it easier for them to then be filed. They have not been filed because they are awaiting space in overcrowded box files. These historical documents are all a mixture of household and work documents, without any clear demarcation between them. The logic purely pertains to the source of the documents, i.e., from a specific bank, from a specific employer, from a specific utility company, and so on. Some older, mostly work-related documents are stored in card folders on an old cabinet and on top of the bookcase next to the box files, awaiting more permanent categorisation and storage. The collection of box files on the bookcase contains household documents, categorised by source. Then, in a filing cabinet and the lower drawer of an under-desk cabinet, there are printed copies of a large number of research-related papers, organised by topic. Tolmie's ultimate intention is to scan all of these and retain just digital versions.

3.1.3.3 Letters Collection (Let)

Over the years, Wilson has kept most of the hardcopy letters he has received. Various storage mechanisms had been used for these, including folders, ring binders, and concertina files; and, as the collection grew, he archived part of it and stored it in his loft. In 2016, Wilson undertook a major digitisation of the collection and reduced 1900 non-email hardcopy letters to just over 400 (Wilson 2016a).

3.1.3.4 Household Documents (HDoc)

In 2016, Wilson investigated all the documents associated with the ongoing management of his house and discovered over 9800 documents residing in 113 files placed in 15 separate locations. 71% of these were in email folders, but even when emails were excluded, 31% of the remainder were still in electronic format (Wilson 2016e).

3.1.4 Research Materials in the Archiving Context

In Chap. 2, we suggested that Archivists are people who look after collections of objects that have been moved from their original locations to long-term storage. We make use of two principal bodies of data relating to this: an ethnographic study conducted by Tolmie at a major film studio; and some observations of Archiving work undertaken by journalists at the Swiss national online news site, SwissInfo.

3.1.4.1 Film Studio Study (Film)

In 2010, Tolmie undertook a study at the post-production suite in a major film production site in the UK as part of a collection of short ethnographic studies conducted within the film and TV production industry to inform the development of a web-based workflow technology. Two distinctive aspects of the post-production suite in question were: (i) post-production was part of a broad set of co-located services designed to support beginning to end film and tv creation; (ii) the main emphasis of the daily work at that time was restoration of 1400 films from a major British Library Archive, which had been hosted at the site for over 20 years. A new company had recently taken over management of the archive, which included clip sales and title merchandising. The archive was kept in temperature and humidity-controlled conditions in two new state-of-the-art cold storage facilities. The film production site was providing most of the film and audio restoration services for the archive, as well as digitisation of an associated stills archive.

To undertake this work, the post-production suite had been more or less entirely reconstructed and had only really begun operating at the beginning of the year. All of the equipment was new, and some staff had been brought in from other places. Thus, the period over which the observations were conducted was a time of ongoing flux. The use of many features had not yet stabilised and there were residual problems with the new technology and its adaptation to local use. On top of this, workflows and work practices had not yet become entirely a matter of routine. Given this, the study inevitably uncovered a large number of issues. A range of activities were observed, including the cleaning, and digitising of materials, the shift from tape-based to digital workflows, archive maintenance, long-term backup, the provision of online access, and sound restoration. The materials were gathered through a mixture of direct observation and non-structured, situated interviews. We will focus here on Archiving activities.

3.1.4.2 SwissInfo Study (Swiss)

In 2014, as part of a European project dedicated to understanding the ways in which organisations handled rumours and misinformation (PHEME, https://www.pheme.eu/), Tolmie undertook two in-depth ethnographic studies in a national news organisation in Switzerland that produces exclusively online content. Despite the focus of the project on rumours, it was considered essential to gain a comprehensive understanding of the journalists' wider body of practices. As a result, the daily work of 15 journalists working on a news desk, together with editorial staff, was closely observed over numerous days to construct a detailed record of everything that was done. Online journalists are obliged to work with content management systems (CMS) that dictate everything from the format of their articles to their length and use of terminology. A key part of this process is the association of current stories with prior related stories in the systems archive, which show on the page as a link. This involves journalists actively searching for prior related stories and then entering the links in the CMS. The journalists are also obliged to archive each story and any associated documents to a cross-organisational repository. This is considered 'filler' work that is done on quiet news days. As a result, there is typically a backlog of such material on most of the journalists' hard drives that they have to actively move to the formal archive. The materials from this research actually sit on the cusp of several collecting contexts—Accumulation, Archiving, Filing, and even, in some ways, the maintenance of a library. As noted, many environments can be said to span several different collecting contexts. These materials allow us to explore that ambiguity in greater depth.

3.1.5 Research Materials in the Museum and Gallery Context

Between 2011 and 2015, Tolmie undertook a range of studies across museums in the UK, France, and Greece, under the auspices of several different projects, most notably the EC-funded project CHESS (https://www.chessexperience.eu/). The studies focused on five sites: the New Acropolis Museum in Athens; the Cité de l'Espace in Toulouse; the Imperial War Museum London; the Imperial War Museum North; and the Tate Modern in London. These studies were wide-ranging in their remit and primarily focused on visitor experiences. However, curatorial staff at each of the sites were also interviewed to gain better insight into curatorial reasoning. We therefore draw upon these materials in our discussion of museum and gallery contexts. The distinctiveness of each of these different sites heavily coloured how they were curated.

3.1.5.1 New Acropolis Museum Study (Acrop)

The New Acropolis Museum was purpose-built between 2004 and 2009 as a showcase for Greek national heritage and archaeology. With pride of place being given to a special gallery constructed to house the Parthenon marbles, the museum is heavily invested in archaeology and conservation.

3.1.5.2 Cite De l'Espace Study (Espace)

The Cité de l'Espace covers an extensive site outside of Toulouse. It concentrates on making the relationship between humankind and space accessible to the public and houses some enormous exhibits, such as full-size replicas of an Ariadne rocket and the MIR space station. Managing access to such large objects and the pedagogic interests of the museum shape its Curation enormously.

3.1.5.3 Imperial War Museum Study (Imp)

The Imperial War Museum aims to present artefacts and first-person experiences that capture the nature of war and its impact. IWM London and IWM North are slightly distinct from one another. At the site in London, much of the exhibition space is organised around conventional galleries and display cases, though some galleries, such as the Holocaust gallery, are organised as fully-fledged walkthrough experiences. The IWM North site in Manchester focuses on providing immersive experiences, so there are fewer enclosed galleries and a heavy use of technology. As a result, the Curation at the two involves a slightly different handling of the objects being curated.

3.1.5.4 Tate Modern Study (Tate)

The Tate Modern houses British Art from the sixteenth century onwards. With its large collection of international modern and contemporary art, it is one of the principal art galleries in Europe. It has an ongoing project to digitise its archive and make its collections accessible online. Its focus on making artworks accessible to a vast international public again gives Curation in the gallery a specific twist.

3.1.6 Research Materials in the Private Curator Context

In Chap. 2, we suggested that Private Curators are individuals and organisations that build valuable collections of original, fine, or rare objects for their own use, though these collections are often also made available to other people, such as members of the organisation or even the general public. Some sources we have already mentioned could also be seen as private collections, for instance, the film archive at the film production site, and the contents of the paid exhibitions displayed periodically at the Tate Modern. However, their character also transcends the above definition, so, for this context, we will use an investigation of The Priory Collection of sporting memorabilia.

3.1.6.1 The Priory Collection (Priory)

The Priory Collection is one of the largest private sporting collections in the world. It contains a collection of jerseys, caps, bats, balls, paintings, the warm-up track from 2012 Olympics, Olympic torches, an autograph book with signatures from Jesse Owens and Joseph Goebbels on adjacent pages, Olympic medals, and numerous other items. It is owned by Nigel Wray, a successful entrepreneur who was, until recently, the chairman of the Saracens rugby football club. Originally founded in the 1990s, the collection is now permanently housed in the Saracens rugby stadium in

London. People can visit the collection in person as part of the Saracens stadium tour, but to publicise its existence and make it available to as many people as possible, Wray has also created two films about the collection which are both accessible from the collection's web site (Wray 2019) (Wray 2023). Our analysis of the collection is based on an analysis of these two films and an interview with the collection's curator, Simon Jones. The materials were all gathered at the beginning of 2024.

3.1.7 Research Materials in the Amateur Collecting Context

Amateur Collecting covers the widest range of possibilities. Basically, this is a hobbyist activity, and people will collect just about anything. It is also pervasive across wide swathes of the worldwide population. We therefore have investigated examples from across the spectrum: at the most arcane level, Wilson's chocolate wrappers collection; at a slightly more commonplace level, stamp and trophy collecting; and, at the most commonplace, the practices surrounding collections of photographs, music, and books.

3.1.7.1 Chocolate Wrapper Collection (Choc)

Wilson started collecting chocolate wrappers when he was about 13 and has done so ever since. Collection items were stuck into a large desk diary and, when that ran out of space, new additions were placed in plastic wallets in a ring binder. It is not particularly organised and has never been digitised. As such, it provides a 'ground zero' basis for investigating the impact of the Icon Age on collecting.

3.1.7.2 Stamp Collection (Stamp)

The development of Wilson's stamp collection spans most of his life. It also spans the pre-digital era in the 1960s to the present day. Several different aspects of it have been augmented by digital capabilities. For instance, when Wilson had filled an album started by his father, he had it printed as a book with a preface describing the digital elements of its creation (see Wilson 2022). This enabled him to give a copy of something indivisible and relatively fragile to both of his grandchildren.

3.1.7.3 Trophies Collection (Trophy)

Wilson had a number of certificates, cups, and other physical tokens of recognition in a bookcase in his office, as well as his collection of published papers in two portfolio boxes. He wasn't prepared to destroy all these objects, but, as he proceeded with his wider policy of digitisation, he decided to consign them to the loft provided

Fig. 3.6 Simulated electronic trophy gallery

he had some physical reminder of them. The idea emerged of a trophy gallery with thumbnails of all the different items that could be displayed on a large electronic wall screen, with each item linked to the digital version of the trophy and related material. As the concept developed, Wilson decided to include significant work products that he had produced or been associated with over the years, all stored in the PAWDOC collection. Without having a wall screen, Wilson instead simulated the Trophy Gallery by assembling the thumbnails and printing them on sheets of A3 paper, which were framed and placed on the wall next to his bookcase as shown in Fig. 3.6 (Wilson 2021).

3.1.7.4 Photographs

We have investigated both Wilson and Tolmie's photograph collection-related practices. As with Filing, this gives us an opportunity to draw upon two quite distinct approaches.

Wilson's Photo Collection (PhotoWil)

Since starting to organise his jumbled personal photo collection around 1978, Wilson pursued the goal of a fully indexed photo collection throughout the following 30 years, over which time digitisation revolutionised photography. By 2013 he had finalised the approach (an Index, a standard structure for photo file titles, a digital folder structure, and standardised albums) and had digitised all of his family's 10,000 + photos. He then set about tackling his parents disparate photo collection which included handed-down photos from previous generations, using the same standardised approach: working with his mother, dates and contents were defined for each of the 7000 + photos, and each photo was indexed, scanned, and given a reference number that reflected the content and date. The physical photos were then put into one of about 19 albums with slip-in tabs (Wilson 2016b).

Tolmie's Photo Collection (PhotoTol)

Almost all of the physical photographs in Tolmie's collection have now been scanned and incorporated into his digital collection. The physical photos are mostly kept in several boxes under a bed as a backup of the digital, as memorabilia, and for their tangibility (occasionally someone in the household wants a physical photo to display somewhere). There is no particular order to the physical photos, though some are kept in albums (that had to be temporarily disassembled for the scanning process).

The organisation of Tolmie's digital photos is far more complex. He has seven different repositories: two stored on external hard drives that are direct copies of one another as a global backup; a separate subset of the overall repository set-up to display as a screensaver on a computer in the living room; a transitory repository on Google Photos, which is made up of a few albums deliberately stored for sharing and to backup the photos taken on Tolmie and his wife's mobile devices; another transitory repository on Tolmie's laptop that is made up of photos scraped from Google Photos that are in the process of being catalogued before storing on the hard drives and assigning to the screensaver; a large separate collection of photos on Tolmie's laptop that is a duplicate of the photographs kept by his wife of her sculptures, which are copied to Tolmie's wife's business website; and, finally, a loose collection of photos Tomie has accumulated across various studies as part of his work, distributed across multiple data folders on his hard drives. The personal photos are all organised in folders by events, settings, or subjects and, where possible, by date.

3.1.7.5 Recorded Music

In the case of music collections, we again make use of both Wilson and Tolmie's collections because they have distinct practices associated with them. In this case, both devote significant effort to their organisation. The differences here arise from the fact that Tolmie is also a musician and a DJ and organises his music, at least in part, around these activities. Note that, as Tolmie's music collection is partly geared towards a more professional activity, he cannot exclusively be thought of as a hobbyist (unlike Wilson, in this case), and his practices elide in some ways into those more associated with Accumulators, Filers, and Librarians.

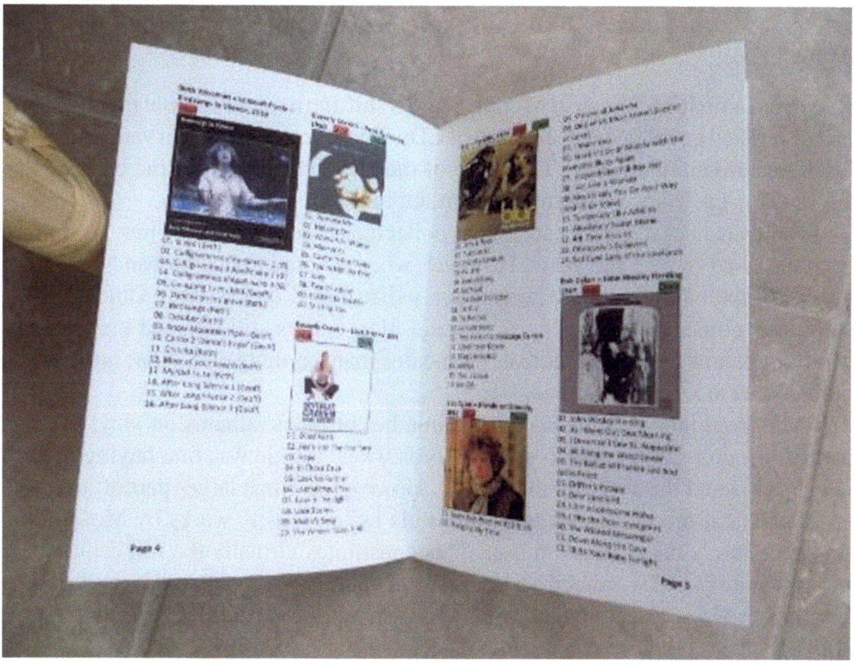

Fig. 3.7 Two of the pages in the 'Sounds for Alexa book

Wilson's Recorded Music Collection (MusWil)

In 2008, Wilson acquired a Numark TTUSB turntable with a USB audio interface, downloaded the free open-source Audacity recording and editing software, plugged in an old ghetto blaster cassette deck, and set about digitising some of the family's LPs and cassettes. The task was completed at the beginning of 2017, shortly after installing an Amazon Alexa speaker. Some items in the collection could be played directly from the Amazon music library and the rest through Alexa. However, as the digital collection lacked the visual characteristics of the physical media, Wilson created a hand-bound book listing the contents of each item together with an image of its cover (see Fig. 3.7) and placed it next to the Amazon speaker. This 'Sounds for Alexa' book includes 335 albums, of which 43 are self-made recordings, special promotional productions, or audiobooks (Wilson 2017a).

Tolmie's Recorded Music Collection (MusTol)

As noted, the most complex, yet perhaps most organised collection in Tolmie's home relates to music. For many years, Tolmie was a musician and music teacher and even now he regularly takes gigs as an amateur DJ. This has resulted in everything relating to matters musical in his home being carefully arranged to support his activities.

First of all, we need to distinguish here between music on physical media and digital music.

Recorded Music on Physical Media: Prior to shifting to purely digital music, Tolmie had developed an extensive collection of CDs. These are still stored in various drawers and cases around the house. The order of these has slipped over time because they are rarely used. They are all labelled but not indexed.

Tolmie also has a somewhat smaller collection of music on cassettes. Many have been disposed of over the years. However, when he used to play in bands, copies of the songs the bands recorded were largely distributed on cassette. Although some were later copied to CDs or purely digital files, he has still retained the cassettes. They might now be viewed more as mementos than anything else. None are indexed, though they are, again, labelled.

Aside from this, Tolmie has a large number of music albums on vinyl. A small part of this collection is made up of records when Tolmie was first buying records, which pre-dated the shift to other media. However, a much larger part of it is made up of classical records he inherited from his father, mostly works by Mozart, who was his father's favourite composer. This constitutes virtually the full catalogue of Mozart's works and is ordered according to '*K*' number (the standard Kochel number assigned to Mozart's catalogue, which is roughly chronological). These albums have not been played in many years but are kept as a sort of family heirloom.

Digital recorded music: At a certain point in time, it made sense for Tolmie to copy most of his CD collection over to iTunes and to acquire music from that point onwards as mp3, m4a, or FLAC files. The selected format partly depended on what was readily available, but also upon concerns about quality. Generally, FLAC is the best format, but the files are very much larger, so, where space was an issue, mp3 was chosen. Over time, Tolmie downloaded a huge quantity of music as part of an ambition to be able to play any song that anyone requested. His store contains over 200,000 songs and, in view of its size, is kept on an external hard drive, that is also regularly backed up to another hard drive. Mostly, because the songs are accessed through iTunes (or, as it is now, Apple Music) the music is kept in automatically generated folders relating to artists and albums in alphabetical order. Because of Tolmie's DJing activities, he manages material through iTunes carefully and, over time, has added metadata regarding the songs (such as BPM, key, genre (if absent), year of release, etc.). This is time-consuming, ongoing work, that also involves amendment of existing metadata, which is frequently incorrect. All of this is done through the iTunes (or Music) interface. As might be expected, the material in this collection spans all genres.

Over the past 5 years, Tolmie has switched to primarily using the music streaming service Spotify and, more recently, Tidal. These services both offer vast catalogues that exceed anything Tolmie is able to store offline, so he has steadily been complementing his original store with songs accessed online (especially new music). These materials are similarly closely managed, reviewed, and assigned to various playlists to support in-the-moment online DJing.

3.1.7.6 Sheet Music (Sheet)

Tolmie has a small collection of paper-based sheet music that is very much organised to support instrumental playing. There is a collection in a cabinet adjacent to Tolmie's piano that consists almost entirely of piano music, another pile of folk songs and guitar music on a bookcase next to where he practises his banjo, and a further pile of old band versions, etc., on the floor in his office. None of this sheet music is particularly organised or indexed. Beyond this, Tolmie also has a very large collection of digital sheet music. This includes music for a wide range of instruments and instrumental groupings, including orchestras. For this reason, at a top level, the music is arranged into folders according to instrument/instrumental grouping. Within these folders, the music is then further arranged into different folders according to composer. This vast reserve of music largely serves the purpose of being there to be printed off when it might prove useful. It is important to note that working directly from digital music when playing an instrument is difficult without a special reader, so the digital versions have little utility until printed.

3.1.7.7 Book Collection (Book)

Around the turn of the millennium, Wilson's office contained an amorphous collection of old books from his childhood, paperbacks, hardback workbooks, and 'mystery' books (pyramids, UFOs, Freemasonry, etc.), which had begun to take up quite a lot of shelf space. Over subsequent years it gradually morphed into an exclusively first edition, hardback collection, such that, in 2014, he digitised his 111 paperbacks, 19 university books, and 56 workbooks. Before cutting the books up to scan them, he took photos of them sitting on their bookshelves to try out the notion of an electronic bookshelf—a flat picture of a bookshelf on a large electronic paper wall screen, on which a book could be selected, and its full text would appear. The photos were turned into posters of various sizes and placed on the study walls, and the full text of each book was produced in a single PDF together with its cover and placed into an iPad (see Fig. 3.8) (Wilson 2014).

3.1.7.8 Electronic Story board Collection (ESB)

In 2018, Wilson digitised 35 University and Work books to make space on his bookshelves. However, in order to preserve what the books meant to him, he analysed his memories and feelings about them and represented those thoughts on a single page with links to more detailed back-end material. The idea was to have the pages digitally represented on a wall screen with the ability to touch the links and have the back-end material displayed. In the absence of a wall screen, Wilson trialled the concept using laminated sheets on the side of a bookcase (see Fig. 3.9). This initial exercise was followed up with a further 35 sheets each representing particular mementos, letters, loft items, photos, music, and books (Wilson 2018).

Fig. 3.8 Digitised books framed on Wilson's study wall, shown on the PC and iPad screens, and on a poster under a desk mat

Fig. 3.9 First set of Wilson's electronic story boards and associated index on the side of a bookcase

3.1.7.9 Display Case Collection (Display)

Wilson's collection of computer artefacts had been built up since the 1980s and had been placed into a display case in 2010, along with a few other items, without any index or organisation. In 2018, Wilson decided to organise all this material and at the same time try to experience the challenges of labelling, describing, and displaying physical objects and of archiving those items for which there was not enough space to display (Wilson 2023).

3.2 Other Resources

We have already noted above that, to enrich our materials, we have drawn from time to time upon various existing blogs, videos, and studies of the collecting contexts we are exploring. This is especially the case with regard to Librarians. However, another resource that has proved invaluable in the assembly of this volume is a personal blog regarding Wilson's approaches to collecting and organising that he has maintained and regularly updated since 2012. The blog, entitled 'Order from Chaos', was originally based upon materials that Wilson began putting together in 2004. As reference will be made to certain parts of this blog throughout, it behoves us to give a little more information about it here.

3.2.1 Order from Chaos Blog (OFC)

At around the time Wilson set up PAWDOC in the early 1980s, he had sorted out a cellar-full of various forgotten objects, and some boxes crammed full of some other person's work files. At home, he was trying to get his photos sorted, and was also encountering the perennial problem confronting all house owners—how to keep the loft accessible while piling stuff into it. These experiences, combined with the more rigorous demands of managing and using PAWDOC, and with personal computers becoming more affordable and versatile, resulted in his growing conviction that technology could be harnessed to help sort out and manage disorganised piles of stuff—any sort of stuff!

In 2004, he decided that there might be a business opportunity in these ideas, and he duly published his thoughts in a White Paper entitled 'Order from Chaos: Organisation, Digitisation, Exploitation' (Wilson 2004). This was closely followed by an OFC Service List and a definition of the standard OFC process. All that was needed at that point was something to test the ideas out on—and the family's loft seemed an ideal candidate—see Sect. 3.1.1.1. After it was completed at the beginning of January 2005, this instance of his loft system remained fully operational for the next 10 years until the Wilson's moved house.

Wilson retired from his job managing bids at CSC UK at the beginning of 2012 and, as part of his retirement, he decided to further develop his Order from Chaos ideas. This included the development of a website in which he could record what he was doing. On 28th April 2012 *pwofc.com* opened for business (http://www.pwofc.com/ofc/). Over the period from then until 2025 it has addressed 29 separate topics, many of which are represented in the Research Materials described earlier in this chapter. One of the items which the OFC Home Page points to is an OFC tutorial (Wilson 2017b), which encapsulates Wilson's approach to managing many of the collections described above.

3.3 Analytic Approach

Below we describe the overall general approach, we have taken to the analysis of our research materials. In subsequent subsections, we describe in turn how we derived the practice hierarchy described in Chap. 4, how we calculated some quantitative measures of the impact of IT on collecting as described in Chap. 5, how we investigated the impact of IT on objects that are collected (as discussed in Chap. 6), and how we have tried to review and check our research findings across the whole of the book.

3.3.1 General Approach

Our general approach has been informed by the following three strategies:

(a) to try to assemble an overall set of research material in the format normally derived from an ethnomethodological investigation as described in Sect. 1.3;
(b) to piggyback upon any pre-existing investigative work that has been undertaken on the research material over the years;
(c) to employ Wilson's material as the primary source of detailed analysis and to use Tolmie's material to compare, augment, and/or adjust the outcomes from the Wilson analytics.

Regarding strategy (a), we considered Tolmie's research materials to already be in an ethnomethodological format because his consultancy work had been contracted to be performed in that way; and for his own personal collections, it was assumed that, given his ethnomethodological credentials, his own personal understanding would be, de facto, from an ethnomethodological perspective. For Wilson's material, however, some specific actions were taken to derive the data. This involved creating a questionnaire of some 52 questions covering the practices involved in assembling, creating and using a collection; and the orientation and reasoning that was performed about the following aspects of the collection: creation, location, ownership/possession, selection of content, development, attraction of potential users, exhibition, consultation, sharing, searching, security and privacy, reference, transmission, preservation/conservation, and deterioration/loss (see Appendix A for further details). The questionnaire was completed for each of Wilson's collections included in the study with the exception of the Household Document collection. This, together with pre-existing information about the collections in papers and in *pwofc.com*, formed the basic set of Wilson's material.

Strategy (b)—to piggyback on existing work—was clearly an important option for Tolmie's consultancy assignments; and Wilson's long-term documentation of his PAWDOC collection and the extensive contents of his *pwofc* blog, also provided much additional material. In both cases, relevant information has been used where appropriate along with a reference to the source publication. An extensive literature search was also undertaken to identify additional relevant materials.

The final strategy (c) entailed using the questionnaire answers referred to above to identify the initial 600 + basic practices from which both the practice hierarchy and IT's impact upon them were derived. Following this, Tolmie's material was used to assess and augment these results and all other chapters in the book.

3.3.2 Development of a Practice 'Hierarchy'

This approach to analysis grew out of a way of working frequently found in ethnomethodological studies that treats a particular activity such as 'going to the shops' as a basic starting point. The activity is then systematically investigated to tease out all of the different phenomena wrapped within it, e.g., 'entering the shop'… 'choosing vegetables'… 'going to the checkout', which are open themselves to yet deeper analysis, e.g., 'picking up a sweet potato'… 'turning the sweet potato round to inspect it for blemishes', and so on. Obviously, this kind of approach is open to infinite regression. However, in practice, it is usually stopped when going to any further level of granularity would cease to offer much in the way of useful insight. Under the auspices of this, each answer in all the completed questionnaires was scrutinised and any phrase or sentence resembling a practice was noted in a spreadsheet. As each practice was recorded, a single word—a verb—was ascribed to the practice to indicate the type of activity that was being performed. These practice identification and activity type choices were made by the authors on the basis of their experience and growing familiarity with the data. As such, the choices made were essentially subjective in nature. However, their intention was not to identify a definitive set of specific practices, but, instead, to provide a large set of raw materials from which the upper levels of a hierarchy of practices could be derived. This was achieved by pursuing a two-stage process:

First, a degree of consistency was achieved across the 600 + basic practices identified, and the types allocated to each one, by an iterative process of adjustment and refinement. With this completed, the second stage extended the type allocations to different levels. For example, for the practice 'Decide what to include in the collection' with a type allocation of 'Define', an upper-level practice of 'Initiate' was identified. This too was an extensive iterative process of deriving higher levels under which specific practices would sit; assessing whether there were other practices to which those higher levels would apply; and finally ensuring the consistent application of the whole hierarchy across the whole set of 600 + basic practices.

3.3.3 Gaining Indicative Measures of IT's Impact on Collecting

After having established the hierarchy of collecting practices, we attempted to identify the impact that Information Technology has had on collecting by considering the following four questions:

- What amount of change has been experienced because of IT?
- Has collecting been made easier or harder by IT?
- Has collectors' workload been increased or decreased as a result of IT?
- What has been the impact of IT on the collected items themselves?

Here, we strayed into the realms of quantitative analysis because each of the questions implied some form of measurement. We therefore decided to try and quantify the impact by first of all using a standard 5 grade Likert type of rating, with 1 as 'little or no impact' and 5 as 'significant impact'. Having made these impact allocations to all the 600 + basic practices, a simple average approach was taken to identify an overall allocation for each particular practice in the practice hierarchy. For example, four instances of Archive (Collect-Maintain-Archive') occurred in the set of basic practices, two with an Amount of Change allocation of '2', one with a '1', and one with a '0'. The overall allocation for this practice was calculated as $(2 + 2 + 1 + 0)/4 = 1.25$ (which was rounded up to 1.3—these indicatory measures only require one decimal point). These impact allocations were made subjectively by the authors and cannot be considered in any sense definitive or even especially robust. However, they do provide an indicative view of the way Information Technology has been affecting collecting across various domains.

3.3.4 Exploring IT's Impact on the Objects that Are Collected

In this final analysis exercise, we have attempted to understand what impact IT has had on both the nature of objects that are collected, and upon the way individuals and society in general, use, relate to, and control those objects. This has largely been achieved by drawing upon our experiences with the research materials described previously, and by the 300 + papers we have read in our literature review.

Table 3.1 Research materials used in this analysis and their abbreviations

Abbreviation	Research material	Abbreviation	Research material
Acrop	New Acropolis Museum study	MusWil	Wilson's Recorded Music collection
Book	Book collection	MusTol	Tolmie's Recorded Music collection
Choc	Chocolate Wrapper collection	OFC	Order from Chaos blog
Data	Research Data collection	PAWDOC	PAWDOC File collection
Display	Display Case collection	PhotoWil	Wilson's Photo collection
Email	Daily Email collection	PhotoTol	Tolmie's Photo collection
ESB	Electronic Story Board collection	Priory	The Priory collection
Espace	Cite de l'Espace study	Sheet	Sheet Music collection
Film	Film Production Studio study	Stamp	Stamp collection
Hdoc	Household Documents	Swiss	Swissinfo study
Imp	Imperial War Museum study	Tate	Tate Modern study
Let	Letters collection	TolDoc	Tolmie' Files
Loft	Loft collection	Trophy	Trophies Collection
MemTol	Tolmie's Memento collection	TVBC	Television Ingest study
MemWil	Wilson's Memento collection		

3.3.5 Verification of Previous Analysis Results

We attempted to verify our analysis results in two ways: First, we used Tolmie's material to assess, verify, and, where appropriate, adjust the practice hierarchy, our assessment of IT's impact, and IT's impact on objects. This was achieved by examining said outputs and making additions and changes where appropriate. Secondly, we sought out other research texts that described collecting practices in various ways, for example, the Spectrum standard practices for museum collection management already mentioned in Chap. 2 (Collections Trust 2024). Here, our concern was to ensure that we had not unwittingly overlooked anything important in our hierarchy. When we analysed this material, the results suggested that only two substantive changes needed to be made to the hierarchy, though the analysis did result in several changes being made to practice descriptions.

In the next chapter, we present the practice hierarchy in detail and examine how it relates to the various research materials we have presented in this chapter. For ease of reference, a list of all the research materials and their abbreviations is provided in Table 3.1.

References

Collections Trust (2024) Spectrum. https://collectionstrust.org.uk/spectrum/. Accessed 04 Nov 2024

Crabtree A, Tolmie P (2016) A day in the life of things in the home. In: Proceedings of the 19th conference on computer-supported cooperative work and social computing, San Francisco, California, USA 26 Feb–02 March 2016. ACM, pp 1738–1750

Mosconi G, Li Q, Randall D, Karasti H, Tolmie P, Barutzky J, Korn M, Pipek V (2019) Three gaps in opening science. Comput Support Coop Work (CSCW) 28(2019):749–789

Straf ML, Martin ME, Fienberg SE (eds) (1985) Sharing research data. National Academies Press

Wilson PA (1984) Towards the electronic pocket diary. Des Stud 5(2):98–105

Wilson PA (1990) Ergonomic aspects of computer supported personal filing systems. In: Lovesey EJ (ed) Contemporary ergonomics 1990—proceedings of the 1990 ergonomics society conference, Leeds, UK, 3–6 April. Taylor and Francis, pp 92–97

Wilson PA (2001) 20 years in the life of a long-term empirical personal electronic filing study. Behav Inf Technol 20(5):395–409

Wilson PA (2004) OFC white paper. Published in the now defunct website www.orderfromchaos.co.uk, 03 Jan 2004, now accessible in the blog post OFC as a service dated 16 July 2017 in the Order from Chaos section in the pwofc website. https://www.pwofc.com/ofc/2017/07/16/ofc-as-a-service/. Accessed 25 Nov 2024

Wilson PA (2012) Memento management. Blog posts in the Memento management section of the pwofc.com website, Nov 2012–Feb 2016. http://www.pwofc.com/ofc/category/journeys-completed/memento-management/page/2/. Accessed 25 Nov 2024

Wilson PA (2014) Electronic bookshelf. Blog posts in the electronic bookshelf section of the pwofc.com website, April 2014–Dec 2014. http://www.pwofc.com/ofc/category/journeys-completed/electronic-bookshelf/. Accessed 25 Nov 2024

Wilson PA (2016a) Letter keeping. Blog posts in the letter keeping section of the pwofc.com website, Jan–Mar 2016. http://www.pwofc.com/ofc/category/journeys-completed/letter-keeping/. http://www.pwofc.com/ofc/category/journeys-completed/letter-keeping/. Accessed 25 Nov 2024

Wilson PA (2016b) Get that old photo collection in order. Watermead village view magazine, Spring issue, 05 March 2016, Watermead Parish Council, Aylesbury. https://www.watermead-pc.gov.uk/village-view-2015---2016.html. Accessed 25 Nov 2024

Wilson PA (2016c) Preservation planning for personal digital collections. Case note published by the digital preservation coalition on its website, 11 April 2016. https://www.google.com/url?client%3Dinternal-element-cse%26cx%3D015383697635205237689:2tx1omaukfw%26q%3D, https://www.dpconline.org/docs/miscellaneous/advice/1509-casenote-pwilson-preservation planning-ver2/file%26sa%3DU%26ved%3D2ahUKEwj6pe_n-faJAxU7RaQEHeIHGXAQFnoECAcQAQ%26usg%3DAOvVaw1wCtv7e09l6ufzQtjgKExn. Accessed 25 Nov 2024

Wilson PA (2016d) Loft management. Blog posts in the loft management section of the pwofc.com website, Sept–Oct 2016. http://www.pwofc.com/ofc/category/journeys-in-progress/loft-management/. Accessed 25 Nov 2024

Wilson PA (2016e) Household file management. Blog posts in the household file management section of the pwofc.com website, Nov–Dec 2016. http://www.pwofc.com/ofc/category/journeys-completed/household-file-mgmt/. Accessed 25 Nov 2024

Wilson PA (2017a) Music management. Blog posts in the music management section of the pwofc.com website, Feb 2017–Feb 2018. http://www.pwofc.com/ofc/category/journeys-completed/music-management/page/2/. Accessed 25 Nov 2024

Wilson PA (2017b) The OFC online tutorial. Blog posts in the order from chaos section of the pwofc.com website, Sept 2017. https://www.pwofc.com/ofc/2017/09/01/u1-the-ofc-online-tutorial-welcome-and-contents/. Accessed 25 Nov 2024

Wilson PA (2018) Electronic story board. Blog posts in the electronic story board section of the pwofc.com website, June 2018–Sept 2022. http://www.pwofc.com/ofc/category/journeys-completed/electronic-story-board/page/2/. Accessed 25 Nov 2024

Wilson PA (2019) Visits 1979–1982. Privately hand-bound and stored in P.A. Wilson's personal library [available for viewing by arrangement with the author]
Wilson PA (2021) Electronic Trophy Gallery. Blog posts in the Electronic Trophy Gallery section of the pwofc.com website, Jan2021 – Jun2022. http://www.pwofc.com/ofc/category/journeys-completed/electronic-trophy-gallery/. Accessed 15 Mar 2025
Wilson PA (2022) Meteor—a story about stamp collecting in the eye of the IT hurricane. Privately published book produced by Blurb, 05 April 2022 [available for viewing by arrangement with the author]
Wilson PA (2023) Display case management. Blog posts in the display case management section of the pwofc.com website, Sept–Oct 2023. http://www.pwofc.com/ofc/category/journeys-completed/display-case-management/. Accessed 25 Nov 2024
Wilson PA (2025) Sorties into the IT Hurricane, 3rd edn. Chapter 9. Self-published in Blurb and distributed by Ingram
Wray N (2019) The Priory collection 2019. https://saracens.com/more/the-priory-collection/. Accessed 25 Nov 2024
Wray N (2023) The Priory collection 2023. https://saracens.com/more/the-priory-collection/. Accessed 25 Nov 2024

Chapter 4
Collecting Practices

Abstract Analysis of the materials described in Chap. 3 identified eight high-level practices that apply to most collections: initiate (starting a collection); equip (putting in place a suitable infrastructure and facilities); acquire (obtaining things); deposit (ingesting things into the collection); use (enjoying and/or making use of the collection); reveal (informing others about the collection and sharing its contents); maintain (keeping the collection in good order); dispose (getting rid of some or all of the collection). All of these high-level practices are broken down into second-level practices, or even third-level practices, and examples are given. Troubles that seem inherent to collecting as an endeavour (i.e., not caused by IT) are also considered.

This chapter focuses on presenting a baseline of collecting practices derived from the research collections and literature review outlined in Chap. 3. Some practices relating to collecting have only evolved as a result of the adoption of IT, but all of these will be presented separately in Chap. 5 so as to make it clearer how computing technology has had an impact on collecting. We begin this chapter by outlining an overall hierarchy that captures eight high-level 'practices'. This forms the backbone of the way we have organised and documented the collecting activities we have identified.[1] In subsequent sections, we describe these practices in greater detail, unpack their constitutive elements, and, through reference to specific phenomena we have observed in our research materials described in Chap. 3, analyse just what it takes for them to look that way. References to our research materials will use either the full name of the material, or the abbreviations specified in Chap. 3 preceded by 'RM', for example [RM: Tate]. The full list of abbreviations is shown in Table 3.1 at the end of Chap. 3.

[1] Note that a digital version of the complete practice hierarchy is available in the book's supplementary material available at 'pwofc.com'.

P. Wilson and P. Tolmie, *Collecting in the Icon Age*,
https://doi.org/10.1007/978-3-031-86470-4_4

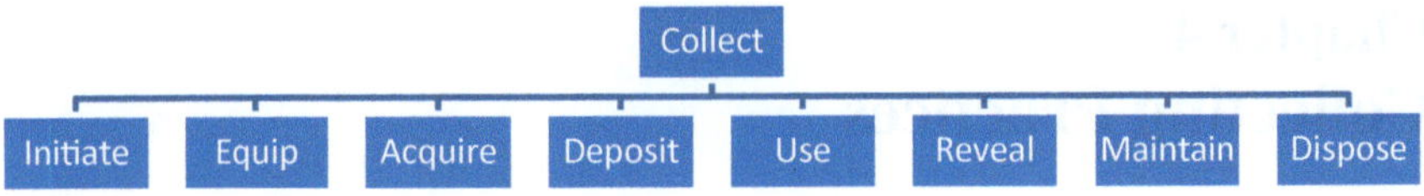

Fig. 4.1 Eight main types of practice associated with collecting

4.1 The Practice Hierarchy

We identified the following eight main kinds of practices associated with collecting: initiate, equip, acquire, deposit, use, reveal, maintain, dispose. For convenience, these can be assembled in the form of a hierarchy, as illustrated in Fig. 4.1, with them encompassing a variety of finer-grained practices.

To elaborate:

Initiate: refers to the various practices involved in starting a collection
Equip: refers to the practices involved in putting in place an infrastructure and the facilities needed to perform the collecting activity
Acquire: refers to obtaining the things that are being collected
Deposit: covers the practices required to ingest items into a collection
Use: refers to everything associated with enjoying a collection and/or making it serve the purpose for which it was intended
Reveal: covers the practices associated with informing other people about a collection and sharing its contents with them
Maintain: refers to all of the practices required to keep the items in a collection in good repair and prevent their deterioration
Dispose: covers the practices implicated by ceasing to be responsible for a collection

Over the remainder of this chapter, we unpack these high-level practices and pull out some of the principal lower-level practices from which we found them to be constituted.

4.2 Initiate a Collection

All collections have to start sometime—though that point may not be very clear: collections often just emerge over a period time (Watkins et al. 2015). However, at some point they are recognised as such and referred to with a name. The name may be very general, such as 'the buckles' or more thought out like 'the Burrell collection'; either way, the collection has become a discernible entity that can be talked and written about. From then on, more details about the collection might be identified or even formally defined and documented, e.g., the owner, what is being collected and why, how much effort and money will be put into creating the collection, who can

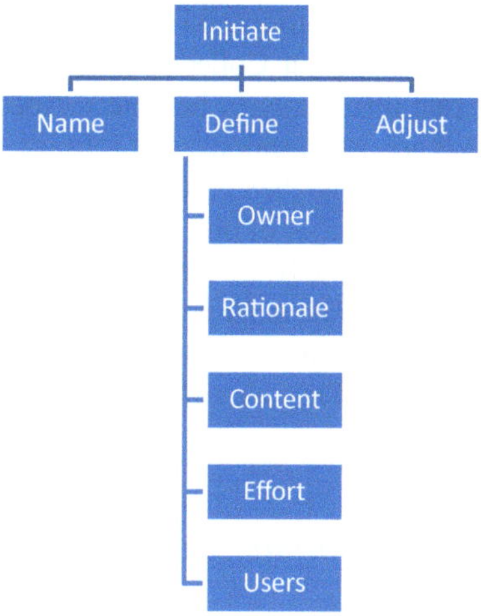

Fig. 4.2 Subsets of 'Initiate'

actually look at and use the objects within it, and so on. However, these details can themselves be subject to change over time, as owners seek (or are obliged) to make adjustments.

Initiating a collection can be seen to be made up of the elements as shown in Fig. 4.2. These are themselves explicated further in the following subsections.

4.2.1 Initiate: Name

Naming a collection provides a shorthand and definitive reference for use when referring to a collection, be that when talking to others, when writing about it, or when labelling materials associated with it. Larger-scale examples we encountered included the Priory Collection and the film archive [RM:Film]. These give an identity to entire organisational entities. Smaller-scale examples include the Mementos, Chocolate Wrappers, and Electronic Trophy Gallery collections, where the reference serves the purpose of just a few people, maybe a household.

Sometimes inappropriate names can cause problems; for example, Electronic Trophy Gallery doesn't immediately convey the idea of publications or work products which are actually included in that collection.

Some names develop over time, and this too can create misnomers, for example, initially PAW/DOC was only one set in the PAW collection. However, over time, the whole collection started to be referred to as PAWDOC because that name seemed an expedient way to convey what it was. Unfortunately, over time, many additional sets were added to the collection (for example, PAW/CD, and PAW/BKS, and PAW/SLI - CDs, Books and 35 mm slides respectively), which has made the name PAWDOC slightly misleading.

Accumulators and Filers are less likely to feel the need to name their collections, while Amateur Collectors and Private Curators who are individuals may create a name informally to be able to speak about what they are doing. Private Curators that are organisations, and Library, Museum, Gallery, and Archive Institutions, will usually name their collections to be able to organise and manage them and to identify discrete bodies of objects within their overall structure (for example, The Parthenon Gallery in the New Acropolis Museum, and the Artist and Society galleries in the Tate Modern). The latter is itself divided up into discrete collections of works and named by different artists or thematic entities that are rotated from their larger archive, for example, 'Deana Lawson' and 'Nation Building'.

4.2.2 Initiate: Define

For most collections, the individual(s) involved have some understanding of what they are doing and why, even if they never explicitly think those things through or write them down. Such things define the parameters within which the collection operates, and they include the following: the *Owner*, the *Rationale* for initiating the collection, the kind of *Content* it should contain, the *Effort* that can be expended upon it, and its anticipated *Users*. Inevitably, organisational and institutional collectors are more likely to maintain up to date and clear written definitions about their collections. However, given the huge numbers of people collecting all sorts of different types of objects, there will be some individual collectors who are just as diligent in managing their collections.

4.2.2.1 Initiate: Define: Owner

Defining the Owner of a collection creates clarity about who takes decisions about the collection, particularly decisions about who is responsible for acquiring new items for the collection, and for its organisation. In collections owned by one individual, the owner is a fait accompli. For family collections, clarity about ownership and responsibilities become more important. For example, in the Mementos collection we examined in this work all the organising, digitisation and indexing is done by one person, but, despite this, there is a clear understanding that the collection is jointly owned by the man and his wife. For larger collections, perhaps operated by organisations with staff, clarity about ownership and decision-making will be essential for the effective management of the collection. In such contexts, obligations and rights to instruct also ride upon understandings of ownership. For instance, in SwissInfo, journalists had a routine understanding that they were obliged to copy material to the company archive whenever they had time on their hands (and were called to account if they failed to do so). In the New Acropolis Museum, the President of the Board of Directors (who themselves represent the Greek Government and, in turn, the Greek people) had the right to instruct the staff in the museum regarding how the exhibitions should be organised.

4.2.2.2 Initiate: Define: Rationale

Collections are often started by individuals simply because they find the items interesting, and reasons for doing so are not explicitly stated or even thought about (Watkins et al. 2015). Other individuals may be prompted to collect because they enjoy discussing the objects with other people (Dillon 2019). However, sometimes there are specific reasons for starting a collection and these may help the owner to figure out what items to keep and how to organise and store them (RM:OFC). For example, understanding the rationale of the PAWDOC collection helped the owner to be clear about his objectives so that he could design, use, and document his use of the collection accordingly. In large collecting institutions, the rationale for a collection is often defined in the form of a Mission Statement (Saponaro and Evans 2019). These may often articulate several contiguous concerns. For instance, the Cite de L'Espace defines its rationales to be '(1) To introduce as many people as possible to all dimensions of space culture; (2) to enhance the region through its active contribution to local, regional, national, and international tourism and cultural policies; (3) to promote the space section, particularly among younger generations and decision-makers' (Cite de L'Espace 2024). In the case of some collections, such as large libraries, the rationales may be even more diverse. The British Library, for instance, considers itself to be simultaneously the custodian of 'the UK's national collection of published, written and digital content', to be there to 'support and stimulate research', to help businesses, to offer 'cultural experiences', to encourage learning, and to advance global 'knowledge and mutual understanding' (British Library 2024).

4.2.2.3 Initiate: Define: Content

Defining what you want in a collection provides clarity about what items are to be included from among the selection you possess already, and what items need to be sought out and obtained. For example, the Wilson Photo collection examined in this work incorporates not only printed still images but also slides and movies. In contrast, the Book collection excludes all but hardbacks. Of course, for some collections what might count as viable content is more evident than it is for others. Thus, for the Chocolate Wrappers collection what is allowable is pretty clear, as it might once have been for cigarette cards, etc., (though the criteria may be steadily refined to exclude things like damaged items or duplicates). However, if one is setting out to collect something like sporting memorabilia, it might be less certain. For instance, does one include tickets? If so, just any tickets? Obviously, for many Private Individual Collectors, what might or might not count as acceptable content will evolve over time and may only come to be explicitly defined after the collection has already been initiated (if at all). Indeed, some collections may only ever be defined in terms of what is excluded.

Some types of collections may have huge numbers of possible items to collect, and this may seem to be too big a task for an owner. Owners employ various strategies to address this. For example, the stamp collection examined in this work, limited the collection to just four countries, as well as filling those album pages on which the father had handwritten the names of 33 other different countries. On the other hand, it may be thought best not to limit the collection, as was the case with the PAWDOC collection for which an explicit decision was made to collect all documents because it was thought to be impossible to know which documents might need to be referred to in the future, and it reduced the amount of time spent on selecting which documents to include (Wilson 1990).

Clarity of content is also necessary to be able to arrange storage for the items, to know how best to organise the items, and to provide for the likely future expansion of the collection [RM:MemWil; Book; Choc; PhotoWil]. Such issues are particularly important in large institutions like Libraries, Archives, and Museums, in which the operational decisions like what items to collect and/or to digitise may be taken by departments or committees rather than individuals (Miller 2022). Such institutions are likely to have an overall collection management policy in place which includes the topics/formats to be collected, the selection criteria, and how the collection is to be evaluated (Saponaro and Evans 2019). For instance, the *Charte documentaire des acquisitions de la Bibliothèque nationale de France* (Bibliothèque Nationale de France 2015 (revision of the 1994 charter) specifies the range of materials the French National Library has an interest in (everything published in French both within France and its ancient colonies, everything published referring to France in other languages, research publications in any language in the natural and social sciences and economics, public documents from around France such as minutes, and so on). Historically, various other publications (for example, Béguet et al. 1999) have then given directives about how this acquisition process should be realised. Along similar lines, Hohn notes that collection management in botanical gardens should include guidelines and standards for acquisitions, accessioning/deaccessioning, collections preservation, and disposal of items in the collections (Hohn 2008).

4.2.2.4 Initiate: Define: Effort

Collecting can be very demanding in terms of time, money, and sheer persistence. Therefore, it can be useful to have some clear limits on the amount of effort one is prepared to expend. This, of course, has ramifications for the preceding set of practices surrounding content. For example, for the chocolate wrapper collection, only those wrappers that were immediately to hand, or which looked particularly unusual or interesting, were acquired despite sometimes seeing many different types for sale that would be good to have in the collection. This decision was made to enable the owner to have a continued small interest in the collection but not to have to go out of his way to add to it. For collecting institutions, the definition of associated budgets and manpower is particularly important (Fieldhouse 2012). Much of this is wrapped up in employment contracts and associated employer expectations. For instance, in SwissInfo, journalists were obliged to maintain the archive when they had no other more pressing concerns regarding generating news output, and they were expected to provide likes to prior relevant content in their document management system when submitting a story. However, no initiatives were introduced to employ additional staff to keep the archive up to date.

4.2.2.5 Initiate: Define: Users

Defining who can use the collection may or may not be an imperative depending on how possessive the owner is. Sometimes it may just evolve. Concerns such as privacy and security may also dictate how much attention is paid to this aspect [RM:Let]. Larger, more valuable, collections owned by organisations may particularly feel the need to control usage. In the case of Galleries such as the Tate Modern, it is commonplace to limit access to certain exhibitions, especially those on loan from other collectors. This may be controlled by charging for entrance or by only admitting members. In Museums, Libraries, and even Archives, certain content may be kept in special areas that are only accessible to those with authorisation. This is especially the case for objects considered vulnerable or fragile or subject to environmental control [RM:Tate; Acrop; Film] (Cornell University Library 2024).

4.2.3 Initiate: Adjust

The process of collecting, by its very nature, changes the content of a collection, and in so doing may change the attitude of its owner towards it. Even when a collection is complete, the owner may start to view it differently over time. Consequently, from time to time, owners may wish to adjust the parameters within which the collection operates—even, on occasion, its name. Where definitions have been formalised, this will probably result in changes to initial documents and policies.

Collection Assessment is a standard activity in many large collecting institutions, particularly Libraries, and the results may well affect their policies about what is collected and why, and the demographic of their users (Saponaro and Evans 2019; Collections Trust 2024). Jamison (2023), for instance, provides a "how to" guide for crafting collection development policies to create equity in Library Collections. After building up and using a collection for a while, all types of owners – institutions and individuals alike - may decide that they wish to spend more or less time, money, and energy on their collections, and may adjust the effort they put into their collections accordingly [RM:Stamp]. Should any objects be removed from a collection as part of this process, then the Collections Trust (2024) has identified the need to undertake an overall deaccessioning and disposal practice (see also Sect. 4.9–Dispose of a collection).

4.3 Equip a Collection

Collecting has always required some sort of equipment to support it—if only to provide a receptacle to store the objects concerned. Sometimes that equipment may already be in place—a shelf or a cupboard perhaps. However, many collections have their own specific equipment requirements ranging from albums to display cases; from filing cabinets to floor to ceiling shelving; from magnifying glasses to microfilm readers; and from special lighting to air conditioning units. The larger the collection, the more these infrastructural requirements ramify.

The equipping practice may well be undertaken when a collection is being first established. However, it is often also carried out throughout the life of a collection as the quantity of items in the collection increases, as old resources wear out, and as new and improved resources become available. At the time it was being studied, the film archive at the film production site was in the process of being moved to new facilities that were better equipped to store vintage film stock. Sometimes the reconceptualisation of what a collection is for can have significant consequences for how it is equipped. The building of the New Acropolis Museum in Athens, for instance, was built to rehouse an existing collection of artefacts as a result of two important shifts in museum-related policy in Greece. First of all, there was a shift in emphasis from purely preservation-focused strategies to a recognition of the importance of providing visiting experiences. Secondly, in response to a set of stringent requirements from the British Museum regarding the possible return of the Elgin Marbles, one whole gallery was constructed specifically to meet those requirements.

The equip practice comprises the elements as shown in Fig. 4.3.

4.3.1 Equip: Consult

For those embarking on a new collection, or rationalising an old collection, they may feel the need to establish how best to handle, organise, stow, and maintain the items, and to understand what tools and equipment are available to help them do so. Some collectors may already possess such knowledge, but most usually like to see what is out there; to see how other people do it; to see what's new; and to understand what best practice is. The most common ways of doing this are by talking to people, reading articles and reviews, and by looking at brochures.

4.3.1.1 Equip: Consult: People

Talking to knowledgeable and experienced people is a reliable way of finding out the norms of how a particular type of collection can be organised and managed and the equipment that is required to do so. Often such people are contacted by

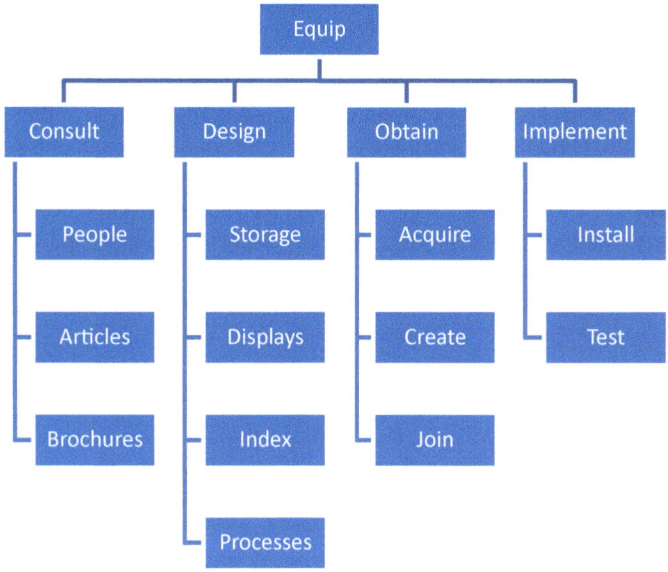

Fig. 4.3 Subsets of 'Equip'

joining a society of like-minded individuals, but this is by no means the only way: knowledgeable individuals can be identified by reputation or recommendation and can be contacted in writing or by phone. This is a relatively easy route to knowledge for common collection types such as stamp collections or classic cars. However, it may be a bit harder to find people who are knowledgeable about collecting more esoteric objects such as firefighter hats. Regardless of the type of collection, collecting institutions are likely to find it easier to take advantage of their size and reputation to arrange in-depth consultations with knowledgeable and experienced people and may well be able to arrange visits to see how other collections are managed. The Cite de l'Espace, for instance, actively explored how certain parts of the Futuroscope theme park in France were set up to inform the construction of some of its larger exhibits.

4.3.1.2 Equip: Consult: Articles

Written treatises on a subject can often provide all the information collectors need and may take the form of general articles, product reviews, reports, guides, or detailed scientific papers. For example, a guide on labelling and marking produced by The Collections Trust, was obtained for use in the revamping of the display case collection [RM:PAWDOC; Display] (Wilson 2023). For larger collections, especially in Museums, Galleries, and Libraries, there are well-established literatures and staff are often recruited on the basis of their prior training and existing knowledge.

4.3.1.3 Equip: Consult: Brochures

Information from manufacturers is often provided in brochures—which is very useful once you know what brochures to obtain and then actually get hold of them. Unfortunately, individual brochures usually just provide information about one single brand or approach, so multiple brochures may be required to undertake a comprehensive review [RM:PAWDOC]. Large organisations often have dedicated procurement departments who typically explore a range of product catalogues and speak to sales representatives prior to purchasing any equipment [RM:Espace].

4.3.2 Equip: Design

The resources required to support and operate a collection may vary enormously depending on the type of items being collected. However, before putting such resources in place, some sort of description of what is required must be thought about or documented. Such descriptions are essentially designs, even at a very broad level such as 'I require some sort of scrapbook into which I can paste the chocolate wrappers'. Although the types of design decisions required will depend on what is being collected, there are some generic design decisions which may be applicable to most collections. These include storage, displays, index, processes.

4.3.2.1 Equip: Design: Storage

Deciding where to keep things, and what to keep them in, is an essential element of the collecting practice. Some collections may only require a designated storage space, such as specified areas within a loft [RM:Loft], or a shelf for music CDs [RM:MusWil]; while others may require storage containers, for example, documents can be stored in filing cabinets [RM:Trophy] (Wilson 1990), and stamps may be stored in albums [RM:Stamp]. The design of storage facilities is a major activity in larger organisations such as Museums, Galleries, Archives, and Libraries. This may involve equipping in terms of having the right delivery or temporary storage facilities [RM:Acrop]. It can also involve having the right kinds of physical resources available for handling acquired objects, for instance ingest apparatus or containers. At the film production site, there was a complex arrangement of apparatus in place for the handling of newly acquired films and videotapes, so that they could be properly treated and sealed prior to ingest into the film archive. Dedicated teams were established to undertake this work.

4.3.2.2 Equip: Design: Displays

For some collections, the storage container may also be a display, for example, a bookcase [RM:Book] or a display cabinet. However, for collections which are larger than the capacity of the display facilities (such as those in Museums), separate storage areas may be required so that part of the collection can be stored while a selected subset is displayed. Even small-scale collections may require both display and storage facilities, for example, a picture frame on a wall displaying the latest Great Britain (GB) stamps before they are put into an album and replaced with newer GB stamps, or the loft storage facilities for those pieces in the display case collection that are not on show [RM:Stamp; Display]. In some settings, the design of displays becomes an important artform that may depend upon the support of professional services. At the Cite de l'Espace, certain exhibitions are changed at the beginning of each new season and professional exhibition designers from across Europe are invited to submit portfolios and provide tenders for the business of constructing the new exhibition spaces. Even once a tender is approved, there is an extensive set of negotiations and meetings with Local Curators before the design is finalised.

4.3.2.3 Equip: Design: Index

Collectors often want to know what they have in their collections, in order to organise or reorganise them; to write or talk about them; to display them; to facilitate the searching of them by themselves or others; to know what new items to obtain or not to obtain for them; to maintain them; or to simply to have an understanding of what they have got [RM:Loft; PhotoWil; Book; Acrop; Espace; Imp; Tate; MusTol; OFC]. Some collections, such as a few classic cars, may be small enough for the collector to have the knowledge in their heads; but larger collections may require some kind of list for the collector to keep a handle on their contents, for example, a collection of office documents [RM:Trophy]. This is even more emphatically the case for large organisations where multiple parties may be involved in assembling, maintaining, and using the collection [RM:Swiss; Acrop; Espace; Imp; Tate]. Any such index has to be recorded on some sort of equipment such as a notebook or index cards or some pages in a looseleaf binder. Such information is usually referred to as a catalogue or an index. Catalogues explicitly document what objects are in a collection (Saponaro and Evans 2019); while Indexes document significant words or terms related to the objects in a collection (Ashikuzzaman 2023). However, these meanings were defined many years before computers emerged; and colloquially their usage has broadened to embrace any information that can be used in a search activity (as will become apparent in subsequent chapters). Therefore, we have elected to use the single term 'index' throughout this book.

In some organisations, the index may be sufficiently large to require storing in a single or even multiple volumes, which themselves need to be designed [RM:Acrop; Espace; Imp; Tate]. The design of the index may also include the structure of a Reference Number [RM:Trophy], and defining what index fields to have (Wilson

1990, 2001). The larger the organisation and the more people who need to have access to the collection, the more formalised the index referencing system is likely to be [RM:Tate]. Some organisations, such as Libraries, are to adhere to existing indexing systems that are well-established in that collecting community (Wellisch 1975).

4.3.2.4 Equip: Design: Processes

The types of items being collected, and the scale of the collection, may require processes to be operated that are specific to their particular needs. This may be particularly true in the area of maintaining the collection. However, almost all collections will undertake some kind of process when they ingest new material into the collection. This may include labelling items, for example writing Reference Numbers onto documents [RM:Trophy] or on tags to accompany items [RM:Acrop] or adding new items into an index [RM:Trophy]. Individual collectors are likely to have such processes in their heads, while collecting institutions and organisations may well document their processes to ensure they are carried out reliably by multiple staff [RM:Acrop; Espace; Tate; Imp]. There is a sense in which the establishment of the whole post-production team studied at the film production site was focused upon the design of the storage workflow for the film archive. While there is clearly a first time through for any such processes or workflows, they are often actively reflected upon to design an 'in principle' way of doing that will only subsequently need to be tweaked [RM:Film].

4.3.3 Equip: Obtain

Having decided what equipment might be required to set up and manage a collection, the equipment has to be physically obtained.

4.3.3.1 Equip: Obtain: Acquire

The acquisition process involves taking the requirements that have been designed, evaluating the equipment that is available, and choosing what best fits the requirements at an appropriate price. For example, in acquiring a filing cabinet, the size and filing system required will narrow down the products available, and an evaluation of each will enable a final selection to be made (Wilson 1990). In some cases, the items being collected will dictate a specific piece of equipment; for example, if stamps of Great Britain are being collected, then an album printed with images of all the Great Britain stamps may be required (as opposed to buying an album with blank pages)[RM:Stamp].

4.3.3.2 Equip: Obtain: Create

Some items needed to support the building of a collection need to be created by the owner, for example indexes, shelving, etc. This work can also be outsourced to others, according to their specifications and the timescales they prefer. A powerful example of this is the example already given above of the creation of exhibition displays at the Cite de l'Espace where, once all of the specifications for a new display have been agreed with external consultants, there is a need to actually construct the new display, which involves the commissioning of a variety of local artisans and professionals (carpenters, painters, electricians, etc.).

4.3.3.3 Equip: Obtain: Join

For any particular type of collection, groups, clubs, societies, trade organisations, or other bodies may exist to bring enthusiasts together and to provide related information, products, and services for its members. This is an important part of equipping oneself with a suitable infrastructure for acquisition by ensuring one is on the right mailing lists, subscribing to the right catalogues, having appropriate notification processes in place, etc. [RM:Sheet]. Many collectors find it useful to join such organisations and take part in their activities. For example, local Philatelic Societies abound in the UK for stamp collectors to join; Museums can join the Association of Independent Museums; and Archives can join the International Council on Archives.

4.3.4 Equip: Implement

Having obtained the required equipment, the collection owner must install them and make sure that they do what is required.

4.3.4.1 Equip: Install

The equipment that has been obtained needs to be put in place and readied for use. For example, having created position labels for the loft collection, the labels needed to be securely mounted in easy-to-see positions in the loft [RM:Loft]. For others, such as Filers who have bought filing cabinets, these need to be placed in their designated places and any hanging files/folders will need to be set up and labelled as per the design. Libraries that have acquired a microfilm reader need to set it up and plug it into a power supply. Museum exhibition spaces have to be physically constructed on the ground such that they both meet the requirements of the projected display and connect up with other existing exhibitions and core infrastructure (e.g., electricity, environment controls, etc.) in appropriate ways [RM:Acrop; Espace].

4.3.4.2 Equip: Test

To test the installed equipment, an owner may do as little as just casting a critical eye over them or may undertake some trial runs. Either way, the objective is to make sure that they work as planned. For example, after installing the position labels for a loft collection, the owner might stand back to check that the position of the label satisfactorily indicates which physical space is being signposted without any ambiguity [RM:Loft]. In a library, equipment such as a microfilm reader will need to be given a trial run to ensure it performs as expected. In complex exhibition spaces, displays are always set-up prior to giving access to the public and often aspects of the display do not quite work as expected and need to be adjusted until Curators are satisfied [RM:Acrop; Espace; Tate].

4.4 Acquire Items for a Collection

Acquiring is a central practice in collecting—collectors usually want more (van den Eede 2010). In the context of Amateur Collecting (and potentially in other contexts, such as Private Curating), the thrill of deciding what objects to go after, of looking for them, of finding them, and of finally actually obtaining them, is what drives many collectors to continue with their pastime. Of course, not all objects have to be hunted down; some may be given by relatives or friends. Many large collections have their origins in donated or loaned objects [RM:Tate; Imp]. In some cases, individuals may create the objects they collect [RM:PhotoWil; PhotoTol; Data] or may subscribe to a service that provides the objects on a regular basis [RM:Stamp; PAWDOC].

The acquire practice comprises the elements as shown in Fig. 4.4.

4.4.1 Acquire: Target

Collectors usually have some idea of what items they would like to add to a collection. Sometimes those targets may only exist in the mind of the owner. In other cases, the targets may be written down in a list. Sometimes, the target list may be very broad, for example, 'I will acquire every single fireman's helmet that I come across'. In other cases, the targets may be very specific, such as the 1923 pair of Japanese stamps commemorating the Crown Prince's visit to Taiwan [RM:Stamp] (Wilson 2022). In large organisations like Libraries, Archives, and Museums, decisions about what to target may need to take into account all the stakeholders including users, managers, suppliers, and publishers (Fieldhouse 2012). It is particularly important to understand what users actually want or need (Xie and Matusiak 2016). As noted in Sect. 4.2.2.3, these decisions may also be strongly shaped by organisational policies (which themselves may reflect an expectation about who they are servicing and to what ends). In such organisations, budget management is also an integral part of

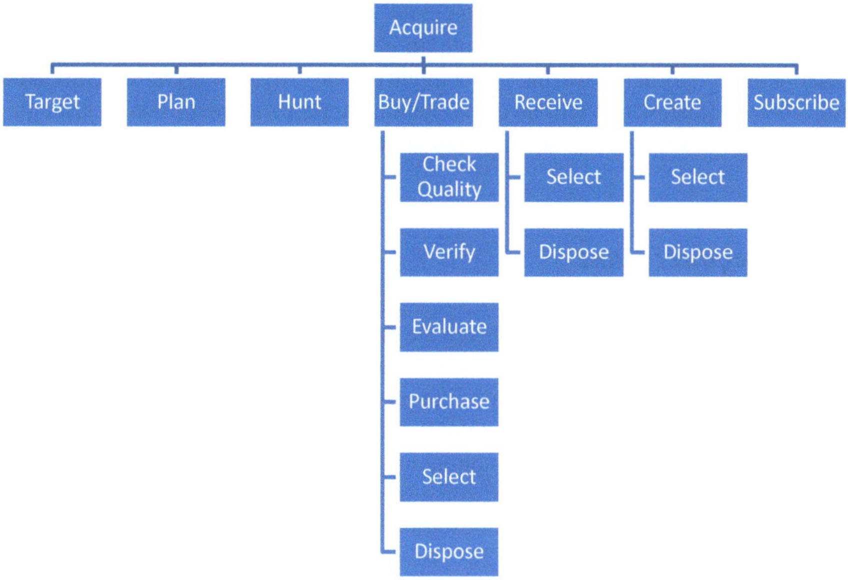

Fig. 4.4 Subsets of 'Acquire'

the targeting activity (Fieldhouse 2012). In addition to all these factors, institutions also have to deal with ethical dilemmas in which personal and professional beliefs and values have to be balanced one against the other (Saponaro and Evans 2019). For institutions dealing with controversial or strongly emotive content, this can be especially challenging [RM:Imp].

4.4.2 Acquire: Plan

Having established what their targets are, collectors may well have some plan in mind for how and where they are going to acquire the items concerned. This may well be just an idea in the back of the mind such as, 'I'm going to go the local car boot sale every weekend and see what turns up'; or it may be rather more specific such as, 'I'm going to work my way through my target list of stamps and, for each item, I'm going to find it and buy it on either eBay, eBid or HipStamps' [RM:Stamp]. Libraries may take a more focused approach by arranging standing orders with suppliers for all titles in a pre-specified category (Saponaro and Evans 2019). For Museums, there may be a need to have mechanisms in place with local and national archaeological organisations, metal detecting societies, and even other Museums, so that they are automatically notified when possible acquisitions become available [RM:Acrop]. Inter-organisational loans of content may be the result of long-term negotiations and planning between different organisations [RM:Acrop; Tate]. In those cases in which the owner is actually creating the items in the collection, a more detailed plan of action may be required, for example, to obtain a collection of data on subjects undertaking certain activities, the owner might decide to make short movie clips of the subjects over time, which will involve obtaining appropriate permissions, arranging appointments, suitably preparing equipment, etc. [RM:Data].

4.4.3 Acquire: Hunt

Some collectors may rely on being given the objects they want, or on subscribing to a service that provides them. However, most collectors have to hunt for the objects they are after. 'The thrill of the hunt' is a commonly used expression in discussions about collecting (Shuker 2010), and individuals seeking out desired objects in auctions, junk shops, car boot sales, etc., is common practice. When the items being sought are moderately difficult to find, and some time and effort have to be spent looking for them, then each sortie can be an exciting voyage of discovery, and it's thrilling when a find is made (Watkins et al. 2015). Of course, this mainly applies to Amateur Collectors and Private Curators, but, nevertheless, individuals within institutions and organisations that are targeting specific items may well also experience the thrill of the hunt. Evidently, this is less likely to be a feature of some collecting contexts, such as Archiving and Filing, where the content making up the collection is already identified or pre-given by its nature. Here, the focus is on mechanisms for ensuring the smooth flow of content into the archive or filing system instead [RM:Film; MusTol].

4.4.4 Acquire: Buy/Trade

One way of acquiring items for a collection is to buy them. There are a wide variety of sources to buy from including, auctions, dealers, and private sellers [RM:Stamp] (Wilson 2022). Regardless of the source of the material, potential purchasers typically want to check the quality of the item, assess its value, and verify its authenticity, before undertaking the purchase. The exception to this is when owners buy in bulk, in which case they will conduct more detailed check of content, quality and authenticity when they sort through the material after the purchase [RM:Stamp]. Large collecting organisations have much more structured and formalised purchasing practices. Libraries, for instance, have tightly specified purchasing arrangements that are often bound up with their collection development policies and that may even be facilitated through consortia to alleviate the pressure on individual libraries (Pye and Ball 1999). The Tate Modern is accountable for all purchases to its Board of Trustees and assiduously documents all of its purchases and the rationales underlying them (Tate 2020).

An alternative to buying something is to exchange it for something you have. While trading is perhaps not widespread, it is a perfectly viable way of acquiring objects. For example, the term 'swaps' has been well known in stamp collecting circles for many years; and it is undertaken in record collecting (Shuker 2010), in the trading card domain (Blume 2019); Upper Deck 2023), and in the UK Vintage Radio Community (Ellis and Haywood 2006). Exchange is attached to the 'Buy' practice because the only difference is in what you are paying for the object being acquired: money or an object of a similar type (or indeed anything else that the buyer will find acceptable). Exchange is also an established practice in the art world, especially among artists themselves who often swap works with other artists and can amass significant collections over time (O'Grady 2019).

4.4.4.1 Acquire: Buy/Trade: Check Quality

When collectors identify an item they want to buy, the most obvious immediate check they can make is to confirm that the quality of the item is up to the standard they require. For example, a tear in a stamp [RM:Stamp], or a price-clipped dust jacket on a book [RM:Book], may or may not be acceptable. Where it is a matter of created content, a check can be made of what has been produced [RM:Data; PhotoWil; PhotoTol]. For larger organisations looking to obtain new items, expert inspection and assessment may well be required [RM:Tate; Acrop].

4.4.4.2 Acquire: Buy/Trade: Verify

The more valuable an item, the more attractive it becomes for a forger to fake it. There are many fakes, particularly among the most well-known collectable artefacts. Awareness of this encourages collectors to verify the authenticity of items. For those knowing how to recognise fakes, careful examination of the item may suffice. However, the best way of ensuring veracity is to buy from reputable dealers. In other words, the work of verification can be pushed off onto third parties and trust invested in those parties instead. Independent verification can be time-consuming and expensive (Wilson 2022). Large organisations purchasing very expensive items on a regular basis such as the Tate, may recruit experts themselves, though there are also many consultancy companies that offer verification services (for example, Richard Polsky Art Authentication[2]).

4.4.4.3 Acquire: Buy/Trade: Evaluate

Once an item has passed the quality and verification checks, collectors must still decide how much they are prepared to pay for it. Of course, there may be occasions when a collector wants an item at virtually any price. However, collectors usually don't want to pay more than the actual market value of an item and would prefer

---

[2] https://richardpolskyart.com/.

to pay less if possible. Clearly, this requires that the market value is known. This can be established in a variety of ways including the use of catalogues (such as stamp catalogues like Stanley Gibbons[3] [RM:Stamp], or for Libraries such as the one offered by Baker and Taylor[4]), or by researching how much various dealers are selling them for or how much they are being sold for in auctions (Wilson 2022).

4.4.4.4 Acquire: Buy/Trade: Purchase

Having decided what to buy and how much to pay for it, collectors may attempt to negotiate the price or other aspects of the deal related to the contents, transport costs, guarantees, etc. Once, the terms have been agreed payment is made. This again can be subject to significant variation, from cash payments made at car boot sales to major international bank transfers ([RM:Tate; Espace; Priory]. Purchasing itself may also implicate a range of other practices associated with banking and accounts management, depending upon the degree to which formal transactions have to be processed, recorded, and subject to audit (Pye and Ball 1999).

4.4.4.5 Acquire: Buy/Trade: Select

In the context of Amateur Collecting and, very occasionally, other forms of collecting, collectors may purchase larger lots of items where the collectors do not necessary fully know the details of the contents. For all such purchases, a degree of sorting and sifting will be required to investigate the contents in more detail and select the items that are to be retained and added to the collection [RM:OFC]. The possibility of finding something special in the course of this sorting process is one of the attractions of making such bulk purchases. For example, cartons of stamps are often sold at auctions, and it is often impossible to know exactly what they contain before bidding on them (Wilson 2022). Even when very specific purchases are made of only a limited number of items, the collector may only want to retain a subset of the items and will select the required items accordingly [RM:Stamp].

4.4.4.6 Acquire: Buy/Trade: Dispose

Some collectors deliberately buy items to sell on (typically to make money so they can buy other items they want for their collections) (Shuker 2010). A classic example here is the resale of trading cards, such as Pokemon cards (Craddock 2004). With reference to the preceding section, some collectors buy a bulk lot and, having selected the items to include in their own collections, want to dispose of the remainder in some

[3] https://www.stanleygibbons.com/shop/publications/stamp-catalogues.

[4] https://www.baker-taylor.com/.

way or other. For instance, book collectors may literally buy books by weight[5] and then sift through those they wish to keep and those they wish to resell. Adjunct practices here include storing them in, for example, an out-of-the-way cupboard. Unwanted collectibles may also be given away. Whichever option is chosen, the objective is to separate them from the collection they have been excluded from.

4.4.5 Acquire: Receive

Some collections consist of items which are received in the normal course of domestic or business activity. For example, a collection of document files [RM:Trophy], a collection of scientific journals [RM:Trophy], video files for ingest [RM:Data; TVBC], or files relating to a news story for archiving [RM:Swiss]. Other collections may acquire items which are given to collectors as either presents, or bequeathments from somebody who has died (DeWitt 1988). This can be in relation to Amateur or Private Collections, but it can also take the form of donations to semi-public or national collections [RM:Tate; Imp]. In some cases, the items received may be something that the collector specifically wants and/or has asked for. For example, a product specification that has been requested may be included in a filing system; a particular first edition book on somebody's target list may make a nice birthday present; or a stamp album someone has looked through enthusiastically might be left to that person in the owner's will [RM:Stamp]. Museums are often specifically known to want certain kinds of objects [RM:Acrop; Espace; Imp]. In other cases, the items received will not have been specifically requested and collectors will need to decide which items, if any, to include in their collections (DeWitt 1988). As with bulk purchase, when objects are bequeathed or gifted to collectors, there are two primary subsets of practices implicated by that: selection and disposal.

4.4.5.1 Acquire: Receive: Select

When incoming items are received in quantity that have not been specifically requested, the collector will need to make a decision about whether to keep or to discard them [RM:Trophy]. The specific selection practices here resemble those associated with the 'Buy/Trade' practice described above, where collectors will check the quality and possibly verify the authenticity of the items and evaluate the merits of including them in their collection. Unwanted items will be disposed of.

[5] https://www.usedbooksfactory.com/buy-second-hand-old-books/category/WHOLESALE-BOOKS-BY-WEIGHT-KILO.

4.4.5.2 Acquire: Receive: Dispose

Unwanted items may be disposed of in a variety of ways such as selling them [RM:Stamp], giving them to charity shops, or simply by putting them in a waste disposal facility. In the case of unwanted gifts, the collector may make take particular care to ensure the donor is not offended (Hurdley 2007). Whatever route is taken, the key objective is to separate them from the collection they have been excluded from.

4.4.6 Acquire: Create

As noted above, for some collections, owners create the items themselves. Common examples of this are the photo collections that many possess in which most, but not necessarily all, of the photos have been taken by the owner [RM:OFC; PhotoWil; PhotoTol]. This may also include the recordings people make of particular music records [RM:MusWil; MusTol]. Creation-related practices can also be found in research settings where data may be recorded [RM:Data]. Artists, writers, and musicians often also build up collections of their own sketches, notes, and jottings (Lucas 2016).

4.4.6.1 Acquire: Create: Select

When owners create things for their collections, even though the content and quality of the objects are under their direct control, the owner may subsequently reject some items for the collection because content or quality criteria are not met satisfactorily. This is particularly the case when certain photos in a film that has been developed are left out of an album; or when cine films are being spliced together and particular frames are excluded [RM:PhotoWil; PhotoTol].

4.4.6.2 Acquire: Create: Dispose

As an adjunct practice to the above, when choices are made about what created items to keep, some or all of those that have been set aside may be simply destroyed or put out with the rubbish [RM:PhotoWil].

4.4.7 Acquire: Subscribe

A final way of acquiring objects for collections is to subscribe to a service that either provides a random selection periodically [RM:Stamp] or that provides information about new items that are available that can then be requested (such as the abstracting service provided by the National Computing Centre in the 1970s). Libraries may use subscription services to order journals and periodicals (Saponaro and Evans 2019).

4.5 Deposit New Items into a Collection

Once an item has been acquired, it needs to be deposited into the collection—a practice that may also be referred to as ingesting or accessioning. Sometimes this may be as simple as placing the item on a shelf. However, often the practices that are carried out are much more involved—particularly in Libraries, Museums, Galleries, and Archives, which will usually create entries in an index and label the objects before placing them into their designated storage. Filers and Private Curators may do the same, while Amateur Collectors are less likely to adopt such formal practices.

The deposit practice comprises the sub-practices as shown in Fig. 4.5.

4.5.1 Deposit: Sort

If a whole set of objects are to be deposited into a collection, the first thing to be done is to sort and organise them into logical groups. This achieves a number of things: it enables an understanding to be gained of what's there; it helps in deciding whether any objects are to be discarded; it provides information for the indexing process; and it provides essential input to deciding what storage is required. For some organisations, a constant supply of new items to be ingested makes this an ongoing process [RM:Acrop; Film; Swiss], and in cases where this is especially intensive, dedicated teams may be involved [RM:TVBC].

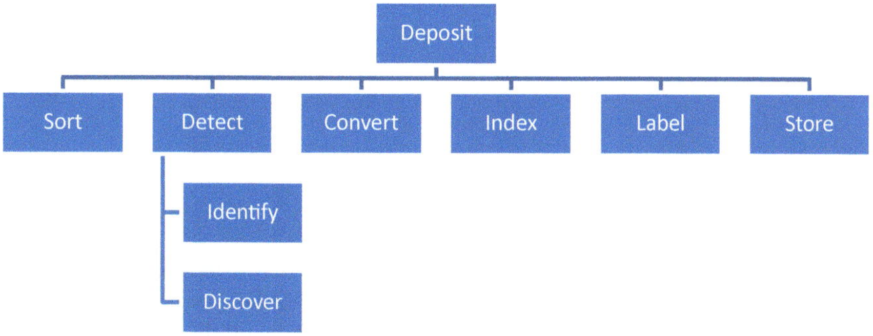

Fig. 4.5 Subsets of 'Deposit'

4.5.2 Deposit: Detect

Upon acquiring an item, a collector often wants to find out information about it, so that the details that are detected can be included with the item when it is stored in the collection.

4.5.2.1 Deposit: Detect: Identify

Many collections contain items that have established names, such as technological space artefacts [RM:Espace] and films [RM:Film]. Others may be listed in catalogues with names and numbers [RM:Stamp] (Wilson 2022). Such items can be identified before being labelled and stored in the collection. For some items, the identification process may take significant amounts of time and energy and involve a range of additional practices on the part of experts potentially using specialised equipment in their own right, such as archaeological finds [RM:Acrop].

4.5.2.2 Deposit: Detect: Discover

For some types of items, it may be evident what type of object they are, but they may have no established names or numbers, in which case information about them will need to be discovered. Photos are one such example, for which even the owner may not know details about the contents without doing research. For old photo collections, which are handed down to younger family members, one of the best ways of discovering the contents of individual pictures can be to talk to older members of the family [RM:PhotoWil; PhotoTol] (Wilson 2016). In the case of things like archaeological finds, even once the type of object has been established, discovering more information about the object may again involve highly specialised kinds of research, potentially across multiple organisations [RM:Acrop]. In the Museum sector, the Spectrum standard for collection management identifies the valuation of collection objects, and the documentation of intellectual property and data protection rights, as key practices (Collections Trust 2024).

4.5.3 Deposit: Convert

Certain types of items may need to be converted in some way before being stored in the collection. For example, stamp collectors who prefer their used stamps to be off the paper they are stuck to will take the trouble to soak them off the paper, and dry and press them [RM:Stamp]. Another type of conversion is undertaken when slide format photos are converted into printed photos [RM:PhotoWil]. In the case of objects for display in Museums and Galleries, there may be a need to undertake restoration work of some kind [RM:Acrop; Tate]. There is a host of other types of conversion activities across various contexts, depending on the type of items concerned and the decisions that owners have taken about how they want to store and access them.

4.5.4 Deposit: Index

An index is a list of names of objects usually with one or more additional pieces of information associated with each object. An index helps collectors (and others) to know what objects are in their collections and to record any amount of additional information that they believe is relevant [RM:PhotoWil].

The design of indexes has already been discussed in Sect. 4.3.2.3. When it comes to creating an index entry for a new item, the collector should then simply need to fill in each of the index fields [RM:Trophy] (Wilson 1990) (Wilson 2001). This process may be assisted by the information identified in the sorting activity described in Sect. 4.5.1 and in the detect activity described in Sect. 4.5.2. Sometimes collectors may subsequently adjust the contents of the index to rectify errors or reflect their changing views (Wilson 2001). Index practices can also change to accommodate new organisational arrangements, such as the need for new kinds of metadata to support changing interests. At the film production site, for instance, although there was a pre-existing index for all the materials in the film archive, new notions of how to commercialise the contents of the archive meant that additional index entries were required, effectively necessitating a complete update of the whole index.

Libraries, Museums, Galleries, and Archives all maintain indexes (sometimes referred to as catalogues) of the contents of their collections. Libraries in particular make use of various indexing schemes to facilitate retrieval. For example, the creation of a thesaurus from which particular words/terms can be included in the index of a particular item (Hoekstra and Evers 1977); and the development of Reference Number schemas such as LCC (Library of Congress Classification), Dewy and Universal Decimal Classification (UDC), which place titles into particular categories. However, there has been debate about the adequacy of such schemas (Manof 2004).

4.5.5 Deposit: Label

Some collections label some or all of the items within them. The information on the label typically, but not always, is tightly bound up with the entries in the index. The label may be physically attached to the item, such as in a loft collection [RM:Loft]; or written on the item concerned as in a document collection [RM:Trophy], whichever is most appropriate [RM:Display]. Alternatively, it may be a separate entity placed next to the item concerned. In some cases, there may be two labels for each item—one written on the item and one placed adjacent to it, such as in a photo collection in an album with slip-in tabs. In this case, each photo is labelled on its back as well as having a separate entry on a slip-in tab [RM:PhotoWil].

Libraries, Museums, Galleries, and Archives all label their objects, while the practice may or may not be performed in other collecting contexts. Museums, Galleries and Archives are careful in their labelling not to detract from the originality of their objects, whereas Libraries are less concerned with defacing a title and more focused on enabling the management of loans, returns, and shelf placement. In the case of archaeological artefacts, the objects themselves are often annotated with references that are largely only meaningful to Curators, while associated labels in display cases are often highly descriptive to promote policies such as education and visitor engagement [RM:Acrop]. In some Museums, the labelling of objects is bound up with other considerations such as the design of exhibition spaces and displays [RM:Espace; Imp], in which case the labelling may vary from space to space. The complexities of labelling are described in some detail in a guide produced by the Collections Trust (Harrison 2020).

4.5.6 Deposit: Store

The final part of the deposit activity is to place the item in its designated storage location as designed in Sect. 4.3.2.1. For example, a new chocolate wrapper joining the collection could be placed in the collection's ring binder storage unit [RM:Choc]; a new memento may be placed in an archive box [RM:MemWil]; a new item in the loft collection may be placed in a certain position in the loft [RM:Loft]; and a new addition to the book collection could be placed in a bookcase [RM:Book]. Collecting institutions often place their new acquisitions temporarily in prominent display positions so that their users can see what's new; and only after that will the objects concerned be placed in their permanent storage locations which, ideally, should also be accessible to users. However, for very large collections, the available display space can limit the number of items that can be displayed at any one-time [RM:Tate; Acrop]. Such organisations often have other storage in which items are kept until they are cycled through exhibition spaces according to various curated themes and circulation policies. In large Museums and Scientific Collections, storage policies can also relate to supporting the development of scientific knowledge, with some items only ever being destined for non-exhibition storage to meet these ends [RM:Acrop].

4.6 Use Items in a Collection

Collectors make use of their collections in a variety of ways. Individuals (Private Curators, Amateur Collectors, and even individuals in institutions such as Archives, Museums, and Galleries) often take pleasure in just looking at their objects. Accumulators and Filers actively use the objects they collect; and Libraries, Archives, Museums, Galleries, and Private Curators that have opened their collections to the public, actively seek to attract the public, or a selected subset, to come and experience their collections. Collection Owners and Users often investigate objects in collections to find out more about them, and in doing so they often collaborate with other people or societies or information sources. They may take copies of objects to enable them to do so. Owners sometime reorganise their collections as a result of what they find or for other reasons. All of these uses often involve searches of the collection and its index in order to locate particular objects.

The use practice comprises the sub-practices as shown in Fig. 4.6.

4.6.1 Use: Authorise

Collection Owners have full rights to enjoy and use their collections as they wish. However, Libraries, Museums, Galleries, Archives, and some Private Curators provide access to some or all of their items to other people, in which case some kind of authorisation process and controls may be enacted. Institutions which allow free access to the public may have very few controls. However, others operate authorisation systems which typically require potential users to provide some sort of information, and possibly payment. In return, they are provided with a card, ticket, or some other signifier of their access rights subject to any accompanying terms and conditions. The nature of controls in different contexts can also vary widely. For some types of objects, touching and even photography may be an issue [RM:Acrop].

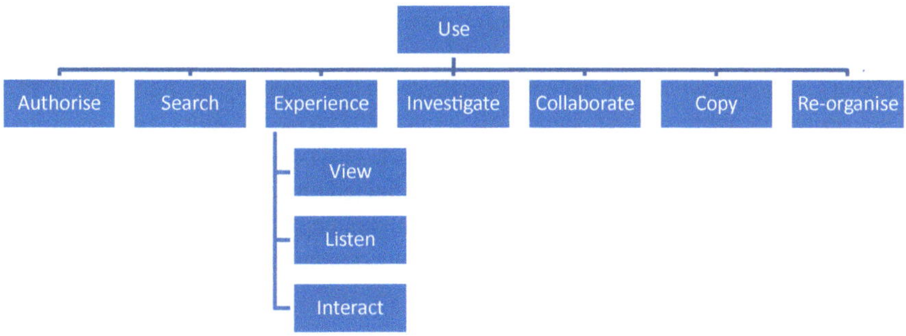

Fig. 4.6 Subsets of 'Use'

In other contexts, direct interaction with objects may be encouraged or even essential [RM:Espace].

4.6.2 Use: Search

Collection users wishing to look at or investigate specific items or groups of items, may not know if such items exist in the collection and/or where the items are located. To find out, they may conduct a search on an index if one exists, or they may conduct a physical search of the collection [RM:Acrop; Espace; Imp]. In some cases, for instance Libraries, users may prefer to undertake physical searches even where an index exists (Ross 1999). If the search is successful, one or more items may be selected and subsequently accessed by the searcher [RM: Trophy]. For example, the filing owner of a large document collection may have need to look for both familiar documents and documents that may or may not be in the collection (Wilson 1990) and may need to conduct the search under several different circumstances such as when in the middle of a piece of work, when speaking on the phone or when talking to a visitor (Wilson 2001). Libraries, Archives, Museums, and Galleries usually have indexes available for their users to search though in some instances, and they may be incomplete: for example, the British Museum has still only catalogued about half of the objects in its collection (The British Museum 2024).

For smaller collections without an index that owners are very familiar with, a quick physical search may be sufficient; for example, a flick through the pages of a stamp album or a chocolate wrapper collection [RM:Choc; Stamp].

4.6.3 Use: Experience

One of the things that people do with their collections is simply to experience the items themselves either by looking at them, listening to them, or interacting with them in some way. They may do this for particular activity-based reasons, as when a Filer reads an item in a work document collection [RM:Trophy], or simply for the pleasure of seeing what they have in the collection and enjoying the items concerned. This primarily applies to Amateur Collectors and Private Curators, but individuals working in Museums, Galleries, or Archives are also open to this. For most people working in large organisations, however, the collected objects are largely experienced in the process of undertaking work related to the upkeep of the collection. For public collections, visitors are open to experiencing the content in similarly varied ways.

4.6.3.1 Use: Experience: View

Many collections contain items that can be used and enjoyed by looking at them. For example, mementos can be experienced by flicking through a folder [RM:MemWil]; a collection of handheld computers can be looked at in a display case [Display]; a collection of images may have photos that can be looked at and movie clips and videos that can be watched [RM:PhotoWil]. For some collections, especially Museums and Galleries, a large part of their mission is to provide for people to view their contents. Thus, in the New Acropolis Museum, one can actively view a large proportion of the Parthenon marbles. In the Cite de l'Espace, one can stand and admire an Ariadne 5 rocket. In the Tate, one can slowly pass through galleries looking at artworks by Modern and Contemporary artists.

4.6.3.2 Use: Experience: Listen

Some collections contain material that can only be experienced by listening to it. These are typically collections of music [RM:MusWil; MusTol], but may also be spoken word collections of audiobooks, or of people talking [RM:MusWil], which Owners and Users can enjoy at their leisure. Most Libraries have collections of audio materials—music and books—which can be obtained on loan, much like books. The British Library Sound Archive[6] is one of the largest sound collections in the world and houses over six million recordings of music, the spoken work, and ambient noise. Further examples of materials designed to be listened to can be found in Museums, where visitors may listen to recordings of historical events [RM:Espace; Imp]. Many Museums also show films as a part of the visitor experience, where, as with the film archive at the film production site, the materials are designed to not only be viewed but heard. In the case of collections of research data, recordings may be uniquely audio-based [RM:Data].

4.6.3.3 Use: Experience: Interact

While viewing and listening in relation to the content of collections requires no particular direct engagement with objects, some collections include items that involve actually interacting with them in some way. For instance, particular types of collections contain machinery that need to be operated to be fully experienced. Examples here would include collections of classic cars or miniature railway engines. Many Museums contain exhibits demanding some kind of interaction [RM:Espace]. Often these are designed to encourage visitor engagement, especially children. Beyond this, collections can be focused around smells, such as the Musee du Parfum in Paris,[7] and some Museums make use of smell to evoke particular kinds of atmosphere, such

[6] https://www.bl.uk/subjects/sound.

[7] https://musee-parfum-paris.fragonard.com/en/.

as the First World War trench exhibition at the Imperial War Museum. Occasionally, touch can also be a specific feature. At the New Acropolis Museum, visitors often display an urge to touch the sculptures, so certain replica exhibits were created that visitors could specifically interact with through touch [RM:Acrop].

4.6.4 Use: Investigate

Having established a collection, one of the activities open to collectors is to find out more about the items it contains. This is essentially research, which may be performed to any level of detail, and which may be documented to some degree or other. Some collectors may just make a cursory investigation into one particular aspect; while others become experts in their fields, for example, a stamp collector known to one of the authors, became an expert in Great Britain pre-Victorian Postal History to and from the continent. In some larger organisations, especially Museums and Galleries, research related to the content is an integral part of their mission [RM:Acrop; Tate] and can lead to the establishment of whole departments dedicated to this purpose.

In collections of written material, the contents are usually the most significant element of the items, and the investigation of their contents and the discovery of information within them, will occur as and when they are accessed. For example, a collection of letters may be investigated to find out something about the writer [RM:Let]; or a selected set of items in a document collection may be used to develop ideas for a journal paper (Wilson 2001); or the contents of a collection of data might be analysed to produce some conclusions [RM:Data]. Libraries housing archival documents and dedicated document archives provide a range of services to support research activities being undertaken by researchers, often from around the world.[8]

4.6.5 Use: Collaborate

Collectors often like to talk to, and collaborate with, like-minded people (Dillon 2019). They might do this informally through conversations, or in more formal circumstances such as at gatherings to hear talks organised by the societies they belong to. Indirect interactions also occur through magazines and communications sent out by clubs and societies (Wilson 2022). Libraries, Museums, Galleries, and Archives may belong to umbrella organisation which may provide opportunities to meet other members, take part in working parties to address contemporary issues, and to present and listen to papers on topics of current interest. Many larger organisations of this kind are also active in participating in research projects, with staff attending international conferences [RM:TVBC; Swiss; Acrop; Espace; Imp; Tate].

[8] See, e.g., https://www.bl.uk/research/ and https://www.nationalarchives.gov.uk/help-with-your-research/.

4.6.6 *Use: Copy*

There may be occasions when a user wants to be able to look at items away from their usual locations. For example, people may copy recorded music to listen to when away from their home sound system [RM:MusWil]; or, when visiting a collector's fair or auction, an owner may take a photograph or photocopy of items in a collection to be clear about what items are missing from the collection. In some instances, copying is a way of sharing parts of a collection with others (see Sect. 4.7.3).

4.6.7 *Use: Reorganise*

When a collector decides to adjust the contents of a collection (see Sect. 4.2.3), or to redesign the storage it is contained in (see Sect. 4.3.2.1), a reorganisation of the collection may be required [RM:OFC]. For example, the owner of a stamp collection may decide to rationalise the collection [RM:Stamp]. Even if no significant changes are being made to the collection's contents or storage, owners may still wish to reorganise the items that they have, such as when an owner decides to prune the household file collection [RM:HDoc]. As described in Sect. 4.2.3, Collection Assessment is a standard activity in many large collecting institutions, particularly Libraries, and may well inspire the reorganisation of a collection. As noted in Sect. 4.3.2.2, Museums and Galleries regularly change their exhibitions and displays as they cycle through their existing content or display newly acquired items. This, too, can lead to significant reorganisation [RM:Acrop; Espace; Imp; Tate].

4.7 Reveal the Items in a Collection

Revealing a collection involves taking steps to inform other people about the collection. This can be for the purposes of sharing the contents with other people, improving their visibility, or exploiting the collection's potential for wider, and possibly more lucrative, usage.

Reveal comprises the sub-practices as shown in Fig. 4.7.

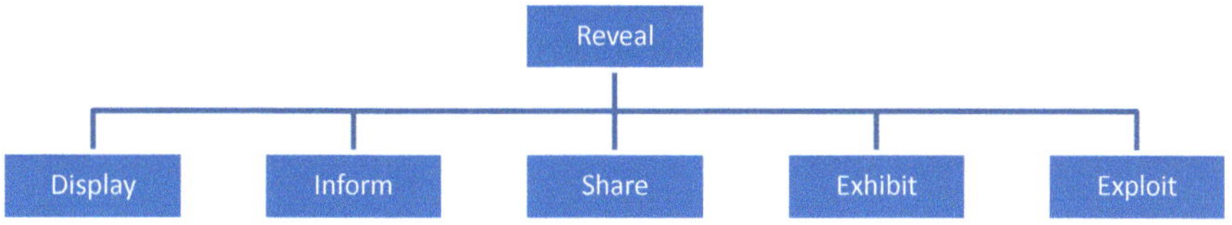

Fig. 4.7 Subsets of 'Reveal'

4.7.1 Reveal: Display

Collectors may display items in their collection either because they want to increase their own experience and enjoyment of the collection, and/or because they want it to be viewed by other people. For example, a display of the latest stamps issued and purchased may be placed on the collector's study wall [RM:Stamp; OFC]; a display of a collector's trophy collection in thumbnail form can be framed and placed on a wall [RM:Trophy]; and a collection of computer artefacts can be placed in a display case [RM:Display]. We have already noted in Sects. 4.3, 4.5, and 4.6 how Libraries, Museums, Galleries, Archives, and even Private Collections may deliberately display their collections for visitors to see and/or use. In such organisations, new acquisitions often have an impact upon the curated themes in order to facilitate their display [Tate][Acrop]. For many of these organisations, promotion and marketing have played an increasingly vital role to get the customers in (Fieldhouse 2012); and, in some cases, may even have dedicated marketing personnel with their own adjunct sets of practices [RM:Espace].

4.7.2 Reveal: Inform

Collectors may inform other people about their collections for a variety of reasons. One such reason is to increase the understanding of users, or potential users, of what the collection consists of and how to find their way about it. For example, it may be necessary to provide guidance to family members on how the loft collection operates [RM:Loft]; or a stamp collector might want to introduce younger members of the family to stamp collecting in general and to the stamp collection in particular [RM:Stamp]. Institutional collectors often make special efforts to provide informative labels about the objects they have on display, and some may provide in-depth guidebooks that go into greater detail than can be accommodated within labels [RM:Acrop; Tate].

Another reason for informing other people is if a collector has conducted detailed investigations of a collection and wishes to make the results known to a wider audience [RM:Trophy]. Indeed, some collectors may enjoy writing in specialist collecting magazines, fanzines, etc., drawing on their collections for pictorial examples; and in some cases, they may even make a living out of doing so by turning their hobby into a job such as journalism (Shuker 2010). Publishing scholarly research about items in collections is a feature of the work in many larger Libraries, Museums, and Galleries, as noted in Sect. 4.6.4.

4.7.3 Reveal: Share

Sharing items in a collection may be done by either sending copies of the collection to other people as is often done with photos [RM:PhotoWil; PhotoTol] or when sharing data with other researchers [RM:Data]. Another approach is to place the collection in full view of the other people you may wish to see it (which may include anyone who visits your home), for example a collection of books [RM:Book] or a music collection [RM:MusTol]. Of course, the latter elides into other practices, such as Display and Exhibit which may also be considered ways of sharing. Here, the distinction often resides in what the collectors consider themselves to be aiming to do.

When it comes to lending, some people may have been put-off doing this in the past because the items concerned haven't been returned. However, others may be enthusiastic about sharing their tastes (or even keen to enhance their status and credibility) (Shuker 2010). Some kinds of collecting contexts are partly premised on the notion of lending, for instance Libraries. Indeed, the spectrum standard for Museum collection management includes the specific practice 'Loans out (lending objects)' (Collections Trust 2024).

4.7.4 Reveal: Exhibit

Collectors may wish to exhibit part or all of their collections at particular events or locations—particularly if the collection contains items of special interest. For example, a chocolate wrapper collection could be displayed in a hobby's exhibition [RM:Choc]. The exhibit may stay in place for varying lengths of time—sometimes for just a day or sometimes for months on end. However, exhibits, unlike displays, are created with a specific, relatively narrow, theme, and usually stay in place for a limited amount of time. In the case of certain contexts, such as Libraries, Museums, Galleries, and (potentially) Private Collections, exhibition is a central feature of how they are organised because there is an understanding that a visiting public will require access and be able to view items on display [RM:Acrop; Espace; Imp; Tate; Priory]. The work involved in conceptualising and organising content within collections as an exhibition has already been discussed in Sect. 4.3.2.2.

An exhibit about a collection doesn't necessarily have to include the actual items in the collection. A good example of this is when a book is created about a collection [RM:Stamp].

4.7.5 Reveal: Exploit

Some collections may contain material that is in demand by the general public. This represents an opportunity to exploit the potential for either kudos or money, an opportunity that may be of particular benefit to collections owned by institutional owners who can incur large expenses in maintaining their collections [RM:OFC]. The ways in which items can be exploited are many and varied and range from post-cards with images of items; books about the collection; and full-size 3D models of items. Many different examples can be found in well-known institutions around the world. Even Amateur Collectors can easily, and relatively cheaply, create books about their collections, using online publishers. For example, a book about how a collection of Italian stamps was assembled, and containing photographs of all the relevant album pages of stamps was created by one of the authors (Wilson 2022). Amateur Collectors may also exploit their collections by using their objects as examples when writing articles on collecting topics (Shuker 2010). The *sine qua non* of collection exploitation is perhaps the gift shops one encounters in Museums and Galleries, with some of the more sophisticated ones offering a vast array of items for sale inspired by the collection, including works of art in their own right (such as photographs and ceramics) [RM:Acrop]. In some Museums, the gift shops are independent enterprises with leasing arrangements, which is effectively another mechanism for such organisations to exploit their collections [RM:Acrop].

4.8 Maintain the Items in a Collection

Many collections require some sort of maintenance to keep them protected and preserved in the long term. Some larger collections may need to keep a proportion of their items in archive storage due to a shortage of main storage space and to undertake periodic checks of the inventory to ensure it doesn't get mislaid. Institutional collectors may also have equipment such as Microfilm Readers which needs to be looked after. For organisational contexts where there is an ongoing need to provide for use, maintenance may encompass a set of routine administrative tasks and updates.

Maintain comprises the various sub-practices as shown in Fig. 4.8.

4.8.1 Maintain: Manage

Institutions such as Libraries and Museums need to manage any specialised equipment such as microfiche readers, special lighting, and air-conditioners to ensure it is

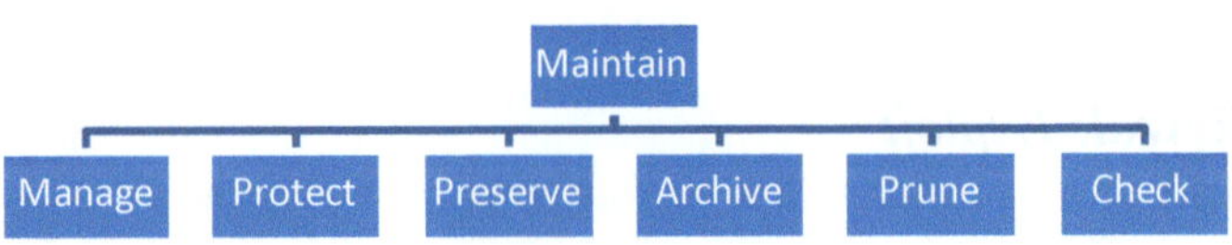

Fig. 4.8 Subsets of 'Maintain'

serviced and continues to be fit for purpose. This may also apply to individual collectors who have specialised equipment such as magnifiers to support their collecting activities. In the case of one of the authors' music collections, managing the content of the collection and its associated metadata requires continual work [RM:MusTol]. Large organisations may also need to maintain their records [RM:Swiss] and to work on keeping them up to date. We have already noted that the British Museum considers the cataloguing of its contents ongoing work and, in the film production site, at the time of study, there was a similar set of routine administrative tasks associated with managing the film archive. Collecting organisations will also need to manage the intellectual property rights and data protection rights associated with objects, reproductions, and information (Collections Trust 2024).

4.8.2 Maintain: Protect

Most collections face the common threats of loss or damage through fire, flood, and theft [RM:OFC], fire being the most destructive of these (Spinney 2022). Less fortunate collections also face the possibility of loss or damage in the course of war. The protections against such events include physical security measures, and insurance (though this latter option won't get the items back) (Wilson 2022). For some large collections, where such a thing is possible, maintenance may involve a continual effort to copy the content and physically move the copies to other locations. This is notably the case with film and sound media [RM:Film; TVBC]. Protection can also implicate a set of regular environment and security checks [RM:Film; Tate; Acrop], as well as planning for what to do in an emergency and how to respond to the damage or loss of objects in the collection (Collections Trust 2024).

4.8.3 Maintain: Preserve

Some types of items, such as paintings, documents, books, and garments, are particularly prone to deterioration for a variety of reasons. In Libraries, the risks include packing the books on the shelving too tightly, inappropriate temperature and humidity, exposure to sunlight, and mould or insects (Saponaro and Evans 2019). Therefore, collectors need to periodically check the condition of their objects (Collections Trust 2024) and to take steps to understand what deterioration their particular items are liable to suffer and to take special measures to prevent this from occurring. For example, keeping photos away from direct sunlight [RM:PhotoWil], and placing an archival cover on book dust jackets [RM:Book]. Collectors may also attempt to repair items that have deteriorated, either by their own efforts or by commissioning an expert. Preservation and restoration are particularly important aspects of the maintenance of Museum and Gallery Collections [RM:Acrop; Tate]. At the time of study, the New Acropolis Museum in Athens was engaged in a major restoration project of the caryatids from one of the temples on the Acropolis and had actually turned the work into a spectator event where visitors could pass through a gallery to watch restorers at work, making this the locus of a number of the different practices we have discussed.

4.8.4 Maintain: Archive

Some collections get too large for the space that is available for them, and it becomes necessary to remove some of the items to archive storage, perhaps on a permanent basis or alternatively on a rotational cycle. For example, a document collection may become too large for the available filing cabinets, and some of the less used items may be placed in archive boxes in a storeroom [RM:Trophy] (Wilson 2001). This has been a particular issue for Museums and Galleries, some of which may have more items in store than on display (Sola 2004; Macdonald 2006). Indeed, for some Museums, there can be more in storage than on display (for example, the British Museum) and their archival role can be considered as important as their public-facing one, especially if they house national collections [RM:Acrop]. Ongoing archive work in many organisations can be built into other routine practices [RM:TVBC]. In others, it may take dedicated effort that is separate to people's other everyday work [RM:Swiss].

4.8.5 Maintain: Prune

An alternative to archiving items in collections that get too big for the storage space is to simply select those items that are no longer needed and to dispose of them in some way. This is often what is done with filing systems, such as collections of household files [RM:HDoc; TolDoc]. Items selected in such a pruning activity are often destroyed, though various disposal options are feasible (see Sect. 4.9 Dispose of a collection). It should be remembered that the process of pruning items from a collection also involves deaccessioning the items concerned from the index records in which they were represented (Hohn 2008), if any such index exists [RM:TolDoc]. Libraries periodically remove old and damaged volumes from their shelves and will often give them away or sell them at massively reduced prices (Golden 1999).

4.8.6 Maintain: Check

Collectors with significant numbers of items can easily lose track of their inventory—particularly if it is being moved around by users and being placed in and out of archive storage [RM:Display]. This is a typical inventory management problem, which a collection's Design practices may have addressed (see Sect. 4.3.2). However, the only way to be sure of what you have at any given moment is to periodically conduct an inventory check (Collections Trust 2024). This will then enable efforts to be focused on tracking down missing items; and will provide the baseline for ongoing use of the collection and for subsequent inventory checks. This is an issue which particularly affects very large organisations. However, Amateur Collections with substantial numbers of objects may also face the same inventory management challenge but are less likely to address it in a methodical way.

4.9 Dispose of a Collection

It can come to pass that individuals may wish to dispose of part or all of their collection or may wish to make provisions for the collection after their death. This can affect Accumulators, Amateur Collectors, Private Curators, and sometimes even Filers. Institutional collectors may also wish to reduce their holdings and dispose of some of their objects, though in some contexts, such as Galleries, this is more likely to fall within the practice of exchange. It is important to note that the disposal of any object from a collection should be accompanied by appropriate adjustments to indexes etc. (see Sect. 4.2.3 Initiate: Adjust). In the Museum sector, the Collection Trust (2024) identifies this as a Deaccessioning and Disposal practice.

Dispose comprises the sub-practices as shown in Fig. 4.9.

4.9.1 Dispose: Donate

One way of disposing of part or all of a collection is to simply give it away, though this does depend on finding a willing recipient. Some people may give a few items to an individual to test out whether they have an interest in them and, therefore, may be somebody to whom they might bequeath the whole collection to (Goode 2002). For small numbers of widely collected items, such potential recipients may be easy to make contact with. However, for large collections, or for unusual or bulky items, it may be more difficult. For example, finding a permanent repository to which the PAWDOC collection can be donated, had proved impossible up to the time of

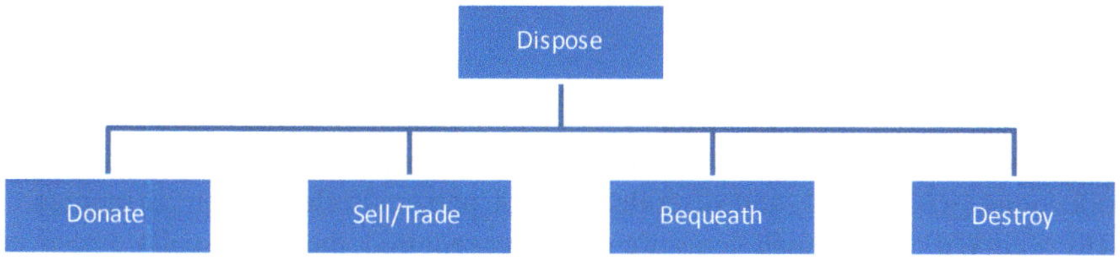

Fig. 4.9 Subsets of 'Dispose'

writing [RM:PAWDOC]. As noted in Chap. 2, some large collections are actually built around donations from various Private Collectors, especially with regard to works of art (van der Grijp 2024), and, in some countries, there can be tax incentives that encourage this practice (Teitell et al. 2019).

4.9.2 Dispose: Sell

Selling all or part of a collection is perfectly feasible provided there is a demand for it. This can be done through auctions or by offering items or whole collections to dealers (see, for instance (Christie's 2023). Inevitably the amount of interest will depend on the price being asked, and if the price is too high the goods may not sell. As noted in 4.8.5, Libraries often sell excess stock by putting them in boxes for visitors to look through. There has been significant debate over the years about the release of items from national or important collections for private sale, which is frequently generative of public outcry (Jingxian 2023).

4.9.3 Dispose: Bequeath

Owners who want something specific to happen to their collections after their death can bequeath them to a family member, or friend, or some organisation, in their wills with whatever provisos they wish to make. Some owners may get their collections valued and provide the information to those to whom the collection is being bequeathed to. The information may be included in a will, attached to the collection, or provided in some other way (Goode 2002). However, inevitably it is the recipient's attitude towards the collection that will dictate what happens to it subsequently [RM:Stamp; MemWil] (Wilson 2022). In some case, owners may not specifically bequeath a collection to an individual but may instead seek reassurance from the 'surviving' partner that the collection will be respected (Goode 2002). Bequests have played an important part in the shaping of many large-scale collections in Museums and Galleries (for example, Mayor 1957).

4.9.4 Dispose: Destroy

Some collections contain items that owners no longer find interesting or useful and which are of no interest to other people either. This is particularly true of document collections [RM:HDoc], and of collections of personal effects such as mementos [RM:MemWil]. When such items are no longer required, they are usually destroyed by either burning them, or throwing them into a waste bin. Sometimes, documents are shredded before being disposed of, for security, confidentiality, and privacy reasons.

For some contexts, especially Museums, Galleries, and Archives, the deliberate destruction of content when collections come to an end is a complex and potentially emotive topic (as with the sale of content) and, in the first instance, other outcomes are more likely, such as the dispersal of content through auction or simple shifting to a warehouse or other storage facility to suffer long-term neglect (Jardine et al. 2019).

4.10 Practice Troubles Unaffected by IT

In the next chapter, we begin to explore the impact that IT has had upon the various collecting practices identified above. As a part of that, we will be looking at various troubles that might be said to have arisen through a shift to using IT. However, before we do that, it is worth noting that some troubles appear to be mostly just inherent to collecting as an endeavour. We present examples of some of these in italics below, drawn from our personal experience. At the detailed level of specific instances, it is not a definitive set, varying as it will from person to person and their different knowledge and circumstances. However, at a broader, more general, level it is indicative of the sorts of troubles that many people are likely to encounter.

Acquiring: One of things that some people wonder about is exactly why they are collecting things.

> Understanding why one is collecting photos is one of those questions with lots of possible answers and it can be quite difficult to nail down exactly why you are doing it [RM:PhotoWil].

Even if they know why they are collecting, people often aren't clear about what they are collecting.

> The easy availability of the year folder means that we just put anything into it that we think there's even the minutest chance of us wanting or needing in the future i.e., we put off any kind of critical appraisal of what we are collecting. As a result, subsequent sorting out took longer and was more difficult [RM:MemWil2].
>
> If you collect stamps by tearing off every stamp that comes in on a letter, you are likely to end up with lots of the same type of the commoner sorts of stamp [RM:Stamp].
>
> Documents are often kept 'just in case' even though it is highly unlikely they will ever be needed again [RM:HDoc).
>
> There is a danger of not limiting the collection enough! Perhaps you have to learn what to collect by just making poor decisions on the subject [RM:Stamp].
>
> To start with I didn't appreciate the difference between a 'First Edition' and a 'First Edition - First Printing'; which resulted in me buying several First edition - 2nd 3rd etc editions which I later had to replace [RM:Book].
>
> Collecting all documents takes a substantial amount of time (probably much more than the average amount of time spent on filing) - though by saying everything will go in, it reduces the amount of time and effort in deciding what to put in; and, in theory, it means that you won't be missing some documents you want later [RM:Pawdoc].

To get a good collection takes some commitment. If the opportunities aren't taken when they arise, collectors may regret the omissions in their collections later.

> Sometimes I see particularly interesting chocolate wrappers for sale which would be good to have in the collection - but I'm just not that dedicated enough to buy them [RM:Choc].

Identification: Of course, collectors don't want to buy any old items—they usually want genuine articles in good condition.

> Sometimes the only way of being certain of veracity is to have an expert inspect the stamp - which is time-consuming and expensive [RM:Stamp].
>
> It's really annoying to suddenly find a flaw in an item you have in your collection [RM:Stamp].

Unfortunately, some of the things that are collected may have flaws which are not immediately obvious.

> I have experienced poor tape quality when borrowing audio books from the library, as well as when buying cassette audio books online. You never know the flaws are there until you listen to the tapes [RM:MusWil].

Even if an item is genuine and of good quality, you may still need some further information about it.

> Sometimes it's difficult to know which country a stamp comes from, or which year it was issued [RM:Stamp].
>
> Establishing the contents of old photos can be very difficult unless there is someone around who remembers – and, even then, memories can be mistaken or forgotten [RM:PhotWil].

Indexing: It may not always be obvious as to whether it's worth indexing a collection.

> Maintaining a manual index is an overhead; and it was generally easier to pull an LP off the shelf than consulting an index first [RM:MusWil].

If a collection has an index, a collector may have a choice about how to include a new item in it.

> A document can be filed independently or with one or more others in the collection. if items are kept together, then the time spent on creating index entries is reduced; and, if an item does not have its own index entry, then it may be more difficult to identify in a search. The difficulty is knowing which of these is the best option [RM:PAWDOC].
>
> Sometimes things do get hard to find because they are packaged up in a container with several other things but classified as a single item [RM:Loft].

Having made an entry in an index, a collector may wish to label the item concerned.

> Each new item for the loft collection had to be labelled with a unique reference number but sometimes it was difficult to find a way of attaching the label to the item [RM:Loft].
>
> Reference info, which is written on the back of a photo, can appear on the front of the photo; and I always worry that biro might affect the photo on the front (and pencil isn't clear enough on photo paper) [RM:PhotoWil].

Storage: An essential pre-requisite for a collection is having somewhere to store it, and this can sometimes be a problem.

> It can sometimes be difficult to find somewhere that is handy, has the necessary space, and is easy to access [RM:HDoc].
>
> It is difficult to find a place to store little used things like trophies and cups in anywhere else but boxes in the loft [RM:Trophy].
>
> It was a bit of a chore having to go up to the loft and sort through boxes and folders to find something [RM:MemWil].

Even the obvious spaces like lofts or cellars or the like may have their problems.

> Difficult to get heavier and bulkier items up the loft ladder and through the hatch. Things too large to go through the hatch simply could not be accommodated [RM:Loft].
>
> We had birds in the loft a while ago and they pooped on things. We also get rodents from time to time but they haven't yet damaged anything [RM:Loft].

Collections are often placed in containers, and it's important that they too don't damage the items.

> I originally used albums with plastic sheets over the whole page, but they didn't do the photos any good [RM:PhotoWil].
>
> Photos in frames tend to fade in the sun and the only way to deal with them is to reprint and replace them [RM:PhototWil].
>
> Putting items into the ring binders resulted in them having holes punched - sometimes obliterating text [RM:Let].

If you want to have easy access to a collection, that aspect needs to be given priority.

> I wanted to be able to access the files while sitting at my desk and to position the upright cabinet accordingly. It was constrained by the room - but I usually found a satisfactory answer [RM:PAWDOC].
>
> Paper filing systems are not portable [RM:PAWDOC].
>
> The collection is in a not very accessible part of my tall cabinet [RM:Choc].
>
> I used to use larger albums which were a pain because they tended to be too big to sit on a standard bookshelf [RM:PhotoWil].

Of course, easy access is also dependent on keeping things in order.

> It was easy to put records back in the wrong place so that the collection became disordered [RM:MusWil].

Some containers are intended to both store items and to display them and may not always work very well.

> Some chocolate wrappers are very big - larger than the ring binder/plastic wallets that I keep most of the wrappers in [RM:Choc].
>
> It's difficult to place new chocolate wrappers in the plastic wallets without either obscuring another wrapper or slipping behind another wrapper [RM:Choc].
>
> Putting stamps into albums with stamp hinges is much fiddlier, and potentially more damaging to the stamp, than putting them into plastic pockets [RM:Stamp].
>
> The storage containers I have don't display the collection very well [RM:Choc].

Successful organisation and display also relies on items being presented in a comprehensible order—which is not always easy.

> It was difficult to guess how much space was needed to accommodate future acquisitions of chocolate wrappers from a particular manufacturer [RM:Choc].
>
> Sometimes there is no obvious place to put a stamp; or the existing storage area is full [RM:Stamp].
>
> The stamps were sometimes placed in inappropriate positions if other stamps were to be included [RM:Stamp].
>
> If the collection includes physical albums organised by date, it may be difficult find a space at the appropriate point [RM:PhotoWil]

However, the most common trouble with storage space is simply that you keep running out of it.

> There is a limited amount of free space of the correct height to accommodate these containers [RM:Choc].
>
> I've run out of space in the new cabinet [RM:Stamp].
>
> It's always a big pain when you run out of space; the process of selecting documents to archive was time consuming and not easy [RM:PAWDOC].
>
> As the collection grew, more and more space was required to store it [RM:Let].
>
> It's a bit of a trial to have to deal with a few folders of stuff every few years when the chest gets too full of folders; As the number of folders build up, the challenge of where to store them increases [RM:MemWil].
>
> As the years go by the storage space required increases relentlessly [RM:MemWil].
>
> I do keep running out of bookcase space - which I believe is a very common problem [RM:Book].

Searching: Unless an item is stored out in the open, a collector may have to search to find it again – which may not be so easy.

> If I did want to find something it would be a bit of a struggle - especially if it was in the plastic wallets which are all of a jumble [RM:Choc].
>
> When you have a lot of material and repositories it's easy to let things get out of hand and to forget where things are [RM:Stamp].
>
> Finding a particular LP amidst the collection on a shelf could sometimes be a bit difficult. Looking at LP spines was difficult because they were so small and sideways and sometimes not at eye height [RM:MusWil].
>
> Searching through boxes and then folders was a chore [RM:MemWil].
>
> Searching through boxes was difficult because they were big and heavy, and you had to take the top ones out to get at items at the bottom [RM:Trophy].

Sometimes you need to find a document while talking to someone else.

> While conversing with a visitor at your desk, you need to judge if you will be able to find the document quickly as it usually won't be acceptable to the other person for you to interrupt the discussion for too long [RM:PAWDOC].
>
> You may need some information while you are on a phone call, but it can be tricky to continue to talk on the phone while simultaneously searching for a document [RM:PAWDOC].

Reorganisation: After a while, collectors sometimes reorganise their collections.

> Sort-outs can often take a long time [RM:Stamp].
>
> It's a joy to configure individual stamps on pages as you get them; but it's a bit tedious to have to reconfigure over 110 album pages all at once; it's a tricky job with the new composition of each page having to be worked out in advance [RM:Stamp].

Sometimes major sort-outs are needed to create new collections.

> If you're given a collection by an elderly or deceased relative, you may need to integrate the new collection into your own [RM:Stamp].
>
> Matching photos to negatives is quite laborious as the negative images are very small and have to be held up to the light to be seen [RM:PhotoWil].

Record-Keeping: Some collectors try and keep records about their collection, but unless they are institutions with employees, it can be easy to forget to do so.

> Updating records of information about the collection is easy to forget to do (though not doing doesn't really cause any problems) [RM:Stamp].
>
> Recording the date of the latest communication with each individual is difficult to remember to do as it is essentially an overhead [RM:Let].
>
> Maintaining a list of stamps that you want for the collection requires that it is constantly updated when new stamps are acquired [RM:Stamp].

As a collection gets more valuable, it might seem prudent to think about protecting it—but it's not always straightforward.

> Conditions of some (possibly most) insurance requires that the collection be stored under lock and key which would reduce the collection's accessibility [RM:Stamp].

Local Buy-in: Collectors are often very enthusiastic about what they are collecting and may be keen to discuss their activity with others, but this can come with its own issues.

> There's always a danger of providing too in-depth and lengthy explanations (illustrated with examples from albums) to people who really aren't that interested [RM:Stamp].

For some family-oriented collections, you need the buy-in of your partner and offspring—which may not always be forthcoming.

> The family is not very interested in understanding how this collection is organised and managed [RM:PhotoWil].
>
> Not sure the family was totally bought into my ideas about managing the loft collection [RM:Loft].
>
> Deciding what to include in the collection can be tricky if multiple owners are involved [RM:PhotoWil].

Bequeathment: When collectors have spent a lot of effort creating a collection, they often like to think it will have a future after their death—but, unlike taxes, there is no certainty of that.

I would like to pass it on to the family but I can't be sure anyone is interested [RM:Stamp].

The next generation doesn't know much about the collection [RM:Choc].

I want to introduce younger members of the family to stamp collecting but need to avoid pushing it too much and putting them off [RM:Stamp].

I can't really predict what people will do with things they inherit [RM:Stamp].

Obviously, the above examples are all drawn from studies of relatively small-scale amateur collections, but even where larger organisations may be able to invest in resources to address some of these issues, they are indelibly bound up with problems that confront anyone attempting to bring together sets of objects in some kind of reasoned and structured way.

References

Ashikuzzaman MD (2023) Difference between cataloguing and indexing. https://www.lisedunetwork.com/cataloguing-versus-indexing/. Accessed 23 Nov 2024

Béguet B, Jouguelet S, Petit C (1999) L'offre de collections à la Bibliothèque nationale de France. BBF 6:18–28

Bibliothèque Nationale de France (2015) Charte documentaire des acquisitions de la Bibliothèque nationale de France. https://www.bnf.fr/sites/default/files/2018-11/Charte%20documentaire%202015.%20Version%20int%C3%A9grale.pdf. Accessed 17 Mar 2025.

Blume J (2019) The rise of the trading cards. In: Lassig S, Weiss A (eds) The world of children: foreign cultures in nineteenth-century German education and entertainment. Berghahn Books, New York, pp 228–251

British Library (2024) About us. https://www.bl.uk/about-us/. Accessed 23 Oct 2024

The British Museum (2024) Collection online guide. https://www.britishmuseum.org/collection/collection-online/guide. Accessed 13 Nov 2024

Christie's (2023) Why Christian Levett is selling a museum-full of art. 21 November 2023, https://www.christies.com/en/stories/christian-levett-property-from-the-mougins-museum-of-classical-art-a84fcc0bcb5c474e8fc56eb3314da081. Accessed 27 Nov 2024

Cite de l'Espace (2024) Who are we? https://en.cite-espace.com/who-are-we/. Accessed 23 Oct 2024

Collections Trust (2024) Spectrum. https://collectionstrust.org.uk/spectrum/. Accessed 04 Nov 2024

Cornell University Library (2024) Rare and manuscript collections. https://rare.library.cornell.edu/collecting-policies/. Accessed 25 Oct 2024

Craddock KD (2004) The cardstock chase, trading cards: a legal lottery? Gaming Law Rev 8(5):310–317

DeWitt DL (1988) Unsolicited marginal gift collections: saying no or coping with the unwanted. Libr Acquis Pract Theory 12(3–4):357–362

Dillon A (2019) Collecting as routine human behaviour: personal identity and control in the material and digital world. Inf Cult 54(3):255–280

Ellis RM, Haywood A (2006) Virtual radiophile (163*): eBay and the changing collecting practices of the UK vintage radio community. In: Hillis K, Petit M, Epley N (eds) Everyday eBay: culture, collecting and desire. Routledge, New York, pp 45–61

Fieldhouse M (2012) The processes of collection management. In: Fieldhouse M, Marshall A (eds) Collection development in the digital age. Facet Publishing, London, pp 27–44

Golden V (1999) Library book sales and auctions, or, you can get more than a dollar for that! Acquis Libr 11(22):143–163

Goode J (2002) Collecting time: the social organization of collecting. In: Crow G, Heath S (eds) Social conceptions of time: structure and process in work and everyday life. Palgrave Macmillan, pp 230–246

Harrison M (2020) Labelling and marking booklet. Collections Trust. https://collectionstrust.org.uk/resource/labelling-and-marking-museum-objects-booklet/. Accessed 24 Nov 2024

Hoekstra W, Evers VHC (1977) Automated microfiche filing system for personal use. IEEE Trans Prof Commun PC-20(4):228–233

Hohn TC (2008) Curatorial practices for botanical gardens. Rowman Altamira

Hurdley R (2007) Objecting relations: the problem of the gift. Sociol Rev 55(1):124–143

Jamison A (2023) Decentering whiteness in libraries: a framework for inclusive collection management practices. Rowman & Littlefield

Jardine B, Kowal E, Bangham J (2019) How collections end: objects, meaning and loss in laboratories and museums. BJHS Themes 4:1–27

Jingxian P (2023) Discussion on should museums sell items from their collections. Int J Front Sociol 5(13):1–7. https://doi.org/10.25236/IJFS.2023.051301

Lucas R (2016) The sketchbook as collection: a phenomenology of sketching. In: Bartram A, El-Bizri N, Gittens D (eds) Recto Verso: redefining the sketchbook. Routledge, pp 191–205

Macdonald S (2006) Collecting practices. In: Macdonald S (ed) A companion to museum studies. Blackwell Publishing Ltd., pp 81–97

Manof M (2004) Theories of the archive from across the disciplines. Portal Libr Acad 4(1):9–25

Mayor AH (1957) The gifts that made the museum. Metrop MusM Art Bull 16(3):85–107

Miller RJ (2022) Metadata for digital collections. Facet Publishing Limited, London

O'Grady M (October 08, 2019) Cash, credit or painting? How, and why, artists exchange work. The New York Times Style Magazine

Pye J, Ball D (1999) Library purchasing consortia in the UK: activity, benefits and good practice. Project report. Capital Planning Information, Bruton

Ross CS (1999) Finding without seeking: the information encounter in the context of reading for pleasure. Inf Process Manage 35(6):783–799

Saponaro MZ, Evans GE (2019) Collection management basics. Libraries Unlimited, Santa Barbara, pp 1–373

Shuker R (2010) Wax trash and vinyl treasures: record collecting as a social practice. Ashgate Publishing Limited, Farnham

Sola T (2004) Redefining collecting. In: Knell SJ (ed) Museums and the future of collecting, 2nd edn. Ashgate Publishing Limited, Farnham

Spinney L (2022) The big idea: could the greatest works of literature be undiscovered? The Guardian, Manchester

Tate (2020) Tate acquisition and disposal policy. https://www.tate.org.uk/documents/1685/acquisition_and_disposal_policy_2020.pdf. Accessed 6 Nov 2024

Teitell C, Weintraub BL, Ricciardi SA (2019) Deducting charitable art donations. Trusts & Estates

van den Eede Y (2010) Collecting our lives online: the use of digital media seen through the lens of collecting practices. Techne Res Philos Technol 14(2)

van der Grijp P (2024) Art collecting and gifts to museums: an anthropology of donations. Taylor & Francis

Upper Deck (2023) Real cards. Real trades. https://www.upperdeckepack.com/. Accessed 30 May 2023

Watkins R, Sellen A, Lindley SE (2015) Digital collections and digital collecting practices. In: Proceedings of CHI 2015, Seoul, Republic of Korea, April 18–23, 2015, pp 3423–3432

Wellisch HH (1975) Dewey decimal classification, universal decimal classification, and the broad system of ordering: the evolution of universal ordering systems. Allerton Park Institute

Wilson PA (1990) Ergonomic aspects of computer supported personal filing systems. In: Lovesey EJ (ed) Contemporary ergonomics 1990: proceedings of the 1990 ergonomics society conference, Leeds, UK, 3–6 April. Taylor & Francis, pp 92–97

Wilson PA (2001) 20 years in the life of a long-term empirical personal electronic filing study. Behav Inf Technol 20(5):395–409

Wilson PA (2016) Get that old photo collection in order. Watermead Village View Magazine, Spring issue, 05 March 2016, Watermead Parish Council, Aylesbury. https://www.watermead-pc.gov.uk/village-view-2015---2016.html. Accessed 25 Nov 2024

Wilson PA (2022) Meteor—a story about stamp collecting in the eye of the IT hurricane. Privately published book produced by Blurb, 05 Apr 2022 [available for viewing by arrangement with the author]

Wilson PA (2023) Indexing arrangements. Blog post in the display case management section of the pwofc.com website, 27 September 2023. http://www.pwofc.com/ofc/2023/09/27/indexing-arrangements/. Accessed 13 May 2025

Xie I, Matusiak K (2016) Discover digital libraries: theory and practice. Elsevier, Amsterdam

Chapter 5
IT's Impact on Collecting Practices

Abstract The Icon Age has created a number of new practices as well as revolutionising others. New practices uncovered were: Equip-Design-Computer System; Equip-Obtain-Subscribe; Deposit-Digitise; Use-Digitise; Maintain-Manage-Digital Systems; Maintain-Protect-Digital Items; Maintain-Protect-Digital Systems; Maintain-Preserve-Digital Items. Examples are provided of the impact that IT has had on collecting practices, and of some of the IT-related troubles that have been experienced. Of the 631 practices that we identified in our analysis of the research materials, over half were found to have been only marginally impacted by IT, if at all. About a third had been revolutionised. The analysis also suggests that IT has tended to make collecting practices slightly easier at the expense of a slight increase in workload. The general conclusion is that that the introduction of IT has resulted in some changes for many collectors but has not had a radical effect on collecting overall.

In this chapter we explore how IT has changed collecting practices since the start of the Icon Age. For each high-level practice, we discuss (where applicable):

- New practices that have been introduced by IT.
- Practices that have been revolutionised by IT.
- IT's impact on the difficulty of performing various practices and the associated workload.
- New Troubles that have arisen in certain practices as a result of the introduction of IT.

5.1 Initiate

Unsurprisingly, there has been almost no impact on the Initiate practice, since it consists mainly of decision making such as naming the collection and defining its contents. Therefore, its hierarchy remains as shown in Fig. 4.2.

P. Wilson and P. Tolmie, *Collecting in the Icon Age*,
https://doi.org/10.1007/978-3-031-86470-4_5

5.2 Equip

5.2.1 New Practices Introduced to the Equip Practice

Two new Equip practices have emerged with the rise of IT: the Design of Computer Systems; and the ability to Subscribe to Collecting Support Services. The updated hierarchy is shown in Fig. 5.1.

The design of Computer Systems: The use of computer technology to support the collecting activity can sometimes be relatively simple, such as getting a Music Management application to organise all the music stored on a computer. All the user has to do is to install the application after which it automatically searches for and presents all the MP4 files it finds; provides them with any album art it can find locally or on the net; categorises them by type or artist; and enables the user to select what to play [RM:MusWil]. This is not radically different when it comes to the download of music streaming applications [RM:MusTol]. However, some computer support can be far more complicated. For example, the design of a system to manage items in the loft collection involved specifying three types of data entities—Positions, Containers, and Items—and building a database to store instances of those entities [RM:Loft]. Sometimes, multiple interlinked systems are used in support of a collection, and this can introduce a high level of complexity which is difficult to manage. For example, the PAWDOC system used an Index in a separate Filemaker database in conjunction with a complex Document Management Product, together with some special control

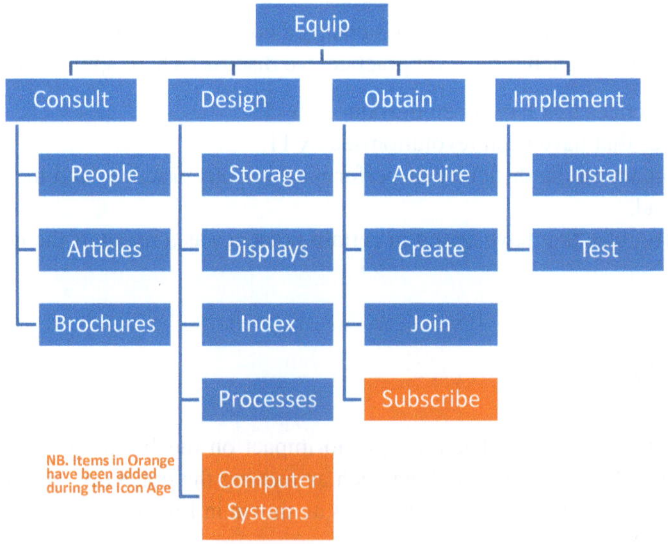

Fig. 5.1 The updated 'Equip' practice hierarchy in the Icon Age

key combinations that had to be set up to make it easier for the user to go from one system to the other [RM:Trophy] (Wilson 2001).

For institutional collectors, a variety of general recommendations relating to the design of computer systems are to be found in the literature, for example, the design of computer systems to support collecting should take into account published research on requirements (Watkins et al. 2015), and should research user requirements and search behaviours in the design of metadata (Miller 2022). However, there are two specific types of system that many institutions are now making use of for which some sort of design is required before purchasing the equipment and software:

- Digitisation systems involving scanners, editing software, and digital storage (Miller 2022).
- Online web sites which require software to create web pages and a web hosting capability.

Interestingly both these types of systems can be implemented and used by individuals as well as institutions (Terras 2010), though on a much smaller scale and therefore requiring rather less formal design work. In all of the institutional contexts studied the design of both back-end and front-end systems to support the development, maintenance, and use of the collections was a focus of significant and ongoing effort [RM:TVBC; Film; Swiss; Acrop; Espace; Imp; Tate]. In several of these organisations, the design effort did not stop at the construction of the systems themselves but also included the design of associated workflows [RM:TVBC; Film; Swiss].

Another significant change with IT implications specifically for Libraries is that the provision of serials (journals, magazines etc.) has changed radically since the 1990s. Most are now available in both electronic and print versions, and, consequently, delivery of the electronic versions to users requires the design and implementation of computer systems and user access management (Fieldhouse 2012). This shift to design for the handling of digital content has also had an impact in media intensive environments (for example, [RM:TVBC; Film; Swiss]), and Museums and Galleries are often now having to equip themselves to handle the provision of hybrid and digital exhibits [RM:Acrop; Espace; Imp; Tate].

Obtaining a Subscription: Some computer systems aimed specifically at collectors are available online, thereby avoiding the need to install any software on a Collector's computer: all that is required is to subscribe to the service. For example, Stanley Gibbons provides its 'My Collection' service which includes an online version of a recent edition of its all-world simplified stamp catalogue, and the ability to document all the stamps you have in your collection and those that you want; all for an annual fee which was less than a sixth of the £299 price of the 2024 hardcopy version of its all-world catalogue [RM:Stamp].

5.2.2 Revolutionary Changes in the Equip Practice

We found that four of the Equip practices have been revolutionised by IT:

- Equip-Consult-Articles
- Equip-Consult-Brochures
- Equip-Obtain
- Equip-Implement-Test.

Articles: While there are still many physical magazines and journals for various types of collecting, a huge amount of similar material is already available on the internet and continues to be generated for online consumption. The first port of call for information for most people is now likely to be an internet search engine such as Google. This is largely the same across all contexts. Even in large organisations, when people need to find collection-relevant information and it is not available from colleagues, the internet is almost always turned to first [RM:Swiss].

Brochures: Although marketing brochures still exist, most businesses now have their own websites where they publish all the details of their products. It is relatively rare now for someone to request that a brochure be sent to them.

Obtain: IT has had a dramatic impact on the way things are now acquired and a significant percentage of purchases are made online. This is, once again, the same for larger organisations, though procurement is more likely to be made using institutional logins on dedicated sites than through consumer platforms such as Amazon [RM:Film; Espace]. In terms of changes to what is purchased, collectors are now buying large amounts of computer equipment and software (though software programmes can also be obtained by either paying somebody to do it for you, or by creating it yourself). This is even more emphatically the case in large organisations where large investments may be made in the development of entire bespoke systems to support the management and development of the collection [RM:Film; Swiss].

Test: Testing collecting equipment in the pre-IT era was rarely required except for large mechanical systems such as moveable filing cabinets. However, the advent of IT has provided a whole range of hardware and software—and often a combination of several such elements—which can support collecting in one way or another. Implementing such technology often involves a fair amount of complexity, and many different ways in which things can go wrong. Therefore, testing and troubleshooting has become an essential element in the process of implementing technology support for collecting. It is often useful to undertake usability testing of a prototype system before finalising the software (Xie and Matusiak 2016). For large organisations, this activity may be devolved to dedicated IT departments staffed by knowledgeable personnel [RM:Tate] or outsourced to specialist companies [RM:Espace]. As these arrangements often elide from set-up to ongoing troubleshooting and support, they may also be considered part of the 'Maintain' group of practices (see Sect. 5.7).

5.2.3 *Difficulty and Workload in the Equip Practice*

In our assessment of whether IT has made practices harder or easier to perform, and of whether it has increased or decreased workload, the Equip practice overall was found to have stayed at about the same level, though four sub-practices were noticeably more difficult:

- **Design-Processes**: Due to the need to deal with an increasing amount of information to file [RM:Trophy] (Wilson 2001).
- **Design-Computer Systems**: Due to the complexities of the technology [RM:PAWDOC; Loft; Let; MusWil]
- **Design-Displays**: Due to the range of possibilities afforded by computer applications [RM:ESB] and the resulting interoperability issues that can therefore arise [RM:Espace].
- **Implement-Test**: Due to the problems associated with integrating different computer applications [RM:ESB] and the highly technical skills that can be required for troubleshooting [RM:Film].

One practice seems to have become a little easier to perform, even if it has increased workload:

- **Subscribe**: It is easier to use an online service, but sometimes there is a lot of set-up to do and a lot of functionality to learn and get used to; and there may be occasions in which problems occur and you need to use additional support such as Help Desks [RM:Stamp].

5.2.4 *Examples of Troubles Introduced into the Equip Practice by IT*

The practicality of using IT has introduced a number of annoying difficulties within many collecting practices. Some examples of those encountered in the Equip practice are described below:

Technology acquisition: While there is a wide variety of technology available to support collecting, it can be challenging to select it and pay for it.

> Acquiring technology that is reliable enough not to require expensive maintenance, is more difficult to do when there is little choice in the market. It is also quite hard work to try and research the performance of particular products [RM:PAWDOC].
>
> The cost of the technology prevented me going down the full RFID route for a loft management system [RM:Loft].
>
> Some systems are easier and quicker to use than others [RM:Loft].
>
> To implement macros to automate the links between applications, required extra software to be purchased and implemented [RM:PAWDOC].

The Sidebooks app won't display JPG files—only PDFs. So, any digital versions of mementos in image format have first to be put into a PDF in order for them to be displayed in Sidebooks. Despite this I decided this was the best free app for the job [RM:MemWil].

Some music management systems had better functionality and better displays than others [RM:MusWil].

While building a music collection in Spotify was very straightforward, it does not support the use of third-party DJ apps, so the collection has had to be rebuilt in Tidal [RM:MusTol].

Reformatting a hard drive to copy over files… "The drives lack RAID or SATA a lot of the time at present. We need better drives" [RM:Film].

5.3 Acquire

5.3.1 New Practices Introduced into the Acquire Practice

No new practices have been introduced into the Acquire practice; therefore, the hierarchy remains the same as shown in Fig. 5.2.

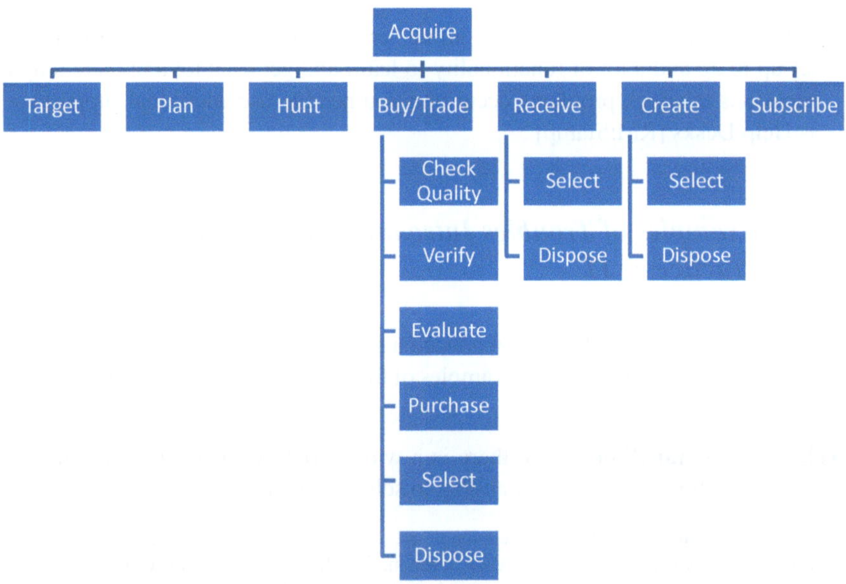

Fig. 5.2 The 'Acquire' practice hierarchy in the Icon Age

5.3.2 *Revolutionary Changes in the Acquire Practice*

We found six of the Acquire practices to have been revolutionised by IT:

- Acquire-Create
- Acquire-Subscribe
- Acquire-Buy-Purchase
- Acquire-Buy-Evaluate
- Acquire-Buy-Dispose
- Acquire-Receive.

Acquire-Create: The emergence of IT has brought with it a huge range of possible digital items that can be created by owners and added to their collections. The obvious example of such things are the collections of files that computer users create and store on their own machines [RM:Trophy]. Other examples are the collections of digital photos that individuals create and store [RM:PhotoWil; Photo]; the collection of Story Boards that Wilson created in PowerPoint format [RM:ESB]; and the collection of video fragments that Tolmie recorded for his 24-h study collection [RM:Data]. Such collections are not confined to individual owners: for example, the Digital Museum of Digital Art (DIMODA)[1] and the Museum of Contemporary Digital Art (MOCDA),[2] both collect and exhibit art created digitally.

Acquire-Subscribe: The notion of a digital collection is clearly cemented in many people's minds simply because they are used to dealing with collections of files on their computers. They have also become used to the idea of remote collections through the commonplace use of Cloud services such as Instagram. With this understanding in place, consumers have been happy to take up streaming services, particularly for music, TV, and film. However, it is music collecting that most clearly demonstrates how this new approach has revolutionised the practice: many people now no longer acquire new additions to their music collections by buying tapes, vinyl, or CDs, but have disposed of their physical media and instead simply subscribe to a streaming service such as Spotify [RM:MusWil] or Tidal [RM:MusTol]. Most serials (journals, magazines etc.) are now available in both electronic and print versions, though a few are still print only (for example, *INQUE*[3]). Given the flexibility and low production costs of digital formats, there are a wide variety of subscription pricing models, many of which incorporate multiple titles (Fieldhouse 2012).

Acquire-Purchase: The pre-digital technology purchasing activity often involved overland mail and the telephone to negotiate prices, terms and delivery arrangement; and payment was made using postal order or cheque. These have largely been superseded by email, messaging, online banking and card payment; and most online marketplaces provide full functionality to support the purchasing process.

[1] https://dimoda.art/.

[2] https://www.mocda.org/.

[3] https://inquemag.com/.

This has affected all contexts, with even large organisational payments having been revolutionised by the shift to digital banking.

Acquire-Evaluate: The ability to compare prices for collectable items has been revolutionised by the availability of shopping web sites and online auction sites. For example, stamps being purchased on an auction web site can be compared with similar stamps on that and other auction sites, and also with stamps in dealer web sites [RM:Stamp] (Wilson 2022). This has had a greater impact in the context of Amateur and Private Collectors. Institutional contexts still largely rely upon the same sources of professional expertise, though their interactions with those experts is now open to being mediated by IT.

Acquire-Receive: The joint accumulation of digital objects such as music or book reviews by an online community is significantly different from receiving objects as an individual. Members of a community can contribute items and the shared collection receives them (Belk 2014). Another major IT impact on the Receive practice is that, in the past, if you didn't want some or all of a collection you had been given (perhaps through inheritance), it was difficult to sell it. Nowadays, however, most items can be offered to anyone in the world via online auctions or social-media systems [RM:Stamp]. Again, this has had a bigger impact on Amateur and Private Collecting than on institutional contexts.

5.3.3 *Difficulty and Workload in the Acquire Practice*

As is the case with the Equip practice, the Acquire practice has largely stayed at about the same level of difficulty and workload, though the following sub-practices were found to be noticeably more difficult:

- **Acquire-Buy/Sell-Check Quality**: Due to the difficulty of checking quality when buying online.
- **Acquire-Buy/Sell-Verify**: Due to the difficulty of verifying that an item is genuine when buying online.

5.3.4 *Examples of Troubles Introduced into the Acquire Practice by IT*

Below are some examples of troubles in the Acquire practice resulting from the introduction of IT.

Buying: As noted above, finding and buying items that you want has become much easier with online marketplaces and auctions. The ability to provide multiple high-resolution photos has also eased the troubles associated with buying items unseen.

However, for some collecting contexts, online purchases bring with them their own troubles.

> You can compare prices across stamp dealer websites and other online sources for stamps you want in your collection—but when doing this it needs to be remembered that prices may be dictated by quality and certainty of authenticity [RM:Stamp].
>
> Price is often dictated by condition, which can be hard to verify absolutely online [RM: Stamp].
>
> You can use automated sniping to buy stamps at auctions (getting a sniping app to put one and only bid in at the last second)—but unfortunately lots of other people also snipe for the items they really want, so you can never be sure if you're going to win an auction until it's over [RM:Stamp].
>
> Postal costs increase the cost of online purchases [RM:Stamp].
>
> It's annoying when a streaming service doesn't have a song you want to hear [RM:OFC].
>
> Streaming services have an irritating habit of suddenly removing songs from their catalogue, meaning that you then have to look for another version, which doesn't always exist [RM:MusTol].

Disposing: Online marketplaces and auctions have certainly eased the old trouble of disposing of unwanted items after buying in bulk or having a clear-out, but such mechanisms often depend on items being shipped through the post.

> If you are sending stamps through the post, there is always the fear that they will get lost (though it has rarely happened to me); and also that the buyer might claim the item is not of good enough quality and/or give you a poor feedback rating [RM:Stamp].

Identification: The internet has many resources to identify items—as long as you can describe them well enough.

> It's difficult to type in the name on a stamp which is in a non-English alphabet [RM:Stamp].

The internet provides a host of information that was previously provided in paper-based catalogues and magazines, which were prone to going out-of-date and that no one may bother to update.

> The Stanley Gibbons website has a stamp catalogue which (at the time of writing) was three years out of date; It's tempting to regard an online catalogue from a trusted source, as being infallible, but, as this case proves, that is not always the case [RM:Stamp].

The Digital File: IT has introduced a new type of item to collect—the digital file—which has brought with it its own challenges.

> Unlike with paper, the amount of information embedded in digital media and files is not immediately apparent and this can make it difficult to judge how much effort is required to deal with them [RM:PAWDOC].
>
> Having to seek out photos in your own and your partner's phone, tablet and social media accounts, to maintain a family photo collection, is challenging [RM:PhotoWil].
>
> Copies of all of the media associated with programmes are ultimately put in an archive folder and backed up on digital tape. However, when different people work on the files, they save duplicates with different codecs. These have to be deleted before the archiving is done. The problem is that different people use the structure in slightly different ways and the duplicates could be in multiple places. It can be hard to find all of the media used from a job and, once things are left, it can be risky to delete them [RM:TVBC].

5.4 Deposit

5.4.1 New Practices Introduced to the Deposit Practice

One new Deposit practice has been introduced as a result of the emergence of IT: the Digitisation of an object. The updated hierarchy is shown in Fig. 5.3.

Deposit-Digitise: The ease of storage and access has inspired huge numbers of people to digitise items as they ingest them into their collections. The primary example of this is the scanning of documents as they are received, which then provides the owner with the option of either retaining the original or throwing it away. Either way the document can be easily stored, transported and viewed [RM:OFC; Trophy] (Wilson 2001; 2014). Other examples are the scanning of old photos to add to a collection [RM:PhotoWil; PhotoTol]; and the digitisation of mementos [RM:MemWil] and letters [RM:Let] as they are received. At the film production site, part of the project associated with managing the film archive included the creation of a whole new set of digital assets to place in the archive that were also open to commercialisation, including original movie posters, stills, and digital copies of the films themselves. This involved intensive scanning, digitisation, and quality control with a number of staff dedicated solely to these activities. As this suggests, large scale digitisation projects require good project management (Hughes 2004). In the Spectrum standard for Museum Collection Management, this activity comes under the heading of 'Reproduction' (Collections Trust 2024).

Overall, the materials we have been analysing suggest that while between a third and two thirds of practices may not have any involvement with digital items at all, those that do tend to involve ***both*** digital originals and digital copies.

A number of other points related to this new Digitise practice are worth noting:

Digital Formats: Digital items, be they originals or copies of physical items, must have a particular format or file type to be operable. The file type defines the characteristics of a digital file, thereby enabling a computer system to know which application the file will run on. File types are typically appended to the end of a file name after a full stop, and they are usually between 3 and 6 characters long. When collecting

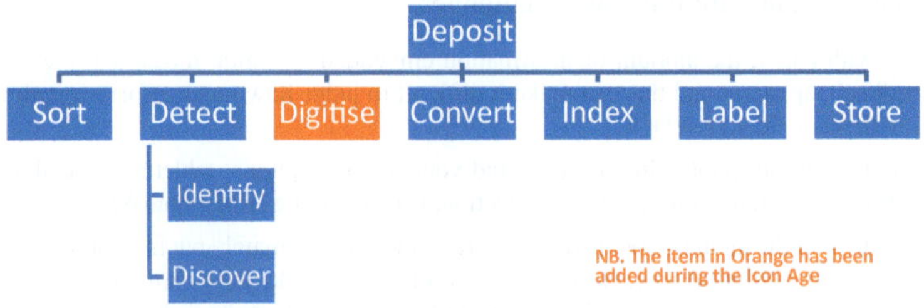

Fig. 5.3 The updated 'Deposit' practice hierarchy in the Icon Age

digital items, there are often choices to be made about what file types to use. For example, photos of items in a pottery collection could be in jpg format or tiff format. JPG is a digital image format which contains compressed image data with a 10:1 compression ratio. Consequently, JPG images are very compact. TIFF files are much larger than JPGs, but they're also lossless, so you lose no quality after saving and editing the file, no matter how many times you do it. Often collectors just adopt the format of the applications they are using. However, collection owners with particular requirements, or with an eye on the long term, may wish to make a more informed choice about the digital formats they use. This is another overhead on collecting introduced by the use of IT. In large organisations, the file types tend to be given. For some organisations, the primary concern is with space [RM:Swiss] and they will ask staff to use compressed formats. For organisations archiving media, the emphasis tends to fall on quality [RM:Film; TVBC]. A great many Museums and Galleries have also developed digitisation strategies in order to facilitate the provision of Virtual Visits [RM:Tate; Acrop; Imp], something that came to the fore during the global Covid-19 pandemic.

The pros and cons of having digital copies of physical originals: Many collections that comprise physical objects, may benefit from producing digital copies of the physical originals. The advantages include:

- Having a security copy in case of damage or theft
- The ability to save space by putting the physical items in archive storage and just using the digital copies
- The ability to view the items on a desktop screen or portable tablet or mobile phone
- The ability to enlarge images on screen
- The ability to engage in manipulations (for example, 3D) that might be difficult with the original object because of its weight or inaccessibility
- The ability to send copies to other people
- The ability to exhibit items on a website.

However, accompanying the advantages of having digital copies of items, are the overheads that go with digital collections:

- The cost of computer equipment
- The need to configure and maintain a computer system
- The need to protect the computer system from intruders and viruses
- The need to undertake digital preservation to ensure that the files are accessible long-term.

The choice between keeping and disposing: Having produced a digital copy of a physical item, owners sometimes think that it's not necessary to have both immediately accessible. In document collections, for example, owners often simply destroy the physical document and rely entirely on the digital copy. However, for some items there may be a dilemma about whether to keep the originals. An investigation of a document collection and a memento collection identified the following reasons for keeping the original once a digital copy had been produced (Wilson 2014):

- Some items need to be put to work in their original form
- There are items for which only the originals can confirm their validity
- Trophy items can be collected and enjoyed in the future
- Large documents may have particular qualities of impact and integrity
- Some publications have fixed spine bindings and/or special papers
- Some publications may mention friends, colleagues or the owner
- Some items may have been published by an organisation or programme that the owner works/worked for
- There can be items that the owner has written, produced, assembled or made a significant contribution to
- There may be physical features which make it difficult to digitise the item and/or to reconstruct it from the digital copy
- Some items illustrate a physical form that has changed due to a development in technology
- Age can provide a quality of uniqueness
- Copying may be explicitly prevented by copyright
- Some items have an aesthetic or artistic quality, such as photos
- Items may need to be used as exhibits
- Items may relate to the legality of an institution
- They may be Executive Policy documents.

Hybrid collections: A collection with some physical originals, some physical originals and their digital copies, and some physical copies with no physical original can be termed a Hybrid Collection. The challenge for collection owners going forward into the digital future is to optimise the hybrid—to decide which of the physical items to dispose of, if any, after digitisation in order to minimise storage space and the overheads of managing physical items. Once thrown away, the unique properties of the physical will be lost, so owners will want to give some thought as to what unique qualities (if any) are particularly important or interesting for the particular items being dealt with. There may be none, of course, in which case none of the physical items need to be retained.

5.4.2 *Revolutionary Changes in the Deposit Practice*

The widespread practice of digitisation has introduced significant changes in the Deposit-Convert and the Deposit-Index practices:

Deposit-Convert: The introduction of digitisation in the Icon Age has been accompanied by the ability to manipulate the resulting files to improve their quality. Such conversion actions may include eliminating scanned dust particles or unwanted noise on audio tapes; and improving contrast and legibility. This has become a major part of the work in some media organisations, leading to investment in highly specialised and expensive equipment [RM:Film]. In the Spectrum standard this practice comes under the headings of 'Collection Care and Conservation' and 'Damage and Loss' (Collections Trust 2024).

Deposit-Index: Indexes in the past were relatively simple constructs with a limited number of fields and designed to be read by humans. For Libraries, this had already started to change with the advent of Machine-Readable Cataloguing information (MARC) in the 1960s. However, the Icon Age brought with it a need for comprehensive and standardised data that could be processed by computers and shared between systems across the world—metadata—and the first metadata standard, the Dublin Core, was introduced in the mid-1990s (Miller 2022). Hence, for all types of collecting institutions (not just Libraries), indexes have now become more comprehensive and frequently resort to the use of programming-type language. Consequently, inputting metadata information for new items being added to a collection has become a significantly different exercise in the Icon Age and is typically achieved using a software application which interfaces to a back-end database (Miller 2022).

For individuals—Amateur Collectors, Private Curators, and Filers—there is no particular need to go down the standardised metadata route. Instead, indexes can be created in a spreadsheet, in a database, or in a myriad of different apps. Consequently, many more such collectors will have a digital index, and the process of including a new item into a collection will involve using a computer to create a new index entry. Things are somewhat different, however, for people working in larger organisations, where a significant emphasis may be put upon the use of standardised metadata [RM:TVBC; Swiss]. This can also apply to Filers where they are working in large organisations with established Content Management Systems. There are also some important exceptions amongst individual collectors. When people build collections of music using streaming platforms, they are obliged to work with the metadata provided by those platforms, regardless of whether it meets their personal needs [RM:MusTol].

Another interesting impact on the Deposit-Index practice relates to the rather niche Icon Age activity of items being collected by an online community (such as music or film reviews, for example). In such cases, if there is an index, there may be more than one view about what information should go in it (Belk 2014) (though note the preceding point about music streaming platforms—even Soundcloud has standardised indexing requirements that users work around by appending annotations to tracks [RM:MusTol]).

5.4.3 *Difficulty and Workload in the Deposit Practice*

Our research suggests that overall, the Deposit Practice has become slightly easier with the introduction of IT, even if the associated workload seems to have become slightly greater. This may or may not be a genuine relationship, but it does seem to reflect a characteristic of computer systems whereby the actual activity, such as typing a document, may be easier on a computer with more flexibility (for making changes etc.), but comes with significant overhead in managing the equipment, software, and files. Having said all that, the new 'Digitise' sub-practice has clearly introduced a high additional workload.

5.4.4 *Examples of Deposit Troubles that Have Been Eliminated by IT*

IT has eliminated or eased several of the collecting troubles of the pre-IT era, as illustrated in the examples below.

> It was tortuous having to write out the title several times—once on the Title Index card and once on each relevant Keyword card [RM:PAWDOC] **[eliminated by the electronic index]**.

> I needed to remember to note down the next Ref No to use before leaving the office [RM:PAWDOC] **[eliminated by the electronic index]**.

> The plastic box took up space and made it a little fiddly to go through the index cards it held. It also eventually became too small, which necessitated having a much bigger and heavier container made up of two steel drawers which took up far too much space on my desk [RM:PAWDOC] **[eliminated by the electronic index]**.

> Managing physical archive boxes is difficult in a confined office space; and if they are placed in another location that reduces their accessibility. On top of that, locating the correct box to find an item is challenging in itself [RM:PAWDOC] **[eliminated by digitising the documents]**.

> It's always annoying when you need a document which is back in the office [RM:PAWDOC] **[eliminated by digitising the documents]**.

> It was a bit of a faff recording cassettes—and it was problematic getting the cassette case to look like the LP [RM:MusWil] **[eliminated by ripping LPs, cassettes and CDs to digital files]**.

> If you didn't have all the gear and the vinyl, DJing for parties used to involve either creating mixtapes or burning tracks to CDs, which then meant you had to work with a fixed playlist [RM:MusTol] **[eliminated by ripping LPs, cassettes and CDs to digital files]**.

5.4.5 *Examples of Deposit Troubles that Have Been Changed by IT*

Some troubles have been changed by the introduction of IT as shown in the examples below.

Indexing: IT has contributed to a huge increase in the amount of paperwork and communications.

> It's become even harder to keep on top of the rising flow of information. It's easy to let things pile up—you have to be diligent to keep on top of getting all the new items into the filing system [RM:PAWDOC].

There's contention with other priority work; it takes an appreciable amount of time to index a document [RM:PAWDOC].

It all gets backed up onto digital tape but then we have to do paperwork to accompany everything as well [RM:TVBC].

IT has made the construction and modification of an index much easier, but it may still be a challenge.

It's difficult to know exactly what filing schema you want until you've been operating a system for a while, and by then you may have built up a sizeable number of entries all requiring updating to the new schema [RM:PAWDOC].

Keeping the number of fields in an index to a minimum may minimise the amount of time and effort it takes to introduce a new document into the collection. However, it may also mean that key information for some items may get missed out of the index [RM:PAWDOC].

In incorporating photos belonging to other family members into the collection, I had to decide whether to have separate indexes and separate albums, or to have a combined index and separate albums [RM:PhotoWil].

The modifications to the Ref No structure were made largely to distinguish between different locations of items (e.g. docs in the filing cabinet and 4 ring binders in the bookcase). However, as the number of different types increased it became difficult to know what types were available and, in some cases to maintain a standardised format [RM:PAWDOC].

There is a Quality Control folder. Once the files have been checked they are marked in green. A second person then checks them again and after that moves the directory to the completed folder. We are double-checking to make sure nothing has been missed. It might be the size or name that is the issue. The most common problem is a file-naming error [RM:Film].

Even an established electronic index may have its own problems.

The Index must be able to provide the means to access the item searched for. Therefore, whatever structure is introduced to achieve that, it must be implemented correctly every time. Sometimes, this didn't happen, and the wrong Ref No was applied to an item, or an item was not stored in the place the index indicated [RM:PAWDOC].

Care has to be taken to create the right words in the index entry; for new topics there is a danger of using inconsistent terminology in different index entries until the field firms up [RM:PAWDOC].

Changing terminology resulted in old index entries using out of date terminology, and this sometimes meant you couldn't find an item when you were searching for it [RM:PAWDOC].

Because the index titles and keywords have never been updated systematically, I'm sure it has affected the effectiveness of my searching. To do it properly would require quite a lot of time and effort [RM:PAWDOC].

Inevitably some information you would like to search on in future gets missed out of some index entries [RM:PAWDOC].

It's easy to just remove something from the collection and to forget to update the database [RM:Loft].

Sometimes offspring just put their stuff in the loft and forget about it even when they get places of their own [RM:Loft].

They use Compressor a lot to change the codecs. However, Compressor appends names, so they then have to rename the files. They use Automator to do the re-naming and have a rename Finder item script they use to replace text. They have to copy the segment that has to go and do a replace with nothing [RM:TVBC].

Storing: The ability to digitise items potentially reduces the amount of physical storage space required. However, that may not always be that clear-cut.

> It is often difficult to decide whether to keep a physical item or not [RM:Let].
>
> Even an established set of retain/destroy criteria can only be a guide: there may be any number of other reasons for keeping a hardcopy document [RM:PAWDOC].
>
> If you apply the principle 'when in doubt, retain don't destroy' that just increases the amount of hardcopy you have to find space for and manage [RM:PAWDOC].
>
> The problem with backing up from LTO4 is that it'll probably be obsolete in 5 to 10 years [RM:Film].

The problems presented by unusual-sized documents presented different challenges in the IT era.

> Unusual shapes and sizes not only caused problems in storing them in hanging folders and archive boxes, but also in scanning them, and sometimes in displaying them on a screen [RM:PAWDOC].
>
> Scanning the photographs of my parents-in-law's wedding album was very nerve-racking. I had to dismantle the whole album and it was very old, fragile, and, for my wife, 'precious' [RM:PhotoTol].

5.4.6 *Examples of Troubles in the Deposit Practice that Have Been Introduced by IT*

Some examples of troubles that have been introduced by IT are described below.

Sorting: Sorting out digital files can be quite demanding.

> Overall, it's more difficult to do sorting of digital files than it is to put physical photos in a pile and make adjustments on the fly [RM:PhotoWil].
>
> Matching photos to negatives is quite laborious as the negative images are very small and have to be held up to the light to be seen. Sorting out hundreds of digital photos is quite difficult without the ability to physically separate them [RM:PhotoWil].
>
> I've been using my periods of free time to go through the household files on my laptop. And what a tedious business it is. At least with paper files you can use your hands and arms to pick up papers and move them around; you can turn your neck to look at papers here and over there; and you can completely change your position to get comfy. But with a screen, you're locked-in with eyes fixed, head in one place, and body stationary staring at an unending stream of similar looking files [RM:HDoc].
>
> Pruning Household Files can be a very tedious business [RM:HDoc].
>
> When sorting out Household Files you have to deal with both hardcopy documents and digital files at the same time [RM:HDoc].
>
> Because I work on so many things at the same time, files tend to end up spread across my desktop. Ideally, I'd like to properly sort those into relevant folders on my external hard drives, but I never find the time. Instead, what usually happens is that I will periodically get fed up with the mess and pull everything into one folder labelled 'Desktop [Date]' and save that instead and start with a clean desktop again. I now have nested desktop folders that have never been sorted on my hard drives that go back years and, the more I do it, the more time it would take to sort everything out, but it can make finding things a nightmare. [RM:TolDoc].

Indexing: Adding entries to the index in the digital era has presented a variety of challenges.

> It was hard work to keep on top of filing—particularly in the face of the rising tide of email which tended to suck any spare time that people had [RM:PAWDOC].
>
> Sometimes album art isn't available and has to be photographed or created: and updating tag properties isn't particularly easy [RM:MusWil].
>
> Sometimes forgot to record the fact that an electronic version of a hardcopy document (or vice-versa) exists within the collection [RM:PAWDOC].
>
> The flexibility of the free-format 'movement' field led to large numbers of different abbreviations being used and information being included in different formats, to record details about the content and state of particular items (e.g. whether an item had been scanned, number and type of electronic files etc). Consequently, over a long period of time the meaning of at least one abbreviation has been lost; and a considerable amount of editing was done later to achieve a relatively standardised format across all instances of this field [RM:PAWDOC].

It's easy to include factual data in the index and file titles, but there are constraints.

> Including substantive information such as phone numbers, book references, and expense claim amounts, in the index entries for a collection can make them very informative; but it can also make them very long to read with the chance that inappropriate information will be included and never used [RM:PAWDOC].
>
> It can be very useful to include the key contents of a file in the title—but it can be difficult to summarise key points in the limited space of a file name [RM:Let].
>
> If you put too much info in a file name, the overall path length limits may be exceeded [RM:HDoc].

The emergence of digital photos has presented its own indexing challenges.

> For old photos the main unit to be indexed was clear—it was each film/set of negatives; but with digital photos you have to decide how to group photos for a single index entry [RM:PhotoWil].
>
> Can be difficult if there is no tag information about the date the photo was taken—or if that date is changed by some spurious system process upon moving or copying the file [RM:PhotoWil].
>
> My wife and I regularly share photos using Google Photo. For my wife's photos, I create back-up copies and enter them into my own photo catalogue. The problem is that, while my own photos have the original dates, the ones from my wife only have the date I copied them over, so it can be hard to decide where to file them [RM:PhotoTol].
>
> It took quite a while to perfect an excel template that fitted the size of the slip-in tabs and that had cut marks printed in the correct places; but it's still a faff having to manually cut up the sheet after it comes off the printer [RM:PhotoWil].
>
> Assembling the list of contents for the album spine labels, and then printing them off, cutting them to size and fitting them on the albums, is a bit of a faff [RM:PhotoWil].

Digitising: Converting items into digital format can be a challenge.

> Some types of negatives were more difficult than others to digitise; disc film negatives were particularly problematic [RM:PhotoWil].
>
> Finding out what the best digital formats to convert things like cine film was a bit tricky [RM:PhotoWil].

To digitise music on LPs and cassette, it was quite an involved activity to assemble the right equipment and software and to get a good result [RM:MusWil].

It takes a lot of time and effort to digitise books [RM:Book].

Copying and pasting emails into word before indexing them was a long winded and time-consuming process which I didn't really want to do—but there seemed no other way of including particular emails in the filing system [RM:PAWDOC].

Relying on the email system's inbuilt filing and searching facilities is fine whilst you are using the same email system; but when you move email system, then all the emails in the previous system are lost [RM:PAWDOC].

A wide variety of difficulties may be experienced in digitising documents.

Digitising legacy hardcopy was a huge additional workload which demanded a huge amount of precious time and effort [RM:PAWDOC].

Ordinary A4 pages weren't a problem to scan; but some items, such as a 4-page article in Computer weekly, were more difficult and time consuming [RM:PAWDOC].

it took an appreciable amount of time to scan a document and put it into the Document Management System [RM:PAWDOC].

The scanner was much too big to carry around with you, so you either had to rely on the place you were at having a scanning capability which you could use; or just pile things up to do the scanning when you got home [RM:PAWDOC].

Sometimes post-it notes are not spotted and go through the scanner without causing a jam—but unfortunately, they often obscure the original text; It can be difficult to find a place close to where the post-it note was originally that doesn't obscure the original text [RM:PAWDOC].

Papers with a variety of different signatures written with different pens and ink colours, don't scan well [RM:MemWil].

Sometimes the scanner grabs multiple pages at once [RM:Book].

I use a Mac laptop and when I scan documents, the standard size they are saved at is huge. If you reduce the quality, they become unreadable. There is a script you can run to reduce the size they are saved at. However, I always forget it, so it's easier to just use an online compressor in the end [RM:TolDoc].

Storage: A variety of problems may be encountered when operating a specialised digital filing system.

Having to put the files into the Document Management System (DMS) was yet another extra task to do after having already created a new index entry for each one [RM:PAWDOC].

Document Management systems are potentially very complicated beasts—often providing a wide range of functionality to control the provision and sharing of information among large groups of people; their complexity is difficult to comprehend and manage [RM:PAWDOC].

I have experienced all the following: Upgrade to laptop requiring the index software (File-maker) and the DMS (Fish) to be re-installed; Optical disc corruption losing some items completely; system crash requiring all the software and filing system data to be completely re-installed; theft of the laptop requiring all the software and data to be re-installed on a new machine; problems in the operation of the Index and DMS software requiring investigation and rectification; problems in scanning (e.g., edges of text cut-off or too dark a copy) requiring a rescan [RM:PAWDOC].

Relying on photo management software means you're locked into the software. If a photo is moved out of the application for whatever reason, there is only the information in the file name and file properties to identify the photo and its contents. Any additional information

> you wish to hold about a set of photos has to be shoehorned into any available aspects of the software application and digital file properties of each photo, despite them not being designed for that purpose [RM:PhotoWil].

Digital items can also be stored in the internet in cloud services.

> The whole business of storing photos in social media sites has brought with it a raft of problems including people stealing identities and photos being published that the people in the pictures do not want published [RM:PhotoWil].
>
> It's annoying not to be able to load your own sounds into a streaming service but to have to play them via another device [RM:MusWil].
>
> While there are lots of advantages to using a music streaming service, the reliance upon having a good internet connection can sometimes cause real issues, including annoying buffering or being completely unable to play anything at all. For DJing, that is just too big a risk, so you end up having to make sure you have local copies anyway [RM:MusTol].

5.5 Use

5.5.1 New Practices Introduced to the Use Practice

One new Use practice has been introduced as a result of the emergence of IT: the Digitisation of an object that is already in a collection. The updated hierarchy is shown in Fig. 5.4.

Use-Digitise: Owners who already have an established collection, may decide to take digital copies of the items for security purpose, to enable the items to be shared or displayed or exhibited over the internet, or simply to provide them with easier access to the items on their desk screens or tablets or mobile phones [RM:OFC]. Examples of this are document collections (though the decision to undertake backfile conversion of a large collection should not be taken lightly) [RM:Trophy] (Wilson 2001); Letters [RM:Let]; Photos [RM:PhotoWil; PhotoTol] (Wilson 2016); Music [RM:MusWill; MusTol]; Books [RM:Book]; Films and Associated Collaterals [RM:Film]; Paintings [RM:Tate]; Museum Exhibits [RM:Acrop].

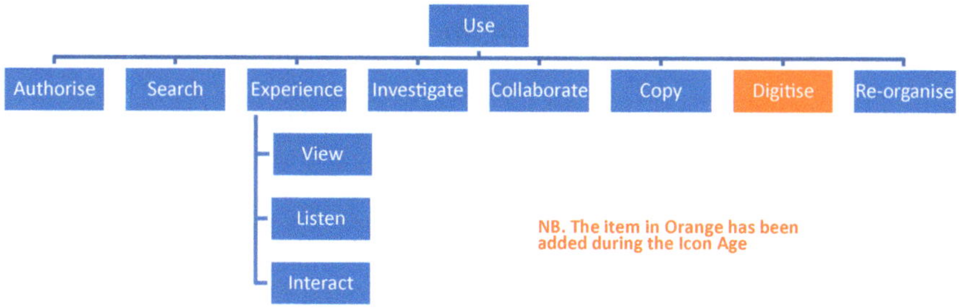

Fig. 5.4 The updated 'Use' practice hierarchy in the Icon Age

Many institutions are now digitising some of their collections and a literature has developed in support of such large-scale projects which are often referred to as Digital Library Projects—though they are not specific to Libraries but apply equally to digitisation projects under taken by Museums, Galleries and Archives. Indeed, the Spectrum standard specifies this activity under the heading of 'Reproduction' (Collections Trust 2024). Some of the key points about undertaking Digital Library Projects are summarised below.

- When digitising objects, decisions have to be made about issues such as what resolution the image is to be captured at, what format the target file will be, and what metadata will be required. In large-scale digitisation projects such features are likely to have been standardised beforehand and fully documented (Miller 2022), as was the case in Tate Modern.
- Before digitisation proceeds in a Digital Library Project, some damaged or deteriorating items may require conservation work to repair them (Xie and Matusiak 2016) (see Maintain-preserve in Chap. 4, Sect. 4.8.3). This has shaped some of the digitisation work at the Acropolis Museum.
- To perform digitisation, the individual(s) concerned need to be able to operate the equipment. A single collector who has acquired a scanner, for example, is likely to have already become familiar with equipment before starting to digitise objects. In large-scale Digital Llibrary Projects however, the staff involved will need to be given training in how to use the equipment, and in other aspects of that part of the digitisation process which they are undertaking (Miller 2022). This was a critical part of the setting up of the facilities at the film production site, where specialist employees were recruited and trained.
- Institutions that are digitising very large numbers of items, and that have formal responsibilities for caring for their collections, need to take a more rigorous approach to ensuring quality and to safeguarding their digital files. They are advised to take copies of master files to form service files upon which quality adjustments can be made to produce a Production master, from which, in turn, production copies can be produced to be accessed by end users (Xie and Matusiak 2016). This was a central part of the processes established at both the Tate Modern and the film production site.

5.5.2 Revolutionary Changes in the Use Practice

We consider four of the Use practices to have been revolutionised by IT:

- Use-Authorise
- Use-Search
- Use-Investigate
- Use-Interact.

Use-Authorise: Authorisation is usually a practice only carried out by institutional collectors. It has become dominated by bar-coded cards, some of which may incorporate chips that can be read by scanners. The cards are associated with back-end databases which provide full details of who has what rights of access. Access to online collections is, of course, managed by digital authentication and password schemes.

Use-Search: Search is no longer limited to searching particular fields with particular keywords: the world has become used to free text searching across the whole set of metadata associated with a collection. Many collecting institutions now have indexes that can be searched in that way, and even Amateur Collectors, Private Curators and Filers may have indexes with a similar capability.

Use-Investigate: The Icon Age has introduced a revolution in how to find out answers to questions. To research any kind of information nowadays, the internet is often the first port of call. The amount and range of collection-related information that can be acquired through a quick internet search far surpasses what could be achieved over many days in previous eras.

Use-Interact: While the Icon Age has not particularly impacted the physical meetings between individuals, for collectors, it has undoubtedly made it much easier to identify like-minded people and groups (through internet searching, or via social media systems), and to interact with them by email, messaging systems and, most especially, through social media. The social media presence of large collecting organisations is now treated as a high priority and a key vehicle for communication with their clients.

5.5.3 Difficulty and Workload in the Use Practice

Our analysis indicates that, overall, the Use practice has become slightly easier, and certainly more diverse, with the introduction of IT, while the associated Workload seems to have stayed about the same. Having said that, the new 'Digitise' sub-practice has clearly introduced a high additional workload.

5.5.4 Examples of Troubles in the Use Practice that Have Been Introduced by IT

Some examples of Use troubles that have been introduced by IT are described below.

Searching: Search in the IT era has become a commonplace activity and takes many different forms but may not always deliver the results you want.

> You can sometimes spend a long time searching for some information on the web just because you think it ought to be there somewhere because everything is on the net [RM:OFC].
>
> Alexa, Amazon's voice recognition interface to its music library and to the internet, often does not understand what you are requesting [RM:MusWil].
>
> The full text of Word or PDF items now stored in Windows folders do get searched in a Windows Explorer search along with all the file and folder names, and this does muddy the results [RM:PAWDOC].
>
> With regard to our old content management system, the location of related material could involve searches of our own site. This, somewhat perversely, used to mean conducting Google searches as opposed to using the system's own search tool, because Google was quicker and more effective. Having acquired relevant titles, however, links still had to be made by searching our local archive [RM:Swiss].

The search capability of an electronic index is very powerful and quick; but those capabilities are not sufficient to guarantee rapid success.

> Successful search depends on having a good description [RM:Loft].
>
> You have to guess at what search terms to use and may have to go through the tedious process of accessing multiple items from the filing system only to find that very few, if any, are what you are looking for [RM:PAWDOC].
>
> Sometimes you have to look through multiple items under one Ref No before establishing that that Ref No is not the solution [RM:PAWDOC].
>
> You may have to undertake several searches. It's easy to get frustrated as the number of unsuccessful search attempts mount [RM:PAWDOC].
>
> If you are unsuccessful in a search, you are uncertain if you are using appropriate search terms or not [RM:PAWDOC].
>
> It's also difficult to know how to adjust your search strategy on the fly. It would be best to have a standard best practice search strategy fully worked out beforehand—but I never produced one of those [RM:PAWDOC].
>
> When successive searches don't identify the desired items, it can be difficult to know when to stop [RM:PAWDOC].
>
> You need to be careful in what search criteria you are limiting yourself to, thereby overly constraining the results [RM:PAWDOC].
>
> When using abbreviated search terms, there is a danger that other terms which have the same short form will be found [RM:PAWDOC].
>
> Machine parts are referred to by their technical names, e.g. 'duplex module', 'finisher', 'upper paper path', 'document feeder rollers', and so on. In addition, technical terminology is also used to describe the faults that occur, such as 'spooling', 'postscript errors', or 'guest authentication pass code lockout error'... If customers are using the knowledge base on their own, they must already have the right kind of terminology available to them. This applies to both searching the knowledge base and interpreting the results of their searches (O'Neill et al. 2005).

Local Buy-in: For some collections you need the buy-in of your colleagues or your family—perhaps even more so in the IT era.

> Other members of the family are not so keen to use the computer system as I am—they just want to put stuff into the loft and take it out [RM:Loft].
>
> Although the collection is jointly owned, I do all the organising, digitisation and indexing [RM:MemWil].

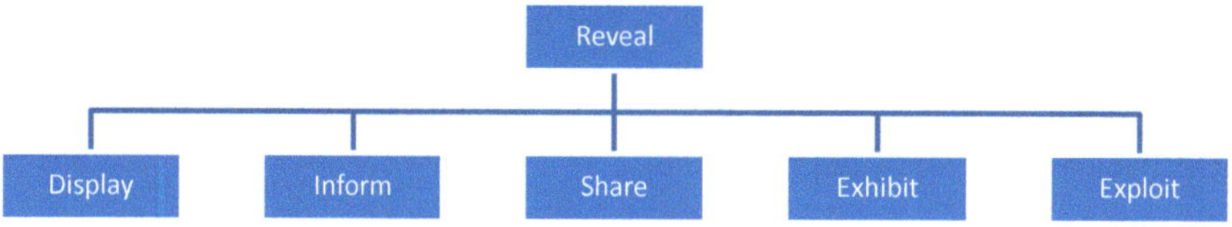

Fig. 5.5 The 'Reveal' practice hierarchy in the Icon Age

> The digital master files are held on my laptop, and a copy of them is on my wife's laptop too but she never really uses them [RM:MemWil].
>
> It's quite difficult to explain what this collection is all about [RM:ESB]!

5.6 Reveal

5.6.1 New Practices Introduced to the Reveal Practice

No new practices have been introduced into the Reveal practice as a result of IT; therefore, the hierarchy remains the same as shown in Fig. 5.5.

5.6.2 Revolutionary Changes in the Reveal Practice

We consider three of the Reveal practices to have been revolutionised by IT: Reveal-Share; Reveal-Exhibit; and Reveal-Exploit.

Reveal-Share: Most serials (journals, magazines etc.) are now available in electronic versions. Therefore, organisations like Libraries that lend out serials need to have appropriate computer systems and user access management functionality in place in order to deliver serials to their users (Fieldhouse 2012). For individual collectors, messaging services, email, and social media systems have made it very easy to share digital objects such as documents and photos, and digitised objects (i.e., scans or photos of collected objects). Across all collecting contexts, the use of social media has had an especially significant impact upon sharing practices. Most organisations now have a variety of social media accounts and will use them to regularly share news about their collections. For Amateur Collections, the use of social media has generated a proliferation of distributed communities dedicated to collecting a huge array of different items, talking to one another about them, and swapping stories and images (Abreu 2013).

Reveal-Exhibit: In the pre-IT era, the exhibiting of a collection was usually undertaken in a specific location. However, IT has hugely expanded the mechanisms and potential audiences for exhibiting collected items. Websites can exhibit lists and digital images of items, for access by either authorised users or by anyone in the world who has an interest. Social media sites, such as Instagram, provide ready-made exhibition space, for photos in general and for images of any type of item [RM:PhotoWil; Acrop; Cite; Imp; Tate].

Reveal-Exploit: IT provides collectors with the ability to create digital images of items and then to manipulate them in all sorts of different ways and to reproduce them in many different forms. An indication of the possibilities is easily established by looking at the variety of offerings from the different photo printing sites on the internet which will produce, very cheaply, large size images and text on canvas, mugs, cushions and plant pots to name just a few [RM:OFC]. These techniques have also been exploited by gift shops in many large collecting organisations [RM:Acrop; Espace; Tate]. The Spectrum standard addresses this practice under the heading of 'Reproduction' (collections Trust 2024). Book production services on the internet enable anyone to create a book with digital images to any level of quality and in any quantity at prices affordable to the individual collector. For example, Wilson created a book containing mementos of all the jobs he has had throughout his life [RM:MemWil], and a book containing the digital images of all the pages in a particular stamp album together with an explanation of its origin and how it was built up and assembled [RM:Stamp] (Wilson 2022).

5.6.3 Difficulty and Workload in the Reveal Practice

Our analysis indicates that, overall, the Reveal practice is the one that has benefited the most from the introduction of IT, with it becoming noticeably easier. However, IT has introduced a small increase in Workload, providing another example of our suspicion that, while IT makes collecting practices easier, it often requires more work. This is illustrated by the Exploit practice: It may be much easier to embark on exploitation work, but the capabilities afforded by IT applications may result in a much greater workload being experienced [RM:OFC]. In large organisations, the new emphasis on sharing news via social media has added an additional activity for some personnel [RM:Swiss] and the use of websites to reveal exhibits has, in some case, necessitated the employment of new personnel [RM:Acrop; Tate].

5.7 Maintain

5.7.1 New Practices Introduced to the Maintain Practice

Four new practices have been introduced into the Maintain practice: Manage-Digital Systems, Protect-Digital Items, Protect-Digital Systems, and Preserve-Digital Items. The updated hierarchy is shown in Fig. 5.6.

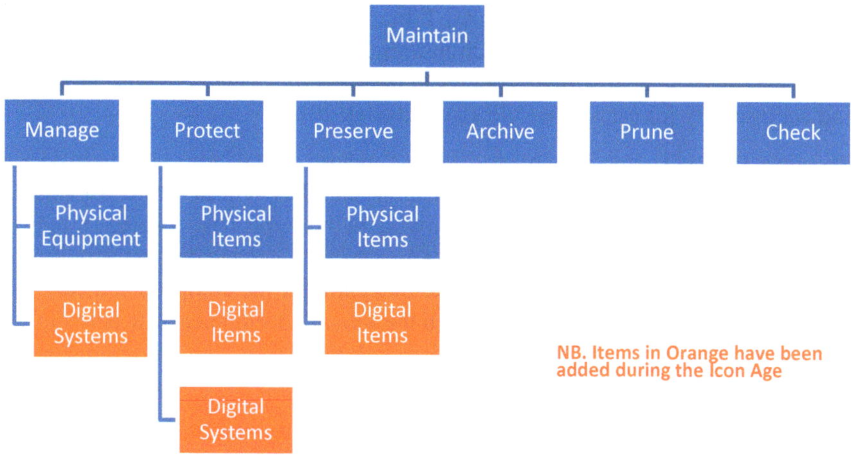

Fig. 5.6 The updated 'Maintain' practice hierarchy in the Icon Age

Manage-Digital Systems: Computer systems cannot just be used for a specific purpose and then forgotten about. They have to be managed and maintained to ensure they are fit for purpose when they need to be used. This applies just as much to small scale systems used by an individual collector, as it does to institutional collectors such as Libraries, Museums, and Galleries, which may be operating large-scale indexes of their collections and providing online access to some of their digitised objects.

Protect-Digital items: Digital data is always vulnerable to corruption or total loss, either by computer malfunction, malicious intervention, or catastrophic events such as fire or flood. To protect against these risks, digital items need to be regularly backed up, and a number of different backup copies retained in different locations depending on how much value is placed on the data. Ideally, this should include at least a local copy, a second copy in another location, and a third copy somewhere else again (Wilson 2001) [RM:Email; Data; Film; TVBC].

Protect-Digital Systems: Digital systems of any type are also vulnerable to system breakdown. To protect against these risks, it has become essential to take the following steps:

- Document the system components, configuration settings, common problems and fixes, and computer support phone numbers, and store this information outside the system concerned—preferably in hardcopy (Wilson 2001)
- Always run security software when connected to the internet to prevent unwanted intrusion by other computers and viruses [RM:Email; Data]
- Take regular backup copies of computer application configuration settings, and all data associated with a collection. Again, for all these backup copies, there need to be local copies, second copies in another location, and third copies in yet another location (Wilson 2001) [RM:Trophy; Loft; Let; Film].

For institutions undertaking Digital Library Projects, best practice is to have master files, service files and production files. The protection and backup arrangements may need to deal with each of these in different ways to optimise protection and accessibility for each type (Xie and Matusiak 2016).

Preserve-Digital Items: The ability to access and use digital Items is entirely dependent on the computer systems and application that they operate on. If the formats they employ, or the application code they were built for, become obsolete, it may be impossible to open the digital items rendering them effectively defunct and useless. These types of problems started to come to light after the computer industry was only some thirty or forty years old. Given the rate of development, the potential for such problems to occur in another 20 years let alone 50 or more years down the line, is quite high. However, there are some simple steps that can be taken to minimise the risk:

- Use common systems such as word processing and spreadsheet applications
- Use common formats such as jpg and mp4
- Keep the operating system up to date
- Keep the applications up to date
- Try opening up the digital items every few years.

A more rigorous approach, which is certainly advisable for large collections of digital items of many different types of formats, is to implement a Preservation Maintenance regime, which periodically assesses the collection and takes steps to rectify emerging problems [RM:Trophy; PAWDOC; Let; Email]. Since the film and television industry has shifted to almost entirely digital formats, a huge amount of energy has been devoted to trying to contend with preservation challenges for large digital media archives [RM:Film; TVBC]. Detailed information about Digital Preservation can be found in an online handbook provided by the Digital Preservation Coalition (DPC 2024) (see also Chap. 7, Sect. 7.2.5).

5.7.2 Revolutionary Changes in the Maintain Practice

Apart from the four new practices, we have not identified any revolutionary changes to the Maintain practice due to the introduction of digital technology.

5.7.3 Difficulty and Workload in the Maintain Practice

Our analysis suggests that Maintain is the only Practice that has been made more difficult by IT. Furthermore, it appears that IT has resulted in the Maintain practice experiencing the greatest increase in workload of all the practices. The likely reason for this is the heavy emphasis on maintaining and protecting computer systems and preserving digital files.

5.7.4 Examples of Troubles in the Maintain Practice that Have Been Introduced by IT

Some examples of Maintain Troubles that have been introduced by IT are described below.

Technology management: The management of technology that has been acquired can be quite demanding.

> The Document Management System (DMS) required that I register each application type before being able to store files of that type [RM:PAWDOC].
>
> The link between the Index and the storage function had to be set up and sometimes didn't work and had to be fixed [RM:PAWDOC].
>
> The dangers of losing large swathes of the collection—or all of it—due to system crashes etc. is far more worrying than it was for pre-digital systems [RM:PAWDOC].
>
> Macros are a bit fiddly to construct (need to understand how the DMS works) and then you need to remember what commands to use to instigate them [RM:PAWDOC].
>
> Documenting system components, configuration settings, little used technology procedures and fixes, and support phone numbers, is an overhead activity and, as such, it is easy to forget to do or to do it inadequately [RM:PAWDOC].
>
> It is difficult to record instructions about things you are not very familiar with in a way that you can follow many months or years hence [RM:PAWDOC].

Backing up: Loss of data is always a concern, so backing up has become a priority activity.

> Making backups requires additional time and energy. Quite often you may run out of space in the course of taking a backup and then you have to spend time sorting out the old backups to make space for a new backup [RM:PAWDOC].
>
> Making manual backups is something that's easy to forget to do; however, automatic back-up systems are an extra expense and have to be setup and configured [RM:PAWDOC].
>
> You need to ensure that backups are performed regularly [RM:MemWil].
>
> Operating a comprehensive back-up regime with a local backup, a secondary backup in another location, and a third backup elsewhere, is an even greater overhead which takes more time [RM:PAWDOC].
>
> I live in an area where the weather can be quite violent, and I have nine old external disc drives next to my desk that were burnt out during storms. I am still hoping to one day recover data from them. It took me quite a while to realise that I needed two external disc drives, one as a copy of the other that is only connected during back-up [RM:TolDoc].

Digital Preservation: Losing the ability to read files in the long term is a risk that can take special effort to mitigate.

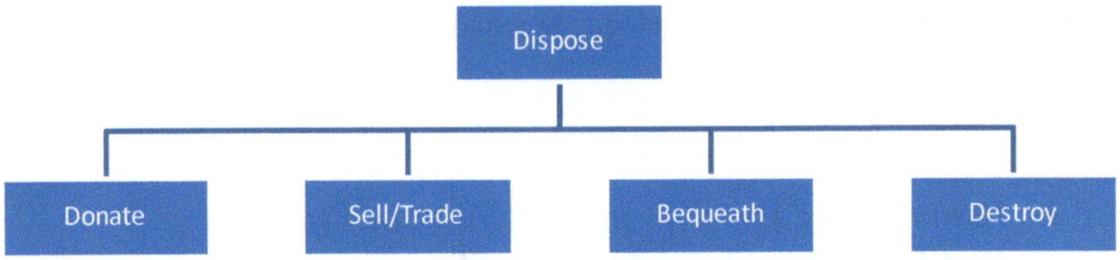

Fig. 5.7 The 'Dispose' practice hierarchy in the Icon Age

Digital preservation activities to prevent files becoming unreadable in the long term, are complicated and time consuming at scale [RM:PAWDOC].

To create and implement digital preservation plans, you need to know what you're doing and to be diligent over long periods of time. This is generally speaking a hassle for anyone who has never done it before—and not one you experience with paper items [RM:PAWDOC].

The internet is a good source of digital preservation advice, guidance and conversion services—but it can be very time-consuming following up large numbers of possible leads about obscure file formats [RM:PAWDOC].

It can be worth finding knowledgeable collaborators who can be asked for guidance—though it may be difficult to know what to ask in the first instance [RM:PAWDOC].

It's easy to forget to label files after they have been converted to a more up-to-date format [RM:PAWDOC].

It's easy to forget to do a regular progress report which may mean that an opportunity to calmly assess what problems exist and how to deal with them, is missed [RM:PAWDOC].

5.8 Dispose

5.8.1 New Practices Introduced to the Dispose Practice

No new practices have been introduced into the Dispose practice; therefore, the hierarchy remains the same, as shown in Fig. 5.7.

5.8.2 Revolutionary Changes to the Dispose Practice

Our research indicates that just one Dispose practice has been revolutionised by IT: Selling/Trading objects in order to dispose of them.

Dispose-Sell/Trade: In the pre-IT era, owners with collections or part-collections to sell were largely limited to offering them to people they knew, by advertising in a magazine or newspaper, or trying to find a dealer who might be interested. IT has revolutionised the possibilities with on-line auction sites and social media systems that now enable both individuals and institutions to try and sell anything world-wide. Stamps for example, can be bought and sold extensively via at least three major auction sites—eBay, Ebid and Hipstamp [RM:Stamp]. Auction sites can also be used to dispose of unwanted items within larger purchases or from spur of the moment purchases which, on reflection, are considered inappropriate (Ellis and Haywood 2006).

5.8.3 Difficulty and Workload in the Dispose Practice

The Dispose practice seems to reflect the general phenomenon described previously that, where IT has made practices a little easier to perform, a slight increase in workload has also been experienced. For example, it may be much easier to sell things in on-line auctions—but the ability to break job lots into smaller units, and the desire to provide potential purchasers with full details and many photos, may result in a greater overall workload [RM:Stamp].

5.9 A Summary of IT's Overall Impact on Collecting Practices

In our analysis of the research collections listed in Chap. 3, we did not identify any generic collecting practice that could be eliminated from the practice hierarchy due to the impact of IT. We did identify a few *specific instances* of practices being eliminated by IT, but these were specific to certain types of collections or mechanisms, and they were all due to one or other of the following four impacts:

- People now using streaming services instead of personally collecting music,
- Card Indexes having been replaced by digital indexes,
- Indexes being carried around on portable devices (laptops, tablets, mobile phones), instead of hardcopy versions,
- Hardcopy masters for photocopying not being needed when digital copies can be printed at will.

Our analysis also suggested that over 50% of the 631 instances of practices at all levels had been changed by IT in only a small way or not at all, and that a significant number operated without involving digital items at all. However, we also found that while between a third and two thirds of practices may have operated without involving digital items at all, those that did involve digital items tended to involve ***both*** digital originals ***and*** digital copies.

Another finding was that about a third of the practices at all levels had been revolutionised by IT. The revolutionary impact came primarily from new practices that have been introduced as a result of IT. These are:

- Equip-Design-Computer System

- Equip-Obtain-Subscribe
- Deposit-Digitise
- Use-Digitise
- Maintain-Manage-Digital Systems
- Maintain-Protect-Digital Items
- Maintain-Protect-Digital Systems
- Maintain-Preserve-Digital Items.

Regarding the difficulty of performing practices and the amount of work they entailed, our findings indicate that IT has tended to make collecting practices slightly easier overall, with the Use and Reveal practices being easier in particular, while the Maintain practice has perhaps become harder. For the Use practice, IT has made it a lot easier to search for items, to index items, and to record information in general about a collection. The Reveal practice has benefited from the ease with which it is now possible to use IT to share information and digital objects, and to display, exhibit and exploit those digital objects. The Maintain practice was adjudged to be harder to perform in the digital era simply because of all the backing up and digital preservation that is required to protect and preserve digital files.

Regarding workload, our findings indicate that IT has slightly increased people's workload overall. We cannot be sure if this is a genuine relationship or just a feature of having potentially subjective and limited sources of data. However, intuitively, many recognise that the more extensive capabilities of IT systems—which seem to make tasks seem easier—often come at the expense of doing a lot more. For example, doing a simple search may seem very easy. However, dealing with all the results and then doing subsequent refinements can significantly increase the workload associated with the exercise.

Generally, we can conclude that the introduction of IT has resulted in some degree of change for most collectors but has not had a radical effect on collecting overall.

References

Abreu A (2013) Collaborative collecting: a literature review. InterActions: UCLA J Educ Inf Stud 9:1

Belk R (2014) Art collecting as personal and public practice in a digital age. In: O'Reilly D, Rentschler R, Kirchner T (eds) The Routledge companion to arts marketing. Routledge, London, pp 243–255

Collections Trust (2024) Spectrum. https://collectionstrust.org.uk/spectrum/. Accessed 04 Nov 2024

DPC (2024) Digital Preservation Handbook. https://www.dpconline.org/handbook. Accessed 01 May 2023

Ellis RM, Haywood A (2006) Virtual radiophile (163*): eBay and the changing collecting practices of the UK Vintage radio community. In: Hillis K, Petit M, Epley N (eds) Everyday eBay: culture, collecting and desire. Routledge, New York, pp 45–61

Fieldhouse M (2012) The processes of collection management. In: Fieldhouse M, Marshall A (eds) Collection development in the digital age. Facet publishing, London, pp 27–44

Hughes LM (2004) Digitizing collections: strategic issues for the information manager, 2. Facet Publishing

Miller RJ (2022) Metadata for digital collections. Facet Publishing Limited, London, UK
O'Neill J, Grasso A, Castellani S, Tolmie P (2005) Using real-life troubleshooting interactions to inform self-assistance design. IFIP conference on human-computer interaction 2005 Sept 12. Springer, Berlin, Heidelberg, pp 377–390
Terras M (2010) Digital curiosities: resource creation via amateur digitization. Literary Linguist Comput 25(4):425–438
Watkins R, Sellen A, Lindley S (2015) Digital collection and digital collecting practice. In: Proceedings of the SIGCHI conference on human factors in computing systems, CHI'15. ACM, New York
Wilson PA (2001) 20 years in the life of a long-term empirical personal electronic filing study. Behav Inf Technol 20(5):395–409
Wilson PA (2014) IV in PIM—the applicability of intrinsic value in personal information management, v1.1, 18 May 2014, Published on www.pwofc.com on 19 May 2014. http://www.pwofc.com/ofc/2014/05/19/the-end-of-this-particular-road/. Accessed 15 Dec 2024
Wilson PA (2016) Get that old photo collection in order. Watermead village view magazine, Spring issue, 05 March 2016, Watermead Parish Council, Aylesbury. https://www.watermead-pc.gov.uk/village-view-2015---2016.html. Accessed 25 Nov 2024
Wilson PA (2022) Meteor—a story about stamp collecting in the eye of the IT Hurricane. Privately published book produced by Blurb, 05 April 2022 [available for viewing by arrangement with the author]
Xie I, Matusiak K (2016) Discover digital libraries: theory and practice. Elsevier, Amsterdam

Chapter 6
The Objects of Collecting

Abstract From time immemorial mankind has had a relationship with objects and we have evolved our capabilities to sense and interact with them. Up to the start of the Icon Age, the types of objects that were collected were limited to Physical Objects (such as jewels or plants) and Information Carrier Objects (such as clay tablets or books). Computing introduced digital files such as programs or data and the Icon Age has significantly expanded the types of objects collected: digitised physical objects in 2D or 3D, with the original being retained or destroyed; physicalised digital objects using 2D or 3D printers; NFTs (Non-Fungible Tokens); physical objects with Internet of Things capability; Big Data; and objects created by AI. The impact of Icon Age technology on the way we interact with all these types of objects is described, and aspects such as ownership and legal issues, and forgeries and fakes, are explored.

Collecting is all about objects. Without objects there is no collecting. So, this chapter explores how we have evolved with objects, what type of objects we collect, what sort of relationship we have with those objects, and how the Icon Age has affected these things.

6.1 Our Evolution with Objects

Our relationship with objects is ancient and intimate. From our earliest days in our pre-Homo Sapiens forms, we have perceived objects and co-existed with them on the earth on which we live. We have developed senses with which to experience some of the many characteristics of these objects—a capacity to detect the visible light radiation that is reflected off them (a sense we call sight); a capacity to detect pressure, vibration, texture, and temperature (a sense we call touch); a capacity to detect chemicals that they emit (a sense we call smell); and a capacity to detect chemicals that they consist of (a sense we call taste). We have also developed a capacity to detect changes in pressure—sometimes caused by objects (a sense we call hearing) (Sherman and Craig 2018). In addition to all these senses, we have

P. Wilson and P. Tolmie, *Collecting in the Icon Age*,
https://doi.org/10.1007/978-3-031-86470-4_6

developed appendages with motors (legs, arms, and hands, accompanied by a variety of muscles) with which we can grasp and move these objects—not least to enable us to acquire and consume the food that we need to sustain ourselves. We have also developed an ability to remember the interactions that our senses have experienced with objects (a capacity we call memory).

As our abilities increased, we started changing some objects to suit our own purposes—such as fashioning spears to hunt with and stones to crack bones (Heylighen 2023; Harari 2014); and we began to assemble objects to support our activities, such as creating a fire hearth (Chazan 2017). We probably started to develop primitive language around the same time, and by 30,000 years ago this had evolved into a mechanism that enabled us to talk to each other not just about physical objects like animals and rivers, but also about imaginary objects like gods and nations (Harari 2014).

We got better and better at fashioning objects and started creating things like pottery (de Saulieu and Testart 2015) and building materials. We created amazing structures like pyramids and temples and tombs (Scarre 1999). By this time, we were actively acquiring, collecting and owning objects. They were obtained either for use in day-to-day living (for example, jars and cooking pots (Frank 2018)); or simply because we enjoyed them (such as jewellery (Grömer 2016)). Of course, we also became very proficient at destroying objects, especially in wars.

Around 3000 BC, we invented written communication and used clay tablets to record the writing (Casson 2001). Different scripts—essentially different languages—were developed around the world (Harari 2014): and with full scripts came the ability to write about non-physical concepts such as ideas, logic and politics (Logan and McLuhan 2016; Casson 2001). Another major script—Arabic Numerals—emerged around 800 AD to enable us to record mathematical information and this was subsequently adopted worldwide (Harari 2014; Logan and McLuhan 2016). A variety of different types of objects, such as clay tablets, split bamboo, papyrus, parchment and modern paper, have been used to record the writings in these different scripts; and, from when writing began, the written-on objects were collected together to provide a record which could be transmitted to our older selves or to others; and to peoples of the future when we die. Eventually these writings came to be assembled in a form we called a book; and, in the middle of the fifteenth century, the printing press was invented which enabled us to create multiple copies of the same book (Heylighen 2023).

From the 1800s onwards, the industrial revolution was well underway and sparked an explosion in manufacturing production which hugely increased both the number of different types of goods being produced, and the number of copies of the same item that were being produced. This combined with the scientific developments of the nineteenth and twentieth centuries produced a consumer society in which possessing large quantities of man-made objects became the norm (Belk 1995).

6.2 Object Affordances

The actions that can be performed upon an object depend upon its physical properties. They are referred to as an object's affordances. Affordances tell you what you can do with an object (Sellen and Harper 2002; Sherman and Craig 2018). For example, the handle of a cup provides the affordance of being able to pick the cup up. In this text, we use a loose interpretation of the object affordance notion, to incorporate all the evolutionary interactions described in the previous section. Table 6.1 summarises the generic object affordances that we learned to undertake with objects as we evolved. These affordances broadly applied at the start of the Icon Age in the early 1980s. Later in this chapter we will revisit them to examine if and how they have been impacted by Information Technology in the subsequent forty-or-so years.

6.3 Features of Our Relationship with Objects

By the start of the Icon Age in the early 1980s, we were interacting with hugely more objects than ever before—a great many of them man-made. We were developing a culture in which a wide range of possessions was seen as a necessity (Belk 1995); and some of the objects themselves were becoming increasingly complex. Within this environment, a number of important characteristics of our relationship with objects were discernible as described below.

6.3.1 The Transmission Triple

We can't transmit our memories, so the ability to write down our thoughts on objects significantly augmented the oral transmittal of information about our activities, thinking, and culture (Hirsch and Spitzer 2006; Heylighen 2023; Logan and McLuhan 2016). Digital objects containing not only writing but also sounds and images, have enhanced this capability (Keilbach 2013). The ability to transmit information to future generations is an important accompaniment to our ability to transmit our genes to new incarnations of ourselves to ensure the continuation of our race. We also transmit non-information objects such as pottery, jewels, cherished possessions, and keepsakes down through the generations (Folkman et al. 2004; Pearce 1998; Clayton 2004). This transmission triple of genes, information and objects is what enables us humans, as a race, to develop and evolve in a world and universe of physical objects. Conversely, experiences, knowledge and culture that are not passed on are likely to play a lesser role in our development (see Wilson (2019b) for an illustration of this point).

Table 6.1 Generic object affordances

Generic object affordances (what humans have learned to do with objects)	Summary
Co-exist with objects	We evolved with objects all around us
Detect objects with sensors we developed	We evolved senses to detect particular characteristics of objects: reflected light (sight), pressure, vibration, texture, and temperature (touch); emitted chemicals (smell); integral chemicals (taste); air pressure (hearing)
Move objects	We evolved legs, arms, and hands, and associated muscles, to grasp and move objects
Remember objects	We evolved an ability to remember the interactions that our senses have experienced with objects (memory)
Change objects	We started changing objects to suit our own purposes
Assemble objects	We began to assemble objects to support our activities
Create objects	We started creating completely new objects such as pottery. Eventually, the printing press enabled us to create multiple copies of books; and the industrial revolution enabled us to produce multiple copies of other physical objects
Talk about abstract objects	We developed language which enabled us to think about non-physical things
Acquire objects	We started to seek out and acquire objects that we wanted
Destroy objects	We became proficient at destroying objects, especially in wars
Record information on objects	We invented written communications and mathematics, and recorded written information on objects
Collect objects	We started to collect objects that we wanted to use and enjoy
Use objects	Some objects we collect to use in our day-to-day lives
Enjoy objects	Some objects we collect to simply enjoy now and in the future
Consume objects	We started buying and using large numbers of manufactured objects

6.3.2 *How Our Minds Comprehend Objects*

A materialistic view of the world explains that the world contains objects and our minds simply explore what is out there and stores knowledge of those objects i.e. this materialistic view claims that the knowledge we have is mind-independent. However, this view doesn't explain why the mind isn't holding massive amounts of detail about the world; nor how the mind deals with abstract objects such as a joke. A more realistic view is that the mind constructs its own version of the world based on what it is sensing. Hence, the existence, names, characteristics, and classifications of objects are all created in the mind and commonly broadcast and accepted through communication and culture (Heylighen 2023; Currall et al. 2004). This process is assisted by the mind's ability to see patterns and to generalise. For example, we can see a model of a car that we've never seen before but still know that it's a car (Sherman and Craig 2018). Inevitably, the individual's own predilections and previous encounters with objects of a similar type will also mould the individual's perception of the object (Pearce 1994e).

Given this state of affairs, we should have no illusions that we fully comprehend the objects we encounter: all we can say is that each one of us has broadly the same set of sensing equipment, and that each of us is interpreting the signals picked up by our sensors and sent through our nerves to our brains. We 'make' the objects in our heads according to what is in the incoming signals AND to what other humans have told us about similar signals, either directly or from a written record. For example, collectively humans have agreed that visible light of wavelength 570–580 nm should be interpreted as yellow. Our knowledge of the objects of the world is entirely constructed within each of our individual heads according to that subset of characteristics which can be detected by our limited set of sensors, and with a lot of help from our living fellow humans and from information transmitted to us by our ancestors. Of course, the condition of synaesthesia, in which senses are mixed—such as tasting colours or seeing sounds—would seriously affect how an individual perceives an object (Seth 2022).

Quite apart from the potential variability in the way we physically sense of objects, there is huge potential for variability in our understanding of what they are. Pearce notes that the meaning of an object is not wholly embedded with the piece itself, nor entirely within the mind of the individual, but in a combination of the two (Pearce 1995b); and Thompson reminds us that objects—and he includes humans and ideas in this observation—have properties conferred upon them as a result of human social life (Thompson 2017). However, regardless of the viewer's persuasions, and the cultural lens through which an object is viewed, it will still possess the history through which it has passed (Pearce 1995b)—though, of course, the way that history is interpreted will itself be subject to the social culture of the individual.

6.3.3 *Impact of Objects on Our Mind and Memory*

Humans could not exist without the material world and the objects within it. Objects influence what we do and who we are (Tobin 2016). When we look at an object, we become an ever-so-slightly different person (Pearce 1995b; Pearce 1994e). Objects interact with memory in three different ways: (a) they form memories that can be recalled, (b) they stimulate the remembering of related memories, and (c) like fragments that speak to archaeologists, they store information which a human can experience and interpret (Kwint 1999). Souvenirs, for example, can have all three impacts, and, consequently, unless the type (c) information is particularly striking, few people are interested in other people's souvenirs (Pearce 1994b). A widely cited illustration of these processes is Benjamin's 1931 essay describing the memories and connections he remembered when unpacking his books from storage crates (Beer 2008; Benjamin 1999). Our memories often associate objects with people. When relationships end through death or for other reasons, one way people may cope is by tending to divest themselves of all such objects except a few which remind them of the good or special times associated with that person (Miller and Parrott 2009).

6.3.4 *Objects Have a Life-Span*

Physical objects have a life-span—though often a much longer span than humans. There is a time when they are new, a period when are in a healthy state, and then they go through a phase of deterioration, which is followed by dissolution (Pearce 1995b).

6.3.5 *Ownership and Legal Issues*

Most man-made objects, and some natural ones, are owned by an individual or group, and this brings with it certain rights. For example, it is the owner's prerogative to physically possess an object and to prevent anyone else from doing so without their permission; and, in some circumstances, patent and copyright laws apply to control the use of objects by non-owners (Carroll 2013). Another characteristic of ownership is that, over time, an object may come to reflect its relationship with the owner—perhaps a scratch here, signs of wear there, and even some personalisation such as the owner's name being inscribed (Banks 2013).

6.3.6 *Representations of Objects*

Those objects that have a physical presence and that we can see, can be easily represented with a photograph or drawing. A photograph puts the viewer in direct perceptual contact with the object, whereas a painting or drawing (or verbal description) only provides a mediated view of the object (Walton 1984). Non-physical entities such as a business or country may require some imagination to represent (perhaps a building for the former and a map for the latter); and some non-physical objects may be harder to represent than others, for example a joke (Sherman and Craig 2018).

6.3.7 *Forgeries and Fakes*

From time immemorial, fakes have been created of the things we value the most. From the Egyptian forgers of the Shabaka Stone whose makers claimed to be copying a worm-eaten document, to the monks who forged supposed charters of Edward the Confessor, the prospect of making easy money from collectors who covert objects so much that their perceptions are influenced by their expectations, has spurred forgers on. Some fakes are better than others, and some are very good indeed making them very difficult to spot. It is a reflection of our times that the thing most faked in the last three quarters of the twentieth century was brand-named goods (Jones 1990)—illustrating that forgeries and fakes are not always made of single unique items. Rare old postage stamps are another such case in point.

6.3.8 *How We Look After Our Objects*

Generally speaking, we keep our physical objects in designated places; and if we keep them indoors, they are usually on shelves or in drawers or cupboards. When we acquire new objects, we assess how we need to care for them and then designate a place to keep them accordingly. Quite often we have too little storage space and things get crammed together. Over time, as we take objects out and put them back, they get disordered and we can't find the things we're looking for.

All the above features applied at the start of the Icon Age. We will revisit them later in this chapter to examine how Information Technology has impacted them in the following forty years.

6.4 Types of Objects Collected Up to the Start of the Icon Age

6.4.1 Physical Objects and Information Carrier Objects

Objects in collections over the millennia have been physical objects. This is an important starting point for our examination of the different types of object available for collecting. It specifically excludes the thoughts and ideas in people's heads. Physical objects have a role or function in the physical world. When writing was invented, an important subset of physical objects was introduced—objects specifically designed to carry information: we will refer to them as Information Carrier Objects – ICO for short. The scope of ICOs was expanded in the first half of the nineteenth century when photography was invented (Wikipedia 2024a) leading first to photographic plates and then to roll film and negatives for both still and moving pictures—all physical objects containing picture information. Sound recording followed on a little later towards the end of the nineteenth century and by the late 1920s the vinyl disc had become firmly established as the standard ICO for stand-alone sound, and sound tracks were being incorporated onto movie film. Magnetic tapes emerged around the 1950s to become another popular ICO for sound (Britannica 2024; Wikipedia 2024b).

Physical objects can be either animate (such as animals or plants) or inanimate (such as rocks, pottery or information carrier objects) (Danet and Katriel 1994). Below are examples of collections of these types of objects:

- Animate physical objects: for example, animals in a zoo, and collections of plants.
- Information Carrier Objects (ICO): for example, the clay tablets on which the Sumerians recorded their commodities, the books in a library, film, vinyl discs, and magnetic tape.
- Inanimate physical objects (non ICO): for example, ancient pottery in a museum, and postage stamps in an album.

From the collecting standpoint, one further distinction is worth making: Information Carrier Objects can either be considered to contain a single work such as the novel Wuthering Heights; or they can contain collections of things—sometimes referred to as anthologies. Such collections could be of ephemeral things that exist in the world such as jokes or tall tales; or be a set of short stories, or song music and lyrics—or any number of other things. An extreme example is the collection of performance art perhaps by acquiring and documenting the rights and means to reperform them (Laurenson and Van Saaze 2014). However, for our purposes, these do not constitute another type of object; they are just another type of content that might appear in an Information Carrier Object.

6.4.2 The Emergence of Computer-Related Objects

In the middle of the twentieth century the modern computer emerged and came into general use in the 1960s (Lavington 2010; Britannica 2023). A computer processes data, and its development introduced a new type of object—the computer program which controls the computing process. Computer programs are information and, in the early days of computing, they often resided on information carrier objects such as print-outs or punched cards. However, when they were put to use in the computer they introduced another new type of object to the world. At that point they were transferred from a tangible, visible, physical, Information Carrier Object onto a new type of digital Information Carrier Object which consisted of electronic equipment containing invisible electrical charges. We eventually chose to cope with this rather complex and mysterious notion by naming the information in its electronic form a Digital File. Although a computer program was the first example of a digital file, computer technology soon became more versatile and, by the late 1970s, Digital Files were holding a wide variety of other types of things including documents and electronic mail messages. A significant proportion of this material was printed out onto hardcopy to become physical versions of the Digital Files.

Data had been a key component of computer programs from the early days. However, as programs became more complex, and the amount of data grew larger, the data tended to be held separately, and by the mid-1960s, the term database had come into general use (Wikipedia 2023a) and the concept of collecting data together had become generally understood among those who worked on or with computers. By the start of the Icon Age, database technology was well established. Like a computer program, a database is stored in a Digital File; but data is very different from other types of Digital File so we will keep it separate.

By the start of the Icon Age, therefore, the generic types of objects that were being collected are shown in Fig. 6.1.

6.5 New Types of Objects Introduced in the Icon Age

6.5.1 Born Digital and Digitised

The start of the Icon Age signified the widespread introduction of the personal computer which resulted in an explosion in the number of Digital Files being created. Around the same time there was a focus on the development of computing technologies to support work in offices. One such development was the digital scanner which was able to create an exact copy of a physical document or page of a book, in a Digital File. This process was referred to as digitisation (Oliver and Harvey 2016), and a number of large-scale electronic filing products were introduced in the 1980s to support the large-scale digitisation and management of office files (Wilson 1986). By

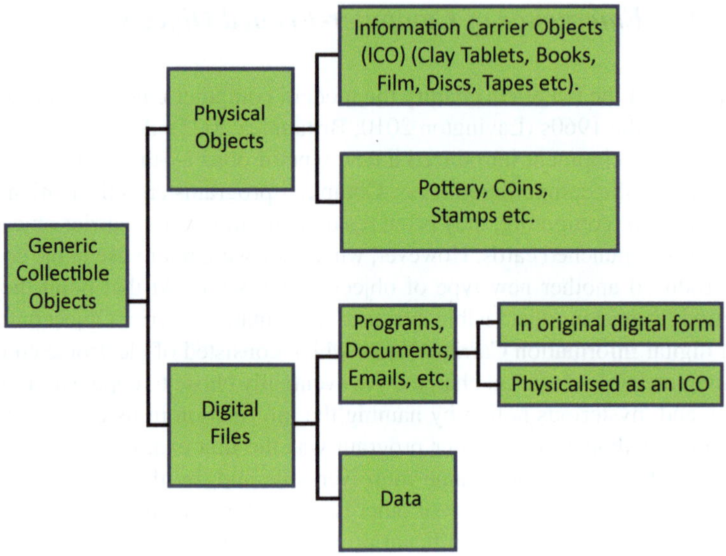

Fig. 6.1 Generic collectible objects before the start of the Icon Age

the 1990s, small scale personal scanners were becoming widely and cheaply available, which led to increasing numbers of paper documents being replicated in Digital Files. The differing routes to a digitised version required different document management processes and systems, and this highlighted a need to distinguish between what had originated on a computer and what had been digitised from a physical object. Librarians, Archivists and Academics also found they needed a distinguishing term, and, by the turn of the century the term 'Born Digital' was in use. It soon became more generally employed as these examples provided by Redwine in 2015 illustrate:

> A Word document, an email and a photograph taken with a digital camera are common examples of Born-Digital items. A digital scan of a Polaroid photograph and an MP3 audio file of a digitally reformatted cassette tape from the 1990s are examples of digitized versions, or digital surrogates, of non-digital items. (Redwine 2015)

It is worth noting a few points about Digitised Objects. The 'Order from Chaos' tutorial advises individuals to bear the following general points in mind before deciding to use a digital approach: (a) Physical objects have characteristics which can't (currently) be replicated digitally; (b) there is a significant difference between the naturalness of physical objects and the engineered nature of their digital equivalents; (c) digital systems have many vulnerabilities; and (d) conversion into digital can sometimes be difficult (Wilson 2017a).

In this text, we continue to separate physical Information Carrier Objects such as documents and books, from digital objects. However, it is of interest that Jones has found it useful to bundle Physical and Digital objects together into a single unit he calls an Information Item. He describes this as a package which encapsulates information in persistent form that can be created, modified, stored, retrieved, given a name, tags and other properties, moved, copied, distributed, deleted and otherwise manipulated. He also provides examples which include paper documents, electronic documents, digital photographs, digital music, digital film and other files, email messages, web pages, and references (for example, shortcuts and aliases) to any of the previous items (Jones 2012). We have not taken that approach because it does not enable us to highlight the significant distinction between an Information Carrier Object and a Digital File: the former is stored on a physical shelf, filing cabinet, cupboard, drawer, or table etc., and to access it you put the book or document in front of your eyes in a well-lit place and read it. The Digital File, on the other hand, is stored inside electronic components of a highly technical appearance and nature, and is accessed by running it on a much larger set of complex electrical and mechanical components combined together into a functioning computer device. Because it is such a peculiar and different thing, there is no need to distinguish it from other types of information carrier objects: the names themselves—Born Digital Object and Digitised Object—imply everything about them—all aspects of how they are stored, accessed, and read/experienced.

Another view of digital objects is provided by the OAIS Open Archival Information System's Reference Model (ISO 2012). This is widely applied by many organisations and institutions to manage their digital objects. OAIS specifies three types of information object: SIP (Submission Information Package), AIP (Archival Information Package), and DIP (Dissemination Information Package). Each information package is made up of a) the digital object to be preserved, b) the metadata required at that point in the system, and 3) packaging information. The AIP is the basic element of the digital repository and is produced by taking the SIP and adding Preservation Description information and representation information to it (Oliver and Harvey 2016).

Note the use of the word 'metadata' in this description. Metadata is information about an object—information that was more often referred to as indexing information in the days before computers when most indexes were human-readable texts. However, in the digital age, it is essential that such information is readable and processable by computers i.e. it needs to be data—hence the word metadata. It also needs to be of good quality and standardised to facilitate it being shared between collections, and to enable effective browsing and search by users. Hence standards such as the Dublin Core (emanating from a workshop held in Dublin, Ohio, in 1995), and MODS Metadata Object Description Schema—an abbreviated version of the MARC 21 Format for Bibliographic data), define lists of what type of data to specify, and provide controlled vocabularies for their contents (Miller 2022). The Open Archive Initiative (OAI—not be confused the OAIS reference model) with also specifies a Protocol for Metadata Harvesting (OAI-PMH) which provides a relatively simple method for collecting organisations to make their internal metadata available to external information services (Miller 2022). Metadata Standards have also been devised to enable objects on the internet to be clearly defined and linked together, instead of just being random words identified by a search engine. Objects can be represented behind the scenes by a globally unique identifier—a URI (Uniform

Resource Identifier)—and can be linked to each other resulting in a Sematic Web (Miller 2022).

6.5.2 *Digitised with or Without the Original*

After an object has been digitised, the vexed question of whether or not to destroy the original may arise. There may be good reason for doing so—to minimise physical storage space requirements is one of the most common. Other considerations may involve the emotions an item evokes, the uncertainty of future need, and a desire to sort out one's legacy (Wilson 2021a). However, some commentators point out that a digitised object is different from the original even if it has some common characteristics, and that while it is easy to have the enjoyment of being able to surround ourselves with physical objects, it's not so easy to do so with digital equivalents (Kirk and Sellen 2010). This fact is highlighted by the list of reasons for keeping documents developed by Wilson out of his experiences with the PAWDOC filing system—see Sect. 5.4.1. However, one of the great benefits of digitisation is that it provides an effective halfway house between keeping a physical object and obliterating it (Wilson 2016a). Despite this, destroying an object one has feelings for, is often difficult, as illustrated by this comment.

> I tore up the physical letters after I had digitised them, and, of course, felt a wrench as I did so. Undoubtedly the physical objects possess characteristics of touch, smell and presence that won't be reproduced in the digital version. However, the digital versions are undoubtedly much more accessible. (Wilson 2016b)

True obliteration, of course, requires the destruction of all originals and copies, physical and digital, including any other objects in which the item appears as a whole (Wilson 2022).

Other concerns have also been raised about destroying physical objects after digitising them. For example, it is suggested that it may be important to record why certain physical documents have been retained while others have been destroyed if only to protect the custodian (Currall et al. 2004). Another concern is that without a physical object, the beliefs and practices around evidence and authenticity may have to change (Knell 2004). Having said all that, if a physical object is digitised, it can emerge in one of two states: Digitised and physical original retained, or Digitised and physical original destroyed.

6.5.3 *Digitised Objects, Optical Character Recognition and Interpretation in General*

When Information Carrier Objects (ICO) such as documents and books, are digitised, their content can be interpreted using optical character recognition software (OCR).

This enables text to be searched, copied, and otherwise manipulated. A digitised document without OCR is essentially just a photo of each page. This is a significant difference so we will distinguish between those files containing Digitised Objects which have been *interpreted,* and those which have not. Note that software to produce text transcripts of audio and video files, became widely available in the late 2010s; though the resulting transcripts were not typically available in a single combined file with the original audio or video content. Nevertheless, the production of such combined files is, in principle a feasible proposition.

6.5.4 2D or 3D Digitised Objects

The most common digitisation technology in the early days of the Icon Age was the scanner. However, as digital photography became commonplace and powerful in the first decade of the twenty-first century, it became equally feasible to digitise a document or physical object with a digital camera. Either way, the result was a two-dimensional rendition of the item. However, that is not the only possibility: more specialist technologies are available which will produce three dimensional (3D) digital images of objects (Haynes 2018; Peinado-Santana et al. 2021), and these are of particular interest to Museums and Galleries who wish to provide virtual access to their digital content. Papers by Kiourt et al. (2016) and Carrozzino and Bergamasco (2010) explore related possibilities and provide case studies for such initiatives. An excellent way to appreciate the potential of the 3D rendition of objects, is to take a look at the African Fossils web site (African Fossils 2024).

Despite such 3D renditions being able to provide excellent all-round views of objects, the observer knows that they are being displayed on a flat screen. However, given sufficient resolution and placed in an appropriate environment, even flat screen projections can appear to be real 3D objects with depth. This was clearly demonstrated in the early 2020s by the highly successful Abba Voyage concerts in London. The 3D images of the band were computer generated, based on a month's worth of recordings of the band's members in motion capture suits; and they were displayed on huge, very high resolution (65 million pixels) screens – one showing life size images and two side ones showing close-ups and supported by a live 16-piece band (Brown 2022). To the audience it looked like a real concert by real people. Despite its realism though, the so-called Abbatars are, like the African fossils, mere 2D renditions of 3D images—and, in any case, such a solution would seem too specialist to work for collections of objects. Another approach which may have more mileage for collecting, arrived on the scene in the 2020s with Proto—a company that projects 3D holograms into booths—one big enough to display a person and another smaller tabletop model some 73 cm high (Proto 2024; Nine 2023). Image capture (both static and video) can be achieved using the Proto app on an iPhone with a 4 K camera, so, in principle, this demonstrates a more viable solution for object collections, as illustrated by the exhibition of Giacometti's Nosea in a Proto booth in the Giacometti Institute in Paris (Binde 2023).

The availability of such technology increases the types of generic objects that might be collected to those listed below:

- Digitised in 2D and physical original retained
- Digitised in 3D (flat screen) and physical original retained
- Digitised in 3D (hologram) and physical original retained
- Digitised in 2D and physical original destroyed
- Digitised in 3D (flat screen) and physical original destroyed
- Digitised in 3D (hologram) and physical original destroyed.

All the above types of object are created from original physical objects. However, Born Digital files can also be either 2D or 3D representations. Some of the most common examples of 2D Born Digital objects are Word Processing documents and digital photos. Born Digital 3D objects, however, are full 3D representations of objects, similar to the renditions produced by the 3D digitisation of a physical object. The distinction is important because of the implications for physicalising Born Digital objects as described in the section below.

6.5.5 Physicalised Digital Objects

Just because an item is Born Digital doesn't mean to say that it is always used on a computer. It is a common practice for people to print out physical versions of 2D Born Digital objects such as word-processed documents, spreadsheets, PowerPoint slides, and emails. The widespread physicalisation of 3D objects is a more recent phenomenon, with low-cost 3D printers only becoming available in the 2010s. However, the range of 3D printing applications in the early 2020s was remarkable and extended from aircraft components and prosthetic eyes to home hobbyists producing backscratchers, coat hooks, etc. (Wikipedia 2023b). Of course, all such items were initially printed from previously created Born Digital objects, though it is probably inevitable that AI programs will eventually be able to create 3D printable files from files of digitised objects—if they are not already doing so.

We can see, therefore, that there are a very significant number of Physicalised Digital Objects in the world and that this number is set to grow even more as 3D printing is used ever-more widely. This makes the question of whether to retain information about which digital objects are physicalised particularly important in order to know what you have, where it came from, what has emanated from it, and whether you have an original or a copy. Wilson, in his use of the PAWDOC filing system, certainly found it necessary to do so, both to know what format was available to use when he searched for an object; and also to be able to manage two sets of material—one in the computer and the other in physical boxes (Wilson 2019a).

6.5.6 NFTs (Non-fungible Tokens)

An NFT (Non-Fungible Token) is a unit of data stored on a blockchain in a decentralised ledger that stores committed transactions as blocks linked together using cryptographic measures (Gadekallu et al. 2022). The blockchain certifies a digital asset to be unique and therefore not interchangeable, while offering a unique digital certificate of ownership for the NFT. The word 'fungible' means something that is easy to exchange or trade for something else of the same type and value (Cambridge Dictionary 2023): conversely, a non-fungible item cannot be exchanged with anything else. The NFT token may store a variety of information including who created it, who previously owned it, and which of the many copies is the original; it may even include contractual elements such as an obligation to pay secondary sales royalties to the creator (Nadini et al. 2021). It is quite feasible to copy an NFT, however that doesn't mean that you own it. Only the person who purchased it, and whose name is in the blockchain, owns it. Furthermore, the copyright remains with the originator unless the purchase expressly transfers copyright ownership to the buyer (Mendis 2021).

In 2017 the first significant sales of NFT images took place within the Ethereum marketplace. Between June 2017 and April 2021 there were at least 6.1 million trades of 4.7 million NFTs in 160 cryptocurrencies. The NFTs were organised in collections such as collectible cards, art masterpieces, and virtual spaces or objects in online games. Potentially any type of digital object can be associated with an NFT including photos, audio sequences, and videos (Nadini et al. 2021).

NFTs are part of the cryptocurrency culture that exploded at the beginning of the twenty-first century. They are undoubtedly the new kid on the block and their future is uncertain as indicated by the downturn in their fortunes in 2022/3 (Hern 2023a). However, they are undoubtedly items that are collected, and, with their distinctive set of characteristics, they are treated as a type of object in their own right as opposed to being classed as a Born Digital object. It is worth noting that, while some NFTs are digital artworks, digital art has been flourishing since the start of the Icon Age and is totally independent of NFTs. It is a burgeoning field in its own right as evidenced by the 3 billion + hits that were returned when we did an internet search on 'digital art' at the end of 2023.

6.5.7 Internet of Things Objects

The Internet of things (IoT) refers to the way in which physical objects can communicate and interact through the internet. To facilitate that goal, virtual objects are created within the IoT as digital representations of the service(s) of the real-world objects. Various architectures can be used: one real object for one virtual object; many real objects for one virtual object; one real object for many virtual objects; many real objects for many virtual objects. Whichever is employed, the virtual objects are able to acquire, analyse, interpret and act on information about their associated real-world object, and will interact with the user and/or a back-end application (Nitti et al. 2015). By the early 2020s, IoT had become an established and rapidly growing technology with applications in many sectors including healthcare, homes and smart cities, and billions of IoT devices in operation (Alsharif et al. 2023; Intel 2025). Since many ordinary objects which people collect may eventually include IoT capabilities, we have included them in the set of generic collectible objects as Physical non-ICO objects in physical form with or without IoT. It is also conceivable that existing physical objects may be retro-fitted with IOT chips (Tebeau 2016).

6.5.8 Program Data and Big Data

As computer systems became an integral part of the operation of most businesses and organisations in the early days of the Icon Age, so every organisation using a computer collected the data that their computer programs required to run their businesses, and stored it in databases. This data is the lifeblood of every organisation: without it they could not operate. We shall call this type of data 'Program Data' to distinguish it from another significant type of collected data—so-called 'Big Data'. This term refers to data sets that are too large or complex to be dealt with by traditional data-processing application software. Such data sets started to emerge in the 1990s and now appear in a great many sectors including healthcare, advertising, government, financial services, urban informatics, meteorology, genomics and physics, to name but a few (Wikipedia 2023c; Mohanty 2015). Data growth statistics illustrate the amount of data we are talking about: in 2018 it was estimated that 2.5 quintillion bytes of data were being created each day, that over 300 million photos were being uploaded to Facebook every day, and that 156 million emails were being sent every minute (Marr 2018).

Big Data became a prominent public issue in the 2010s and 2020s in two respects: first with the amount of personal data that social media sites were able to harvest and use (Ben-David 2020; Zeller 2015); and secondly with respect to the training of AI systems as described below.

6.5.9 Born Digital Material Created by AI

Towards the end of 2022, the free-to-use artificial intelligence tool, ChatGPT, was launched by the OpenAI company, closely followed a few months later by equivalent products from Google (Bard) and Microsoft (Bing Chat) (Hern 2023b). Stories abounded about CHATGPTs ability to write articles and poetry, to create graphics and paintings, and to write music and song lyrics—all at the instruction of a brief sentence stating the requirement. The quality of the output was often convincing (though occassionally wrong), and there was a growing concern among professionals such as artists, designers, photographers, voice-over actors, authors, and musicians that their jobs might be simply taken over by AI (Thorpe 2023).

However, concerns about the accuracy and impact of AI generative systems are peripheral to our focus in this chapter. The fact is that such systems are producing Born Digital objects, and therefore we must now distinguish between Born Digital objects created by Humans and Born Digital objects created by AI.

6.5.10 A Summary of the New Types of Object Introduced in the Icon Age

Figure 6.2 summarises the changes described above and highlights in yellow the new objects introduced by the Icon Age.

The significance of the new objects introduced to the collecting world during the Icon Age, lies in their impact on the generic affordances and features of objects outlined earlier in this chapter, and on the practices conducted with the various Collecting Contexts. The former is discussed below; the latter are discussed in Chap. 7.

The probable usage of Icon Age Generic Objects by the different Collection Contexts described in Chap. 2 is indicated in Table 6.2. The allocations have been made in accordance with the experience of the authors, but would need to be verified by surveys. Usage has been indicated only where the authors believe it to be widespread. Short forms are suggested for each type of generic object to make it easier to refer to them.

In Table 6.2, we have specified that Big Data is only encountered in the Archiving context (by media organisations or internet archives, for example). However, this is not the whole story. Big Data is also *accumulated* by large commercial organisations and institutions to support operations such as marketing or surveillance. When gathered for these purposes, the collection and use of Big Data is a very specialised area, managed by Data Processing professionals, and with few similarities to other collecting practices. Consequently, we have excluded those uses from this text.

6.6 Generic Object Affordances Forty Years into the Icon Age

In this section we assess the impact that these new types of object are having on the object affordances described earlier in this chapter.

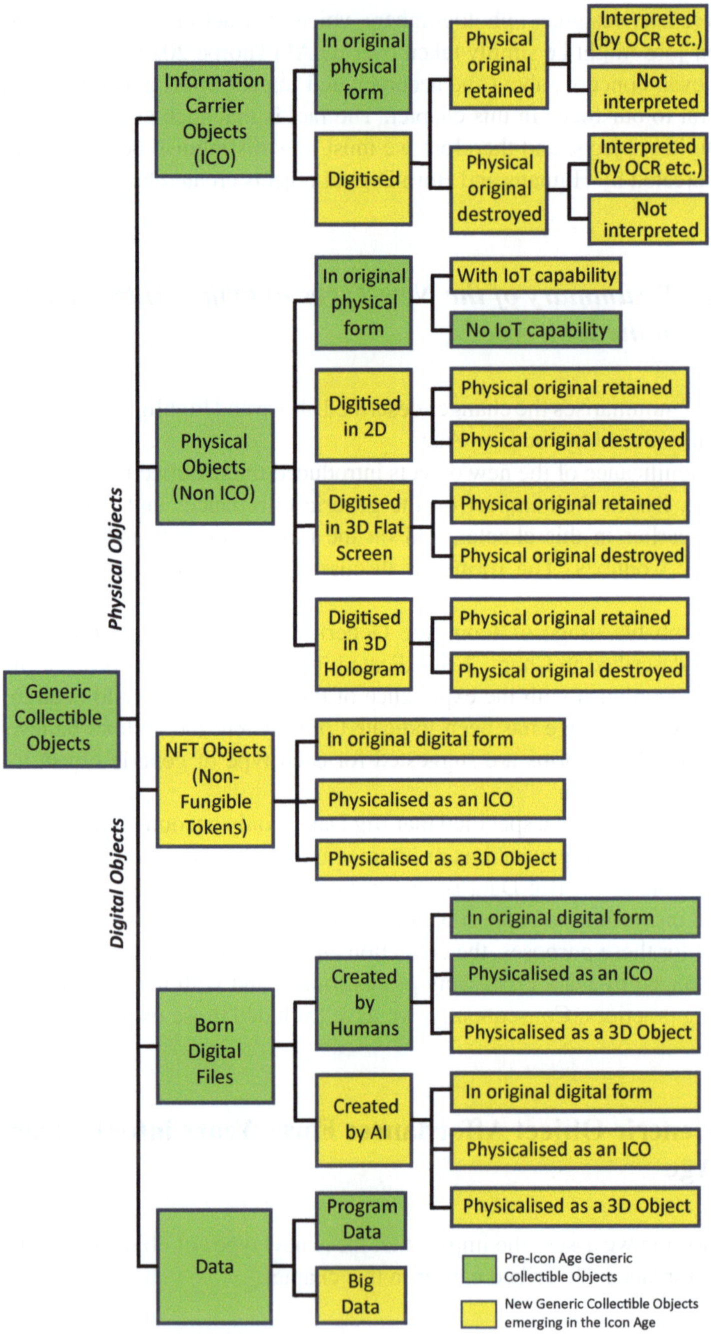

Fig. 6.2 New generic collectible objects that have emerged since the start of the Icon Age

Table 6.2 Generic collectible objects in place after forty years of the Icon Age

Generic collectible Objects forty years into the Icon Age	Accumulators	Librarians	Filers	Archivists	Museums/ Galleries	Private Curators	Amateur Collectors
Information carrier objects (ICO)							
• In original physical form	x	x	x	x	x	x	x
• Digitised with original retained NOT OCR'd		x	x	x	x	x	x
• Digitised AND OCR'd with original retained		x	x	x	x	x	x
• Digitised with original destroyed NOT OCR'd			x				x
• Digitised AND OCR'd with original destroyed	x	x	x				x
Physical objects (non-ICO)							
• In original form NO Internet of Things capability	x			x	x	x	x
• In original form WITH Internet of Things capability	x						
• Digitised in 2D and original retained				x	x	x	x
• Digitised in 2D and original destroyed	x						x
• Digitised in 3D (flat screen) and original retained					x	x	?
• Digitised in 3D (flat screen) and original destroyed					?	?	?
• Digitised in 3D (hologram) and original retained					x	x	
• Digitised in 3D (hologram) and original destroyed					?	?	
NFTs (Non-fungible tokens)							
• In digital form	x				x	x	x
• Physicalised as an ICO						x	x
• Physicalised as a 3D object						?	?
Born Digital Files							
• Created by Humans in Original form	x	x	x	x	x	x	x
• Created by Humans and physicalised as an ICO	x		x				x
• Created by Humans and physicalised as a 3D object			x		x	x	x
• Created by AI in original form	x	x	x	x	x	x	x

(continued)

Table 6.2 (continued)

Generic collectible Objects forty years into the Icon Age	Accumulators	Librarians	Filers	Archivists	Museums/ Galleries	Private Curators	Amateur Collectors
• Created by AI and physicalised as an ICO	x		x				x
• Created by AI and physicalised as a 3D object			x		x	x	x
Data							
• Program Data	x	x	x	x	x	x	x
• Big Data				x			

Note that '?' in the right-hand columns of this table indicates that such objects are feasible in the specified contexts, but that examples had not been encountered at the time of writing

6.6.1 Co-existing with Objects

We still do have objects all around us—probably more than ever before. At the same time, however, some of the previously visible objects in the home—books, music, and photos for example—are being moved into the digital domain. As one commentator puts it:

> Home continues to be important to us, but is being stripped of an important physical layer that reminds us of our connection to others and to our past, that tells visitors something about our interests and personality, and that simply acts to create a domestic aesthetic. (Banks 2013)

On the digital front, it's clear that humans have embraced the digitised world—a world in which most digital objects are currently represented by icons on screens. The screens may be large and sitting on desks; or housed in laptop computers; or small in the now ubiquitous mobile phone. They may be being used by highly educated people working in complex organisations in soaring cities; or by people who work the land with little investment, in small undeveloped villages. Either way, the individuals concerned understand how to use the devices and have grasped the concept that they contain digital objects which they can use.

6.6.2 Detect Objects with Sensors We Developed

Too little time has passed to enable evolution to adapt our bodies to the Icon Age (whatever that might have involved); so, instead, we have created digital objects with facets that can be detected with our existing senses. Our digital objects are presented as images which we can see on a screen. They have names and properties (metadata) which can be viewed, or, for those without sight, can be heard when spoken. We have developed surrogate sensors in the form of coded programs, to help us explore that metadata—and, indeed, the contents of the digital objects. Such program objects are becoming increasingly sophisticated as we find out more about the field we refer to as AI—Artificial Intelligence.

As the Icon Age grows to play an ever more central role in our lives, so we have started to try to integrate physical objects into the digital world by either putting digital components into them which emanate signals that can be picked up, and/or interrogated by the parent system; or by creating digital copies of physical objects by scanning or photographing them. In such ways we are endeavouring to be able to sense and interact with our physical objects within the digital environment.

6.6.3 Move Objects

In the Icon Age we have built several different mechanisms to move objects—one of them enabling our own hands to use a 'mouse' to move images of our digital objects around a screen. The other mechanisms are coded programs such as 'Copy' and 'Paste' to perform local moves; and communication mechanisms such as email or FTP (File Transfer Protocol) to perform moves over longer distances.

6.6.4 Remember Objects

Unfortunately, the Icon Age has merely placed more demands on our ability to remember objects while providing few mechanisms to help us to do so. Unlike physical objects which have a wide variety of discernible characteristics, and which are usually perceived in a physical world environment rich in content, digital objects in the Icon Age are singularly uniform and small, and exist in a bland, standardised, environment. We are left to utilise our memory of content to remember the vast and growing range of digital objects that we are generating and receiving.

6.6.5 Change Objects

Our ability to repurpose objects is as capable as ever—only these days there are many more types of object which potentially have multiple uses. We have made even greater strides in the Icon Age in our ability to take physical raw materials or component objects and to turn them into other physical objects (see Create objects below). In our digital systems, we are able to change our digital objects using the same coded programs that we used to create them.

6.6.6 Assemble Objects

Individuals receive large numbers of digital objects in the Icon Age, and they assemble them in hierarchical folders, named and ordered to suit their specific purposes. Digital technology has also been harnessed to assist with the assembly of physical objects, for example, on car assembly lines (Bogue 2022) or in automated warehousing systems such as those operated at scale by Amazon and other retailers (Lorson et al. 2023).

6.6.7 Create Objects

The Icon Age has brought with it an increasingly powerful capability to create new objects. Manufacturing in all its many guises is becoming increasingly computer controlled (Dotoli et al. 2018) to produce more complex objects faster, more precisely, and in volumes that can vary to meet demand. The discovery of new properties of materials is also being significantly assisted by AI, thereby enabling new objects such as medicines to be produced (Paul et al. 2021). In our digital systems we are able to create new digital objects at will using coded programs such as Word Processors, Spreadsheets, and Digital Cameras; and if we want to fashion a significantly different digital object, we simply build a new program to do the job (though we may re-use some of the underlying coded routines). It is also very simple to make copies of items, a capability which has significantly increased the amount of information that is being shared and the speed with which it is distributed. The ability to duplicate items has also made it possible to safeguard digital items in alternative secure places; and to bequest the same digital items, such as photos, to all members of a family instead of having to single out an individual (Banks 2013).

6.6.8 Talk About Abstract Objects

Our language enables us to talk about an ever-greater number of abstract concepts, not least those associated with lies, truth, honesty, anger, hardship, mental health, and the future; and our verbal and written communication systems ensure that a very widespread audience are party to such conversations.

6.6.9 Acquire Objects

The ability to acquire objects has been greatly enhanced by the emergence of electronic mail and the internet. In the Icon Age, digital objects such as newsletters, brochures, photos, reports etc. can be sent by email; and the World Wide Web (WWW) has made it easy and quick to seek out and acquire a huge variety of digital objects including music, books, scientific papers and digital programs. The Web and the Internet's on-line auction and social media systems have also provided significant new mechanisms for the acquisition of physical goods, and these systems are widely used by a large percentage of the earth's human population. As a consequence, the role of dealers as trusted middle person between vendors and collectors is becoming less critical in the art market (Belk 2014) and probably in most other areas of collecting.

6.6.10 Destroy Objects

We now destroy physical objects for many reasons other than war (though war is still producing an awful lot of destruction). The prevalence of consumer goods has resulted in our becoming a throw-away society, and waste disposal has become a massive challenge. Not so in the digital world, however, where destruction is a much simpler affair. To erase the visibility of a Digital File is a matter of selecting the delete command. Total obliteration requires the selection of further commands depending on the system being used.

6.6.11 Record Information on Objects

Objects containing information are the very essence of the Icon Age. Indeed, it was the desire to produce information using coded programs that spurred the development of digital technology. Another defining characteristic of the Icon Age is the way digital technology is used to produce paper versions of digital objects in a huge variety of formats including documents, books, photos, posters and tickets. Indeed, the technology has proved so successful that it is now not only the mechanism of choice for just recording information, but also for creating content primarily intended for use in or on physical objects.

6.6.12 Collect Objects

Individuals collect digital objects such as digital photos, digital music and eBooks, and have been doing so for more than 20 years. Some people are now starting to collect NFTs. Information technology is also used to digitise collections of physical objects such as printed photos, paper documents, and mementos in many different forms. In some cases, owners are satisfied with the new digital versions and destroy the original physical objects. However, it's also worth noting that for streamed music and video, there is actually no object, either physical or digital, available to collect unless special measures are taken (Wilson 2023a).

Dedicated collecting institutes such as Museums, Galleries and Libraries, have also made extensive use of imaging technology to enable their physical objects to be viewed remotely over the internet. Furthermore, the range of digital objects now existing, and their importance to our lives, has prompted such institutions to collect digital objects; for example, the British Library started collecting web sites in 2005 (British Library 2023). In addition, a whole variety of new institutions have been established specifically to collect Born Digital objects, for example, the Berlin Computer Games museum (Computerspielemuseum 2023); the Museum of Computer Art (MOCA 2023) based in New York State, USA; and the Internet Archive organisation which collects not only worldwide web sites through its Wayback Machine, but also a wide variety and staggering quantity of other digital objects, all of which can be accessed online (Internet Archive 2023).

6.6.13 Use Objects

In the same way that we collect physical objects/tools for use in our day-to-day lives, so too, in the Icon Age, we collect digital objects/tools to use in our digital world activities. Such objects are usually coded programs and include word processors, spreadsheets, graphics packages, media players, and a myriad of other more specialist tools. We have also augmented some of our physical objects (such as vacuum cleaners, lawnmowers and doorbells) with a digital capability thereby enabling us to incorporate them into our digital world and to use them through our screens.

6.6.14 Enjoy Objects

Among the digital objects we collect to simply enjoy are digital photos, digital music, videos and ebooks. There is also the hugely popular genre of computer games which are played by very large numbers of people for significant lengths of time (Palma-Ruiz et al. 2022). Individuals don't necessarily have to collect such objects on their own machines since much of this sort of material is held on computer servers somewhere in the internet cloud, and can be streamed from there to the individual's screen or playing device.

6.6.15 Consume Objects

Economic growth continues to feed the consumer society with a bewildering array of physical objects; and advertising and culture continues to stimulate the public to buy and possess. This also applies to computer-related products such as mobile phones and laptops; though, interestingly, the mobile phone's photo-taking capability has decimated the consumer camera market. There has been an equivalent rise in our consumption of digital objects as more and more business operations have gone digital and as social media systems have gone mainstream.

6.7 IT's Impact on Features of Our Relationship with Objects

In this section we assess the impact that IT is having on the relationships we have with objects as described earlier in this chapter.

6.7.1 The Transmission Triple

More and more of our information is being held in digital form, and this greatly enhances the spread of information among those who are living via mechanisms such as email, websites and portable storage devices. However, the transmission of digital objects to our future selves, or to others after we are gone, is a more challenging practice simply because of the rapidly changing technology. Objects in old formats may not play on new machines with new versions of programs; old programs may not play on new computer hardware; and the media on which digital objects are stored may become obsolete and inaccessible. To mitigate against these problems, and to ensure that digital objects can be accessed many years in the future, demands periodic and detailed maintenance of both the objects themselves and the equipment they are run on—which is not an activity many people are motivated to undertake or are qualified to do (DPC 2023).

6.7.2 How Our Minds Comprehend Objects

Information Technology contributes hugely to our ability to undertake science to understand our bodies and minds and the world about us. Hence our knowledge about how we comprehend objects continues to increase as demonstrated by works such as 'Being You—A New Science of Consciousness' (Seth 2021). Seth argues that our view of the world is a series of best guess predictions and that all incoming perceptions are calibrated against the previous best guess; and that, consequently, we live in a 'controlled hallucination' which is constantly being reshaped in an endless cycle of prediction and correction. Consequently, there is no guarantee that we are all seeing objects in the same way. An illustration of this occurred in 2015 when millions of social media users expressed different views about the colour of a dress in a photo. Some said it was white and gold and others said it was black and blue (Wikipedia 2023d). Seth suggests that this and similar experiences could be transformational for the human race by helping us to understand our inner diversity (Seth 2022).

Regarding the Icon Age's objects, there are some that people will probably see in very much the same way: the screen icon being a case in point. However, there are others, such as NFTs, which may well be perceived in different ways by individuals—if they are recognised at all. However, there is a general point to be made here about information technology: it is undoubtedly prevalent across the world, and therefore it is likely that some of its central and simpler objects—App icons, word documents, and digital photos—will be comprehended in much the same way by a large percentage of people; perhaps by a larger percentage of people than has ever been the case for particular objects. However, there is no doubt that many IT-related objects are very complex and/or obscure—system files or macros, for example—and will be comprehended in different ways by different individuals.

6.7.3 Impact of Objects on Our Mind and Memory

Recent work on memory reported by Ed Young indicates that, in much the same way that our mind comprehends objects, our mind remembers objects in a constant cycle of reframing them as a consequence of the context we are living at any one time (Young 2016; Rogers 2022). Rogers also reported a conversation by Prof Catherine Loveday, a neuropsychologist at the University of Westminster, who said that any experience (such as encountering an object) generates a unique set of neurons firing, and when the same neurons fire together a few times they become functionally linked as a pattern that can be recognised in the future. So, when enough of the neurons in the pattern are activated the whole set fires up (Rogers 2022). Hence, the suggestion that we don't store memories – only the external cues that prompt the reconstruction of memory (Broekhuijsen et al. 2017).

In whatever way memory is achieved, the question remains of whether replacing a physical object with a virtual object changes the impact it has on our minds and memories. Well, clearly it does, because our mind must also engage with the interface to some sort of physical computing device in order to experience the virtual object (Beer 2008). Beyond this however, there is no reason why a virtual object shouldn't inspire memories and connections in the same way that everything else we encounter in life does. This seemed to be the case in Wilson's second Electronic Storyboard exercise in which the thoughts inspired by seven different types of objects were teased out and used to create displays; three of these were primarily physical objects (mementos, letters, loft items) and three were digital objects (photos, digital music albums, and digitised books). There was no noticeable difference in the process and outcomes associated with the physical and digital objects (Wilson 2020a, b).

Unfortunately, we live within a moving sea of continually accumulating daily experience and cues, and this can affect our memories of people and events (Wilson

2018a). Multiple instances have been recorded in the *pwofc.com* website: for example, remembering poor air conditioning in a holiday room whereas, in fact it was another holiday (Wilson 2020a), and thinking he had instigated a project whereas in fact it was someone else. Whatever the nature of our 'record', be it memory, or a selection of the relevant items that you have, or all of the items that you have, or, indeed, all the relevant items that exist in the world, we should always remember that it may not be the whole story. (Wilson 2018b). Having said that, it is simply a fact of life that a written record, although just the particular version of an event noted at a particular time, is inevitably likely to gain more long-term credence than memory and word of mouth (Wilson 2020a, b).

6.7.4 Objects Have a Life-Span

Digital objects have a life-span, though generally much shorter than physical objects. The media on which they reside may start to deteriorate after only 3 years in the case of hard discs; and even Solid-State Drives (SSDs) may not last much more than twenty years or so. Other storage mechanisms with longer lifetimes do exist but they are specialised, expensive, and not in widespread use—for example, nano-structured glass (Zhang et al. 2014). However, media longevity is only one of the factors limiting the life-span of a digital object. As described above in the section on the Transmission Triple, the continually changing technology may result in unreadable Dgital Files due to obsolescent hardware and/or software. Given the gathering pace of our switch into digital from physical, this shortcoming is a serious concern; and dealing with it will become an increasingly important priority. Perhaps AI will be recruited to help in this endeavour, though, given its criticality, we would need to be constantly checking to make sure it was being done effectively.

6.7.5 Ownership and Legal Issues

Regulations and laws designed to apply to physical objects are inevitably extensive and complex, and their equivalent versions, adapted and extended to apply to digital complicated—not least because Digital Files are so easy to copy and the distinction between original and copy disappears (Zeller 2015). Furthermore, the continuing rapid development of the technology and its applications make it difficult for the law to keep up as illustrated by the lag between problems emerging with the use of social media in the 2010s and the scramble by politicians in countries around the world to introduce legislation to deal with them (Stokes 2019; Bassan 2021; Suzor 2019).

For individuals, the flexibility of the technology places them in numerous situations in which their actions flirt dangerously with the law. For example, the ease with which the internet can be searched for text and images which, once found, can then be incorporated into other documents, may be infringing copyright rules. The copying of music and films is widespread. Keens provides another example in the field of disco music editing, and writes about how difficult it is to track down the legal rights owners of obscure songs. He notes that:

> ...the line between reverential edit and shameless, exploitative bootleg can be uncomfortably slim at times...'. (Keens 2022)

In Social Media systems, some individuals seem drawn to authoring vitriolic, phobic, and threatening posts whilst the dispatch of similar material in hardcopy letters might have previously been considered to be too serious to overlook. In terms of protecting their own material, individuals can apply a Creative Commons licence which is a:

> free, simple, and standardized way to grant copyright permissions for creative and academic works; ensure proper attribution; and allow others to copy, distribute, and make use of those works'. (Creative Commons 2023)

Even if this licence is specified, no doubt there are occasions when attribution is either deliberately omitted or simply forgotten. There appears to be a general understanding that individuals who digitise material they actually own and keep it for their own use are not at risk of being prosecuted—though such individuals would be well advised to follow Wilson's example and keep the originals to be able to demonstrate ownership (Wilson 2023b).

6.7.6 Representations of Objects

Objects in computer systems are typically referred to as Virtual Objects. Up to this point, forty years into the Icon Age, work on virtual objects has been mainly undertaken for three different environments: computer and mobile phone screens, computer games, and virtual reality systems.

The icons we see on our computer screens and mobile phones are familiar to billions of people worldwide. Fundamental inputs to the design of icons were work on semiotics and symbols, such as that by Eco (1976). In the following decades a great deal of human factors work was done specifically on the design of screen icons and how to evaluate and refine them; and this information is now available to those creating new icons in texts such as 'Interaction Design' (Preece et al. 2015).

The representation of virtual objects by the computer gaming industry takes a completely different approach. Here, the norm is for objects to look like the real thing, and to operate like the real thing. Even if the object has no equivalent in the real world, it is represented in full detail. Icons and symbols representing objects have no place in the vast majority of these worlds. The constant development of new games, and the huge numbers of people who play them worldwide, mean that the industry has a great deal of knowledge and experience in the design of virtual objects.

In many ways it is a similar situation in Virtual Reality (VR) systems. However, although VR objects are designed to look and act like the real thing, VR designers pay a great deal of attention to ensuring the realism of the objects, both in terms of their appearance and their affordances. VR has been defined as:

> a medium composed of interactive computer simulations that sense the participant's position and actions and replace or augment the feedback to one or more senses, giving the feeling of being mentally immersed or present in the simulation (a virtual world). (Sherman and Craig 2019)

VR started to gain public prominence at the start of the Icon Age when the company called VPL research was established in 1984 (Lanier 2017). Since then, it has become a mainstream technology with uses in education, training, engineering, retail, museums, and medicine to name but a few (Greengard 2019). Much published work has been done on VR in general and on how the virtual objects with the VR world should be represented and should operate. A comprehensive exploration of the topic is provided in Sherman and Craig's 800-page book 'Understanding Virtual Reality' (2018) (see Sect. 9.2 for more details about VR).

Some commentators note some ways in which digital objects are inferior to their physical equivalents: they lack the authority and aura of the original; they fail to engender the same sense of wonder as the physical original; and, if they are three dimensional objects like sculptures, they are difficult to fully comprehend the object as a whole (Belk 2014). Zeller goes one step further saying that virtual objects are merely 'temporary actualizations of a binary code' and 'a momentary realisation of information, not objects anymore' (Zeller 2015). Despite some of these being valid points, we do still comprehend, make use of, remember, and collect virtual objects—think of digital photos, for example.

6.7.7 Forgeries and Fakes

To make convincing forgeries of physical objects still requires the hand of a skilled human to work on the physical material despite the widespread availability of 2D and 3D printing. Though, undoubtedly, the ease with which high quality images can be captured, edited and printed out has made that part of forgery and fakery a much less skilled activity. However, the forging and faking of digital objects such as emails, and social media posts is very easy and consequently the internet has been awash with them for years. For example:

- Phishing emails: These purport to come from a supplier used by the recipient and aims to get them to log into a dummy website so that their username and password can be acquired and subsequently used illegally.
- Fake adverts: These have been prominent in the holiday industry. Details of genuine properties or hotels are copied off the net and then advertised with false owners. Booking monies are paid to the scammers, but the booking itself is dud.
- Fake news: The skilful analysis of social media data has enabled individuals to gradually subvert the thinking of large groups of people on social media systems

by the placement of a series of fabricated posts by fake individuals (Cadwalladr and Graham-Harrison 2018; Hajli 2024)

Interestingly NFTs are, in principle, not affected by forgery because proof of ownership of the NFT is contained within a blockchain. However, it has yet to be seen whether the ability for individuals to take screenshot copies of an NFT, or to register the same NFT with another blockchain platform, will affect the long-term viability of the NFT market.

6.7.8 How We Look After Our Objects

Forty years into the Icon Age, the options we have for dealing with physical objects are changing. Where we once chose paper, we might choose to go paperless; where we once filed, we might choose to scan; where we once kept an object we might choose to simply keep a photo; and where we once may have simply destroyed an object we now might digitise it first and then destroy it. Behind many such decisions is the significant difference between physical and digital displays of larger collections: all items in a collection can be made accessible digitally, but may be too great in number to be presented physically to the viewer (Wilson 2023c). Huge numbers of people are now making choices like those listed above, quite often; and they will inevitably have potential impacts such as those listed below (Wilson 2021a):

- All these choices affect the number of physical objects in the world.
- The changing mix of physical/virtual objects in the world, and people's perception of both types of objects, are probably going to affect what people collect and the composition of collections eventually acquired by Curating institutions.
- When we choose the virtual as an alternative to creating a physical object, we are reducing the number of physical objects that our future progeny will encounter.
- When we choose to replicate a physical object virtually, and then destroy the physical object, we both reduce the number of physical objects that our future progeny will encounter, and prevent our future progeny being able to experience the physical essence of the object—something will have been lost.

With respect to digital objects, we also have another choice to make: whether to keep them locally or remotely. The tablet now provides a very effective and portable means of storing and viewing our digital collections locally (Wilson 2023c). However, huge numbers of people now use cloud storage, which is a very new and different way of possessing things. While it has some advantages, people get concerned that they don't really have a handle on what they have in the cloud, that they might not be able to access it, and that deleting it might not completely get rid of it (Odom et al. 2012).

In 2014, the English translation of the widely read book 'The life-changing magic of tidying' (Kondo 2014) appeared, and this directly addressed the question of how we should look after the objects we possess. Kondo's approach can be summarised as follows: take a category of your belongings; assemble EVERY item in that category from EVERY part of your house, into a big pile; take each item, hold it in your hand, and decide if it gives you a spark of joy—If it does, keep it, and if it doesn't, discard it; assign a specific space to store everything you keep; when you store things, make them as visible as possible, and avoid piling things one on top of the other. This process is intended to be a one-off, all inclusive, exercise to be done on every possession you have. In Kondo's experience it usually takes about half a year (Wilson 2017b). Kondo's book is about organising all of an individual's possessions, and it makes hardly any reference to digitising things. In contrast, the Order from Chaos tutorial (Wilson 2017c) provides guidance on how to deal with any set or subset of objects, and on how the power of digitisation can help in the process.

References

African Fossils (2024) Explore the lab. https://africanfossils.org/. Accessed 26 Nov 2024

Alsharif MH, Jahid A, Kelechi AH, Kannadasan R (2023) GreenIoT: a review and future research directions. Symmetry 15(3):757. https://doi.org/10.3390/sym15030757.Accessed26Nov2024

Banks R (2013) Our technology heritage. In: Hawkins DT (ed) Personal Archiving: Preserving Our Digital Heritage Information Today Inc.

Bassan F (2021) Digital platforms and global law. Edward Elgar Publishing

Beer D (2008) The iconic interface and the veneer of simplicity: MP3 players and the reconfiguration of music collecting and reproduction practices in the digital age. Inf Community Soc 11(1):71–88

Belk RW (1995) Collecting in a consumer society. Routledge

Belk RW (2014) Art collecting as personal and public practice in a digital age. In: O'Reilly D, Rentschler R, Kirchner T (eds) The routledge companion to arts marketing. Routledge, London, pp 243–255

Ben-David A (2020) Counter-archiving Facebook. Eur J Commun 35(3):249–264

Benjamin W (1999) Unpacking my library. In: Benjamin W (ed) Illuminations. Pimlico, London, pp 61–69

Binde J (2023) A hologram of the "Nose" emerges at the Giacometti Institute. Beaux Arts Magazine No 475, 06 Oct 2023. https://www.beauxarts.com/grand-format/un-hologramme-du-nez-surgit-a-linstitut-giacometti/. Accessed 26 Nov 2024

Bogue R (2022) The changing face of the automotive robotics industry. Ind Robot 49(3):386–390

Britannica (2023) History-of-computing. https://www.britannica.com/technology/computer/History-of-computing. Accessed 06 Apr 2023

Britannica (2024) Motion picture technology: introduction of sound. https://www.britannica.com/technology/motion-picture-technology/Introduction-of-sound. Accessed 11 Nov 2024

British Library (2023) UK web archive. https://www.bl.uk/collection-guides/uk-web-archive. Accessed 02 Apr 2023

Broekhuijsen M, van den Hoven E, Markopoulos P (2017) From PhotoWork to PhotoUse: exploring personal digital photo activities. Behav Inf Technol 36(7):754–767

Brown L (2022) We've been thinking about holograms all wrong: forget reanimating dead musicians. This tech is for living performers who can't stand their bandmates, vulture, 11 Oct 2022. https://www.vulture.com/2022/10/abba-voyage-london-holograms.html. Accessed 22 Jan 2024

Cadwalladr C, Graham-Harrison E (March 17, 2018) Revealed: 50 million Facebook profiles harvested for Cambridge Analytica in major data breach. The Guardian, Manchester, UK

Cambridge Dictionary (2023) Fungible. https://dictionary.cambridge.org/dictionary/english/fungible. Accessed 29 Mar 2023

Carroll E (2013) Digital inheritance: tackling the legal and practical issues. In: Hawkins DT (ed) Personal archiving: preserving our digital heritage. Information Today Inc.
Computerspielemuseum (2023) Welcome to the Computerspielemuseum. https://www.computerspielemuseum.de/1210_Home.htm. Accessed 20 Apr 2023
Carrozzino M, Bergamasco M (2010) Beyond virtual museums: experiencing immersive virtual reality in real museums. J Cult Herit 11(4):452–458
Casson L (2001) Libraries in the ancient world. Yale University Press
Chazan M (2017) Toward a long prehistory of fire. Curr Anthropol 58(Supplement):16
Clayton N (2004) Folk devils in our midst? Collecting from 'deviant' groups. In: Knell SJ (ed) Museums and the future of collecting, 2nd edn, Ashgate, Farnham
Creative Commons (2023) What we do. https://creativecommons.org/about/ Accessed 01 Apr 2023
Currall J, Moss M, Stuart S (2004) What is a collection? Archivaria 58(August):131–146
Danet B, Katriel T (1994) No two alike: play and aesthetics in collecting. In: Pearce SM (ed) Interpreting objects and collections. Routledge, Chapter 28, pp 220–239 (This paper first appeared in Play and Culture, 1989, 2(3):255–271)
de Saulieu G, Testart A (2015) Innovations, food storage and the origins of agriculture. Environ Archaeol 20(4)
Dotoli M, Fay A, Miśkowicz M, Seatzu C (2018) An overview of current technologies and emerging trends in factory automation. Int J Prod Res 57(15–16):5047–5067
DPC (2023) Preservation issues. Digital Preservation Coalition, https://www.dpconline.org/handbook/digital-preservation/preservation-issues. Accessed 06 Apr 2023
Eco U (1976) A theory of semiotics. Indiana University Press
Frank T (2018) Household food storage in Ancient Israel and Judah. Archaeopress Publishing Ltd.
Folkman C, Price LL, Arnould E (2004) How individuals' cherished possessions become families' inalienable wealth. J Consum Res 31(December):609–622
Gadekallu TR, Huynh-The T, Wang W, Yenduri G, Ranaweera P, Pham Q, da Costa B, Liyanage M (2022) Blockchain for the metaverse: a review. arXiv:2203.09738 (cs.SI), 21 Mar 2022. https://arxiv.org/abs/2203.09738. Accessed 26 Nov 2024
Greengard S (2019) Virtual reality. The MIT Press
Grömer K (2016) The art of prehistoric textile making. Natural History Museum Vienna
Hajli (2024) Election disinformation: how AI-powered bots work and how you can protect yourself from their influence. The Conversation, 09 April 2024. https://theconversation.com/election-disinformation-how-ai-powered-bots-work-and-how-you-can-protect-yourself-from-their-influence-227174.. Accessed 25 March 2025
Harari YN (2014) Sapiens. Harvill Secker, London
Haynes R (2018) Eye of the Veholder: AR extending and blending of museum objects and virtual collections. In: Jung T, Claudia M, Dieck T (eds) Augmented reality and virtual reality. Springer
Hern A (March 28, 2023a) UK government drops plans for NFT made by Royal Mint. The Guardian, Manchester, UK
Hern A (March 21, 2023b) TechScape: the AI tools that will write our emails, attend our meetings—and change our lives. The Guardian, Manchester, UK
Heylighen F (2023) Mind, brain and body: an evolutionary perspective on the human condition. Lecture Notes 2022–2023, Vrije Universiteit Brussel, pp 1–217
Hirsch M, Spitzer L (2006) Testimonial objects: memory, gender, and transmission. Poetics Today 27(2):353–383
Intel (2025) IoT Solutions Connect the World. https://www.intel.com/content/www/us/en/internet-of-things/overview.html?wapkw=internet%20of%20things.. Accessed 18 March 2025
Internet Archive (2023) Internet Archive. https://archive.org/. Accessed 02 Apr 2023
ISO (2012) Space data and information transfer systems—open archival information system—reference model. Standard 14721, International Organisation for Standardisation, Geneva
Jones M (1990) Fake? The Art of Deception. British Museum Publications Ltd: London, pp 11–16

Jones W (2012) The future of personal information management, part I: our information, always and forever. Morgan & Claypool
Keens O (July 13, 2022) Cutting up the dancefloor: the glorious, dubious history of the disco edit. The Guardian, Manchester
Keilbach JA (2013) Collecting, indexing and digitizing survivors—holocaust testimonies in the digital age. In: Bangert A, Gordon RSC, Saxton L (eds) Holocaust intersections: genocide and visual culture at the new millennium. Legenda, pp 46–63
Kirk DS, Sellen A (2010) On human remains: values and practice in the home archiving of cherished objects. ACM Trans Comput-Hum Interact 17(3):10.1–10.43
Kiourt C, Koutsoudis A, Pavlidis G (2016) DynaMus: a fully dynamic 3D virtual museum framework. J Cult Herit 22(Nov-Dec):984–991
Knell SJ (2004) Altered values: searching for a new collecting. In: Knell SJ (ed) Museums and the future of collecting, 2nd edn. Ashgate, Farnham
Kondo M (2014) The life-changing magic of tidying. Hirano C (Transl), Vermilion, London
Kwint M (1999) Introduction: the physical past. In: Kwint M, Breward C, Aynsley J (eds) Material memories. Berg
Lanier J (2017) Dawn of the new everything. Bodley Head, pp 1–351
Lavington S (2010) A brief history of British computers: the first 25 years (1948–1973). https://www.bcs.org/articles-opinion-and-research/a-brief-history-of-british-computers-the-first-25-years-1948-1973/. Accessed 06 Apr 2023
Laurenson P, Van Saaze V (2014) Collecting performance-based art: new challenges and shifting perspectives. In: Remes O, MacCulloch L, Leino M (eds) Performativity in the gallery: staging interactive encounters. Peter Lang Ltd., Oxford, pp 27–41
Logan R, McLuhan M (2016) The future of the library. Peter Lang
Lorson F, Fugener A, Hubner A (2023) New team mates in the warehouse: human interactions with automated and robotized systems. IISE Trans 55(5):536–553
Marr B (May 21, 2018) How much data do we create every day? Forbes. https://www.forbes.com/sites/bernardmarr/2018/05/21/how-much-data-do-we-create-every-day-the-mind-blowing-stats-everyone-should-read/?sh=384b4e1960ba. Accessed 30 Mar 2023
Mendis D (2021) When you buy an NFT, you don't completely own it—here's why. The Conversation, 14 August 2021. https://theconversation.com/when-you-buy-an-nft-you-dont-completely-own-it-heres-why-166445. Accessed 28 Mar 2025
Miller D, Parrott F (2009) Loss and material culture in South London. J R Anthropol Inst 15(3):502–519
Miller RJ (2022) Metadata for digital collections. Facet Publishing Limited, London
MOCA (2023) MOCA museum of contemporary art. https://moca.virtual.museum/. Accessed 02 Apr 2023
Mohanty H (2015) Big data: an introduction. In: Mohanty H, Bhuyan P, Chenthati D (eds) Big data—a primer. Springer, New Dehli
Nadini M, Alessandretti L, Di Giacinto F, Martino M, Aiello LM, Baronchelli A (2021) Mapping the NFT revolution: market trends, trade networks, and visual features. Sci Rep 11:20902. https://doi.org/10.1038/s41598-021-00053-8.Accessed26Nov2024
Nine A (2023) This startup can turn almost anything into a hyper-realistic hologram. ExtremeTech, 07 August 2023. https://www.extremetech.com/electronics/this-startup-can-turn-almost-anything-into-a-hyper-realistic-hologram. Accessed 24 Jan 2024
Nitti M, Pilloni V, Colistra G, Atzori L (2015) The virtual object as a major element of the Internet of Things: a survey. IEEE Commun Surv Tutor 18(2):1–1
Odom W, Sellen A, Harper R, Thereska E (2012) Lost in translation: understanding the possession of digital things in the cloud. In: Proceedings of the SIGCHI conference on human factors in computing systems, CHI'12, Austin, Texas, USA 5–10 May 2012, pp 781–790
Oliver G, Harvey R (2016) Digital curation. Facet Publishing

Palma-Ruiz JM, Torres-Toukoumidis A, González-Moreno SE, Valles-Baca HG (2022) An overview of the gaming industry across nations: using analytics with power BI to forecast and identify key influencers. Heliyon (01Feb2022):e08959
Paul D, Sanap G, Shenoy S, Kalyane D, Kalia K, Tekade RK (2021) Artificial intelligence in drug discovery and development. Drug Discov Today 26(1):80–93
Pearce SM (1994b) Collecting reconsidered. In: Pearce SM (ed) Interpreting objects and collections. Routledge, Chapter 26, pp 193–204 (This paper first appeared in Kavanagh G (ed) (1991) Museum Languages, Leicester University Press, pp 135–53)
Pearce SM (1994e) Objects as meaning; or narrating the past. In: Pearce SM (ed) Interpreting objects and collections. Routledge, Chapter 4, p 19–29 (This paper first appeared in Pearce S (1990) New research in museum studies: objects of knowledge. Athlone, London, pp 125–40
Pearce SM (1995b) On collecting: an investigation into collecting in the European Tradition. Routledge
Pearce SM (1998) Collecting in contemporary practice. Sage Publications
Peinado-Santana S, Hernández-Lamas P, Bernabéu-Larena J, Cabau-Anchuelo B, Martín-Caro JA (2021) Public works heritage 3D model digitisation, optimisation and dissemination with free and open-source software and platforms and low-cost tools. Sustainability 13(23):13020. https://doi.org/10.3390/su132313020
Preece J, Rogers Y, Sharp H (2015) Interaction design—beyond human-computer interaction. Wiley
Proto (2024) Making digital real: proto delivers a truly lifelike holographic experience so viewers see, hear and interact with others anywhere in the world. https://protohologram.com/. Accessed 24 Jan 2024
Redwine G (2015) Personal digital archiving. DPC technology watch report 15-01, Digital Preservation Coalition, pp 1–33
Rogers J (Apr 03, 2022) Music, memory and my dad: how songs define and shape us. The Guardian, Manchester, UK
Scarre C (ed) (1999) The seventy wonders of the world. Thames & Hudson Ltd., London
Sellen AJ, Harper RHR (2002) The myth of the paperless office. The MIT Press
Seth A (2021) Being you—a new science of consciousness. Faber & Faber
Seth A (2022) The big idea: do we all experience the world in the same way? The Guardian, Manchester, UK, 03 Oct 2022
Sherman WR, Craig AB (2018) Understanding virtual reality, 2nd edn. Morgan Kaufmann
Stokes S (2019) Digital copyright—law and practice. Bloomsbury Academic
Suzor NP (2019) Lawless: the secret rules that govern our digital lives. Cambridge University Press
Tebeau M (2016) Engaging the materiality of the archive in the digital age. Collections 12(4):475–487
Thompson M (2017) Rubbish theory—the creation and destruction of value, New. Pluto Press, London
Thorpe V (2023) ChatGPT said I did not exist': how artists and writers are fighting back against AI. The Guardian, Manchester, UK, 18 March 2023
Tobin BF (2016) Introduction: consumption as a gendered social practice. In: Goggin MD, Tobin BF (eds) Material women, 1750–1950: consuming desires and collecting practices. Routledge, pp 1–16
Walton KL (1984) Transparent pictures: on the nature of photographic realism. Critical Inquiry 11(December), The University of Chicago
Wikipedia (2023a) Database: 1960s, Navigational DBMS. https://en.wikipedia.org/wiki/Database. Accessed 28 Mar 2023
Wikipedia (2023b) 3D printing. https://en.wikipedia.org/wiki/3D_printing. Accessed 29 March 2023
Wikipedia (2023c) Big data. https://en.wikipedia.org/wiki/Big_data. Accessed 29 Mar 2023
Wikipedia (2023d) The dress. https://en.wikipedia.org/wiki/The_dress. Accessed 31 Mar 2023

Wikipedia (2024a) History of photography. https://en.wikipedia.org/wiki/History_of_photography. Accessed 11 Nov 2024

Wikipedia (2024b) History of sound recording. https://en.wikipedia.org/wiki/History_of_sound_recording. Accessed 11 Nov 2024

Wilson PA (1986) Electronic filing—products and suppliers. NCC Publications, Manchester

Wilson PA (2016a) One of digitisation's advantages. Blog post in the scribble keeping section of pwofc.com, 18 August 2016. http://www.pwofc.com/ofc/2016/08/18/one-of-digitisations-advantages/. Accessed 26 Nov 2024

Wilson PA (2016b) The 'A's—first impressions. Blog post in the letter keeping section of pwofc.com, 25 January 2016. http://www.pwofc.com/ofc/2016/01/25/the-as-first-impressions/. Accessed 26 Nov 2024

Wilson PA (2017a) U3.4 why do it?—Why use digital technology to organise your collections? Blog post in the order from chaos section of pwofc.com, 17 September 2017. http://www.pwofc.com/ofc/2017/09/17/u3-4-why-do-it-why-use-digital-technology-to-organise-your-collections/. Accessed 26 Nov 2024

Wilson PA (2017b) The life changing magic of tidying. Blog post in the order from chaos section of pwofc.com, 31 July 2017. http://www.pwofc.com/ofc/2017/07/31/the-life-changing-magic-of-tidying/. Accessed 26 Nov 2024

Wilson PA (2017c) U1. The OFC online tutorial—welcome and contents. Blog post in the order from chaos section of pwofc.com, 01 September 2017. http://www.pwofc.com/ofc/2017/09/01/u1-the-ofc-online-tutorial-welcome-and-contents/. Accessed 26 Nov 2024

Wilson PA (2018a) Insights prior to creating the boards. Blog post in the electronic story board section of pwofc.com, 4 August 2018, http://www.pwofc.com/ofc/2018/08/08/insights-prior-to-creating-the-boards/. Accessed 26 Nov 2024

Wilson PA (2018b) A few insights and conclusions. Blog post in the keeping work stuff section of pwofc.com, 14 Dec 2018. http://www.pwofc.com/ofc/2018/12/14/a-few-insights-and-conclusions/. Accessed 26 Nov 2024

Wilson PA (2019a) PAWDOC: hardcopy/electronic mix. Blog post in the personal document management section of pwofc.com, 20 August 2019. http://www.pwofc.com/ofc/2019/08/20/pawdoc-hardcopyelectronic-mix/. Accessed 26 Nov 2024

Wilson PA (2019b) Doggie tales. Blog post in the order from chaos section of pwofc.com, 17 May 2019. https://www.pwofc.com/ofc/2019/05/17/doggie-tales/. Accessed 23 May 2025

Wilson PA (2020a) Building observations. Blog post in the electronic story board section of pwofc.com, 4 Dec 2020. http://www.pwofc.com/ofc/2020/12/04/building-observations/. Accessed 26 Nov 2024

Wilson PA (2020b) Laptop story board musings. Blog post in the electronic story board section of pwofc.com, 17 Dec 2020. http://www.pwofc.com/ofc/2020/12/17/laptop-story-board-musings/. Accessed 26 Nov 2024

Wilson PA (2021a) Musings on physical/virtual objects. Blog post in the object obliteration section of pwofc.com, 28 July 2021. http://www.pwofc.com/ofc/2021/07/28/musings-on-physicalvirtual-objects/. Accessed 26 Nov 2024

Wilson PA (2022) Obliteration findings. Blog post in the object obliteration section of pwofc.com, 03 June 2022. http://www.pwofc.com/ofc/2022/06/03/obliteration-findings/. Accessed 26 Nov 2024

Wilson PA (2023a) Musings about video collections. Blog post in the DVD management section of the pwofc.com website, 19th August 2023. https://www.pwofc.com/ofc/2023/08/19/musings-about-video-collections/. Accessed 13 May 2025

Wilson PA (2023b) Choosing rationales. Blog post in the DVD management section of the pwofc.com website, 7th November 2023. https://www.pwofc.com/ofc/2023/11/07/choosing-rationales/. Accessed 13 May 2025

Wilson PA (2023c) The digital display case. Blog post in the display case management section of the pwofc.com website, 17th October 2023. https://www.pwofc.com/ofc/2023/10/17/the-digital-display-case/.. Accessed 13 May 2025

Young E (2016) Memory lane has a three-way fork. The Atlantic. https://www.theatlantic.com/science/archive/2016/10/memory-lane-has-a-three-way-fork/505250/. Accessed 31 Mar 2023

Zeller C (2015) From object to information: the end of collecting in the digital age. Arcadia 50(2):389–409

Zhang J, Gecevičius M, Beresna M, Kazansky PG (2014) Seemingly unlimited lifetime data storage in nanostructured glass. Phys Rev Lett 112:033901

Chapter 7
IT Impacts on Collectors Forty Years into the Icon Age

Abstract Major technology developments in the Icon Age have included the internet, the mobile phone, social media, streaming services, and video games. Five topics affect every organisation and individual collecting digital objects: the necessary infrastructure; Digital Curation; file naming; backing-up; and digital preservation planning. The impact of IT on each of the seven contexts—Accumulations, Libraries, Files, Archives, Museums/Galleries, Private Collections, and Amateur Collections—is discussed in two parts: the new digital objects being collected; and IT support.

At the beginning of the book, we explained what we meant by 'The Icon Age' and how it started roughly in the early 1980s. We then described the status of 'Collecting' and seven types of Collectors—Accumulators, Librarians, Filers, Archivists, Museum and Gallery Curators, Private Curators, and Amateur Collectors—up to the start of the Icon Age. In subsequent chapters we explored how collecting practices and the objects that are collected have been affected by the first 40 years of the Icon Age. Now we return to the types of collectors and assess how the overall impact of the Icon Age has affected them up to the time of writing in 2024. These summaries almost certainly do not present a complete view of what has happened. Inevitably, they are limited by what we have elected to include, and by the fact that we know more about some aspects than others. However, our aim is to provide an indication of the changes that have occurred. First, though, we summarise the main technology developments of relevance to collecting, that have occurred since the early 1980s.

7.1 Information Technology Developments Since the Early 1980s

First, and most importantly, we can say that the Icon Age is still with us. The Graphical User Interface is still very much alive and well within the three primary operating systems in use around the world: Microsoft Windows, Apple IOS, and Google

P. Wilson and P. Tolmie, *Collecting in the Icon Age*,
https://doi.org/10.1007/978-3-031-86470-4_7

Android. Objects are still represented by icons within a flat interface; although, in some cases, the application icon is replaced by a thumbnail of the first page of the file as shown in Fig. 7.1.

These operating systems have surfed two huge technology waves since the 1980s. One was the arrival and exponential growth of the World Wide Web. The first web page was published in August 1991, and by 2014 the Internet Archive, which collects web sites, was holding 376 billion archived web pages (Costa et al. 2016). This has given access to information, shopping, and services to anyone connected anywhere, and has also enabled individuals and organisations to publish their own collections of material. Another highly significant impact of the internet is that it has educated a huge number of people regarding how to undertake free text searching which has led in turn to a widespread belief that this is the way they should be able to access any information store (Moss and Thomas 2018).

The other technology wave was the take up of the increasing powerful mobile phone, giving portable access to worldwide communication services, and to the World Wide Web. Although the first commercial mobile service was launched in 1983 (Harris and Cooper 2019), it wasn't until the early 2000s that handsets like the blackberry started to sport larger screens and icon-style interfaces. In 2007, Apple introduced the first of its iPhones with a large touch sensitive screen and no keypad (Wikipedia 2023a). By the end of 2022 the United Nations agency for digital technologies, the International Telecommunications Union (ITU), was reporting that, of the world's 8 billion people, three quarters of the population aged 10 years or

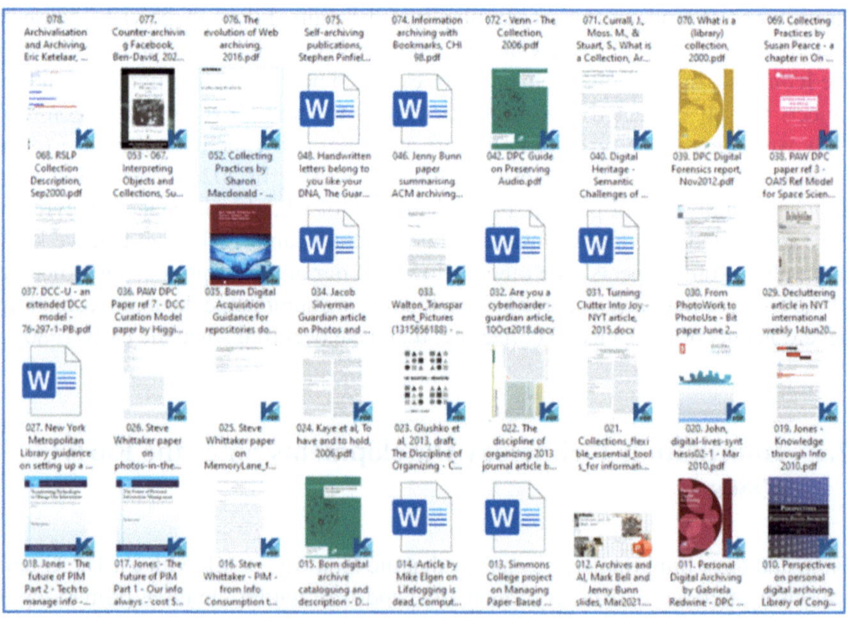

Fig. 7.1 Example of some application icons being replaced by first page thumbnails

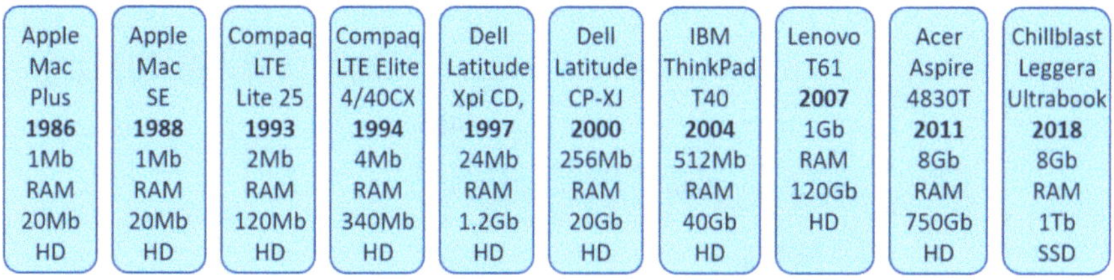

Fig. 7.2 Memory and storage specifications for the PAWDOC platform 1986–2023

more owned a mobile phone (ITU 2022). The communication services afforded by the mobile phone are not limited to voice, but also include emails and text messages, both of which are assembled in huge collections by most users. The combination of these two waves of development has changed the way people live and the way the world operates—and how we go about collecting, as we will discuss shortly.

The computing devices we are now using have been continuously advancing in speed, storage, and general capability, year on year, as illustrated in Fig. 7.2 by the memory and disc drive specifications of the machines used to host the PAWDOC collection from 1986 to 2023. The cost of local disc storage in 2010 was a mere 1% of what it had been in 2000 and 0.001% of what it had been in 1990 (Yeo 2018). Disc sizes of both Hard Discs (HD) and Solid State Drives (SSD) continue to increase and the cost per Gigabyte continues to drop.

The developments in technology have spurred a revolution in Business and Government. At the beginning of the 1980s, office professionals used support staff—typing pools, secretaries, and admin support staff—to perform their administrative tasks. However, as office technology became widespread, professionals were equipped with desktop or laptop computers and started to create their own Born Digital Files. Support staff became a luxury and were increasingly cut to reduce budgets. At the time of writing, only very senior management have secretaries, and office workers are expected to be self-sufficient and fully competent in the use of all hardware and software relevant to their work. This includes the management of large and growing collections of Digital Files on their computers. Over the same period, hot desking and home working have become widespread, and scanning technology has become reliable and cheap. This has stimulated the practice of digitising paper documents—adding to the collection of files to be managed on employee computers.

The same is true for home computer users: they too have large collections of Born Digital and digitised files to manage on their computers. However, they have also been affected by another development—the near complete replacement of print and cine film photography, and dedicated cameras, by digital photography using mobile phones. This is illustrated by the family photo collection belonging to one of the authors. Using the information in the collection's index, the usage of different file formats over time was plotted in the graph in Fig. 7.3. This shows that old-style print photography was last used by the author in 2004 and that he now only takes digital photos.

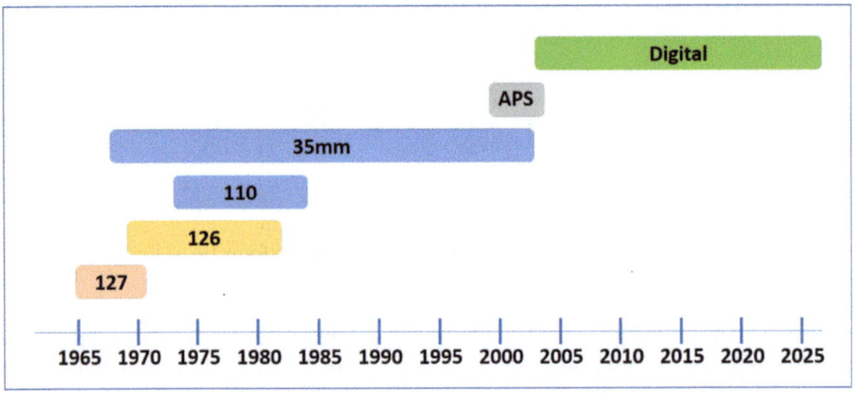

Fig. 7.3 Use of film formats by Wilson—digital format only from 2004 onwards

People now take huge numbers of photos and videos for a variety of reasons—often to communicate rather than just record: the 'selfie' self-portrait has become commonplace (Boogh 2013). Individuals maintain sizeable collections of the resulting digital images, either locally on phones or computers, or in the cloud. Despite this change, very large numbers of old hardcopy prints and cine film still exist and it is commonplace for these retro items to be either digitised and retained, or digitised and destroyed—even for institutional collections (Edwards and Morton 2015). If originals are retained, hardcopy prints are likely to survive longer than cine film.

In a similar vein, the distribution of music, films, and TV programmes has been revolutionised by streaming services. The Vinyl LP was replaced by the CD which in turn was superseded by streaming music over the internet from a central point in 'the cloud'. Likewise, the consumption of films: VHS and Betamax video tape was superseded by DVDs which were in turn superseded by streaming services. Various online platforms now provide huge amounts of material once distributed by conventional TV broadcasters. All this streamed material is in digital form and, in principle, could be collected, as was the case with LPs, CDs, VHS tapes, and DVDs. However, that would somehow negate the benefits of streaming. Perhaps it will take some years to see if people really are satisfied just to stream and not to actually possess such items. Certainly, some people do not find streaming to their liking (Pelly 2022). In the meantime, a great many of the retro versions still exist in home collections and in places like charity shops, and some people do still collect the old formats (Kaba and Özalpman 2021; Shuker, 2010). Indeed, in the case of LPs, a substantial number of people actually prefer them to the digital versions (Ferguson 2022). However, all these retro items require specific equipment to play them on.

A third major change that has had a significant impact on the general public is the emergence of Social Media systems such as Facebook, Instagram, and Tik-Tok. Their growth has been rapid and widespread. For example, in 2008 Facebook had over 100 million users, and by the end of 2021, this had risen to 3 billion monthly users, with some 2 billion using the service daily. The material which people put into these systems, and the posts that they see, are not actively collected by them, but, nevertheless, are retained and managed by the system and consequently do represent significant collections of material relating to each individual user. A great many photos are shared in social media systems—particularly in image-heavy systems such as Instagram. So much so that at least one commentator believes that, for many people, photos have become more about communicating with other people than about memorialising their lives (Silverman 2015).

While streaming services and social media systems take up a substantial amount of people's time, we should not underestimate the impact that computer games have also had on people's lives. This was a $282 billion + worldwide industry in 2024 with over 3 billion players (Exploding Topics 2025). The Entertainment Software Association estimated that over 60% of the US population played video games in 2024 (ESA 2024). Even the numbers of players of individual games are big: a 2022 newspaper article reported that Fortnite attracts 250 million active players a month; gaming platform Roblox has more than 200 million visitors a month; and Minecraft has 170 million visitors a month (Rose 2022). While such games immerse users in specially created virtual worlds, an alternative approach is to superimpose characters and objects on the real world using Augmented Reality techniques on a mobile phone or tablet screen. Pokemon Go was the first mainstream game to take this approach and required users to move around the real world to find virtual 'Pokemon' creatures and other digital objects. The game had rapid worldwide success when it was launched in 2016 with over 65 million users (Mardon and Belk 2018). Wikipedia reported that this had risen to 147 million active users by May 2018, and had grossed more than $6 billion in revenue by 2020 (Wikipedia 2023i). Interestingly, a substantial part of the revenue from video games comes not from the sale of the games but from the sale of collectables within the environments in which the games are played.

Video game virtual environments, and virtual reality social media systems such as Second Life (Bailenson 2018), have inspired some people to envisage a Metaverse—the internet populated by interlinked virtual worlds (Ball 2022). One of the most prominent enthusiasts for this concept has been Mark Zuckerberg, the founder of Facebook (now renamed Meta), who said in May 2021:

> We want to get as many people as possible to be able to experience virtual reality and be able to jump into the metaverse and... to have these social experiences within that. (Sparkes, 2021).

We will discuss the possible impact of the Metaverse a little further in Chap. 9.

The final point to note about technology developments since 1980, is that a high percentage of young people have grown up as 'ipad native' (Ball 2022); i.e. they know nothing about the precursors to the internet, laptops, tablets, mobile phones and text messaging. Obviously, their number is growing. For them, the digital world is their natural world and their collecting practices are digitally oriented and un-tempered by pre-digital experiences and constraints (Gomez 2008).

7.2 IT's Impact on Every Type of Collector

The need to deal with digital objects in our collecting activities has brought with it a whole range of tasks and issues. Some are specific to particular types of collecting and they are dealt with later in this chapter. This section, however, addresses topics which apply to every organisation and individual collecting digital objects.

The overall activity of collecting digital objects is referred to as 'Digital Curation' and its professional characteristics are described below. However, within the overall topic we believe there are 4 considerations that are so fundamental to the collection of digital objects that they are worth highlighting in their own right, so we have also provided each of them with their own sub-sections. They are:

- Essential infrastructure
- File naming
- Backing-up
- Digital Preservation Planning.

7.2.1 Digital Curation

Professional Digital Curation can be considered to include:

> ...all activities involved in managing data from planning its creation, best practice in digitisation and documentation, and ensuring its availability and suitability for discovery and re-use in the future (Abbot 2010).

This description was provided by the Digital Curation Centre (DCC)—just one of several organisations and programs established from the mid-1990s onwards when concern about the risk of not being able to access Digital Files in the future had been raised in a 1996 US report called Preserving Digital Information. A comprehensive history of those events and initiatives is provided in Sara Higgin's paper 'Digital Curation: The Emergence of a New Discipline' (Higgins 2011).

In 2008, the DCC published its Curation Lifecycle model to help organisations ensure that all necessary steps are taken to ensure successful Curation and preservation of data (Higgins 2008). The steps are described as follows:

- **Conceptualise**—Conceive and plan the creation of digital objects, including data capture methods and storage options.
- **Create**—Produce digital objects and assign administrative, descriptive, structural and technical archival metadata.
- **Access and use**—Ensure that designated users can easily access digital objects on a day-to-day basis. Some digital objects may be publicly available, whilst others may be password protected.
- **Appraise and select**—Evaluate digital objects and select those requiring long-term Curation and preservation. Adhere to documented guidance, policies and legal requirements.

- **Dispose**—Rid systems of digital objects not selected for long-term Curation and preservation. Documented guidance, policies and legal requirements may require the secure destruction of these objects.
- **Ingest**—Transfer digital objects to an Archive, trusted digital repository, data centre or similar, again adhering to documented guidance, policies and legal requirements.
- **Preservation action**—Undertake actions to ensure the long-term preservation and retention of the authoritative nature of digital objects.
- **Reappraise**—Return digital objects that fail validation procedures for further appraisal and reselection.
- **Store**—Keep the data in a secure manner as outlined by relevant standards.
- **Access and reuse**—Ensure that data are accessible to designated users for first time use and reuse. Some material may be publicly available, whilst other data may be password protected.
- **Transform**—Create new digital objects from the original, for example, by migration into a different form.

The way these steps map onto the Practice Hierarchy described in Chap. 4, is shown in Table 7.1.

Table 7.1 Mapping of the DCC digital preservation steps to the collecting practice hierarchy

Practices DCC Steps	Initiate	Equip	Acquire	Deposit	Use	Reveal	Maintain	Dispose
Conceptualise	Define	Consult/ design						
Create			All	Index/ label/ store				
Access and use					All			
Appraise/ select			All					
Dispose								All
Ingest				Index/ label/ store				
Preserve							Preserve	
Reappraise			All					
Store							Protect	
Access and reuse					All			
Transform					Re-organise	Exploit		

NB. Entries in the cells are practices and sub-practices from this book's collecting hierarchy

While there is a degree of crossover between the DCC steps and the practices outlined in Chap. 4, it is by no means a comfortable match. For example, the DCC activities 'Create' and 'Appraise/Select' seem to address the collecting practice 'Acquire' which has been identified in this book. The reason for this may well be in the origins of the two sets of material. The DCC was established to support the management of *Research Data* by organisations and consortia (indeed, the strap line on the DCC website reads 'Because good research needs good data'); whereas the Collecting Practice Hierarchy is intended to apply to the collection of any type of object by both individuals and organisations across all the collecting contexts. This wider remit is implied by the comprehensive 2016 volume 'Digital Curation' which, despite being based around the DCC model, notes that:

> Digital curation involves a wide range of stakeholders cutting across disciplinary boundaries: as well as cultural heritage organizations such as Libraries, Archives, and Museums, it also involves funding agencies, government bodies, national data centres, institutional repositories, and learned societies (in fact, Digital Curation is the concern of all who create and use data) (Oliver and Harvey 2016).

Although the word 'data' is still used in this definition, we believe that Digital Curation is now more broadly understood to mean the collection and management of all kinds of Digital Files, some of which have been Born Digital and others that are digitised versions of physical papers or objects. In the latter case, a choice will have been made as to whether to digitise or not. Hence, an appropriate starting point for Digital Curation activities might well be to consider the relative advantages and disadvantages of physical objects versus digital objects. The strengths of managing digital information, as compared to paper-based information are itemised by Ashenfelder (2015) as follows:

- Easier management
- Vast storage space
- Accessibility
- Findability
- Ability to have multiple copies
- Perceived longer lifespan.

We would add to the above list: 'Portability—the ability to carry your complete digital collection around with you in a laptop or even in your mobile phone' (Wilson 2019f; g).

According to Ashenfelder (2015), the weaknesses of managing digital information when compared to paper-based information include:

- Difficulty in taking notes
- Loss of physical interaction
- Decreased readability
- Less portability
- Need to have a machine/device to access information
- Loss of personal sentiment.

Harrison et al. (2017) identify the following additional disadvantages of digital collections:

- No space constraints make it easier to create large and unmanageable collections
- Ease of archiving/deleting may lead to more hidden/lost items
- More forgettable because they are not meaningfully showcased.

Where there is a need to undertake any kind of extensive repetitive work with Digital Files, we would add the following: with a screen, you're locked-in with eyes fixed, head in one place, and body stationary staring at an unending stream of similar looking files. At least with paper files you can use your hands and arms to pick up papers and move them around; you can turn your neck to look at papers spread in front of you; and you can completely change your position to get comfy. Although often more focussed on the use of paper versus digital in collaborative work, these points resonate with the insights offered in Sellen and Harper's seminal book, *The Myth of the Paperless Office* (Sellen and Harper 2002).

Yeo (2018) points out that the lack of space constraints with digital material means that we may be moving into an era where there is a tendency to keep everything, and he identifies the following pros and cons of doing so:

Advantages of keeping everything:

- No loss of documentary relationships/context.
- No subjective selection of what to remove.
- Elimination of the time-consuming/costly task of selection.
- Reduction in digital preservation costs.
- Difficult of ensuring all copies are eliminated.

Disadvantages of keeping everything:

- There can be a massive amount of content.
- The digital preservation work can be huge.
- The environmental impacts of huge amounts of computing.
- Difficulties in identifying/retrieving relevant material.

For Digital Curators of publicly available collections, including, Archives, Lbraries, Museums, and Galleries, who wish to ensure maximum awareness and use of their collections in the Icon Age, some special measures such as those documented below by Ladd (2015) may need to be considered:

- Take into account search engine and social media user behaviour when creating metadata.
- Take special measures to be noticed—perhaps by highlighting a steady flow of new additions.
- Seek out potential users wherever they might be rather than waiting for them to find the collection.
- Recognise that the audience will no longer be a local one but instead, potentially, global.

Plenty of other advice and guidance is available for the aspiring Digital Curator:

- The DCC website contains guidance and lists of publications (DCC 2023).
- The Library of Congress website has a Personal Archiving page which contains links to various useful brochures, guides and resources (Library of Congress 2023).
- The DPC website contains a very comprehensive handbook which, despite it being aimed at Digital Preservation, includes much of use to the Digital Curator (DPC 2023a).
- The UK Joint Information Systems Committee (JISC)'s Digital Preservation Email List provides a steady stream of information about ongoing activities and issues in the Digital Curation and Preservation fields (JISC 2023).

7.2.2 Essential Infrastructure

Digital Files are not totally intangible objects without a physical presence (Mardon and Belk 2018). To access Digital Files, it is essential to have appropriate equipment and a supply of electricity. We make no apologies for highlighting this rather obvious point, because it is the most significant differentiator between physical and digital objects. Such requirements do not apply to clay tablets, books, pottery vases or sets of Lego bricks. If you choose to go down the digital route, you accept the attendant challenge of providing and maintaining these two essential items in all circumstances, and across the whole of the timescale you wish your collection to survive. No ifs and buts. That's it. Full stop.

7.2.3 File Naming

The names given to files are just one of many types of information recorded about specific digital objects. All such material is known as *metadata* and includes tag information held within the Digital File itself as well as information held externally in an index. The information may describe the object, or provide the technical detail required to use the object, or record what has happened to the object as it moves through the Curation lifecycle (Oliver and Harvey 2016).

So why is the file name being singled out for special treatment here? There are three reasons:

(a) it is the collected digital object's unique identifier;
(b) it is immediately visible when you come across a digital object;
(c) it can store very useful information.

Consider the following example: when the PAWDOC collection was using a Document Management System (DMS), it contained a file which the DMS named

'1DF.ppt'. After the collection was moved out of the DMS into a Windows folder called 'PAW-DOC-4268–02', the file name was changed to:

PAW-DOC-4268-02 Slides used for housing Corporation presentation, ORIGINAL, 26-05-2002, 1DF.ppt.

The latter is still unique, is immediately visible when encountered, and informs the viewer not only that its name in the DMS used to be 1DF but also that it is an ORIGINAL file that has been subsequently updated to a new version of PowerPoint. That new version is present alongside it in the Windows folder with the following file name:

PAW-DOC-4268-02 Slides used for housing Corporation presentation, UPDATED, 02-04-2018.pptx.

This is a salient point for collectors—particularly institutions—who choose to use application packages which apply their own proprietary file names to manage digital objects. There may well be significant benefits in using such an application, but it is best to have an understanding of the consequences if, for whatever reason, it becomes necessary to access and manage the files independently of the package.

Going back to the example above, note also the all-important Reference Number which provides the link between the Digital File, its location, and its index entry and/or an equivalent physical object.

The ability to use the file name to record information commonly looked-up, is very easy to achieve and can provide a sort of visible database as illustrated in the three file names shown below:

2020-07-19—Privilege car insurance policy for 12 months from 19July2020 £306.pdf.
2021-07-19—Privilege car insurance policy for 12 months from 19July2021 £291.20.pdf.
2022-07-19—Privilege car insurance policy for 12 months from 19July2022 £281.76.pdf.

Similarly, a collection of communications with friends can be helpful if salient information about their content is recorded in the file title:

2006-11-04—Second Life Computer History Museum proposal.rtf.
2007-06-13—My house is sold—I am homeless.doc.
2007-06-30—Speaking at the royal institution next week.doc.

As all these examples illustrate, the file name can be used in many different ways to enhance a collection of digital objects. Another more prescriptive approach could be to always include the name of the source, the year of publication, and some keywords to aid retrieval (Seehusen 2004). Whatever approach is adopted to file naming, it typically involves some effort (Balogh et al. 2022).

7.2.4 Backing-Up

Despite there being widespread awareness of the need to backup Digital Files, its importance is rarely fully appreciated until you actually lose some files. This may not happen very often, so it's easy to get lulled into a false sense of security. For example, over the 43 years of the existence of the PAWDOC collection there have only been the following 4 instances of data loss—but all were traumatic:

- **1998 MO disc corruption:** When I first started using a Document Management System (DMS), I was using Magneto-Optical (MO) drives to store the files. However, when subsequently moving the files onto CD-ROM discs I discovered that one of the MO drives was partially corrupted. After extensive and time-consuming investigation, I established that 6 files had been lost—2 pages from an 18-page document (at that time the scanned documents were being stored as a separate TIF file for each page) and 4 Word documents.
- **2004—theft of briefcase and laptop** (Wilson 2025): This entailed that the PAWDOC collection and its associated DMS and Index software had to be completely reconstituted on a new laptop. The backups enabled this to be achieved successfully, though it is possible that some index entries and Digital Files may have been lost due to the backups having been taken some days before the theft occurred. A few physical documents which had not previously been scanned, were also in the briefcase. Overall, there were undoubtedly some losses of a few collection items; however, the back-ups did enable most of the overall collection to be successfully reconstituted.
- **2017—blue screen** (Wilson 2025): One afternoon I switched on my laptop and got a screen saying Windows wouldn't start. Despite going through System Startup Repair, going into Administrator mode, and scouring the net for advice, I couldn't get round the dreaded Blue Screen. The system was totally inaccessible, and I had no option but to put my trust in a PC repair shop. Luckily Fix My PC in Bedford was able to completely recover all my files and to reinstall Windows; but I had to reinstall all the software applications, including my DMS software which was exceptionally complex, difficult and time-consuming. However, I managed it in the end and no items were lost from the PAWDOC collection.
- **2021—battery expansion**: One day I noticed that the top of my laptop wasn't closing fully, caused by a hardly noticeable bump in the casing. I was bemused. The next day, however, the bump had become substantial and I deduced that something was happening to the battery—something that was potentially dangerous. I shut down and disconnected from power immediately, contacted the supplier, and arranged for the laptop to be picked up and repaired. Some 5 weeks later, I got the machine back with all applications and files unaffected.

These are just a few of the problems that can occur. There are many other possibilities, and they can just as easily occur to more powerful machines in data centres/the cloud (Ubois 2013). Malevolent hacking is also a serious threat: in a 2024 article written by an ex-head of the UK National Cybersecurity Centre, it was suggested that ransomware is now so widespread, unpreventable and unpoliceable, that system owners should put tested plans in place to be able to recover quickly from such an event (Martin 2024). Regardless of the effort it can entail to maintain effective backups, it is becoming ever more essential to back up collections of Digital Files; and to periodically practice reconstituting files from the backups to confirm that it can be done successfully.

Organisations with IT departments will find it easier to have back-ups performed reliably according to pre-planned schedules. However, individual collection owners can forget, or let the activity slip down their priority list. Automated backup software, preferably with two mirrored NAS (Networked Attached Storage) discs, can overcome this problem. However, for non-automated processes, there can be a need for something like a checklist showing back-up dates planned and completed, displayed prominently in the individual's work space (Wilson 2019a).

7.2.5 Digital Preservation Planning

To open a Digital File, you need hardware and software that are capable of processing it. Unfortunately, the technology is developing at such a pace that, over a period of just ten to fifteen years, the hardware and software being used may not have that capability. Even the media on which the file is stored may not be capable of working with the hardware; and, furthermore, the media itself may only have a limited lifetime before it starts to degrade. Any or all of these problems may mean that a digital file can't be accessed and used. So, the purpose of digital preservation work is to identify and overcome such risks. If one intends to keep a collection of digital objects for anything more than about ten years, it has become advisable to undertake digital preservation initiatives.

A wealth of information and guidance on how to conduct preservation planning can be found in the Digital Preservation Coalition's Handbook (DPC 2023a). Much of this is aimed at large institutions and organisations, for which a wide a range of services and tools are available. Its contents also provide excellent background for individual collectors, but do not give a simple clear-cut way of conducting preservation planning on a relatively very small scale. Indeed, Wilson spent some time trying to find such a methodology in order to undertake digital preservation on the PAWDOC collection (Wilson 2016a), but couldn't find anything suitable and ended up developing a set of document templates with embedded guidance, to do the job (Wilson 2021a).

7.3 IT's Impact on Accumulators

Accumulators collect objects out of functional necessity and make use of the items in their collections.

7.3.1 New Digital Objects Being Collected by Accumulators

Before discussing the sorts of new digital objects that are being collected by Accumulators, it's worth noting that, forty years into the Icon Age, consumption in general has continued to gather pace. This was already being pointed to in the early 90s, as illustrated by a light-hearted newspaper article entitled 'The importance of stuff' (which we would say has more than an element of truth in it), where the author argued that:

> Life is all about acquiring stuff, then acquiring more stuff, maybe changing your stuff round a little, then acquiring even more stuff, then getting a bigger place because there's no room for all your stuff, getting rid of some stuff, then getting a smaller place because you haven't got as much stuff. Then you die. (Kelner 1993)

There has been no let-up since, as illustrated by a lady who photographed all of her 12,795 possessions (Lane 2023). Another graphic example of this is the BBC TV programme 'Sort your life out' that first aired in 2021, which helps families declutter their homes (IMDB 2023) (BBC 2023). Some of the items that regularly turn up in this show are the physical media associated with digitised film and music—DVDs, and CDs. These things proliferated in homes during the 1990s and 2000s. Interestingly, however, the trend reversed in the 2010s with the widespread take-up of streaming services such that CDs and DVDs now litter the charity shops. In a similar vein, video recorders were popular over the same period, enabling people to set TV programmes to be recorded and subsequently watched at their leisure. The collection of unwatched material would build up over time depending on the capacity of the disc in the recorder. The use of video recorders, too, started to decline when TV streaming services became prevalent from the 2010s onwards. At the same time, the digital economy now makes it very easy to purchase digital music and video, and conversion programs enable such material to be converted from the original media, so many people have collections of digital music, video files and even books. However, a physical book, CD, or DVD have a tangible presence in the world, whereas a software file is just about invisible, so our collecting habits associated with physical and digital media will never be the same (Wilson 2023a, 2023b).

Text messages are new objects that have emerged in huge volumes since the start of the Icon Age. They are accumulated by many individuals after reading them, within their particular messaging applications on their mobile phones (for example, Samsung Messages, Google Messages, Apple's iMessage, and WhatsApp). No action is required to keep them, whereas deleting them does take a little bit of effort; therefore, many people just leave them and have them there in case they should subsequently want to re-read the contents or check when they communicated with somebody.

Email usage has also experienced huge growth since the start of the Icon Age. Users who store the emails they have read, in particular folders, are discussed in the Filers section. However, some studies have found that many people allow all their email to simply pile up in the inbox (Henderson and Srinivasan 2011; Fisher et al. 2006; Whittaker and Sidner 1996).

Mobile phone apps are another type of object that many people tend to accumulate indiscriminately. Their icons proliferate over several screens, many only to be used a few times before being forgotten about. Similarly, some people accumulate icons on their PC desktops (Hern 2018).

One of the largest accumulations found on mobile phones is of photos. People now take photos for all sorts of reasons—one of the main ones being to share what they are doing with their friends on social media (Silverman 2015). The ease with which photos can be taken with a mobile phone, the high quality of the results, and the usefulness of the features provided to manage and present the photos on the phone, has resulted in it being commonplace for people to have hundreds, if not thousands, of photos accumulated on their devices. No active Curation is required—a huge advantage since most people lack the time and motivation to organise their collections (Broekhuijsen et al. 2017; Frohlich et al. 2002). Some people prefer to have their phones automatically transfer their photos to a cloud service where they can be accumulated in even larger quantities—though storage space on mobile phones continues to increase and reduce in cost. Cloud photo services may provide even more automatic Curation-type functionality than a phone Photo app—from being able to identify images of certain types such as 'dog', to being able to trim a large set of, say, 500 holiday photos down to the 'best' 50 (Hern, 2018). However, this distinction between cloud and on-device services is rapidly vanishing: in 2024, one of the authors' phones was able to find instances of dogs, weddings, butterflies etc. Phones' photo management features are continually expanding and improving—as is just about everything in the digital arena in the twenty-first century.

Huge numbers of people around the world accumulate vast quantities of material—often of a quite personal nature—in social media systems and the cloud. This is a different kind of collecting: the items are created, not acquired; and they are publicly shared, not deposited into a private space in the way that entries about experiences, events and reflections used to be made in a private diary. Studies indicate that motivations for this sharing of personal data include the forging and preservation of social links, engendering kudos, managing identity, impression management, self-display, creating 'social capital', maintaining trust, preserving memories and encouraging recollection, and facilitation of various kinds of transactions (Tolmie and Crabtree 2018). Harari neatly summarises this behaviour as:

> Writing a private diary… sounds to many present-day youngsters utterly pointless. Why write anything if nobody else can read it? The new motto says: 'If you experience something - record it. If you record something - upload it. If you upload something - share it. (Harari 2016).

Unfortunately, it seems that people often lose track of what they have where in these systems, and sometimes lose material altogether (Lindley et al. 2013).

On a much smaller scale, e-books are growing in popularity, spurred on by the fact that they do not necessarily require a specialist reading device such as a Kindle, but can be read on any of the millions of tablet computers in current use. Whichever technology is used, readers tend to accumulate the books they have bought, on the device in question, in much the same way that they might accumulate physical books. Of course, the term e-books covers a wide variety of formats including magazines and comics: the Kindle store on Amazon claimed to be able to list over 30,000 Kindle e-book *magazine* titles and over 50,000 Kindle e-book *comic* titles when a search was conducted in May 2023. Overall, Amazon was estimated to have nearly 9 million different Kindle e-book titles of all types listed in 2021 (Haines 2023). Another commentator noted in 2021 that digital text was well on its way to becoming the predominant form of printing (Byers 2021). While e-books are text-based, audio books and podcasts are also widely used, and these are probably accumulated in the same way by many people. Interestingly, the terms and conditions of sale of e-books and other digital entertainment products such as streamed music and films, are usually on a loan basis meaning that there is no transfer of ownership, only a limited right to use (Bellamy et al. 2014).

We have made no mention of souvenirs and mementos so far, because they continue to be collected largely in physical form. However, they do appear prominently in various studies on the home and its contents that have been carried out since the 1990s (Kirk and Sellen 2010) (Kalnikaitėa and Whittaker 2011; Petrellia et al. 2014). Some of these studies have attempted to identify digital alternatives to the functions being performed by some of the objects identified, and, in some cases, prototypes have been designed and evaluated (Banks 2013; Kirk and Sellen 2010). Of the digital mementos and souvenirs that have been identified, most are in the form of Born Digital photos or messages which we have already discussed above, though some instances have been recorded of people keeping digital work documents, and gifts of digital art work, as valued mementos (Kirk and Sellen 2010). A study of the virtual possessions of teenagers identified a wide range of items including homework assignments, blog entries, status messages from social networking systems, archived SMS messages, various self-made digital artworks, as well as expansive collections of digital video, digital photos, and digital music (Odom et al. 2011) (for digital music it's worth noting that particular songs may be accumulated on the mobile phone itself or in an individual's personal playlists stored in a streaming service—both are valid forms of Accumulated Collections). Despite a paucity of exploration of this in the literature, there are most probably large numbers of physical mementos, souvenirs, and other types of Accumulated Objects, which have been digitised either to make space and/or to display them in some way or other. For example, photographing an old collection of university books on the shelf before cutting the spines off and scanning them. Although this destroyed the physical books, they are still visible in a photo under a transparent blotter and the contents are still accessible in the digital PDF versions on a laptop and an iPad (see Fig. 7.4) (Wilson 2014b).

Fig. 7.4 Photos of old university books before being digitised; and of the book PDFs on an iPad after being digitised

Finally, we should mention the phenomenon of lifelogging whereby individuals record every aspect of their lives using an automated camera which takes a photo every few seconds. This was first started as a Phd experiment at MIT in 1994 and was then taken up by Gordon Bell in the MyLifeBits project in 1999 when he was working at Microsoft. Over the following years Bell's camera took a photo every 20 seconds during his waking hours, he constantly recorded his GPS coordinates, and he stored all his documents and emails as well as scanning the legacy documents he had from his career as a computer engineer (Zeller 2015). We have classed this as Accumulating because it is indiscriminate—everything is collected regardless of context or purpose. However, it is a somewhat minority pursuit, not least because of the very lack of a clear purpose. When interviewed in 2016, Bell was no longer wearing his camera and said that the whole lifelogging project "wasn't something that was bringing a lot of value to my life" (Elgan 2016).

7.3.2 *IT Support for Accumulators*

Probably the most convenient source of support for Accumulators forty years into the Icon Age, is the mobile phone app. Among the many millions of apps in the various app stores, are to be found programs relating to a bewildering range of consumer items and activities. For example, an hour's searching the Apple App store identified the following:

- Gardenize: Log the plants in your garden and get reminders and advice on caring for them.
- CLZ Music: Keep track of your CD and vinyl collection.
- Homer: Save and manage all the information about your home in one place.

- Recipe Keeper: Keep all your recipes in one place and get shopping and meal planner advice.
- WearTracker: Manage your wardrobe and keep track of what you wear, sizes, repairs etc..
- PetNote + : Manage your pet's conditions, notes and expenses.
- Book track: Track all the books you own and the ones you want to read in the future.
- Clever Baby: Track your baby's well-being, growth and development.
- My Car: Track all aspects of your car's fuel consumption, service history, and other expenditure.
- KeepTrackMed: Keep all the health information about you and your family in one place.
- Spending Tracker: Log expenses and income, and track your spending against a budget.

For many of the above, this is just one of several apps doing the same job. We have no idea if these apps are any good—but it's clear that for most Accumulations some sort of app is probably available to help manage them. We don't know how intensively such apps are used—people often download them to try them out for a little while and then just lose interest.

For some types of Digital Files, specialist PC software is available. For example, for photos there are several such products, most of which not only organise the photos but also include powerful image editing capabilities. A net search for 'X management applications', where X can be a Photo or any other type of object, will probably return several review websites listing currently available products. Having said that, relying on specialist applications has some disadvantages including:

- the need to upgrade it from time to time.
- moving a file outside the app means there is only the filename to identify it.
- any additional information you want to add has to be shoehorned into the facilities provided in the application.

Wilson declined to do this for his photo collection and instead created an index in Excel and applied a standard structure for each photo's filename—Ref No, Free text title, Date (Wilson 2012b). In practice, a spreadsheet can be used to record and manage the contents of just about any type of collection.

The above discussion is concerned with collections of, or about, specific things. However, another, very general type of Accumulation has become very prevalent: the stuff that builds up in people's lofts, attics, garages, and outhouses. These usually contain a very diverse range of objects that are being stored for possible future use. To try to understand how such collections might be managed, a long-term experiment initiated in 2004 by one of the authors, entailed numbering each item, dividing a loft into distinct positions, and keeping a laptop database of what items were in each position (Wilson 2016b). The intention was to eventually attach RFID tags to each item so that their locations could be automatically pointed out by a reading device. This was never fully achieved, but the original laptop database was replaced by a mobile phone database app in 2016, which proved very successful—particularly when using the app on the phone while in the loft; and being able to take a mobile phone photo of each object within the app itself (Wilson 2016c).

7.4 IT's Impact on Librarians

Librarians collect works recorded on portable media, and provide their customers with access to them.

7.4.1 New Digital Objects Being Collected by Librarians

One of the most visible digital objects in Libraries has been the physical media—DVDs and Blue-Ray discs—associated with their film collections. CDs containing Music and Audiobook Digital Files are also prominent. However, while audiobook usage remained strong through the 2010s, Library Music Collections became less popular due to the growth of streaming services and the practice of listening to music on devices such as mobile phones (Saponaro and Evans 2019). Audio digital files are also used to hold a variety of other types of collection such as the StoryCorps Archive in the American Folklife Center at the US Library of Congress, which contains 45,000 interviews of individuals across over 30,000 hours of audio files (Ubois 2013).

Many Libraries collect serials—newspapers, magazines, journals, yearbooks and the like. Many serials now either produce a digital version as well as a print version, or are just produced electronically (Fieldhouse 2012). E-serials can be among the most heavily used of a Library's resources—especially because, unlike print versions, they are easy to search (Saponaro and Evans 2019).

CDs, DVDs and the transfer of serials to electronic formats are all illustrative of a general move to the digital in many of the items collected by Libraries—a move that simply reflects the world's growing dependence on electronically transmitted information. Librarians could not afford to ignore this change without being marginalised: they had to give their new generations of users the information they wanted in either print or electronic form (Lee 2000; Logan and McLuhan 2016; Saponaro and Evans 2019). In one way, the move to digital content is particularly apt for organisations whose main function is to lend items to people: a physical information carrier object (ICO) can only be lent to one person at a time, whereas a digital ICO can be used by multiple people simultaneously (Lewis 2013). Consequently, many Libraries now offer online access to their collections of films, music, and audiobooks through services such as Overdrive which, according to its website in 2025, was providing digital content to over 92,000 libraries and schools in 115 countries. Libraries can build their individual digital collections from Overdrive's catalogue of more than 3 million titles, and users are able to access that content, provided they have a library card, through Overdrive's 'Libby' app any time day or night. Overdrive also enables

Libraries to provide e-books to their users as well as databases and streaming video (Overdrive 2025). So, many Libraries have a full range of both print and digital material to offer and to manage and their content selection practices have to ensure an appropriate balance between the two (Saponaro and Evans 2019).

Libraries that wish to actually own and build up their own special collections of e-books are likely to face a variety of challenges including digital preservation issues, non-standard file formats, unclear and short-term licencing agreements, and the possibility of the content changing (Bigelow, 2021). There is a view that simulation technology may be a better approach for preserving e-books in the long-term, i.e., rather than trying to ensure that a Kindle will work in 100 years-time, it may be better just to maintain a simulation of what it would have been like to read an e-book title on a Kindle device. Such a simulation could be a useful way to exhibit e-books in the future (Bigelow 2021).

Of course, the internet now acts as one vast library (Logan and McLuhan 2016), and since the start of the new millennium Libraries have provided computers for their users to access it. However, as internet usage became more widespread from home and via mobile phones, there has perhaps been less demand for such facilities. On the other hand, Libraries have found other ways of adding value to this computing capability. For example, some have taken to providing links to material on the net that they believe is particularly useful and accurate (Saponaro and Evans 2019), and some are reported to have provided access to programs that enable users to make their own information packages or books, or to undertake 3D printing (Logan and McLuhan 2016). All such activities require Libraries to deal with a wide variety of Digital Files.

Another sort of collection held by some Libraries is the set of manuscripts produced by an individual of note. Such collections began to contain more and more digital material in the 1990s, so much so that the British Library created a post for a Curator of eManuscripts in 2003 (Williams and Rowland 2009), and an authoritative guide for donors and repositories was produced in 2013 by representatives from a number of well-known Libraries and institutions (Redwine et al. 2013).

For libraries associated with academia and research, the Icon Age has spurred another set of demands: for many years, such institutions had made attempts to obtain so-called 'Grey Literature'—essentially unpublished working papers shared among researchers. The ease with which individuals can now collaborate around the world has increased the amount of such material and has perhaps increased awareness of its existence. Consequently, since 2000 there has been a move to establish Institutional Repositories (or expand existing repositories of final form texts) to collect this information and to make it available to authorised personnel. There is also a growing number of pre-print databases such as arXiv[1] that support the sharing of such materials. Some institutions also preserve physical computers and their file contents in the repositories (Saponaro and Evans 2019; Cahoy 2013). Research data, in particular, needs to be available for use and reuse by scholars around the world, but, in practice, there appear to be many obstacles to overcome before this becomes a reality (Oliver

[1] https://arxiv.org/.

and Harvey 2016; Mosconi et al. 2018). However, it is reported that some Academic Libraries are actually purchasing data sets from commercial operators, on behalf of their users for text and data mining (Saponaro and Evans 2019).

Accompanying the initiatives around Institutional Repositories has been a movement to provide Open Access to journal articles whereby researchers deposit an electronic copy online for anyone to access free of charge (Logan and McLuhan 2016). Of course, there are many obstacles to such a practice becoming commonplace (Pinfield 2004)—not least quality control, and the fact that journals charge a subscription to obtain and read them. Nevertheless, the Open Access movement has prompted some publishers to modify their policies such that, in a review of 107 publishers, the number allowing some form of Self-Archiving had increased by 12%, to 97 over the 12-year period to 2015. However, over the same period the restrictions imposed on how, where and when Self-Archiving was allowed to take place had increased 119%, 190% and 1000% respectively (Gadd and Covey 2019). Over the same period and beyond, many academic Libraries have ceased to collect physical copies of journals, but instead provide their users with access to the relevant publisher databases (Lewis 2013) or to services such as JSTOR (simply standing for Journal Storage), which at the beginning of 2024 was claiming to hold full runs of more than 2800 journals in the humanities, social sciences and sciences plus 100,000 scholarly books (JSTOR 2024).

As well as the Icon Age introducing Libraries to new types of data, it has also introduced a new type of Library: Virtual Libraries that have no physical location, and that only exist on the internet. Virtual Libraries typically digitise books that are out of copyright and provide digital books and papers for use by internet users in general. Some examples are Project Gutenburg, Manybooks, Feedbooks, the Internet Archive, the HathiTrust and Google Books (Byers 2021). The last of these—Google Books—originally had perhaps the largest digitisation operation which also included books still in copyright. By March 2012 they had scanned 20 million of the 130 million books they estimated were in existence (Lewis 2013). However, following several court cases, the scanning operation was all but shut down towards the end of the 2010s (Saponaro and Evans 2019). Google is also the Curator of Google Scholar, which is an extensive database of the titles and very brief synopses of scientific research papers and books, with links to the actual documents and volumes where they exist digitally on the net. This had become widely used by the early 2020s. We should also mention Wikipedia, the online encyclopaedia, which can be considered to be a vast online library of articles in its own right. When we accessed the Wikipedia stats page in June 2023 it was reporting that it contained 6.6 million articles and was receiving billions of page views every month (Wikipedia 2023k). Investigations have shown that Wikipedia content is at least as good as that of the Encyclopaedia Britannica (Logan and McLuhan 2016).

It seems clear that, for many Libraries, digital material is now at least as important as print material. However, there are significant differences between the two types of content, and these will have a continuing effect on the services which Libraries offer and the way they develop. The book 'Collection management basics' lists them as follows (Saponaro and Evans 2019):

- A Library rarely owns its electronic materials.
- E-resources often come with a restrictive licence or contract.
- Licence restrictions often go against Library philosophies of open access or sharing with others.
- Decision to purchase often comes after a trial period.
- Acquisition by Library consortiums is more complex with trials and deals based on numbers that may vary if some members eventually drop out.
- Assessment often depends on vendor-supplied data which may not reflect what the Library wants to evaluate.
- There is a lack of permanence since the Library often does not own the product/service.

7.4.2 IT Support for Librarians

IT has revolutionised the way Libraries are operated and managed. Library users have their membership details recorded electronically, and are issued with a membership card and/or tags that can be recognised automatically. They can access the library's information system over the internet, either from a desktop machine or via an app on their mobile phones. They can interrogate the index, request or reserve items, and take out digital items, any time day or night (Logan and McLuhan 2016). Many Libraries now have self-check-in/out machines that enable users to take out or return physical items themselves without needing a member of staff for the process. Most physical items are now labelled with either bar codes or RFID tags that enable them to be automatically recognised. RFID tags also enable an alert to be sounded if an item passes through the exit without having been checked out.

All these customer-facing facilities are supported by back-end systems that are provided largely by a variety of service providers: the Capterra Software review website was listing 103 library automation software suppliers in 2023 (Capterra 2023). However, many Libraries are now looking for cheaper alternatives to their legacy systems. One way of achieving this is for libraries to become part of a consortia and to invite system providers to bid for the business (Chad 2021). Another trend is for Libraries to change to cloud-based library management software because it is scalable, relatively cheap and easy to upgrade (Technavio 2024).

Many Libraries have collections of legacy image materials such as reel film, filmstrips, slides, and printed photos; and they are digitising them to make space and to eliminate deterioration problems (Saponaro and Evans 2019). Libraries are also digitising other hardcopy material, such as very old texts, historical documents, and works of eminent people (Ubois 2013; Martin 2009)—but in these cases the objective is to make them more easily available to users over the internet, and the originals are retained. The use of Optical Character Recognition (OCR) software in the course of the digitisation process enables the full text of the documents to be searched. Many Libraries are using turnkey software packages such as CONTENTdm and Greenstone to support such projects by specifying the necessary metadata based on standards such as Dublin Core, and by providing the necessary database and web access functionality (Miller 2022). Of course, Libraries may well still possess legacy material in other formats such as newspapers on microfilm. In these cases, and for any such specialist material that they collect in the future, Libraries will have to retain the necessary equipment/software to be able to continue to access such items (Grenoble and Whaley 2002).

The concept of Inter-Library Loans has been around for many years. However, these are now managed through IT systems; as are so-called 'floating collections', whereby items are requested from one library and delivered to a patron in another. When the item is returned, it stays in the patron's library until it is requested by another user (Saponaro and Evans 2019). A more ambitious application of this approach is the notion of a distributed library, such as that envisaged by Australian Librarians who started promoting the idea of a National Distributed Library in 1988 (Lee 2000). Similar initiatives are operational in the USA and Europe. The DPLA (Digital Public Library of America) aggregates metadata from Libraries, Museums and institutions around the country thereby enabling users to search through a single interface (DPLA 2025). In Europe, Europeana displays digital cultural heritage material drawn from over 2000 different institutions across Europe (Europeana 2025; Capurro et al. 2023). These two operations provide access to items from many other institutions apart from Libraries and demonstrate how digital technology enables material from multiple institutions to be drawn together and accessed through a single interface.

Beyond all this support for Library operations, there has also been a growing realisation that developing AI capabilities could have a major impact on the creation of metadata and on the ability to search and find information. Consequently, some Libraries have set up initiatives to familiarise their staff and their customers with AI, for example, the AI Lab established in 2018 by the Library of the University of Rhode Island (Dekker et al. 2022); and the 2019 AI workshop programme at the University of Toronto (Toane et al. 2022). Other Libraries have been running projects that explore how AI can be harnessed for use in Libraries for activities such as the classification of images (Coleman et al. 2022), the digitisation of handwritten texts (Terras 2022), and research discovery (Hervieux and Wheatley 2022).

7.5 IT's Impact on Filers

Filers collect factual information assembled on a specific media, that they may wish to refer to and/or use later

7.5.1 New Digital Objects Being Collected by Filers

The arrival of the personal computer had a massive impact on the number of people who are Filers. The provision of a folder-based filing system in both major platforms—MS Windows and Apple MAC OS/iOS—encouraged the majority of users to create folder names and hierarchies into which they could deposit their Digital Files. In so doing, they all became Filers. Only those unceremoniously dumping all their files into a single folder could escape this label.

Digital Filing is such a widespread activity that several studies have been conducted investigating the folder structure strategy of individuals (Henderson and Srinivasan 2011; Whittaker and Massey 2020; Khoo et al. 2007; Fastrez and Jacques 2015).

The types of Digital Files that are placed into folders include those containing text, images, sounds, datasets, and software (Powell et al. 2000). These are either created by the user, or received in emails, or downloaded from the internet. Many PC users also undertake completely separate folder-based Filing within their email systems, which operate as silos within their computing environment (Whittaker and Sidner 1996; Fisher 2006; Henderson and Srinivasan 2011). They may also set up folders in the bookmarking facilities in their browsers (Abrams et al. 1998) and in internet/cloud-based file sharing services such as Dropbox.

This Folder-Filing practice is now conducted so universally that it has become part of common culture. It has been spurred on by the huge growth in the number of digital documents we create, receive and obtain: a phenomenon that many commentators believe to have resulted in widespread information overload and anxiety (Ketelaar 1999; Logan and McLuhan 2016; Whittaker and Hirschberg 2001; Elgan 2016; Kaye et al. 2006). Shoving Digital Files into folders may be one way in which people try to cope. Certainly, storage has now become so cheap and plentiful that lack of space has ceased to be a motivation to delete all but the largest types of digital files (such as video) (Whittaker 2011; Williams et al. 2009).

Of course, paper has also proliferated over this period, and to manage it people have taken to digitising it using either scanners or cameras. This has introduced another kind of Digital File to the mix, and another decision to be made by the Filer: 'should the original paper document be retained or destroyed?'—a question that has been explored in some detail for the PAWDOC collection (Wilson 2014a). If a paper-based collection is being converted to a digital collection, there will also be the question of whether to just digitise all new documents, or to also undertake backfile conversion on the legacy collection. Backfile conversion should not be undertaken lightly: it can take a lot of time and can act as a drag on the new collection (Wilson 2019d).

All the above points are related to anybody who uses a Personal Computer (PC). However, there are some impacts on PC users that are different depending on whether the user is a home user or a work user. In particular:

- **Domestic Filing**: While most houses kept some paperwork prior to the 1980s, in the Icon Age, with its digitised information and services, the management of collections of files—both digital and paper—has become a significant and essential domestic activity. However, whereas at work this is part of the job, at home it's up to the individuals concerned whether they do it and how they do it.

- **Document ownership**: The Digital Files that a home user handles belong to the home user (usually); whereas the Digital Files used at work may well belong to the employing organisation. In the work context, this has implications for both caring for the existence of the file, and for what happens to the file when the user leaves the organisation. Some commentators point out that the lines between work and private life are blurring (Kim 2013). However, the employer has the power, and the rules they impose and the technology they provide their employees, will dictate what individuals have to do.
- **Reuse and sharing**: While there are many uses that digital files may be put to in both home and work environments, there are two uses which occur primarily in the work environment: reuse of the contents and the sharing of items with colleagues (Marshall 2013; Kaye 2006).
- **Departmental versus Personal Filing**: In the work context the user may have use of a departmental file system to facilitate the sharing of Digital Files. For example, a shared repository in an academic department for teaching materials (Kung et al. 2004). Users may find this a complicating factor when it comes to Filing their own documents. Indeed, the debate about whether it is best to have several Personal Filing systems, or one central system has been going on a long time (Tonne 1946). Even if there is no group repository, users may wish to keep copies of publicly available documents in their own files for any one or more of the following reasons: so that the item is immediately available to them; to use the item to remind them to do something; because they don't trust external stores; and for sentimental reasons (Whittaker 2011).

Companies, institutions, corporations and government, all have a need to manage their overall collection of information in physical paperwork and Digital Files in order to operate, share information effectively, and to meet legal requirements for document retention. Some choose to perform that function by having a central digital repository for the organisation as whole or for specific groups, for example the content database of a newspaper (Proctor et al. 2014). Such bodies also curate some particularly significant collections of information. One is the vast swathes of information about individuals and their activities that are gleaned from sales and other sources. Another is medical records data. These are special, not only because of the privacy requirements associated with the management such data, but also because of their potential value for data mining (Lynch 2013). Other important collections of medical-related information include genome databases such as MGI-Mouse, and the Protein Data Bank (Oliver and Harvey 2016). Companies and corporations also curate databases of digital objects to sell to customers, for example, online image libraries, and libraries of news content which journalists may use in their stories (Proctor et al. 2014). These are just a few examples to illustrate the very broad range of information collections that are owned and managed by organisations in the 2020s.

Whether at home or at work, Filing takes time and is rarely a priority activity (Kaye et al. 2006; Marshall 2013). Nevertheless, some people may decide that a simple hierarchical file system does not enable them to control and use their files as they would wish. Such people may choose to introduce an index in which various information is recorded about each file, a link to the file is itself included in the record, and facilities are provided to search all the records. In the PAWDOC system, the following minimal amount of information was recorded in the Index (text in brackets provides a view of the usefulness of the field after 38 years of use) (Wilson 2019b):

- Reference Number (essential).
- Title (free format description and keywords) (essential).
- Creation Date (useful).
- Movement Status (very useful—originally for recording the whereabouts of items, but its use has expanded to include other status information such as whether there is a physical file).
- Date Last Accessed (only useful if you particularly need it).
- Publication Date (not very useful).

Note that these index fields enable both digital and physical items to be included, and for more than one Digital File to be associated with each record—both principles found to be essential over the life of the system (Wilson 2019c). The PAWDOC index started off on physical cards but went electronic in 1987 (see the PAWDOC architecture in Sect. 3.1.3.1). The vast majority of indexes today will also be electronic—yet another type of Digital File that Filers have had to become acquainted with.

While the notion of Filing usually brings documents to mind, another field in which it is important to devise appropriate filing and indexing structures is academic research data. In this endeavour, without detailed planning of how the data are to be interrogated and analysed, its storage in the course of it being generated can become chaotic and unhelpful, and even obstructive to the aims of the project. Alternatively, a well-designed system of data management can enable new combinations of techniques: quantitative and qualitative; case study and pattern-seeking; theory construction and theory testing (Richards and Richards 1994).

A rather different type of file that is collected around the world is software code files. These contain sets of programme code, and are assembled together to produce an operational software system. Various versions of the files are produced as a result of testing which identifies errors, and in order to implement changes in requirements. At any one time a particular subset of the overall collection may be in use. So-called Software Configuration Management systems control all the files and their various configurations at particular points in time (G2 2023).

Finally, we should mention the vast numbers of blogs that exist in the world—over 600 million in 2022 by some estimates. These are essentially web sites consisting of a series of informal diary-style text entries commonly referred to as posts, typically following some sort of theme, and presented in date order (Wikipedia 2023j). The *pwofc.com* website belonging to one of the authors is a typical example. Since they are organised and managed collections, blog owners can be considered Filers. Rather than use a blog, some people achieve the same sort of result with a general web site. The Grazian Archive is an extraordinary example of what can be achieved—though since Alfred de Grazia's death the web site has become, de facto, an Archive (de Grazia 2023). Another type of website that is halfway between a Filing system and an Archive, is the Online Memorial—a facility offered by many service providers. We found a list of at least ten such providers by doing a net search for 'Online memorial' (Everplans 2023). These enable individuals to record their thoughts, stories and photos of loved ones or friends who have died and to have the full record available for, potentially, many years for those who want to remember the person (Odom et al. 2010). As people make their contributions they are Filing; but eventually, when contributions stop coming and the site has been inactive for a few years, the collected material becomes an Archive.

7.5.2 IT Support for Filers

We have already described the folder software in the major PC platforms, which have not so much provided support for Filers but rather turned huge numbers of people into Filers. However, for those wanting a more sophisticated solution, Document Management Systems (DMSs) emerged in the 1990s to provide a self-contained environment in which Digital Files can be indexed in some way, stored, and searched for. DMSs are typically heavyweight software programmes that are built to scale across whole organisations and are capable of looking after large numbers of items with extensive metadata associated with each one and which may exist in several versions. A DMS will also possess sophisticated search and retrieval functionality, will manage access rights for each item, and will control who is able to get into the system and what they are able to see. Different organisations may use a DMS in different ways: some may use it for documents currently in use (so-called 'hot' files); some may use it for documents associated with activities in the past (so-called 'cold' files). At least one commentator believes that DMS functionality is more suited to cold files (Sellen and Harper 2002)—which in our classification would be an Archive.

DMSs usually include features enabling them to be integrated with scanners—with the primary objective of enabling paper documents to be digitised and included in the DMS. The PAWDOC collection used such a DMS for some 20 years—though with a separate index in a Filemaker database. The index was used to identify the appropriate Reference Number and that was then used to find the document in the DMS. The experience was instructive: the software had a comprehensive set of functions—more than was needed—and consequently was complex to install and maintain. The need to install new versions of the software over the years to keep up to date with upgrades to the software and the operating system, and to move the system from old to new laptops, was difficult to achieve, often required direct support from the supplier, and was an unwanted pressure (Wilson 2012a). Consequently, in 2018, all the files were moved—some 27,000 of them—out of the DMS into Windows Folders, with each folder being labelled with a Reference Number. It was a great success. The new system was very effective and easy to use; and required no specialist maintenance work at all. The computing power available in the PCs and laptops of the late 2010s was more than adequate to enable rapid scrolling through thousands of folders to find a file (Wilson 2018a).

The experience confirms what is probably self-evident: a DMS is overkill for personal collections. They are intended primarily for groups and organisations which have high usage and/or legal and regulatory requirements (Wilson 2018b) and now come in a variety of shapes and sizes—some suited for small businesses and others designed to support organisations with thousands of people. Some are applications that reside on a PC, and others are cloud-based applications that store the files somewhere on the internet.

Unlike the DMS, the PAWDOC index has been found to be essential throughout the PAWDOC collection's existence. The index is held in a Filemaker database—but that is purely historical. It was the most suitable software when it was created in 1986 and it has been used ever since. Filemaker is a little expensive and it does require updating every few years, but it is easy to install and requires no special maintenance. However, for any Filer wanting to establish an Index today, spreadsheets often suffice and can be designed to record whatever fields are required and provide an adequate search capability (Wilson 2017).

Search and retrieval is an essential function for Filers, and it, too, like folders, has become an established part of our culture. Billions of people throughout the world now know what it means to search for something because they are doing so all the time when they search the internet in their browsers. The phrase 'Google it' has become commonplace. This sets our expectations for search functionality, and spreadsheets don't quite come up to that standard. However, the PAWDOC experience revealed that search and retrieval success is not only dependant on functionality and power; a target document has to be correctly identified and selected from among many others, and this requires a match being achieved between what is in the users' mind and what is in the records being searched. Problems that may prevent this occurring include the passage of time and changing terminology (Wilson 2019e).

Most of the above discussion has been framed around documents. However, the collection of information in smaller chunks might also be considered to be Filing. A variety of software applications have been designed specifically for this purpose. Evernote is one of the primary examples of such systems and can capture, store, and organise digital materials in virtually any format—documents, photos, video clips, or webpages (Hawkins 2013). A comprehensive list of 37 such Note-Taking applications, is provided in a Wikipedia entry where it is noted that each app organises its contents by using one or more of the following: trees, tags, notebooks, colours, chronology, and stacks. Functions may include: outline bulleting, web clipping, annotation, whiteboard, ink-pen input, character recognition, spellcheck, search, print, import/export (Wikipedia 2023b).

For the Filer in the 2020s, the ability to digitise documents is an essential capability, and the technology to do so is widely available. Scanning technology has advanced considerably since the 1990s, and high resolution, colour scanners are now plentiful and cheap. A scanning capability is usually built into multi-function printers, and into larger photocopying machines. However, scanning is no longer the only way people capture documents. The cameras in mobile phones are of such high resolution that they too can capture images of high quality. This is especially useful for things like white boards or flip charts which won't fit in a scanner. In fact, the ease of taking digital photos may well have prompted additional materials being included in Digital Filing Systems—a picture is often a useful accompaniment to some documentation. Optical Character Recognition (OCR) software is widely available and is easily applied to digitised documents to enable the searching of the full text of documents. Once digitised, such documents are usually easy to work with on screen (Wilson 2019h).

7.6 IT's Impact on Archivists

Archivists look after collections of objects which have been moved from their original locations and placed into long-term storage

7.6.1 New Digital Objects Being Collected

The emergence of email as a significant and voluminous method of communication, presented one of the Icon Age's most significant challenges to the classic Archival institution—the national archives of particular countries. Where once they collected only paper-based memos and documents passed between their politicians and leaders, they now had to collect and manage not only digital documents but also email messages as well. For example, the US Government National Archives and Records Administration in Washington, DC, was faced with the problem of preserving, organising and cataloguing the 16–24 million electronic messages accumulated by the Clinton Administration (Featherstone 2006). The massive growth in popularity of the text message in the 2010s and beyond has presented a further challenge.

The other communication mechanism that has seen explosive growth is social media, the systems of which, by the 2020s, had so many users and so much material that they contained, de facto, significant evidence of personal lives and the culture of our time (Ben-David 2020). There may have been no Archives with a specific mandate to collect such data, but at least one commentator believes that public institutions have a role to play in doing so—despite major issues such as access and privacy needing to be overcome (Marshall 2013).

Yet another huge set of material that arrived with the Icon Age is the World Wide Web with contents even more diverse and voluminous than social media systems. The importance of this material for future reference was recognised as early as 1996 when a USA-based non-profit foundation called The Internet Archive started to collect web pages in its 'Wayback Machine'. When we checked the Wayback

Machine in 2023, it was claiming to hold 808 billion web pages (Internet Archive 2023a). It isn't the only organisation collecting web sites: a study in 2016 identified 68 Web Archiving initiatives across 26 countries (Costa et al. 2016). Despite these efforts, a large amount of material may never make it into any Archive because it is simply too large and elastic; because a substantial number of websites such as family history operations are privately owned and accessible only on a subscription basis (Moss and Thomas 2018), and because a significant number of pages are lost every day (DPC 2023b; Costa et al. 2016).

The Internet Archive does not restrict itself to web sites. In 2025 it also contained over 20 million freely downloadable books and texts (Internet Archive 2025); an Open Library catalogue (an open, editable library catalogue, building towards a web page for every book ever published); several video collections including TV news; and a host of collections uploaded by users, one of the best known being the Live Music Archive (LMA), which contains concert recordings provided by authorised recorders or by the musicians themselves (Ximm 2013). In 2023 the LMA contained over 258,000 recordings (Internet Archive 2023b).

Another Archiving initiative in the arts is the UK National Video Archive of Stage Performance—part of the Victoria and Albert Museum's Theatre and Performance Archives. In 1992, a unique agreement was reached with the Federation of Entertainment unions to enable archival recordings to be made without the payment of fees to the artists. Each member of the performing company must give their permission, and the recordings are strictly confined to Museum premises (Fowler 2004). In 2023 the collection contained recordings of over 300 performances (V&A 2023).

We will turn now to a totally different type of Digital Archive—research data. As Strasser makes clear, the collection of research data simply follows on from a long tradition originating in the collection of specimens—both activities being fundamental to the expansion of scientific knowledge and understanding (Strasser 2012). The potential benefits of sharing research data include the ability for other researchers to scrutinise results and methodologies; the data can be built on in further research, and duplication can be avoided (Oliver and Harvey 2016). This is reflected by the fact that, as discussed earlier in this chapter, the Digital Curation Centre was established to support the management of research data; and the OAIS Open Archival Information Systems Reference Model (which many organisations use to manage all kinds of Digital Archives) was created by the Consultative Committee for Space Data Systems specifically to enable the storage and sharing of Space Data Archives. It is not surprising, therefore, that one of the most extensive examples of a Data Archive is to be found at NASA—the US National Aeronautics and Space Administration. Its Space Science Data Coordinated Archive is accessible via a vast web site that offers information across the following high-level categories: Astrophysics, Heliophysics, Solar System Exploration, and Image Resources (NASA 2023). As one would expect, a wide variety of spreadsheet, database, image and video files are available throughout the site and it has many links to associated Archives.

Many other Research Data Archives exist and are integral to scientific endeavour. In the biological sciences, for example, databases of protein structure and DNA sequences are now an integral part of laboratory experimental work. Various Journals require that their authors store their reported data in a Public Archive (Strasser 2012), as do certain funding agencies. Examples of other Archives can be found in Wikipedia (2023c) and in the University of Bath's Library web page on 'Archiving and sharing data: Choosing an archive' (University of Bath Library 2023).

Its worth noting here that there are other types of Data Archives that may be constructed not for research but for the purpose of surveillance and information gathering. While such databases may be used operationally on a day-to-day basis, they may also be fed data about individuals and groups that are stored long-term and for no immediate purpose. The existence of such archives has given rise to some concern by certain commentators about the general use of data archives to exert power and control over populations (Eliassen 2022).

Turning to the domestic environment, the ability to digitise important documents such as birth and death certificates has not only made it easier to ship them to other organisations when required, but has also provided an alternative way of storing them for the long term, and perhaps passing copies through family generations. Researchers have also been looking into the notion of digital heirlooms, storytelling, and Family Archives in general (Kim 2013). In relation to this, a massive recent surge in interest in using DNA databases to find one's ancestry has spawned a host of Family Archives with associated photographs and documents, largely hosted online (see, for instance, Family Tree DNA[2] and Ancestry[3]).

Over the period that the Icon Age has been impacting the establishment and contents of Archives, the meaning and general understanding of the terms 'Archive' and 'Archivist' may have been further extended and altered beyond the lack of clarity described previously in Sect 2.4. Whether this is due to the impact of IT or not, commentators have noted that it has become commonplace for people to describe themselves as Archivists despite having no qualifications at all (Proctor 2010); for movie plots to involve Archives of truth and hidden knowledge; for newspapers and radio stations to refer to their archives (Ubois 2013); for the term 'Archive' to have *'become a kind of loose signifier for a disparate set of concepts'* (Manof 2004); and for personal papers to have become Personal Achives (Williams et al. 2009). Despite this general fluidity in the meaning of the words, we continue to regard the contents of Archives as being unchanging thereby ruling out the inclusion of general filing systems, operational databases, and the internet. We believe this is the best approach, particularly in the light of concern expressed in some quarters that such entities threaten the integrity of the overall archival practice (Hogan 2015; Laermans and Gielen 2007). For a definitive view of what contemporary Archiving is all about, the international Council on Archives (ICA) and its primary serial publication, COMMA, the International Journal on Archives, are good sources of information. ICA's web site states that 'Archives are the documentary by-product of human activity retained for their long-term value' (ICA 2024).

---

[2] https://www.familytreedna.com/.

[3] https://www.ancestry.com/dna/.

7.6.2 IT Support for Archivists

In order to fully comprehend the range of IT technology that Archives are now drawing upon, it is helpful to understand the impact that IT technology itself has had on society as a whole—archives included. First, as discussed earlier in this chapter, internet users across the world have come to expect easy, online, access to information and, by extension, to archives in general. Second, IT is continually enabling cheaper solutions with more efficient systems requiring fewer people to operate them. Archives, like every other endeavour, are feeling the pressure to embrace such advantages and to operate on lower budgets. A third phenomenon is that the rapid and all-pervasive communications enabled by social media systems has undermined faith in the integrity of knowledge and records of all kinds, with some claiming we are now in a so-called 'post-truth' era—a term chosen by the Oxford English Dictionary as its Word of the Year in 2016 (Duranti 2018; Gauld 2018). One commentator believes that all these changes presage a future for Archivists that abandons custodial preservation activities to paraprofessionals, and instead involves data science, research, education and the identification of materials to include in the collection (Theimer 2018; Duranti 2018). Such activities will involve the support of a variety of IT capabilities including:

- The ability to work across collections and large volumes of records (Ranade 2018).
- The enrichment of content by OCR, speech recognition and image analysis Ranade (2018).
- Automatic identification of connections between records (Ranade 2018).
- Crowdsourcing of content and classification (Theimer 2018).
- The use of blockchains to store and verify records (Lemieux 2018).
- The provision of access by both humans and machines.

To this list we should add the provision of Artificial Intelligence (AI) capabilities to manage collections and to respond to questions about their contents. For example, a special issue of Digital Humanities Quarterly explored the potential of AI to unlock the contents of Image Archives (Jaillant 2024). The long-term impact of AI is likely to be huge if somewhat unpredictable (Gauld 2018) (AI is further explored in Chap. 9).

This, then, is the background to the various specific examples provided below.

A particularly significant technology development for Archivists has been the massive increase in storage capacity, and its reduction in cost, that has occurred in recent years. This applies both to local storage (either within devices such as PCs or servers, or external storage units), and to cloud-based services. So, storage need not be a constraint for all but the very largest Archives—and its easy availability may even have stimulated the retention of extra digital material in Archives (Hogan 2015; Yeo 2018).

As is the case with Libraries, technology support for Archives comprising or including digital items is now widely available in the form of application packages. Some of these are described as Document Management Systems, though these are primarily aimed at supporting the operations of commercial organisations. Packages that are truly aimed at Archives usually comply with the OAIS standard—the revised DPC introductory guide to OAIS identifies half a dozen such packages (Lavoie 2014). However, a wide variety of other suitable software packages are available such as those identified in a Unesco guide to institutional repository software. This compares the following features of 6 different products: Infrastructure, Front-end Design, Content Organisation and Control, Content Discovery, Publication Tools, Reporting, Multimedia, Social Features and Notifications, Interoperability, Authentication, Accessibility, and Preservation (Bankier and Gleason 2014). While most digital repository systems support the specification of metadata based on standards such as Dublin Core and MODS to enable browsing and searching; some may augment or replace those functions by facilities such as free text searching throughout the file titles and contents of text documents, or by pattern searching in music or image collections (Miller 2022; Ernst 2004). Such facilities are what users want and expect of Archives—online access and user interfaces that minimise the effort required to access them (Gauld 2018).

For Archivists wishing to capture and store web sites, a variety of tools are available that will crawl pre-specified web sites periodically and capture their contents. For those organisations not wishing to acquire and operate their own Web Archiving technical infrastructure, several third-party services are available which will do the job for them. The DPC Preservation handbook provides a good summary of both these approaches and some of the available tools and services (DPC 2023b).

Many Archives possessing old/rare hardcopy documents and books are now digitising their items both to protect them from damage due to use or disaster, and to provide easier access to a wider audience. The application of Optical Character Recognition (OCR) software during the digitisation process enables the subsequent searching of the full text. Specialist high-resolution scanning solutions are available on the market to enable documents to be scanned from overhead, and books to be held in a cradle so that they don't have to be flattened. There are also several organisations providing such a service. Examples of both can be found by searching the net using a term such as 'high resolution scanning of rare books'. Small cultural heritage organisations may not have the expertise or funds to go down either of these routes, so it is interesting to note the use of a mobile digitisation kit in a project undertaken by the Metropolitan New York Library Council (METRO). The project spent a maximum of two weeks at each of 10 different organisations—Local Libraries, Archives, Academic Institutions or Historical Societies—digitising specific collections. Descriptions and photographs of the equipment used are provided in the project write-up (METRO 2016).

Providing access to digitised material is usually done through websites, though there are various ways of doing it. An innovative example is to be found in the Virtual Tour of the Public Record Office of Ireland. The office was destroyed at the start of the civil war in 1922. However, this is a 3D reconstruction of the building and in it can be seen some of the documents that were eventually recovered from the rubble or duplicates of those that were lost (Treasury of Ireland 2023). A rather different approach involved the creation of a mobile phone app by the Center for

Public History and Digital Humanities at Cleveland State University. This provided stories about the city and its history and guides users on pre-defined tours of parts of the city or helps them to create their own tours related to particular topics (Tebeau 2016). Such innovations illustrate the myriad ways in which archive contents can be delivered to users.

7.7 IT's Impact on Museum and Gallery Curators

Museum and Gallery Curators collect objects and cultural phenomena and display them for public viewing

7.7.1 New Digital Objects Being Collected by Museums and Gallery Curators

Many Museums and Art Galleries seem to have taken the opportunity to digitise some or all of their collections (Belk 2014). To check this out, we took a Timeout list of the twenty best Museums and Galleries in the world (Dickinson 2021) and visited the website of each one. One of them—the Hermitage in St. Petersburg—was inaccessible. Four of them didn't appear to have collection catalogues online; but all the rest did have online catalogues that displayed digital images of their collections. We assessed eight as probably having images of everything, and seven as having images for more than 80% of their collections. The fifteen had a combined collection of over 1.5 million items (though some 1.2 million of those were from just two institutions—the RijksMuseum in Amsterdam and the Louvre in Paris).

The majority of the images were single views of the objects. However, eleven of the institutions provided some way of magnifying the image—a simple box that could be clicked, or a thumbnail of the image, or multiple images taken from different views of the object. In a few cases, some 3D images were available. When selected, these were typically downloaded to your local browser together with appropriate software (only taking about ten seconds) after which you could manipulate the object very quickly and smoothly in any direction. Just two of the institutions provided a few 3D images which entailed clicking on an image to load the 3D (which only took a few seconds) and then manoeuvring the object with the mouse. However, many other Museums and Galleries do provide 3D images on their websites, including 27 that are listed in a Forbes article (Fink 2020). For example, at the time of writing the Scottish Maritime Museum had over 45 such models (Scottish Maritime Museum 2023); the Smithsonian Institution had 312 models in its online website (Smithsonian 2023a); and Niederösterreich, the Lower Austria website of monuments and Roman Archaeology, had over 1000 models (Niederösterreich 2023).

Only one of all the Museum websites that we looked at presented audio objects. These were recordings of interviews in the National Museum of African American

History and Culture, Washington DC (2023). Video objects were more common, with over 1000 appearing across four of the institutions, but all were just represented as single photos (or a blank image)—none were available to play or download.

While the practice of digitising Museum and Gallery objects might seem to be primarily to enable collections to be viewed remotely, other things have been happening in the Museum and Gallery world over the first 40 years of the Icon Age that have also affected attitudes and action. One is a lack of space to accommodate growing collections (Sola 2004; Macdonald 2006). Another is the growing awareness that it is worthwhile, or perhaps absolutely necessary, to collect some of the vast array of contemporary consumer society objects in order to tell the story of the current era to future generations (Macdonald 2006). This was highlighted by the success of the UK's People's Show's in the early 1990's, the first of which displayed what 63 local residents collected—a hugely diverse range of objects including eggcups, Hindu religious pictures, clip-on furry toys, and tea-towels (Mullen 1994). Another way of collecting contemporary material is to invite the public to contribute items (Terras 2010). For example, the National September 11 Memorial Museum in the USA enables families and friends of victims to contribute photos and other digital artefacts to the commemorative arm of the museum (Drakakis 2020), and the Stockholm County Museum provides a portal for the public of the greater Stockholm area to upload images of their choice (Boogh 2013).

A third phenomenon has been a growing understanding that many objects in current collections should perhaps be back where they were taken from (Addley 2023)—or at least able to be viewed online in their originating countries where appropriate (Belk 2014)—and that Museums and Galleries should get better at telling the political and cultural stories behind the objects that are sometimes just presented as isolated examples of craftsmanship or things that exist (Marshall 2020; Macdonald 2006).

These considerations have suggested to some commentators that Museums should shift their emphasis from collecting physical objects to digitally recording the existence of the objects and the part they play in society (Knell 2004; Macdonald 2006). Such an approach might even turn the process of returning physical objects to their originating peoples into an innovative event eagerly curated and displayed with pride in full multimedia glory.

We should turn now to those digital objects that are at the very heart of the IT revolution: computer programs and games. These too are collected by Museums: for example, the Computer History Museum in California has over 18,000 software items in its catalogue (CHM 2023); and Wikipedia lists over thirty Video Game Museums (Wikipedia 2023d). There are also over 120 Museums around the world collecting the computer hardware upon which such programs run (Wikipedia 2023e), not least The National Museum of Computing at Bletchley Park which operated some of the world's earliest computers during the second world war (The National Museum of Computing 2023). Computers aren't digital objects, but Museums that house physical computers inevitably have to manage and preserve the digital software that operates them, and the combined hardware and software system has to be preserved if video games are to be able to run successfully in the future (Winget and Murray 2009).

There are also several Virtual Computer Museum websites that simply provide photos and information about their exhibits (Wikipedia 2023e). Likewise, there are several Virtual computer game Museums (Wikipedia 2023d). In fact, the arrival of the digital object has enabled many new Museums to be created as entirely virtual entities with no physical location (Wikipedia 2023f). For example, the Digital Atlas of Ancient Life has an extensive collection of fossils and related objects that can be viewed in 3D (Digital Atlas of Ancient Life 2023), and the (virtual) Mobile Phone Museum has photos and information about over 2600 different models (Mobile Phone Museum 2023). All Virtual Museums will, de facto, be managing digital objects of one sort or another.

Another type of digital object that Museums have started to explore are digital art creations designed to be viewed by either Virtual Reality (VR) or Augmented Reality (AR). For example, the Australian Centre for the Moving Image in Melbourne set up an Audience Lab, where AR or VR video-game makers or artists could test out their work with visitors. The first three VR commissions were done with performing-arts practitioners who adapted work they had made to VR. The Centre then commissioned visual artists who already had an established Gallery practice to do their first VR work (Sedgwick 2020). In another example, AcuteArt in London launched Olafur Eliasson's Wunderkammer as a mobile phone app around 2020. This enabled users to download objects that can be virtually placed in the camera image of one's living room. You can, for example, place the sun next to your dog, or your sofa. The app has been used by hundreds of thousands of people (Birnbaum 2020).

The rise of the Digital Museum/Gallery Object has inevitably led to discussion about how the physical should relate to the virtual and the relative merits of each. This debate was given an extra twist when New York's Museum of Modern Art announced it would sell 29 of its physical paintings to provide money for digital art and supporting technology (Malik 2022). Combine that with a view that perhaps records in sound, image and words may be better than unprovenanced, decaying objects (Kavanagh 2004), and the digital would seem to be gaining ground. However, others would argue that objects have the power of the real thing and remain a uniquely tangible primary source (Clayton 2004). As Kenan Malik put it:

> *...no degree of sophistication of a digital experience can reproduce the actuality of seeing a work of art in front of you* (Malik 2022).

Despite that, Museums are continuing to collect digital items and are developing expertise to manage them as illustrated by the 'Toolkit for Managing Digital Collections' produced by the London Museum Documentation Network (Digital Collections Toolkit Working Group 2023).

7.7.2 IT Support for Museum and Gallery Curators

Like most organisations, Museums and Galleries of any size are making use of IT for their backend operational systems such as Accounts, HR and Payroll. To advertise their existence and interact with their customers, most Museums and Galleries have a website. As well as providing information about the organisation and what it offers, this may also manage the sale of tickets to visit the physical location in which its collection is housed. Access to the collection index, and even to a digital version of some or all of its collection contents may also be provided as discussed in the previous section. Like Libraries and Archives, many Museums and Galleries provide such functionality using turnkey software products that enable the definition of metadata, the storage of digitised objects and web access. For collections comprising art or architecture, the VRA's (Visual Resources Association) Core Categories are often used to guide the specification of their metadata (Miller 2022).

The technology to digitise paintings, artworks and museum objects advanced considerably during the first two decades of the twenty-first century. By the 2020s ultra-high-definition images of paintings hanging on walls could be acquired by mounting computer-controlled photographic equipment on special gantries (see, for example, the equipment used by Haltadefinizione (2023)). 3D scanning technology has also made significant advances with several different techniques available to achieve the end result. The broad approach is to take a whole series of photos of the object from every direction, and then to use software to stitch them together. Viewing software is then used to manipulate the object and to display it from any viewpoint (Wikipedia 2023g). Museums and Galleries can acquire the systems and undertake the digitisation activity themselves, or can contract the work out to specialist organisations.

Museums and Galleries are increasingly employing a range of IT systems such as mobile applications, websites, audio guides, and social networking sites, to aid the presentation and appreciation of their collections (Scaglia and Falakeh 2023). These can include displays presenting information and videos about the collection; and self-guided audio tours listened to through headphones. Virtual tours of the physical buildings and their contents had also become available in several institutions by the 2020s (Wilson A 2020). Augmented Reality or virtual reality displays are also being explored to enhance the visitor experience by providing information relating to the object that is in view or bringing objects to life (Neuburger and Egger 2018). This was already being explored in several of the Museums we studied in the early 2010s [RM:Acrop; Espace]. These may employ headsets, smart glasses or even mobile phones. For example, in 2021, the Muséum National d'Histoire Naturelle in Paris started a project that enabled visitors to use Microsoft's Hololens headset to come face to face with extinct animals. Meanwhile, the Smithsonian has a downloadable app that, when the mobile phone is pointed at some of the skeletons in the Bone Hall, puts skin and muscle on the skeletons and shows how the animals might have moved (Charr 2024; Smithsonian 2023b). There has also been research on providing the ability to create virtual exhibitions comprising objects from multiple repositories (Kiourt 2016).

As well as using digital technology to present their own objects to the public, some Museums are providing network access to their combined digital collections. As discussed in the section on libraries, the DPLA (Digital Public Library of America) aggregates metadata from Libraries, Museums and institutions around the country

(DPLA 2025), and in Europe, Europeana displays digital cultural heritage material drawn from over 2000 different institutions across Europe (Europeana 2025; Capurro et al. 2023). Such initiatives are only likely to increase as more and more objects are digitised, though progress may be slowed by a lack of suitable transdisciplinary data standards and data models (Sturm et al. 2022).

Beyond this, most Museums and Galleries have some sort of computer-controlled security systems to protect their collections. These can include video surveillance cameras in the viewing areas, a central control room in which the video streams are displayed, and burglar alarm systems throughout the building.

Finally, we shouldn't forget IT support for one of the most important elements of a Museum/Gallery's operation: the shop. Stock Control and Point of Sale systems support the physical shop; and equivalent systems support the online version within the organisation's website along with systems to support order picking, packaging, delivery and returns. In addition, many institutions now enable customers to buy replicas of some of their objects, and these are usually produced using either 2D or 3D printers, which may be operated in house, or, more likely, by external contractors.

7.8 IT's Impact on Private Curators

Private Curators are individuals and organisations that build valuable collections of original, fine or rare objects for their own use

7.8.1 New Digital Objects Being Collected by Private Curators

Almost by definition, Private Curators continue to be focussed on physical objects in the Icon Age. However, they may digitise their objects, not because of a lack of space (they either have, or can acquire, as much space as they need), but primarily for insurance purposes and/or to be able to view the objects on digital devices. Some collectors, however, may simply want to share their collections with a wider circle of friends or the public at large in order to gain respect and admiration and acknowledgement of the collection's significance or value (Scaraboto 2016).

There is, however, one new type of digital object that some Private Curators are collecting: the NFT (Non-Fungible Token). As described in Sect. 6.5.6, an NFT is a data file that provides a unique certificate of ownership and that is held on a distributed database called a Blockchain. While NFTs can represent both digital and physical objects, and can be used for a diverse range of items such as virtual objects in computer games and sports collectibles, Private Curators in the early 2020s were primarily collecting NFTs of images. For example, in 2021 an NFT by the artist known as Beeple, sold for $69.3 million at Christie's (Nadini et al. 2021).

As well as producing a new type of object (the NFT), the Icon Age has also produced a new type of Private Curator: companies or corporations who provide social media services. Their primary business is: the provision of facilities that enable users to create and publish their own material and to interact with each other; the harvesting and analysis of user data for commercial purposes; and the management of advertising and other types of services for clients. All data associated with these activities can be considered Accumulations as discussed in Sect. 7.3. However, the data that users create and place inside social media platforms are of no intrinsic interest to social media organisations. They curate it because it is what users want, and so that they can harvest user data from it. Yet, these vast collections of user-generated material contain detailed tapestries of contemporary human life. Unfortunately, commercial operations are driven by commercial considerations, so if it is no longer viable to maintain the contents of a social media system, commercial organisations will have no compunction about simply eliminating it. Such was the fate of some early examples of sites with User-Generated Content—namely GeoCities, Friendster, and Google Video (Hogan 2015). If users want to be sure they will have long-term access to the material they input to social media systems, they have to make their own backup arrangements and store the material elsewhere. Unfortunately, the status of social media content is further complicated by Data Privacy regulations which, while being a good thing for individual users, disincentivise service providers from making such content available for research or from Curating it long-term. An example of this was when Facebook removed the ability of researchers to extract large amounts of data for analysis, due to the CambridgeAnalytica scandal, when it appeared that such data had been used to influence elections (Ben-David 2020). An exception to this was the Library of Congress acquisition of the Twitter Archive in 2010 (Redwine 2015), though this may have been achieved simply because the many issues around social media content had not yet surfaced at that time.

7.8.2 IT Support for Private Curators

Private Curators with larger collections of physical objects may maintain a sophisticated digital index in a specialised application. However, whatever the size of the collection, the objects will almost certainly be listed in some form or other together with their digitised images for insurance purposes.

The other main use that Private Curators may make of IT is in protecting their collected physical objects. The more expensive the objects, the more sophisticated the security measures are likely to be. They may range from video surveillance systems to locking systems, motion sensors, pressure pads, laser beams, alarms, and other sophisticated detectors or mechanisms. Whatever systems are used, they are likely to be computer controlled.

7.9 IT's Impact on Amateur Collectors

Amateur Collectors decide what they want to collect as a hobby, and then seek out and assemble appropriate pieces at their leisure

7.9.1 New Digital Objects Being Collected by Amateur Collectors

As a preface to this discussion about the impact of IT on Amateur Collectors, we note that the popularity of collecting as a hobby appears to be unabated in the 2020s. Mardon and Belk's 2018 paper repeats previous findings that about one third of consumers claim to be collectors, and that:

> '…collecting has been found to occur in virtually all cultures and eras, and across ages and genders', (Mardon and Belk 2018).

Furthermore, there was no shortage of 2020s articles on the subject when we conducted an internet search for 'Collecting as a Hobby'. One of the articles we came across was '200 + Cool Things to Collect' (Don 2023), which included some very unusual items ranging from Accordions to Zoo Warning Signs, though there were only two comprising any kind of digital object—Computers and Video Games. However, a 2010 paper reported that many Amateur Collectors were creating pools of digitised objects ranging from dress making patterns to book cover artwork, as well as using blogs, wikis or photo sharing sites. Its survey of 100 such collections identified that the contents were always beyond the scope of traditional memory institutions and that they would not be available at all unless they were online (Terras 2010). Other papers document how people are digitising old comics (Wright 2008), and some music fans specialising in rare or bootlegged material have taken advantage of the ability to store, manipulate and share music digitally (Anderton 2016).

This, of course, is what we intuitively know in the mid-2020s: the internet is awash with digitised images and information on just about any type of object you care to mention. However, an increasing number of Amateur Collectors are collecting Born Digital material. A 2022 online article recounts how an individual, during the Covid pandemic, collected about 1600 bookmarked links separated into over 20 folders with various tags; a collection of articles, essays and interviews in the course of a project named '100 days of things I've learnt'; and a collection of random fun links, sites and videos in a project called '100 Days of Just for Fun' (Tang 2022).. Perhaps these give an indication of what might be going on out there: there's certainly no shortage of diverse content within the net and people who are using it.

Two particularly prominent types of Born Digital objects being collected by Amateurs in the 2010s and beyond are digital objects within video games and virtual worlds and Digital Trading Cards (Mardon and Belk 2018). The collecting of digital objects in video games and virtual worlds is on a very large scale simply because video games are played by billions of people as described in Sect. 7.1. Of course, not every video game has things to be collected and not every player sets out to collect in-game digital objects. Nevertheless, many companies make huge amounts of revenue from the sale of digital objects. For example, even in 2010, the revenue tables from Zynga, the company that sold Farmville and other simulation games, showed revenue of over half a billion dollars, the vast majority of which came from the sale of virtual goods (Bailenson 2018); and, more recently, the Fortnite game, from its launch in 2017 to the end of 2021, generated an estimated $20 billion in revenue, the majority of which was from sales of digital avatars, backpacks, and dances (also known as "emotes")(Ball 2022). A 2016 survey identified the following categories of things that video game users collect: rewards, modifications to game rules, and personalisation items such as clothing. The specific types of objects that were collected were GEAR (34:4% of the responses), CRITTERS (21.2%), MISCELLANEOUS objects which included object types unique to a specific game and sets of finite collectible objects (20.6%), CHARACTERS (7.4%), SKINS (7.4%), VEHICLES (4.2%), and INFORMATION (2.1%) (Toups et al. 2016). Such items are often provided in so-called loot boxes which are bought without knowing what they contain. Some commentators believe this is an unregulated form of gambling because the items can also be bought or sold in online marketplaces, with some items fetching thousands of dollars; so, players may spend large amounts of money in the hope of acquiring an object which can be sold at a profit (Davies 2024).

An example of digital trading cards is Topps Trading cards which started selling physical cards in the 1950s, and entered the market for digital cards in 2012. Over the next seven years their card sets included various sports (such as baseball and soccer), The Walking Dead, Marvel, Disney, and Star Wars (Wikipedia 2023h). It was a lucrative business valued at $329 million in the US in 2015 compared to $1.4 billion for physical cards (Cook 2016). Topps isn't the only company selling digital trading cards. Its competitors include Panini and Upper Deck. The latter offered a hybrid solution in the 2020s with the initial sale of e-packs of digital cards being supplemented by the option to have the physical cards shipped to you at any time (Upper Deck 2023a).

While on the surface, the reproducibility, ease of transmission, intangibility, and durability would seem to reduce the attractiveness of collecting digital objects, a variety of marketing techniques have been developed to address these characteristics. They include limiting the quantities available, limiting the time period of availability, requiring time, effort and skill to find objects, and providing metadata to record object histories (Mardon and Belk 2018).

The newest type of digital object that an Amateur Collector might encounter is an NFT (Non-Fungible Token) as described in the preceding section. All three of the trading card companies mentioned above were selling NFT versions of their cards in the early 2020s. In April 2023, Upper Deck announced its NFT trading site Evolution and included in the announcement that:

> Today's release of Preview Packs gives a sneak peek of three upcoming Fleer Showcase drops and boasts 25 top players from the original 2015-16 product. Each of the 9,000 packs contain one NHL® and NHLPA licensed NFT trading card limited to 320 or fewer. Collectors

> who complete the Base Set can earn an Evolution® Update Achievement Set. (Upper Deck 2023b).

In May 2023, the Topps NFT website was reporting 12,800 owners and $125.3 K sales; and encouraging readers to:

> Celebrate YOUR fandom. Digital collectibles offer you a chance to collect key moments and star players that define a baseball season – from Opening Day through the Postseason. Chase Facsimile Signatures, Slabs, and more to build the ultimate Topps digital collection. (ToppsNFT 2023).

Also in May 2023, Panini was offering 2022–23 Panini NFT Prizm Basketball Packs (145,002 packs left) at $10 each, as well as seven exclusive 1 of 1 s 'Legendary' cards of NFL and NBA players at $71,102.04 and dropping at intervals until a sale is made (Panini, 2023) (at $71,000, a buyer might be considered to be more of a Private Curator than a mere Amateur Collector).

Of course, Trading Cards aren't the only type of NFTs being collected by Amateurs. OpenSea, which claimed to be the world's first and largest digital marketplace for crypto collectibles and non-fungible tokens (NFTs), was offering items in the following categories when we looked at it in May 2023: Art; Gaming; Memberships; PFPs (Profile Pictures); Photography; Domain Names; Music; Sports Collectibles; and Virtual Worlds. Completed transactions over the previous 2 min were on too many screens to count (no overall Tables were provided) and sale prices seemed to vary between 1c to $3600. However, there was no way to identify if humans or bots were undertaking these transactions. The sales were being recorded in one or other of the following eight Blockchains: Arbitrum, Avalanche, BNB Chain, Ethereum, Klaytn, Optimism, Polygon, and Solana (OpenSea 2023). Another NFT marketplace, VeVe, offers even more sophisticated objects:

> VeVe digital collectibles are 3D sculptures that live in the digital space and are viewed, displayed and interacted with through VR and AR' and 'VeVe's Augmented Reality allows you to scan your own surroundings, then tap to drop your digital comic collectible in AR. Move, rotate and scale your digital collectibles and comics to make them 1:1 size, then capture it all in a photo. (VeVe (2023)

The details in these last two paragraphs are provided merely to illustrate this brave new digital object, rather than to provide any sound statistics or survey of capabilities. An indication of the potential of NFTs to impact collecting in general is the collaboration between VeVe and Stanley Gibbons, the world's longest established stamp dealer, to issue 8468 NFTs of various Penny Black stamps. Apparently, these sold out within minutes (Stanley Gibbons 2024; VeVe 2024).

Coming back to more mundane digital objects, the Amateur Collector may also have reason to digitise some or all of a physical collection by either photographing or scanning the items. This may be simply to have a record in case of disaster, or perhaps to have some images to look back on if the collection is disposed of. Another reason might be to create a display as Wilson has done: pages of a stamp collection with country titles written by his father, were scanned and assembled in a self-published book of which three physical copies were made, one to keep for himself and two to provide to each of his two great-grandchildren (see Fig. 7.5), accompanied by an e-book version (Wilson 2024). In fact, the latter is an example of another particular type of digital collection—the digital legacy. Individuals are assembling together sets of digital material to pass on to their heirs (Doyle and Brubaker 2023). Such collections may suffer even more than physical objects from the turn-off syndrome: at some point, the size of the collection and/or the opaqueness of its contents, may tip the recipient's attitude from curiosity to disinterest. Furthermore, Icon Age people expect to be able to search digital material, so bequeathed digital collections without adequate metadata may be an even bigger turn-off. Such legacy collections might never be enjoyed and may just be retained as background answer machines (searched by AI) unless their owners undertake some specific project that necessitates their consultation.

An associated legacy phenomenon is the online memorial in websites or social media systems, in which information, memories and thoughts about a deceased individual are collected together and remain accessible for an indefinite period (Doyle and Brubaker 2023).

Fig. 7.5 Wilson's book of scanned images of a stamp collection produced for grand-children

7.9.2 IT Support for Amateur Collectors

The book shown in Fig. 7.5 includes some pages at the front describing how IT had affected Wilson's stamp collecting hobby and how it had been used to facilitate the production of the book (Wilson 2022). We will use these as the basis for the following notes about IT support for Amateur Collectors:

Club communications: Most communications from clubs and societies relating to Amateur Collecting now come via email and/or text messaging.

Auctions: Many auctions of collectibles are now online, though in some cases physical catalogues are still sent out.

Dealers: Many dealers have their own websites listing the items they are selling and their prices. This makes it easier to find and buy items and to compare prices.

Buying and selling: The online buy/sell auction sites (of which eBay is a prime example) have made a huge impact on the Amateur Collector. They make it much easier to find items and to obtain the cheapest prices in a worldwide marketplace (Ellis and Haywood 2006). Equally significant is that such sites make it possible for Amateur Collectors to sell items—particularly important if people buy bulk lots of items and wish to retain only a few of them.

Identifying objects: Some sort of information about hard-to-identify items can usually be found on the internet. The ability to put an image into a search engine and have it find similar items can improve the chance of success.

Determining veracity and quality: There may be web sites on the internet dedicated to listing forgeries and providing advice on how to identify them. Some such sites facilitate conversations between users, so a question about veracity can be asked. Alternatively, similar items can be found on the net and their images expanded enabling a comparison with the item in question.

Recording collection information: For certain hobbies, such as book collecting, dedicated mobile phone apps can be downloaded to record details of a collection. However, Word processing, spreadsheet and database applications enable collection information of all types to be compiled and indexed in any way a collector wants. This may include consolidating metadata information from different collections into a single index to facilitate management and searching (Wilson 2023c).

On-line catalogues: Detailed catalogues of the items being collected may be available online, either for free or for the payment of an annual fee.

Creating a display: The ability to digitise objects using photography or scanning, enables a whole host of possibilities for displaying collections of either physical or digital items, or a combination of the two. These include screen savers that present different images on screen at pre-determined intervals; posters and collages of images, which can be created on a computer and then sent to a specialist photo printing company for printing on paper, canvas, cushions or a variety of other materials or objects; books that can be compiled using word processing or specialist desktop publishing software, downloaded and printed by specialist online book publishers; and websites that can be used to display whole collections together with associated information about the objects.

A detailed study of 70 vinyl record collectors identifies the use of similar IT support mechanisms (Shuker 2010) where it was found that:

- Collectors now seem to be comfortable with hunting and purchasing records via the internet.
- Websites, some with offerings from dealers, enable thousands of collectible records to be browsed through. Online rare record and memorabilia auctions abound. Online discographies and collector groups informs collectors about what is available and new releases, and which aids the process of record buying through establishing what is available and comparative shopping.
- About half of the 70 collectors interviewed had no catalogue, but eight had more thorough cataloguing practices using a mix of computer databases and with printed lists.
- Collectors are using websites and You-Tube to show off their collections, and to share their knowledge about how to maintain their collections and where to find records.

It is also important to recognise the widespread and heavy use being made of social media systems to enable collectors of specific types of objects to communicate and socialise together, and perhaps to undertake elements of all the activities already described in this section, as illustrated by an investigation into collectors of fountain pens (Ferasso et al. 2022), and a paper describing how collectors of Melissa shoes share their Curation activities via You-Tube videos (Scaraboto et al. 2016). Indeed, it has been suggested that such systems enable a group of like-minded collectors to collaborate across all collecting practices. For example, the practice of enabling any member of a group to categorise or tag items to produce a so-called Folksomony (as opposed to a taxonomy), has become a widespread phenomenon (Belk 2014).

Not all Amateurs want to share their collections with the world; many want to be able to enjoy their digital collections on their own private screens. Software applications enabling the management and display of a variety of specific types of objects are available—notably for books and photos. Other more generic apps are also available. For example, Wilson has used the SideBooks app extensively to display books, mementos, publications, reports and awards. Functionality specifically to support the collection and display of photos of physical objects by Amateur Collectors, has also been explored by a team from UCL and Microsoft Research Labs. They developed the Thinga.Me app, which was tried out in 2016 by over 500 active users who added over 5000 objects in 650 different collections. Users particularly liked the feature enabling them to 'cut out' the objects concerned from the photos they had taken (Harrison et al. 2017).

Finally, various tools are now available to support digital legacies (Yamauchi et al. 2021). Digital Legacy Management Services are designed to help individuals plan what happens to their collections of digital material after death. Examples that were advertising their services in 2024 were SecureSafe, Everplans, and DGLegacy. Online Memorial Services provide facilities for people to collect together information and memories about someone they know who has died. Examples documented in a 2021 review included Memories, HeavenAddress, and ForeverMissed (Peter 2022).

References

Abbot D (2010) What is digital curation? Digital Curation Centre, Edinburgh

Abrams D, Baecker R, Chignell M (1998) Information archiving with bookmarks: personal web space construction and organization. In: Proceedings of the SIGCHI conference on human factors in computing systems CHI 98, Los Angeles, USA, 18–23 April 1998. ACM, pp 41–48

Addley E (2023) How one Derbyshire museum took initiative in returning Indigenous artefacts. The Guardian, Manchester, UK, 13 Feb 2023

Anderton C (2016) Sonic artefacts: "Record collecting" in the digital age. IASPM J 6(1):85–103

Ashenfelder M (2015) How academics manage their personal digital and paper information in their digital work space. Post in the signal blog, Library of Congress, 07 July 2015. https://blogs.loc.gov/thesignal/2015/07/how-academics-manage-their-personal-digital-and-paper-information-in-their-digital-work-space/. Accessed 29 Nov 2024

Bailenson J (2018) Experience on demand. W. W. Norton & Company

Ball M (2022) The Metaverse and how it will revolutionize everything. Liveright Publishing Corporation

Balogh M, Billingsley DP, Kennan MA (2022) Attributes of personal electronic records. Arch Manuscr 50(1):47–70

Bankier JG, Gleason K (2014) Institutional repository software comparison. UNESCO. https://unesdoc.unesco.org/ark:/48223/pf0000227115. Accessed 30 Nov 2024

Banks R (2013) Our technology heritage. In: Hawkins DT (ed) Personal archiving: preserving our digital heritage. Information Today Inc.

BBC (2023) Sort your life out. https://www.bbc.co.uk/programmes/m00116n4. Accessed 31 May 2023

Belk RW (2014) Art collecting as personal and public practice in a digital age. In: O'Reilly D, Rentschler R, Kirchner T (eds) The Routledge companion to arts marketing. Routledge, London, pp 243–255

Bellamy C, Arnold M, Gibbs M, Nansen B, Kohn T (2014) Consumer issues for planning and managing digital legacies. IEEE Technol Soci Mag 33(3):26–31

Ben-David A (2020) Counter-archiving Facebook. Eur J Commun 35(3):249–264

Bigelow J (2021) The steward of book history in the digital age: the struggles and rewards of collecting e-Books for special collections institutions. RBM A J Rare Books Manuscr Cultural Heritage 22(2):63–70

Birnbaum D (2020) Museums & technology. In: Szanto A (ed) The future of the museum—28 dialogues. Hatje Cantz Verlag GmbH, pp 255–264

Boogh E (2013) Samtidsbild/Contemporary Images – a method of collecting vernacular photography in the digital age. Museum Int 65(1–4):54–67

Broekhuijsen M, van den Hoven E, Markopoulos P (2017) From PhotoWork to PhotoUse: exploring personal digital photo activities. Behav Inform Technol 36(7):754–767

Byers R (2021) The private library. Oak Knoll Press

Cahoy ES (2013) Faculty members as archivists: Personal Archiving practices in the academic environment. In: Hawkins DT (ed) Personal archiving: preserving our digital heritage. Information Today Inc.

Capterra (2023) Library automation software. https://www.capterra.co.uk/directory/30022/library-automation/software. Accessed 07 May 2023

Capurro C, Plets G, Verheul, J (2023) Digital heritage infrastructures as cultural policy instruments: Europeana and the enactment of European citizenship. Int J Cultural Policy 1–21. https://doi.org/10.1080/10286632.2023.2193401

Chad K (2021) Trends in the library technology market—a UK perspective. CILIP website, 17 Feb 2021. https://www.cilip.org.uk/news/news.asp?id=552340&hhSearchTerms=%22chad%22Accessed. Accessed 19 Mar 2025

Charr M (2024) How Museums are using Augmented Reality. Museum Next, 10 April, 2024. https://www.museumnext.com/article/how-museums-are-using-augmented-reality/. Accessed 30 Nov 2024

CHM (2023) Catalog search—Search the Catalog 'Software'. https://www.computerhistory.org/collections/search/?s=software&f=software.Accessed 22 May 2023

Clayton N (2004) Folk devils in our midst? Collecting from 'deviant' groups. In Knell SJ (ed) Museums and the future of collecting, 2nd ed. Ashgate, Farnham

Coleman CN, Engel C, Thorsen H (2022) Subjectivity and discoverability: an exploration with images. In: Hervieux S, Wheatley A (eds) The rise of AI: implications and applications of artificial intelligence in academic libraries, Association of College and research Libraries, pp 83–93

Cook J (2016) Thousands of people are spending money on virtual trading cards that don't actually exist. Business Insider, 02 Sep 2016. https://www.businessinsider.com/people-are-spending-hundreds-on-virtual-trading-cards-that-dont-actually-exist-2016-8. Accessed on 30 Nov 2024

Costa M, Gomes D, Silva MJ (2016) The evolution of web archiving. Int J Digit Libr 18:191–205

Davies R (2024) 'It's rotting young people's brains': the murky world of gambling in video games. The Guardian, Manchester, UK, 04 Feb 2024

DCC (2023) DCC Website, https://www.dcc.ac.uk/. Accessed 12 May 2023

De Grazia (2023) Welcome to all the works of Alfred de Grazia. https://grazian-archive.com/index_2.htm. Accessed 03 June 2023

Dekker H, Ferria AG, Mandal I (2022) URI Libraries' AI Lab - evolving to meet the needs of students and research communities. In: Hervieux S, Wheatley A (eds) The rise of AI: implications and applications of artificial intelligence in academic libraries. Association of College and research Libraries, pp 15–34

Dickinson S (2021) The 20 best museums and galleries in the world. TimeOut, 21October 2021, https://www.timeout.com/arts-and-culture/best-museums-and-galleries-in-the-world. Accessed 30 Nov2024

Digital Atlas of Ancient Life (2023) Virtual Collection. https://www.digitalatlasofancientlife.org/vc/. Accessed 22 May 2023

Digital Collections Toolkit Working Group (2023) Toolkit for managing digital collections. London Museum Documentation Network, April 2023. Collections Trust website. https://collectionstrust.org.uk/resource/toolkit-for-managing-digital-collections/. Accessed 30 Nov 2024

Don (2023) Collecting ideas: 200+ cool things to collect. HobbyLark, 09 May 2023. https://hobbylark.com/collecting/things-to-collect. Accessed 29 May 2023

Doyle DT, Brubaker JR (2023) Digital legacy: a systematic literature review. In: Proceedings of the ACM on human computer interaction, 7, CSCW2, Article 268 (October 2023). ACM, pp 1–26

DPC (2023a) Digital preservation handbook. https://www.dpconline.org/handbook. Accessed 01 May 2023

DPC (2023b) Content-specific preservation: web-archiving. https://www.dpconline.org/handbook/content-specific-preservation/web-archiving. Accessed 16 May 2023

DPLA (2025) Frequently Asked Questions. https://dp.la/about/frequently-asked-questions. Accessed 19 March 2025

Drakakis A (2020) From the material to the digital: reflections on collecting and exhibiting grief at the 9/11 memorial museum. In: Zucker EM, Simon DJ (eds) Mass violence and memory in the digital age. Palgrave Macmillan Memory Studies

Duranti (2018) Whose truth? Records and archives as evidence in the era of post-truth and disinformation. In: Brown C (ed) Archival futures. Facet Publishing

Edwards E, Morton C (2015) Between art and information: Introduction. In: Edwards E, Morton C (eds) Photographs, museums, collections: between art and information. Bloomsbury Academic, pp 3–23

Elgan M (2016) Lifelogging is dead (for now). Computerworld, 04 April 2016

Eliassen KO (2022) The archives of michel foucault. https://www.academia.edu/5473534/Archives_of_Michel_Foucault. Accessed 01 Dec 2022

Ellis RM, Haywood A (2006) Virtual radiophile (163*): eBay and the changing collecting practices of the UK Vintage radio community. In: Hillis K, Petit M, Epley N (eds) Everyday eBay: culture, collecting and desire. Routledge, New York, pp 45–61

Ernst W (2004) The Archive as Metaphor. Open 7:46–52

ESA (2024) 2024 Essential facts about the U.S. video game industry. https://www.theesa.com/resources/essential-facts-about-the-us-video-game-industry/2024-data/. Accessed 28 Nov 2024

Europeana (2025) Europeana. https://www.europeana.eu/en/about-us. Accessed 19 March 2025

Everplans (2023) The top 10 online memorial websites. https://www.everplans.com/articles/the-top-10-online-memorial-websites. Accessed 03 June 2023

Exploding topics (2025) How Many Gamers Are There? (New 2024 Statistics). 23 February 2025. https://explodingtopics.com/blog/number-of-gamers. Accessed 18 March 2025

Fastrez P, Jacques J (2015) managing references by filing and tagging, human interface and the management of information. Information and knowledge design. Springer

Featherstone M (2006) Archive. Theory Cult Soc 23(2–3):591–596

Fieldhouse M (2012) The processes of collection management. In: Fieldhouse M, Marshall A (eds) Collection development in the digital age. Facet publishing, London, pp 27–44

Ferguson A (2022) 7 Reasons why people still prefer listening to vinyl records. Decker & Sons website, 16 Mar 2022. https://www.deckersons.com/blog/why-people-prefer-vinyl. Accessed 27 Nov 2024

Ferasso M, Gallon S, Pauli J (2022) Social interactions and collecting practices mediated by the cyberspace: a nethnography with fountain pens collectors. Res Soc Develop 11(9):1–13

Fink C (2020) Realistic 3D objects from famous museums. Free. Forbes, 25 Feb 2020. https://www.forbes.com/sites/charliefink/2020/02/25/realistic-3d-objects-from-famous-museums-free/?sh=21a0af3d5bf4. Accessed 30 Nov 2024

Fisher D, Brush AJ, Gleave E, Smith MA (2006) Revisiting Whittaker & Sidner's "Email Overload" ten years later. In: Proceedings of the 2006 20th anniversary conference on Computer supported cooperative work, Banff, Canada, 4–8 Nov 2006. ACM, pp 309–312

Fowler J (2004) Collecting live performance. In: Knell SJ (ed) Museums and the future of collecting. Second Edition, Ashgate, Farnham, UK

Frohlich DM, Kuchinsky A, Pering C, Don A, Ariss S (2002) Requirements for Photoware. In: Proceedings of the CSCW'02 Conference on computer supported cooperative work, New Orleans, Louisiana, USA, 16–20 Nov 2002. ACM, pp 166–175. https://www.g2.com/categories/configuration-management. Accessed 22 July 2023

G2 (2023) Best Configuration Management Tools, https://www.g2.com/categories/configuration-management. Accessed on 22nd July 2023

Gadd E, Covey DT (2019) What does 'green' open access mean? Tracking twelve years of changes to journal publisher self-archiving policies. J Librariansh Inf Sci 51(1):106–122

Gauld C (2018) The end of archival ideas? In: Brown C (ed) Archival futures. Facet Publishing

Gomez J (2008) Print is dead: books in our digital age. Macmillan, Basingstoke

Grenoble LA, Whaley LJ (2002) Archiving electronic journals. Linguistic Discovery 1(2)

Haines D (2023) How Many ebooks are there in the Kindle Store on Amazon? https://justpublishingadvice.com/how-many-kindle-ebooks-are-there/. Accessed 02 May 2023

Harari YN (2016) Homo Deus. Harvill Secker

Haltadefinizione (2023) We digitize works of art. https://www.haltadefinizione.com/en/we-digitize-works-of-art/. Accessed 23 May 2023

Harris A, Cooper M (2019) Mobile phones: Impacts, challenges, and predictions. Human Behav Emerg Technol 1:15–17

Harrison DBP, Banks R, Regan T, Grayson M (2017) Presenting physical things digitally: new collecting practices. In: Proceedings of the 3rd Biennial research through design conference RTD2017, Edinburgh, UK, 22–24 Mar 2017, article 25, pp 389–405

Hawkins DT (2013) Software and services for personal archiving. In: Hawkins DT (ed) Personal archiving: preserving our digital heritage. Information Today Inc.

Henderson S, Srinivasan A (2011) Filing, piling & structuring: strategies for personal document management. In: 44th Hawaii international conference on system sciences, 04–07 Jan. IEEE

Hern A (2018) Are you a 'cyberhoarder'? Five ways to declutter your digital life—from emails to photos. The Guardian, Manchester, UK, 10 Oct 2018

Hervieux S, Wheatley A (2022) Introduction. In: Hervieux S, Wheatley A (eds) The rise of AI: implications and applications of artificial intelligence in academic libraries. Association of College and research Libraries, pp ix–xii

Higgins S (2008) The DCC curation lifecycle model. The Int J Digital Curation 3(1)

Higgins S (2011) Digital curation: the emergence of a new discipline. Int J Digital Curation 2:78–88

Hogan M (2015) The archive as dumpster. Pivot 4(l):7–38

ICA (2024) What are archives? International Council on Archives web site—About us. https://www.ica.org/discover-archives/what-are-archives/. Accessed 16 Oct 2024

IMDB (2023) Sort your life out. https://www.imdb.com/title/tt14254752/. Accessed 31 May 2023

Internet Archive (2023a) Wayback machine. https://archive.org/web/. Accessed 16 May 2023

Internet Archive (2023b) Live music archive. https://archive.org/details/etree. Accessed 16 May 2023

Internet Archive (2025) eBooks and Texts. https://archive.org/details/texts.. Accessed 20 March 2025

ITU (2022) Measuring digital development: facts and figures 2022. https://www.itu.int/hub/publication/d-ind-ict_mdd-2022/. Accessed 01 May 2023

Jaillant L (2024) Introduction to the special issue: using visual AI applied to digital archives. Digital Human Quart 18(3). https://www.digitalhumanities.org/dhq/vol/18/2/000752/000752.html. Accessed 30 Nov 2024

JISC (2023) JiscMail - DIGITAL-PRESERVATION@JISCMAIL.AC.UK. The Subscribe/Unsubscribe page for the JISC Digital Preservation email list. https://www.jiscmail.ac.uk/cgi-bin/WA-JISC.exe?SUBED1=DIGITAL-PRESERVATION&A=1. Accessed 12 May 2023

JSTOR (2024) What's in JSTOR. https://about.jstor.org/whats-in-jstor/. Accessed 08 Jan 2024

Kaba S, Özalpman D (2021) Non-theatrical film experience and film collecting practices in the digital age. Quart Rev Film Video 38(4):354–368

Kalnikaitėa V, Whittaker S (2011) A Saunter down memory lane: digital reflection on personal mementos. Int J Human-Comput Stud 69(5):298–310

Kavanagh G (2004) Collecting from the era of memory, myth and delusion. In: Knell SJ (ed.) Museums and the future of collecting, 2nd ed. Ashgate, Farnham

Kaye J, Vertesi J, Avery S, Dafoe A, David S, Onaga L, Rosero I, Pinch T (2006) To have and to hold: exploring the personal archive. In: Proceedings of the CHI 2006 conference, Montréal, Québec, Canada, April 22–28. ACM, pp 275–284

Kelner M (1993) Exchange with mart: Martin Kelner's theory of the meaning of life: Part 3—The importance of Stuff. The online archive of the independent newspaper, 14 May1993, 23:02 BST. https://www.independent.co.uk/money/exchange-with-mart-martin-kelner-s-theory-of-the-meaning-of-life-part-3-the-importance-of-stuff-2323050.html. Accessed 05 May 2024

Ketelaar E (1999) Archivalisation and archiving. Arch Manuscr 26(1):54–61

Khoo CSG, Luyt B, Caroline E, Jamila O (2007) How users organize electronic files on their workstations in the office environment: a preliminary study of personal information organization behaviour. Inform Res 11(2)

Kim S (2013) Landscape of personal digital archiving activities and research. In: Hawkins DT (ed) Personal archiving: preserving our digital heritage. Information Today Inc.

Kirk DS, Sellen A (2010) On human remains: values and practice in the home archiving of cherished objects. ACM Trans Comput Human Interact 17(3)(Article 10):10.1–10.43
Kiourt C, Koutsoudis A, Pavlidis G (2016) DynaMus: a fully dynamic 3D virtual museum framework. J Cult Herit 22:984–991
Knell SJ (2004) Altered values: searching for a new collecting. In: Knell SJ (ed) Museums and the future of collecting, 2nd ed. Ashgate, Farnham, UK
Kung S, Lapid MI, Philbrick KL (2004) an electronic filing cabinet for "classic" articles and other teaching materials: something old, something new. Acad Psychiatry 28(2):140–143
Ladd M (2015) Access and use in the digital age: a case study of a digital postcard collection. New Rev Acad Librariansh 21(2):225–231
Laermans R, Gielen P (2007) The archive of the digital an-archive. Image and Narrative 17(April)
Lane G (2023) 12,795 possessions! Meet the woman who photographed every single thing she owns, The Guardian, Manchester, UK, 20 July 2023
Lavoie B (2014) the open archival information system (OAIS) reference model: introductory guide, 2nd ed. Digital preservation coalition. https://www.dpconline.org/docs/dpc-technology-watch-publications/technology-watch-reports-1/1359-dpctw14-02/file. Accessed 30 Nov 2024
Lee H (2000) What is a collection? J Am Soc Inform Sci 51(12):1106–1113
Lemieux V (2018) The future of archives as networked, decentralised, autonomous and global. In Brown C (ed) Archival futures. Facet Publishing
Lewis DW (2013) From stacks to the web: the transformation of academic library collecting. Coll Res Libr 74(2):159–176
Library of Congress (2023) Personal archiving. page on the Library of Congress website. https://digitalpreservation.gov/personalarchiving/. Accessed 12 May 2023
Lindley S, Marshall CC, Banks R, Sellen A, Regan Tim (2013) Rethinking the web as a personal archive. In: Proceedings of the 22nd international conference on World Wide Web (2013) WWW'13, Rio de Janiero, Brazil, May 13–17. ACM, pp 749–760
Logan R, McLuhan M (2016) The future of the library. Peter Lang
Lynch C (2013) The future of personal digital archiving: defining the research agendas. In: Hawkins DT (ed) Personal archiving: preserving our digital heritage. Information Today Inc.
Macdonald S (2006) Collecting practices. In: Macdonald S (ed.) A companion to museum studies. Blackwell Publishing Ltd., pp 81–97
Malik K (2022) The web has expanded the reach of art but nothing beats standing in front of a Picasso. The Guardian, Manchester, UK, 18 Sept 2022
Manof M (2004) Theories of the archive from across the disciplines. Portal Libraries Acad 4(1):9–25
Mardon R, Belk R (2018) Materialising digital collecting: an extended view of digital materiality. Mark Theory 18(4):543–570
Marshall CC (2013) Social media, personal data, and reusing our digital legacy. In: Hawkins DT (ed) Personal archiving: preserving our digital heritage. Information Today Inc.
Marshall A (2020) What is a museum? A dispute erupts over a new definition. New York Times, 06 Aug 2020. https://www.nytimes.com/2020/08/06/arts/what-is-a-museum.html. Accessed 30 Nov 2024
Martin C (2024) On the matter of the British Library cyber incident. Ciaran's Crispy Cogitations, 20 Jan 2024. https://ciaranmartin.substack.com/p/on-the-matter-of-the-british-library. Accessed 24 Jan 2024
Martin M (2009) Collecting against the tide: building a new collection of rare books in the digital age. Austral Library J 58(2):147–159
Miller RJ (2022) Metadata for digital collections. Facet Publishing Limited, London
METRO (2016) Culture in transit toolkit. https://mnylc.github.io/cit-toolkit/.Accessed 18 May 2023
Mobile Phone Museum (2023) Home page. https://www.mobilephonemuseum.com/catalogue. Accessed 22 May 2023
Mosconi G, Li Q, Randall D, Karasti H, Tolmie P, Barutzky J, Korn M, Pipek V (2018) Three gaps in opening science. Comput Support Cooper Work (CSCW) 28:749–789

Moss M, Thomas D (2018) The accidental archive. In: Brown C (ed) Archival futures. Facet Publishing

Mullen C (1994) 'The People's Show'. In: Pearce SM (ed) Interpreting objects and collections. Chapter 34, p 287–290 (This paper first appeared in Vis Sociol Rev 6(1):47–49 (Summer 1991))

Nadini M, Alessandretti L, Di Giacinto F, Martino M, Aiello LM, Baronchelli A (2021) Mapping the NFT revolution: market trends, trade networks, and visual features. Sci Rep 11(1):20902

NASA (2023) Space science data coordinated archive. https://nssdc.gsfc.nasa.gov/. Accessed 17 May 2023

National Museum of African American History and Culture (2023) Collection search results. https://nmaahc.si.edu/explore/collection/search?edan_fq()=online_media_type%3A%22Sound+recordings%22. Accessed 22 May 2023

Neuburger L, Egger R (2018) Augmented reality: providing a different dimension for museum visitors. In: Jung T, Claudia M, Dieck T (eds) Augmented reality and virtual reality. Springer

Niederösterreich (2023) Niederösterreich 3D. https://www.noe-3d.at/index.php. Accessed 22 May 2023

Odom W, Harper R, Sellen A., Kirk D, Banks R (2010) Passing on & putting to rest: understanding bereavement in the context of interactive technologies. In: Proceedings of the SIGCHI conference on human factors in computing systems CHI'10, Atlanta, Georgia, USA, 10–15 April 2010. ACM, pp 1831–1840

Odom W, Zimmerman J, Forlizzi J (2011) Teenagers and their virtual possessions: design opportunities and issues. In: CHI'11: Proceedings of the SIGCHI conference on human factors in computing systems 7–12 May 2011, Vancouver, BC, Canada. ACM, pp 1491–1500

Oliver G, Harvey R (2016) Digital curation, 2nd ed. Facet Publishing

OpenSea (2023) Activity stats. https://opensea.io/activity. Accessed 03 May 2023

Overdrive (2025) Overdrive. https://company.overdrive.com/. Accessed 19 March 2025

Panini (2023) NFT packs & Exclusive 1 of 1's. https://nft.paniniamerica.net/nft-store/nft-pack.html?sport=UFC and https://nft.paniniamerica.net/nft-store/limited-edition-nft.html?s=0. Accessed 30 May 2023

Pelly L (2022) 'There's endless choice, but you're not listening': fans quitting Spotify to save their love of music. The Guardian, Manchester, UK, 27 Sept 2022

Peter D (2022) Top 11 Online Memorial sites for 2022. https://devon-peter.medium.com/the-top-7-memorial-websites-in-2019-232766561a9a. Accessed 08 Jan 2024

Petrellia D, Bowen S, Whittaker S (2014) Photo mementos: designing digital media to represent ourselves at home. Int J Human-Computer Studi 72(3):320–336

Pinfield S (2004) Self-archiving publications. In: Gorman GE, Rowland F (eds) International yearbook of library and information management 2004–2005: Scholarly publishing in an electronic era. Facet, pp 118–145

Powell A, Heaney M, Dempsey L (2000) RSLP collection description. DLib Mag 6(9)

Proctor M (2010) What's an 'Archivist'? Some nineteenth-century perspectives. J Soc Arch 31(1):15–27

Procter R, Tolmie P, Bruttin C, Burger C (2014) D8.1 Requirements gathering, use case design and interface mock-ups. Deliverable 8.1 of the EC FP7-ICT Strategic Targeted Research Project Pheme (No. 611233): Computing veracity across media, languages, and social networks. Available on the PHEME website. https://www.pheme.eu/deliverables/. Accessed 30 Nov 2024

Ranade S (2018) Access technologies for the disruptive digital archive. In: Brown C (ed) Archival futures. Facet Publishing

Redwine G et al (2013) Born digital: guidance for donors, dealers, and archival repositories. CLIR Publication No. 159, Council on library and information resources, Washington, USA, pp 1–37

Redwine G (2015) Personal digital archiving. DPC technology watch report 15-01, Digital Preservation Coalition, pp 1–33

Richards L, Richards T (1994) From filing cabinet to computer. In: Bryman A, Burgess GR (eds) Analizyng qualitative data. Routledge, pp 146–172

Rose S (2022) 'The metaverse will be our slow death!' Is Facebook losing its $100bn gamble on virtual reality? The Guardian, Manchester, UK, 07 Dec 2022

Saponaro MZ, Evans GE (2019) Collection management basics. Libraries Unlimited. Santa Barbara, California, pp 1–373

Scaglia I, Falakeh D (2023) Framing the future: the museum experience and digital technology. School of Engineering, Jonkoping University, Sweden

Scaraboto D, Ferreira MC, Chung E (2016) Materials matter: an exploration of the curatorial practices of consumers as collectors. Res Consum Culture Theory 18:217–243

Scottish Maritime Museum (2023) Scanning the horizon—explore our collections in 3D. https://www.scottishmaritimemuseum.org/3d-collections/. Accessed 22 May 2023

Sedgwick K (2020) Immersive experiences. In Szanto A (ed) The future of the museum—28 Dialogues. Hatje Cantz Verlag GmbH, pp 265–275

Seehusen DA (2004) Creating an electronic filing cabinet. Fam Pract Manag 11(1):65–67

Sellen AJ, Harper RHR (2002) The myth of the paperless office. The MIT Press

Shuker R (2010) Wax trash and vinyl treasures: record collecting as a social practice. Ashgate Publishing Limited, Farnham

Silverman J (2015) 'Pics or it didn't happen'—the mantra of the Instagram era. The Guardian, Manchester, UK, 26 Feb 2015

Smithsonian (2023a) 3D models. https://www.si.edu/search/3d-models?edan_q=3D%20objects&. Accessed 22 May 2023

Smithsonian (2023b) Skin and bones. https://apps.apple.com/us/app/skin-bones/id929733243. Accessed 24 May 2023

Sola T (2004) Redefining collecting. In: Knell SJ (ed.) Museums and the future of collecting, 2nd ed. Ashgate, Farnham

Sparkes M (2021) What is a metaverse and why is everyone talking about it? New Scientist (Technology), 11 Aug 2021

Stanley Gibbons (2024) A new digital age for the world's first postage stamp. Dispatches section of the Stanley Gibbons website, Oct 2024. https://www.stanleygibbons.com/collecting-stamps/dispatches/new-digital-age-worlds-first-postage-stamp. Accessed 17 Oct 2024

Strasser BJ (2012) Collecting nature: practices, styles, and narratives. Osiris 27(1):303–340

Sturm U, et al. (2022) Anthropocenic objects. Collecting practices for the age of humans. Res Ideas Outcomes 8:e89446. 12 Jul 2022

Tang C (2022) The art of collecting. UX Collective, 12th Mar 2022. https://uxdesign.cc/the-art-of-collecting-ead79c5f5e49. Accessed 29 Mar 2023

Tebeau M (2016) Engaging the materiality of the archive in the digital age. Collections 12(4):475–487

Technavio (2024) Library management software market analysis North America, APAC, Europe, Middle East and Africa, South America - US, UK, China, Russia, Canada - Size and Forecast 2024–2028. https://www.technavio.com/report/library-management-software-market-industry-analysis. Accessed 30 Nov 2024

Terras M (2010) Digital curiosities: resource creation via amateur digitization. Literary Linguistic Comput 25(4):425–438

The National Museum of Computing (2023) Explore the galleries. https://www.tnmoc.org/galleries. Accessed 22 May 2023

Theimer K (2018) The end of the archival profession as we know it and I feel fine. In: Brown C (ed) Archival futures. Facet Publishing

Toane C, Doucette L, Rousseau P, Serafin M, Spence M, Kim C (2022) The 99 AI challenge: empowering a university community through an open learning pilot. In: Hervieux S, Wheatley A (eds) The rise of AI: Implications and applications of artificial intelligence in academic libraries. Association of College and Research Libraries, pp 3–14

Tolmie P, Crabtree A (2018) The practical politics of sharing personal data. Personal Ubiquitous Comput 22:293–315

Tonne HA (1946) The organization and management of records. The Journal of Business Education, June 1946

ToppsNFT (2023) What's new in Major League Baseball. https://toppsnfts.com/collection/MLB. Accessed 30 May 2023

Toups ZO, Crenshaw NK, Wehbe RR, Tondello GF, Nacke LE (2016) "The collecting itself feels good": towards collection interfaces for digital game objects. In: Proceedings of CHI PLAY '16–19 Oct 2016, Austin, Texas, USA. ACM, pp 276–290

Treasury of Ireland (2023) Virtual tour of the public record office of Ireland. https://vrtour.virtualtreasury.ie/. Accessed 18 May 2023

Ubois J (2013) Personal digital archives: what they are, what they could be, and why they matter. In: Hawkins DT (ed) Personal archiving: preserving our digital heritage. Information Today Inc.

University of Bath Library (2023) Archiving and sharing data: choosing an archive. https://library.bath.ac.uk/research-data/archiving-and-sharing/choosing-an-archive#s-lg-box-wrapper-17405040. Accessed 17 May 2023

Upper Deck (2023a) Real cards. Real trades. https://www.upperdeckepack.com/. Accessed 30 May 2023

Upper Deck (2023b) Upper Deck inveils Evolution—a new marketplace for authentic digital collectibles. http://www.upperdeck.com/Corporate/News-And-Events/2023-04-25.aspx. Accessed 30 May 2023

V&A (2023) Theatre and performance archives: national video archive of performance (NVAP). https://www.vam.ac.uk/info/theatre-performance-archives#national-video-archive-of-performance-nvap. Accessed 17 May 2023

VeVe (2023) 'Your collection in your pocket' and 'Bring your collectibles to life with Augmented Reality'. https://www.veve.me/. Accessed 31 May 2023

VeVe (2024) Stanley Gibbons—Penny Black, VeVe website. https://www.veve.me/collectibles/en/series/1060345b-45e6-4ebd-b886-f24bace4546c. Accessed 17 Oct 2024

Whittaker S (2011) Personal information management: from information consumption to curation. Ann Rev Inf Sci Technol 45(1):1–62

Whittaker S, Hirschberg J (2001) The character, value, and management of personal paper archives. ACM Trans Computer-Human Interact 8(2):150–170

Whittaker S, Massey C (2020) Mood and personal information management: how we feel influences how we organize our information. Personal Ubiquitous Comput 24:695–707

Whittaker S, Sidner C (1996) Email overload: exploring personal information management of email. In: Proceedings of the conference on human factors in computing systems: common ground, CHI '96, Vancouver, BC, Canada, 13–18 April 1996. ACM, pp 276–283

Wikipedia (2023a) Smartphone. https://en.wikipedia.org/wiki/Smartphone. Accessed 23 April 2023

Wikipedia (2023b) Comparison of note-taking software. https://en.wikipedia.org/wiki/Comparison_of_note-taking_software. Accessed 13 May 2023

Wikipedia (2023c) Research data archiving. https://en.wikipedia.org/wiki/Research_data_archiving. Accessed 17 May 2023

Wikipedia (2023d) List of video game museums. https://en.wikipedia.org/wiki/List_of_video_game_museums. Accessed 22 May 2023

Wikipedia (2023e) List of computer museums. https://en.wikipedia.org/wiki/List_of_computer_museums. Accessed 22 May 2023

Wikipedia (2023f) Virtual Museum. https://en.wikipedia.org/wiki/Virtual_museum. Accessed 22 May 2023

Wikipedia (2023g) 3D scanning. https://en.wikipedia.org/wiki/3D_scanning. Accessed 23 May 2023

Wikipedia (2023h) Topps. https://en.wikipedia.org/wiki/Topps. Accessed 29 May 2023

Wikipedia (2023i) Pokemon Go. https://en.wikipedia.org/wiki/Pok%C3%A9mon_Go. Accessed 31 May 2023

Wikipedia (2023j) Blog. https://en.wikipedia.org/wiki/Blog. Accessed 01 June2023

Wikipedia (2023k) Wikipedia: statistics. https://en.wikipedia.org/wiki/Wikipedia:Statistics. Accessed 02 June 2023
Williams P, John JL, Rowland I (2009) The personal curation of digital objects: a lifecycle approach. ASLIB Proc 61(4):340–363
Wilson A, (2020) 10 of the world's best virtual museum and art gallery tours. The Guardian, Manchester UK, 23 Mar 2020.
Wilson PA (2012a) A new, simpler, cheaper filing system. Blog post in the Personal Document Management section of the pwofc.com website, 20 Dec 2012. https://www.pwofc.com/ofc/2012/12/20/223/. Accessed 13 May 2025
Wilson PA (2012b) Indexing photo collections. Blog post in the Organising Family Photos section of pwofc.com, 10 Sep 2012, https://www.pwofc.com/ofc/2012/09/10/indexing-photo-collections/. Accessed 13 May 2025
Wilson PA (2014a) IV in PIM - The Applicability of Intrinsic Value in Personal Information Management, v1.1, 18 May 2014, Published on www.pwofc.com on 19 May 2014. http://www.pwofc.com/ofc/2014/05/19/the-end-of-this-particular-road/. Accessed 15 Dec 2024
Wilson PA (2014b) Electronic bookshelf. A completed journey in the pwofc.com website, http://www.pwofc.com/ofc/category/journeys-completed/electronic-bookshelf/. Accessed 29 Nov 2024
Wilson PA (2016a) Preservation planning for personal digital collections. Case Note published by the Digital Preservation Coalition on its website, 11 Apr 2016. https://www.google.com/url?client=internal-element-cse&cx=015383697635205237689:2tx1omaukfw&q=https://www.dpconline.org/docs/miscellaneous/advice/1509-casenote-pwilson-preservationplanning-ver2/file&sa=U&ved=2ahUKEwj6pe_n-faJAxU7RaQEHeIHGXAQFnoECAcQAQ&usg=AOvVaw1wCtv7e09l6ufzQtjgKExn. Accessed 25 Nov 2024
Wilson PA (2016b) Loft phase 2—maybe with RFID this time, and Spec for uGrokit system. Two blog posts in the Loft Management section of pwofc.com, dated 05Sep2016 and 07Oct 2016. http://www.pwofc.com/ofc/category/journeys-in-progress/loft-management/. Accessed 29 Nov 2024
Wilson PA (2016c) First feelings for the Grok app. Blog post in the Loft Management section of pwofc.com, 13 Oct 2016, https://www.pwofc.com/ofc/2016/10/13/first-feelings-for-the-grok-app/. Accessed 13 May 2025
Wilson PA (2017) U5.4.2 Digitise—titles, metadata, indexes and labelling. Blog post in the Order from Chaos section of the pwofc.com website, 03 Oct 2017. http://www.pwofc.com/ofc/2017/10/03/u5-4-2-digitise-titles-metadata-indexes-and-labelling/. Accessed 30 Nov 2024
Wilson PA (2018a) Retrospective preservation observations. blog post in the Preservation Planning section of the pwofc.com website, 08 Mar 2018. https://www.pwofc.com/ofc/2018/03/08/1401/. Accessed 13 May 2025
Wilson PA (2018b) Relief. Blog post in the Personal Document Management section of pwofc.com, 09 March 2018, https://www.pwofc.com/ofc/2018/03/09/relief/.. Accessed 13 May 2025
Wilson PA (2019a) BackupBolstering. Blog post in the Personal Document Management section of the pwofc.com website, dated 30 Jan 2019. https://www.pwofc.com/ofc/2019/01/30/backup-bolstering/.. Accessed 13 May 2025
Wilson PA (2019b) PAWDOC: Indexing (and the Accession process). Blog post in the Personal Document Management section of pwofc.com, 09 August 2019. https://www.pwofc.com/ofc/2019/08/09/pawdoc-indexing-and-the-accession-process/.. Accessed 13 May 2025
Wilson PA (2019c) PAWDOC: Hardcopy/electronic mix. Blog post in the Personal Document Management section of pwofc.com, 20 Aug 2019. https://www.pwofc.com/ofc/2019/08/20/pawdoc-hardcopyelectronic-mix/.. Accessed 13 May 2025
Wilson PA (2019d) PAWDOC: deciding what to file. Blog post in the Personal Document Management section of the pwofc.com website, 06 August 2019. https://www.pwofc.com/ofc/2019/08/06/pawdoc-deciding-what-to-file/.. Accessed 13 May 2025

Wilson PA (2019e) Searching. Blog post in the Personal Document Management section of the pwofc.com website, 17 Aug 2019. https://www.pwofc.com/ofc/2019/08/17/pawdoc-searching/.. Accessed 13 May 2025

Wilson P (2019f) PAWDOC: relationship between work patterns and filing activities. Blog post in the Personal Document Management section of the pwofc.com website, 21 Aug 2019. https://www.pwofc.com/ofc/2019/08/21/pawdoc-relationship-between-work-patterns-and-filing-activities/.. Accessed 13 May 2025

Wilson PA (2019g) Portability. Blog post in the Personal Document Management section of the pwofc.com website, 26 Aug 2019, https://www.pwofc.com/ofc/2019/08/26/pawdoc-portability/.. Accessed 13 May 2025

Wilson PA (2019h) Scanning. Blog post in the personal document management section of the pwofc.com website, 15 Aug 2019. https://www.pwofc.com/ofc/2019/08/15/pawdoc-scanning/.. Accessed 13 May 2025

Wilson PA (2021a) Preservation planning document templates v3.0, 16th Nov. 2021. Files embedded in a blog post entitled 'Templates v3.0: DONE (after a 7-year journey)' dated 18 Nov 2021 in the Preservation Planning section of the pwofc.com website. https://www.pwofc.com/ofc/2021/11/18/templates-v3-0-finished-after-a-7-year-journey/. Accessed 13 May 2025

Wilson PA (2022) Meteor: a story about stamp collecting in the eye of the IT hurricane. Self-published book using the Blurb service, 05 Apr 2022

Wilson PA (2023a) Conversion alternatives. Blog post in the DVD Management section of the pwofc.com website, 13th Sept 2023. https://www.pwofc.com/ofc/2023/09/13/conversion-alternatives/. Accessed 13 May 2025

Wilson PA (2023b) Choosing rationales. Blog post in the DVD Management section of the pwofc.com website, 7th Nov 2023. https://www.pwofc.com/ofc/2023/11/07/choosing-rationales/. Accessed 13 May 2025

Wilson PA (2023c) Indexing arrangements. Blog post in the Display Case Management section of the pwofc.com website, 27 Sept 2023. https://www.pwofc.com/ofc/2023/09/27/indexing-arrangements/.. Accessed 13 May 2025

Wilson PA (2024) Turning a stamp album into a book. Blog post in the 'Exploit - in Books' section of the pwofc.com website, 27 Mar 2024, https://www.pwofc.com/ofc/2024/03/27/turning-a-stamp-album-into-a-reference-book/.. Accessed 13 May 2025

Wilson PA (2025) Sorties into the IT Hurricane, 3rd edn. Self-published in Blurb, distributed by Ingram

Winget MA, Murray C (2009) Collecting and preserving videogames and their related materials: a review of current practice, game-related archives and research projects. Proc Am Soc Inform Sci Technol 45(1):1–9

Wright F (2008) How can 575 comic books weigh under an ounce?: Comic book collecting in the digital age. J Electron Publ 11(3):1–9

Ximm A (2013) Active personal archiving and the Internet Archive. In: Hawkins DT (ed) Personal Archiving: preserving our digital heritage. Information Today Inc.

Yamauchi EA, Maciel C, Mendes FF, Ueda GS, Pereira VC (2021) Digital legacy management systems: theoretical, systemic and user's perspective. In: Filipe J, Śmiałek M, Brodsky, A, Hammoudi S (eds) Proceedings of the 23rd international conference on enterprise information systems (ICEIS 2021), Vol. 2. Virtual Event, 26–28 April 2021, pp 41–53

Yeo G (2018) Can we keep everything? The future of appraisal in a world of digital profusion. In: Brown C (ed) Archival futures. Facet Publishing, pp 45–63

Zeller C (2015) From object to information: the end of collecting in the digital age. Arcadia 50(2):389–409

Chapter 8
The Slide Towards Collecting Context Conformity

Abstract The historical background to collecting described in Chap. 2, suggests that the contexts central to this book were very distinct domains prior to the Icon Age. However, the analysis reported in this book suggests that, with the arrival of the Icon Age, the gap between the contexts has been narrowing. This becomes apparent when digital objects form part of collections, when digital indexes are employed, and when IT systems are designed to enable better access to collections and to information about them. Instances where narrowing has occurred within particular elements of the practice hierarchy, are described. The overall conclusion is that the gap has narrowed between the different contexts, and that this is due to a combination of the following: contemporary internet facilities; easily accessed software facilities and cloud services; the ease with which objects can be digitised; and the uniformity of IT activities.

In Chaps. 1 and 2, the historical background to the various types of collecting gives the impression of some very distinct domains and a lack of unanimous certainty about what can be called 'proper' collecting. Accumulators are not seen to possess true collecting motivations; Filing is not really embraced within the collecting field; Libraries seem to be side-lined in discussions of more contemporary collecting which seem to focus more on the collection of material objects; and Archiving is becoming an increasingly fluid concept.

We perceive this situation to have existed to some degree or other right up to the start of the Icon Age. In contrast, the evidence documented in this volume seems to suggest a narrowing of this disjoint—so much so that we suggest that the affordances of the Icon Age have resulted in a unification of many of the practices undertaken in all the collecting contexts. To explore this claim, we will first review some instances of the narrowing gap between specific domains, and then investigate if there is a growing similarity in how each of the 7 types of collectors are using the practices identified in Chaps. 4 and 5.

P. Wilson and P. Tolmie, *Collecting in the Icon Age*,
https://doi.org/10.1007/978-3-031-86470-4_8

8.1 Examples of the Narrowing Gap Between Collecting Contexts Due to Digital Innovations

8.1.1 The Relationship Between Accumulating and Filing/ Amateur Collecting

Computer users tend to be Accumulators rather than Filers: In Chap. 7 we described most computer users as Filers due to their extensive use of folders. However, the mass of digital material most people are faced with often makes the Filing of individual documents more of a hasty action or afterthought. One commentator observed that many people treat their digital items with a mixture of benign neglect and unrealized ambitions to do better because (a) a wide range of unfamiliar Curatorial activities are required to do the job properly, (b) we now have much more storage so that many things that used to be transient are now kept indefinitely, and (c) to properly Curate the growing flood of digital items would take too much time away from people's other activities (Marshall 2013).

Apps may turn Accumulators into Filers or Amateur Collectors: As described in Chap. 7, mobile phone apps seem to exist for almost everything. If someone deliberately goes out of their way to identify an app (say the Recipe Keeper app to record details of all their recipes), download it, and install it, then that would be a deliberate act of Filing. However, many people just download apps to take a look at them or to just try them out. The acid test is whether they continue to use the app long-term—say six months or more; and whether they use it for their complete collection of whatever it is—or at least a specific subset. A temporary flirtation with an app does not change an Accumulator; but a long-term engagement with an app can convert an Accumulator into a Filer or an Amateur Collector.

Photo/Message Accumulators benefit from in-phone apps: The 2020's mobile phone has tailor-made apps to manage photos and messages. The messages apps typically file messages by date and recipients or groups; and the photo apps file photos by date and may be able to distinguish between different types of photos. For example, a 2023 iPhone can identify location (by GPS tags in each photo), some types of images, and significant events (such as weddings)—information which is often provided in indexes. The Accumulator gets the benefit of all this index-type information without having to do any of the work which a Filer would normally have to do to create it.

Photos can be Accumulated in social media: Transferring photos into social media doesn't turn an Accumulator into a Filer; the photos simply accumulate in another system. Indeed, having duplicate photos in two or more systems can become quite confusing.

8.1.2 The Relationship Between Filing and Archiving

Archives can become immediately accessible: Archives seem to have been traditionally viewed as containing items which are inactive. For example, the record lifecycle developed by the US National Archives and Records Administration (NARA) envisaged ageing records becoming inactive and being stored separately until they are eventually moved to a separate Archive store (Kim 2013). However, Archives that have been digitised, and/or contain Born-Digital Files, can cease to depend on storage as their defining characteristic, but can become a virtual store which is immediately accessible 24 × 7 over the internet (Featherstone 2006).

Email folders become Archives: Most email systems enable users to set up folders in which to store messages that have been dealt with. The way that individuals manage their email varies: Whittaker and Sidner identified three approaches in 1996—the 'no filers' who don't use folders at all, the Frequent filers' who clean their inboxes every day, and the 'spring cleaners' who periodically clean their inboxes. Research some ten years later confirmed that this was still the case (Whittaker and Sidner 1996; Fisher et al. 2006). Both of these studies appear to refer to the email archive as a combination of both messages in inboxes and messages in folders, so it is a little difficult to distinguish between what is actually an archived item set aside for some unspecified future activity, and what is just a filed item available for possible scrutiny within the foreseeable future. In fact, the 2006 study did identify that the mean number of folders was 133 compared to the average 47 identified in 1996; that nearly half of the email archive was older than 3 months; and that the participants were actively using relatively few of their folders, suggesting that they were keeping' substantial archives' (Fisher et al. 2006). The implication from these results is that, while users may be initially filing emails in folders to provide easy access in the future, some people may just be leaving them there indefinitely to become an Archive. Wilson's experience confirms this possibility. His folders in 2023 contained approximately 39,000 messages with the earliest dating back to 2006. Some of this material has been referred to within a few months of putting it in folders but some has only been looked at many years after putting it in folders—if at all. This is clearly both a File and an Archive.

Websites and blogs can become Archives: As noted in the section on Filers in Chap. 7, the extraordinary Grazian archive (de Grazia 2023) probably started out as Alfred de Grazia's filing system, but since his death must now be considered an Archive. In the case of the *pwofc.com* blog, Wilson has been placing posts in it since 2012. They are in one of two main sections—'Journeys in progress' and 'Journeys Completed'. Material in the 'in progress' section are most definitely in the Filing category; items moved to the 'completed' section can be initially considered to have been filed, but as time goes by, they gradually mutate into Archives.

Online memorials start as files and change to Archives: As also pointed out in the section on Filers in Chap. 7, individuals file their memories and thoughts about departed friends and relatives in Online Memorial applications, and these are read and commented on by the other users of the facility. However, as contributions and visitors dry up, the memorial becomes an Archive—a shrine to the departed individual.

Personal files can turn into archived items: If you make the effort to file a document, you are unlikely to throw it away unless there is a real need such as a lack of space—and huge increases in cheap storage capacity have eliminated that issue for digital files. Consequently, filed documents often just turn into archive material, lying dormant but safely stored for possible scrutiny in an unknown future. This seems to be becoming an accepted fact. For example, one commentator regards Personal Digital Archiving as part of everyday record keeping with the objective of preserving documents in the long term and possibly beyond the owner's lifetime (Kim 2013). Another paper suggests thinking about Personal Archives as something 'live' which can be drawn upon to be reused in both the near future and long term (Marshall 2013). Even in the academic environment it has been said that 'Personal scholarly archiving has become a dynamic process rather than a rote exercise at the end of a faculty member's career' (Cahoy 2013).

Archived items can be turned into accessible files: This is a widespread phenomenon as Archives digitise their contents and make them available online (see Sects. 5.5.1 and 7.6.2) The PAWDOC experience illustrates this point: in its early days when it was mainly paper-based, the upright cabinet in which it was housed regularly ran out of space and an Archiving exercise was conducted to select little-used items and place them into archive boxes. Between 1986 and 1988, at least 7 such sessions were carried out which, overall, removed some 700 items to boxes, freeing up approximately 180 cm of cabinet space. In 1994, 32 boxes were removed to the Box-IT document storage service, where they stayed until being returned in 2001, placed in a garden shed and garage, and gradually scanned into the filing system. By 2016 they were all scanned and the collection was totally digitised (Wilson 2025). Up to that point, PAWDOC had two parts: a filing system with accessible items, and an Archive with items which were identifiable in the index but which were located elsewhere and only accessible with considerable effort. From 2016 onwards, however, there was no archive. Every item in the collection was immediately accessible on the laptop. This applied equally to the very first document placed into the collection on 1st June 1981 and to the very latest item in the collection. All were current no matter how little or often they were accessed and looked at.

8.1.3 The Relationship Between Libraries, Museums/ Galleries, and Archives

Objects cease to be differentiated after they are digitised: When objects are digitised, they all have to be managed in the same way; they are all displayed remotely within the constraints of the online media; they must all be given explanations using the digital facilities of the net; and they can all be searched for using standard search facilities. So, as Libraries, Museums/Galleries, and Archives digitise their objects and display them in digital form online, there becomes less reason for users to differentiate between the institutions on the basis of the objects they collect (Manof 2004; Navarrete 2022) (though people working in the institutions may have other perspectives…). This might also apply to Private Curators and Amateur Collectors who display their collections online.

The notion of a Digital Library takes hold: In 2005, a 32-page paper outlined a step-by step process to create a digital repository (Chopey 2005). In 2016, a 388-page book called 'Discover Digital Libraries: Theory and Practice' put more flesh on the bones of this activity and highlighted the term 'Digital Library' with the following description:

> Digital Libraries encompass a wide range of materials, from books to representations of three-dimensional artefacts. The content is either created digitally or converted from a variety of analog sources through digitization. Extensive digitization efforts have accompanied the construction of Digital Libraries to transform the wealth of traditional scholarly and cultural materials held in Libraries, Archives and Museums into a digital format. (Xie and Matusiak 2016)

Miller's gargantuan 536-page 2nd edition of 'Metadata for Digital Collections' came out in 2022 and emphasises in no uncertain terms the significance and complexities of digital collections in the modern world of Libraries, Museums, Galleries and Archives. The book defines a digital collection to be:

> …a collection of digital resources, along with metadata about those resources, made available online through an interface that allows users to search and/or browse the contents of that collection and retrieve displays of the digital resources and their metadata. (Miller 2022)

It's clear from these texts—and indeed from the many examples of digital collections described in Chap. 7—that Digital Collections/Digital Libraries are clearly discernible entities in their own right with their own very clear requirements for construction and operation. As such, they eliminate the distinction between whichever type of Collecting Context—Library, Museum/Gallery, Archive, Private Curator (and even Amateur Collectors with online content)—that creates them.

8.1.4 The Relationship Between Indexing/Search and All the Collecting Contexts

Digital indexes can be applied to all types of collections: Libraries, Museums and Archives have long since digitised their catalogues and now enable the public to access and search their indexes online. It matters little that the underlying indexing application is different, or that the fields of information—the metadata—are different: to the user it's simply a source of information which can be searched using free text.

Having said that, the LODLAM initiative (Linked Open Data for Libraries Archives and Museums) has promoted the creation of rich sets of metadata in standard formats and making that openly available (Tebeau 2016). For other types of collectors—Filers, Private Curators and Amateur Collectors—the notion of an index is well understood, and easy to put into practice: there are a plethora of software products that can be hired or acquired, and the highly flexible spreadsheet can provide a very cheap and effective solution. In summary, the digital index has become a commonplace object widely used and understood not only by collectors but all parts of society—part of a new culture which recognises the importance of ordering, listing and searching (Andersen 2018).

Search is potentially applicable to all collections: While people have always searched for information, the internet and Google have turned search into a mundane everyday activity. We now make sense of the world by the information we receive from the searches we conduct (Andersen 2018). It is what people expect to be able to do when interacting with collections—and they expect to be able to do it in roughly the same way for any and every type of collection: a free text search producing a selection of search results from which they can select items to further investigate (Ladd 2015). Having said that, what the average user is unlikely to be aware of is that the results being generated are entirely dependent on the algorithms being applied to select items and to order their presentation (Andersen 2018), and are not without human influence—they do their creators' bidding. Indeed, every search conducted has the potential to benefit those who amass, shield, and sell information (Zeller 2015). It has also been pointed out that digital search generates transient collections—a group of items which have been collected together by the selection of specific elements of the information (metadata) held for each item (Currall et al. 2004). This is particularly obvious—and mundane—when a web search is conducted: but, in the collecting context it could be seen as a way in which new collections can be created at the press of a few buttons. This might be a significant capability in very large collections such as the British Museum or the Rijksmuseum in Amsterdam.

8.1.5 Digital Design, Curation, and Access in All the Collecting Contexts

Standard approach to digital design is feasible in all collecting contexts: Organisation has always been at the heart of collecting: organisation of the physical objects and organisation of the information about those objects. However, different disciplines—library science, information science, computer science, informatics, and information systems—took different approaches to their organisation of objects and information prior to the Icon Age, and have continued to do so to a large extent despite the general changes in thinking and culture that IT has stimulated. Differences also occur depending on whether it is IT architects, analysts, programmers, or, indeed, co-opted Curators, who are tasked with designing collection-related systems; each will draw on their own training, experience, and methods to do the job. However, a groundbreaking book—'The Discipline of organizing' (Glushko 2013)—has unified the underlying concepts of all these different disciplines and perspectives with a new set of terminology; with descriptions of the relationships and interactions which constitute organising; and with associated design principles. This combined with substantive volumes on metadata for digital collections (Miller 2022, 544 pages) and on how to undertake Digital Curation (Oliver and Harvey 2016, 242 pages), suggests that, as far as digital design is concerned, all types of collections could utilise the same constructs.

All collecting contexts with digital objects will need to perform Digital Curation practices: Whatever the type of collection, if it contains digital objects then Digital Curation practices will need to be performed. This will include the particularly important practice of digital preservation to ensure that the objects can continue to be viewed/used in the future.

All types of digital collections can be accessed using the same technology: Access to information about a collection, and/or to digital collections, can usually be achieved using the same technology—PC, laptop, tablet, or (hugely significantly) the mobile phone. There may be exceptions such as very large Archives using off-line tape storage, for example. However, most collections wanting to enable such access will design their facilities in broadly the same way to take advantage of particular technology capabilities and to avoid constraints.

Table 8.1 provides a snapshot overview of examples of the narrowing gap between Collecting Contexts that we have made so far in this chapter. The points that can be immediately drawn from it are:

- It seems that when Accumulations, Files and Archives contain Digital Files, there can be slippage between those three categories such that Accumulations can become Files and Files can become Archives.
- When Librarians, Filers, Archivists, Museums/Galleries, Private Collectors and Amateur Collectors deal with digital objects, the traditional differentiation between those Collecting Contexts can be diluted.
- For all Collecting Contexts other than Accumulators, IT has resulted in most of them performing a number of practices in a similar way, namely the use of a digital index, the performance of Digital Curation activities, and the design of systems to optimise access to their collections by PC, laptop and mobile devices.

Table 8.1 Examples of the narrowing gap between collecting contexts due to digital innovations

Contexts digital innovation	Accumulators	Librarians	Filers	Archivists	Museum and Gallery Curators	Private Curators	Amateur Collectors
Increased volume of information	Filers tending to be Accumulators		Filers tending to be Accumulators				
Mobile apps for everything	Accumulators tending to be Filers		Accumulators tending to be Filers				Accumulators tending to be Filers
In-phone photo apps	Photo/message Accumulators get filing benefits with no effort		Photo/message Accumulators get filing benefits with no effort				
Photos put into social media systems	Photo Accumulators stay Accumulators						
Archives become virtual			Archives become like files	Archives become like files available 24×7			
Email systems with folders	Accumulations become Archives			Accumulations become Archives			
Websites and blogs			Files may become Archives	Files may become Archives			
Online memorials			Files become Archives	Files become Archives			

(continued)

Table 8.1 (continued)

Contexts digital innovation	Accumulators	Librarians	Filers	Archivists	Museum and Gallery Curators	Private Curators	Amateur Collectors
Large amounts of digital storage			Some files become Archives	Some files become Archives			
Digitisation of archive content		Archives become accessible files	Archives become accessible files	Archives become accessible files	Archives become accessible files		
Objects can be digitised		Objects cease to differentiate contexts	Objects cease to differentiate contexts	Objects cease to differentiate contexts	Objects cease to differentiate contexts	Objects cease to differentiate contexts	Objects cease to differentiate contexts
Digital Libraries		Creation of a Digital Library	Creation of a Digital Library	Creation of a Digital Library	Creation of a Digital Library	Creation of a Digital Library	Creation of a Digital Library
Digital indexes		Use of Digital index	Use of Digital index	Use of Digital index	Use of Digital index	Use of Digital index	Use of Digital index
Culture of Search		Provision of search facility	Provision of search facility	Provision of search facility	Provision of search facility	Provision of search facility	Provision of search facility
Universal approach to Digital Design		Could use standard approach	Could use standard approach	Could use standard approach	Could use standard approach	Could use standard approach	Could use standard approach
Digital curation (DC) Practices		DC practices will need to be followed	DC practices will need to be followed	DC practices will need to be followed	DC practices will need to be followed	DC practices will need to be followed	DC practices will need to be followed
Access via PC, laptop, mobile phone		Systems designed to enable easy access	Systems designed to enable easy access	Systems designed to enable easy access	Systems designed to enable easy access	Systems designed to enable easy access	Systems designed to enable easy access

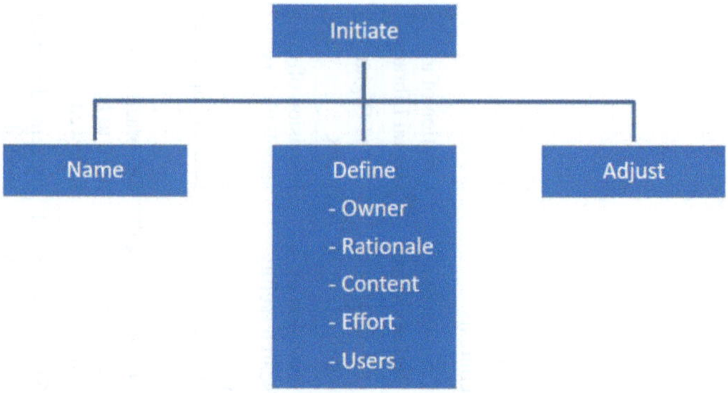

Fig. 8.1 The 'Initiate' practice in the Icon Age

8.2 IT's Impact on Collecting Practitioners

Having identified some of the digital innovations that are narrowing the gap between Collecting Contexts, we now examine ITs impact on the collecting practices identified in Chaps. 4 and 5 (Initiate, Equip, Acquire, Deposit, Use, Reveal, Maintain, Dispose),[1] and highlight further illustrations of narrowing.

8.2.1 *IT's Impact on Initiate Practitioners*

The main elements of the Initiate Practice are shown in Fig. 8.1.

Name: Unaffected by digital technology across all the Collecting Contexts.

Define and Adjust: In the Icon Age, all Collecting Contexts, with the exception of Accumulators, need to consider the format of the **Content** they propose to collect. Those Contexts which provide public access to their collections also need to define which **Users** are going to be enabled to access the collection online.

8.2.2 *IT's Impact on the Equip Practitioner*

The main elements of the Equip Practice are shown in Fig. 8.2.

Consult: Practitioners of all Collecting Contexts will likely take advantage of the internet to seek out relevant **People** and to communicate with them; and to find

[1] Note that a digital version of the complete practice hierarchy is available in the book's supplementary material available at 'pwofc.com'.

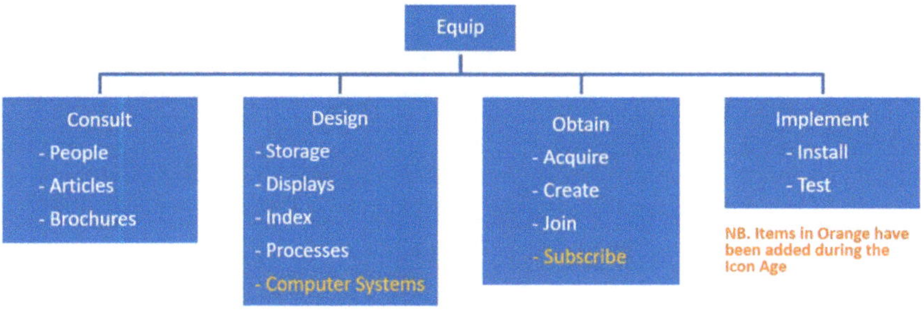

Fig. 8.2 The 'Equip' practice in the Icon Age

relevant **Articles** and information in, not just magazines, journals and **Brochures**, but also in web sites.

Design: All types of Collectors, with the exception of Accumulators and some Amateur Collectors, will likely be defining the use of a computerised **Index** or set of equivalent metadata, running on appropriate **Computer System** hardware and software.

Obtain: All Collecting Contexts, will be using the internet to establish what products are available and how much they are. They may even place online orders to **Acquire** such products. Similarly, most Collectors will use the internet to establish what relevant clubs, societies, or associations, exist, and in some cases to **Join** one or more of them. Most collectors will use the internet to identify any services (such as an online catalogue) that they require, and to **Subscribe** to them.

Implement: Given that all collectors (with the exception of Accumulators and some Amateur Collectors) will be using a computerised Index/metadata on appropriate computer systems, then they must also **Install** the hardware and software and **Test** it.

8.2.3 IT's Impact on the Acquire Practitioner

The main elements of the Acquire Practice are shown in Fig. 8.3.

Target: Unaffected by digital technology across all the Collecting Contexts.

Plan: The development of plans made by all types of collectors will probably include the use of the internet to investigate possibilities and constraints. Some collectors—especially collecting institutions—will document their plans in Digital Files, spreadsheets etc.

Hunt: All types of collectors except for Accumulators and Filers are likely to use the internet search facilities and websites to seek out the objects they are looking for.

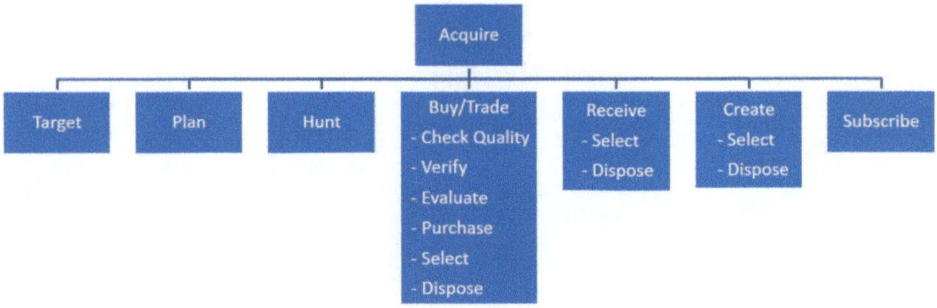

Fig. 8.3 The 'Acquire' practice in the Icon Age

Buy/Trade: Online auction sites such as eBay have made a huge impact on the buying practices in all the Collecting Contexts other than Accumulators and Filers—and particularly on Amateur Collectors. Not only have they provided huge marketplaces with lots of choice, they have also provided different versions with which to compare the **Quality** of the item being considered. Should it be necessary to **Verify** the authenticity of the item concerned, there may be web sites available which focus specifically on explaining how to detect a fake; alternatively, the web sites of respected dealers may be offering the same item against which the item in question can be compared. In similar vein, the price of the item in question can be **Evaluated** by comparing it with the prices of equivalent items in auction and dealer sites. Online marketplaces usually provide functionality to facilitate the **Purchase** activity, and card payment and online banking have eliminated the need to transfer cash or cheques to pay for things. Finally, the unwanted remains of a bulk lot can usually be easily **Disposed** of in an online auction site.

Receive: As in Buy/Trade, unwanted items can be **Disposed** of in online auction sites. Such facilities may be used in all the collecting contexts except for Filing.

Create: IT may or may not be involved in this practice depending on what is being created.

Subscribe: Accumulators and Amateur Collectors in particular, may wish to subscribe to, say, a music streaming service. There may also be other types of online services which all types of Collectors may wish to subscribe to.

8.2.4 IT's Impact on the Deposit Practitioner

8.2.5 The main elements of the Deposit Practice are shown in Fig. 8.4.

Sort: All contexts will probably need to undertake this practice at one time or another. It may or may not involve digital items.

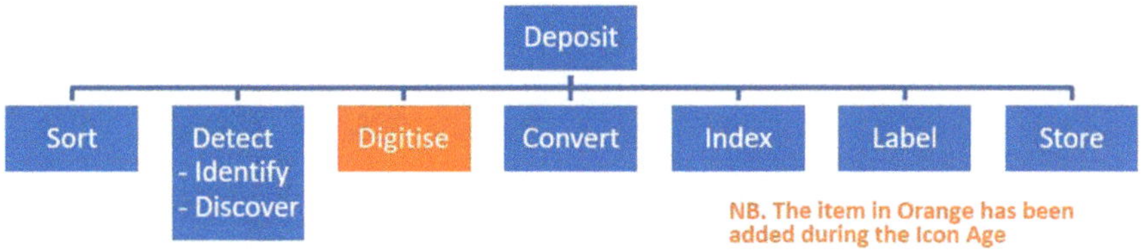

Fig. 8.4 The 'Deposit' practice in the Icon Age

Detect: The internet may be used in all the Collecting Contexts to find out information about an item, though it may be a more fruitful search when trying to **Identify** what an object is, rather than when trying to **Discover** details about a single specific item.

Digitise: All but Accumulators may wish to digitise their physical objects.

Convert: All but Accumulators may undertake some type of conversion work - though some types will be purely from one physical form to another (such as removing stamps from paper). Digital conversion activity may include converting from one file format to another.

Index: All types of Collectors, with the exception of Accumulators and some Amateur Collectors, will probably be using a computerised index or an equivalent set of metadata.

Label: Librarians, Filers, Archivists, and Museum/Gallery Curators are all likely to label the objects they are dealing with. Private Curators may do so as well depending on the size of their collection. A percentage of Amateur Collectors may also do so. The labelling may be purely physical, for example a stringed label on which the identification is handwritten. In some cases, however the label will still be a physical entity but be computer printed - or may even be a physical digital device such as an RFID tag which is widely used by Libraries. Of course, a digital item will be labelled with a Digital file name and possibly with additional metadata.

Store: Items are stored in all Collecting Contexts. Physical items will be placed in a physical store, and digital items will be placed in a digital store.

8.2.5 IT's Impact on the Use Practitioner

8.2.6 The main elements of the Use Practice are shown in Fig. 8.5.

Authorise: This practice is performed mainly by institutions who wish to control access to their collections—Libraries, Archives and Museums/Galleries—though it doesn't preclude Filers, Private Curators and Amateur Collectors from doing so. The authorisation practice typically involves people making requests for authorisation, being granted authorisation (and possibly being given a signifying token), and the

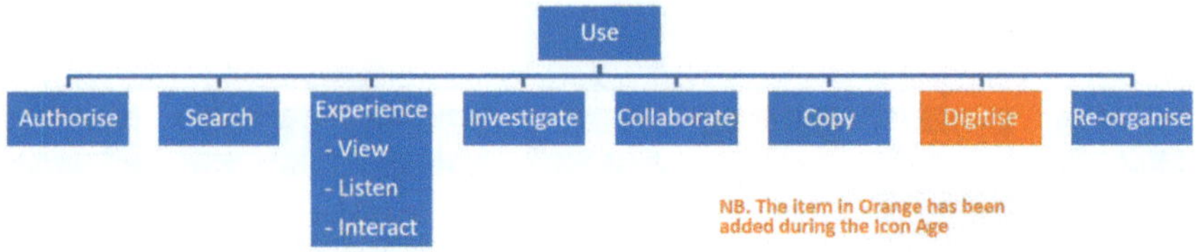

Fig. 8.5 The 'Use' practice in the Icon Age

control of access according to who has been authorised. All of these steps may be of varying sophistication, but may well involve some sort of IT support including email, digitised tokens, and digital access controls.

Search: All types of collectors may conduct a search from time to time for one or more of their items. It may simply involve looking through the collection to find something; or, for collections with an index (all Collection Contexts except for Accumulators and some Amateur Collectors), a digital search may be conducted.

Experience: All types of collectors, with the exception of some Accumulators, usually like to experience the items in their collections. If the items are in digital form they may be **viewed** on a screen or **listened** to via loud speakers or headphones. Some institutions may provide digitally controlled **interactive** experiences associated with the objects in their collections.

Investigate: Research into the contents of a collection may well involve searching the internet for information. A percentage of all types of collectors, with the exception of Accumulators, may conduct such investigations from time to time.

Collaborate: All types of collectors may want to collaborate with other people to find out about other collections and collecting practices and how they compare with their own. While this need not involve IT at all, many people use the internet to find out about magazines, societies, talks and other people in the field; to use email to communicate with individuals; and even to attend online talks etc.

Copy: All types of collectors may wish to make a copy of some of their collected items, in order to take them away to show friends or colleagues, to buy similar items, to show potential buyers etc. Copies in the 2020s are made by either photocopying, scanning or photographing—all digital processes.

Digitise: All collectors apart from Accumulators may wish to digitise their physical objects.

Re-organise: If significant changes are made to a collection's contents—then a major re-organisation may be required of the way it is arranged, stored and documented, including any of the collection's digital elements. This will apply to all collectors apart from Accumulators and some Amateur Collectors.

8.2.6 *IT's Impact on the Reveal Practitioner*

The main elements of the Reveal Practice are shown in Fig. 8.6

Display: Collectors wishing to display their collections may digitise physical objects to be able to display them, and/or may use digital technology to achieve the display (in a web site, for example). This applies to all types of collectors apart from Accumulators who will either just be displaying physical objects, or else will be accumulating Digital Files which they will not want to display.

Inform: All types of collectors may wish to inform other people about their collection—either to pass on information within the family, or to inform viewers of the collection, or to provide information about the collection to a club or society, or even to publish information and/or research results to the public at large. IT may be involved in many of the methods that may be used, for example, email, Word Processing software, PowerPoint slides, or even the compilation and publishing of a book.

Share: Sharing a collection involves actively passing one or more items to someone else. For this to involve IT, it requires that the object is either digitised (such as a scanned copy of a document) or is already a Born-Digital item (such as a digital photo). Sharing a collection might be performed by all types of collectors apart from Accumulators.

Exhibit: All kinds of collectors, with the exception of Accumulators and Filers, may wish to exhibit their collection for one reason another. If the items are digital then the mechanism of display will involve IT. If the items are physical then the information for the exhibit might be assembled using IT (and items may be digitised in the process), and the actual display itself might be digital.

Exploit: Institutional collectors such as Museums/Galleries may wish to exploit their collections to help fund their operation. However, not all exploitation involves making money. Sometimes it may just involve using digitised collection items to make something to give to someone, for example, a coffee mug with a photo for Father's Day. Or, for a Filer, it may involve creating a spreadsheet list of disparate items in the collection which might be relevant to a particular long-term interest. Any type of collector might want to exploit collection items, and might employ Information Technology to do so.

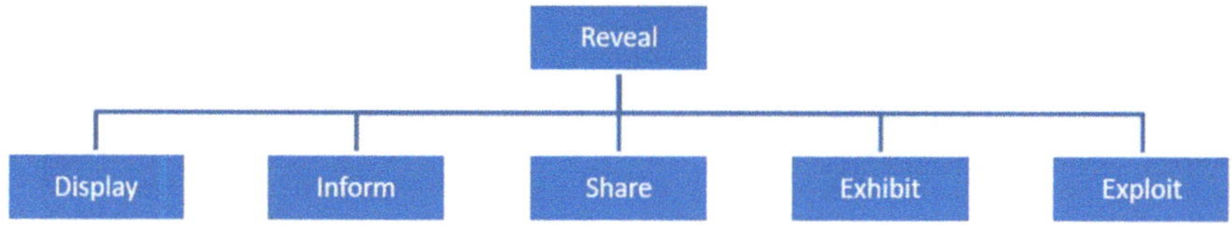

Fig. 8.6 The Reveal practice in the Icon Age

8.2.7 IT's Impact on the Maintain Practitioner

The main elements of the Maintain Practice are shown in Fig. 8.7.

Manage: All Collection Contexts may have **Digital Systems**, and, if so, they need to be managed to ensure they are fit for purpose and fully operational.

Protect: All Collection Contexts may have **Digital Items** and associated **Digital Systems**, and, if so, they need to be protected from system failure and malicious hacking.

Preserve: All Collection Contexts may have **Digital Items** which may cease to be accessible in the long term due to the obsolescence of digital hardware and software. Therefore, steps need to be taken periodically to upgrade hardware, software and the files themselves in order to preserve those files and ensure that they can be read in the future.

Archive and Prune: All Collection Contexts may end up with a collection of Digital Files that is too large to fit the available storage, or which contains individual items which are simply obstructing the effective use of the majority of the rest of the items. In these cases, the best strategy may be to remove those items and archive them in some other store. An alternative to Archiving is to simply select those items that are no longer required at all and to prune them from the system i.e. to remove and destroy them.

Check: All collections of any size may lose track of, or simply lose, physical or digital items from time to time. It's just a feature of large collections in which various different kinds of activity is going on. Those collections which have some sort of index or inventory of the items in their collections (this excludes Accumulators and some Amateur Collectors) may want to conduct inventory checks periodically to ensure that they have all the items they are supposed to have, and to identify the ones that have gone missing and need to be tracked down.

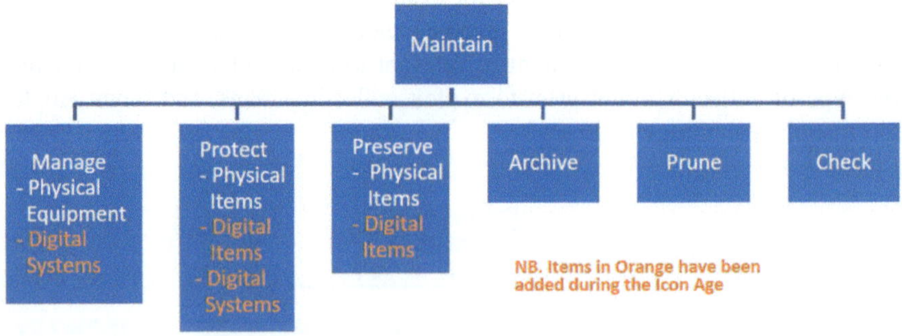

Fig. 8.7 The 'Maintain' practice in the Icon Age

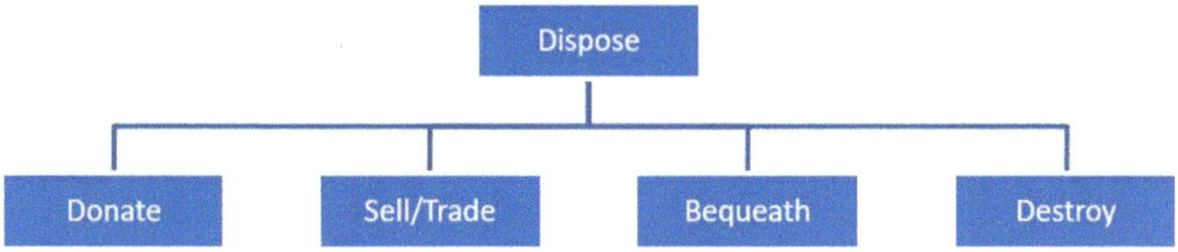

Fig. 8.8 The 'Dispose' practice in the Icon Age

8.2.8 IT's Impact on the Dispose Practitioner

The main elements of the Dispose Practice are shown in Fig. 8.8.

Donate: This practice need not involve any IT element.

Sell: All types of Collectors apart from Filers may wish to sell all or part of their collections, and might do so using the various online auction sites such as eBay or other more specialised auction services which also operate on the internet.

Bequeath: When bequeathing items, Accumulators, Filers, Private Curators and Amateur Collectors may document the bequest in a digital document of some sort or other.

Destroy: All types of collectors may utilise computer 'delete' functionality for digital objects.

8.2.9 IT's Overall Impact on Collecting Practitioners

The table below summarises the overall impact of IT on collecting Practices in the first forty years of the Icon Age.

The most prominent points suggested by Table 8.2 are:

- IT has affected Accumulators and some Amateur Collectors less than the other Collecting Contexts.
- When IT affects collecting it does so in broadly the same way for all the Collecting Contexts affected in the vast majority of cases.
- Internet search is prominent with 6 instances across all the practices listed in the table.

Table 8.2 Summary of the impact of IT on collecting practices

Contexts practice	Accumulators	Librarians	Filers	Archivists	Museum and Gallery Curators	Private Curators	Amateur Collectors
Initiate: name							
Initiate: define		Content/Users	Content	Content/Users	Content/Users	Content	Content
Initiate: adjust		Content/Users	Content	Content/Users	Content/Users	Content	Content
Equip: consult	Search	Search	Search	Search	Search	Search	Search
Equip: design		Index	Index	Index	Index	Index	Some
Equip: obtain	Search	Search	Search	Search	Search	Search	Search
Equip: implement		Systems	Systems	Systems	Systems	Systems	Some
Acquire: target							
Acquire: plan							
Acquire: hunt	Search	Search		Search	Search	Search	Search
Acquire: buy/trade		Online		Some	Some	Online	Online
Acquire: receive: dispose	Online	Some		Some	Some	Online	Online
Acquire: create	Digital items	Some	Digital items	Some	Some	Digital items	Digital items
Acquire: subscribe	Online	Online	Online	Online	Online	Online	Online
Deposit: sort	Sort/Organise	Sort/Organise	Sort/Organise	Sort/Organise	Sort/Organise	Sort/Organise	Sort/Organise
Deposit: detect	Search	Search	Search	Search	Search	Search	Search
Deposit: digitise		Digitise	Digitise	Digitise	Digitise	Digitise	Digitise
Deposit: convert		File format	File format	File format	File format	File format	File format
Deposit: index		Index	Index	Index	Index	Index	Some
Deposit: label		RFID/Filename	Filename	Filename	Filename		Some

(continued)

Table 8.2 (continued)

Contexts practice	Accumulators	Librarians	Filers	Archivists	Museum and Gallery Curators	Private Curators	Amateur Collectors
Deposit: store	Digital store	Digital store	Digital store	Digital store	Digital store	Digital store	Digital store
Use: authorise		Token/Controls		Token/Controls	Token/Controls		
Use: search		Index	Index	Index	Index	Index	Some
Use: experience		View/Listen/ Interact	View/Listen/ Interact	View/Listen/ Interact	View/Listen/interact	View/Listen/ Interact	View/Listen/ Interact
Use: investigate		Search	Search	Search	Search	Search	Search
Use: collaborate	Search	Search	Search	Search	Search	Search	Search
Use: copy	Scan/photo	Scan/Photo	Scan/Photo	Scan/Photo	Scan/Photo	Scan/Photo	Scan/Photo
Use: digitise		Digitise	Digitise	Digitise	Digitise	Digitise	Digitise
Use: re-organise		Make changes	Make changes	Make changes	Make changes	Make changes	Some
Reveal: display		Digitally	Digitally	Digitally	Digitally	Digitally	Digitally
Reveal: inform	Digital doc	Digital doc	Digital doc	Digital doc	Digital doc	Digital doc	Digital doc
Reveal: share		Digital File	Digital File	Digital File	Digital File	Digital File	Digital File
Reveal: exhibit		Digital exhibit	Digital exhibit		Digital exhibit	Digital exhibit	Digital exhibit
Reveal: exploit	Create	Create	Create	Create	Create	Create	Create
Maintain: manage	Update etc	Update etc	Update etc	Update etc	Update etc	Update etc	Update etc
Maintain: protect	Backup etc	Backup etc	Backup etc	Backup etc	Backup etc	Backup etc	Backup etc
Maintain: preserve	Digital preservation	Digital preservation	Digital preservation	Digital preservation	Digital preservation	Digital preservation	Digital preservation
Maintain: archive	Move files	Move files	Move files	Move files	Move files	Move files	Move files
Maintain: prune	Destroy files	Destroy files	Destroy files	Destroy files	Destroy files	Destroy files	Destroy files

(continued)

Table 8.2 (continued)

Contexts practice	Accumulators	Librarians	Filers	Archivists	Museum and Gallery Curators	Private Curators	Amateur Collectors
Maintain: check		Stocktake	Stocktake	Stocktake	Stocktake	Stocktake	Some
Dispose: donate							
Dispose: sell	Online	Online		Online	Online	Online	Online
Dispose: bequeath	Document		Document			Document	Document
Dispose: destroy	Digital objects	Digital objects	Digital objects	Digital objects	Digital objects	Digital objects	Digital objects

8.3 The Relationship Between Collecting Contexts in the 2020s

Our conclusion from the material we have reviewed in this chapter is that there has indeed been a narrowing of the gap between the various Collecting Contexts, though less so with respect to Accumulators and some Amateur Collectors. This seems to have been brought about by the following phenomena:

- **General capabilities afforded by the internet**: the internet has provided the ability to search for information about people and things, to buy and sell objects, to communicate quickly and easily with anyone connected, and to publicise and exhibit capabilities, products, possessions, and characteristics. Such general capabilities have impacted every aspect of human activity, and collecting, in all its guises, no less than any other.
- **Specific functionality afforded in the Icon Age**: The practices associated with managing collections are now ably supported by a full range of software applications and cloud services. Whereas previously, indexes may have been seen as specialist entities, they can now be realised for any type of collection using the simple spreadsheet, a database, or by numerous applications and cloud services provided for specific types of collections. Integral to such applications are metadata concepts and standards, search and retrieval, and the ability to modify and extend the contents. Photographs can be taken, documents can be scanned, and the resulting images can be included, if required, in particular applications. Control sheets, background descriptions, and information of any sort about collections and the objects they contain, can all be created and maintained using software applications. The divide of practice that used to exist between the various major strands of collecting, has been substantially narrowed by the generalisability of the computing tools that can be used to assist them.
- **The digitisation of objects**: The emergence of digital objects has had three effects. First, the fact that most computer users—hundreds of millions of people, both at work and at home, have collections of Digital Files to organise and manage, has brought Filing and Archiving closer to the other strands of collecting. Secondly, the distinction between Accumulations, Files, and Archives is substantially diminished when they deal with digital objects: all three may exist in a single collection. Thirdly, the facts that (a) there are now digital objects to collect as well as physical objects; (b) that physical objects can be digitised; and c) that digital objects can be made physical, have all impacted all types of collecting. The objects of Digital Collecting—Digital Files—now all look the same in all the Collecting Contexts.
- **The uniformity of IT practices:** Within the IT environment, the hardware and software infrastructure, and the methods used to apply and manage them, are largely the same regardless of industry or application. Consequently, when dealing with digital items, all collecting contexts can use the same design methodologies and Digital Curation practices, giving the impression of—and probably confirming—a similarity in purpose and activities.

These four phenomena have affected all types of collecting: institutional and individual, material objects and information objects, work and home. They have brought each aspect into the view of one another, and they have resulted in common practices being applied across all the Collecting Contexts. This homogeneity encourages and enables the whole field to be examined as an overall homo sapiens practice of collecting.

References

Andersen J (2018) Archiving, ordering, and searching: search engines, algorithms, databases, and deep mediatization. Media Cult Soc 40(1)(016344371875465):1–16

Cahoy ES (2013) Faculty members as archivists: personal archiving practices in the academic environment. In: Hawkins DT (ed) Personal archiving: preserving our digital heritage. Information Today Inc

Chopey MA (2005) Planning and implementing a metadata-driven digital repository. Cat Classification Q 40(3/4):255–287

Currall J, Moss M, Stuart S (2004) What is a collection? Archivaria 58(August):131–146

De Grazia (2023) Welcome to all the works of Alfred de Grazia. https://grazian-archive.com/index_2.htm. Accessed 03 June 2023

Featherstone M (2006) Archive. Theory Cult Soc 23(2–3):591–596

Fisher D, Brush AJ, Gleave E, Smith MA (2006) Revisiting Whittaker & Sidner's "email overload" ten years later. In: Proceedings of the 2006 20th anniversary conference on computer supported cooperative work, Banff, Canada, 4–8 November 2006. ACM, pp 309–312

Glushko RJ (ed) (2013) The discipline of organizing. MIT Press

Kim S (2013) Landscape of personal digital archiving activities and research. In: Hawkins DT (ed) Personal archiving: preserving our digital heritage. Information Today Inc.

Ladd M (2015) Access and use in the digital age: a case study of a digital postcard collection. New Rev Acad Librariansh 21(2):225–231

Manof M (2004) Theories of the archive from across the disciplines. Portal Libr Acad 4(1):9–25

Marshall CC (2013) Social media, personal data, and reusing our digital legacy. In: Hawkins DT (ed) Personal archiving: preserving our digital heritage. Information Today Inc.

Miller RJ (2022) Metadata for digital collections, 2nd edn. Facet Publishing Limited, London, pp 1–544

Navarrete T (2022) Libraries, archives and museums of the future—educational programs in Europe. In: Stuart LA, Clareson TFR, Ray J (eds) Economic considerations for libraries, archives and museums. Routledge, pp 91–103

Oliver G, Harvey R (2016) Digital curation, 2nd edn. Facet Publishing, pp 1–242

Tebeau M (2016) Engaging the materiality of the archive in the digital age. Collections 12(4):475–487

Whittaker S, Sidner C (1996) Email overload: exploring personal information management of email. In: Proceedings of the conference on human factors in computing systems: common ground, CHI '96, Vancouver, BC, Canada, April 13–18, 1996. ACM, pp 276–283

Wilson PA (2025) Sorties into the IT Hurricane, 3rd edn. Self-published in Blurb, distributed by Ingram

Xie I, Matusiak K (2016) Discover digital libraries: theory and practice. Elsevier, Amsterdam

Zeller C (2015) From object to information: the end of collecting in the digital age. Arcadia 50(2):389–409

Chapter 9
Notes on Collecting in the Digital Future

Abstract This chapter explores particular IT-related developments that may have a significant impact on collecting. Thus, while Icons, Displays, and Digitisation are likely to stay pretty much the same, the latter two may become more powerful. Virtual Reality will continue to increase in affordability and effectiveness. Such systems may enable digital collections to be viewed and described in great detail and remotely. However, the need to wear a helmet may prove to be a drag on widespread acceptance. Artificial Intelligence (AI) is already having a huge impact in all fields, as well as generating significant concerns about its long-term safety. For collecting, AI may both create new objects for collecting, and also significantly improve the searching and management of collections. Should the internet eventually morph into something like a Metaverse, collecting organisations are likely to take their place within it. Unfortunately, the risk of wars, climate change and other disasters, affecting the supply chain of computers, will remain present, with a huge potential impact on collectors. Beyond this, at some point brain-machine interfaces will probably become feasible, and AI will have become a commonplace and powerful adjunct to the human. At that point the impact on collecting is difficult to foresee, though it will doubtless continue in some form.

Trying to foretell the future is a risky business—especially in an era in which developments, and the flux they create in the cultural mix, are occurring at an increasingly rapid rate. With this in mind we have chosen to headline this chapter as merely 'notes'—some thoughts and ideas about how the things we know today might pan out going forward. The future undoubtedly has huge numbers of IT developments in store—too many and too difficult to predict. So, we have elected to look at a few specific areas which we believe will have a progressive impact on collecting in particular up to the middle of the twenty-first century. They are:

- Icons, Displays, and Digitisation
- Virtual Reality
- Artificial Intelligence
- The Metaverse

P. Wilson and P. Tolmie, *Collecting in the Icon Age*,
https://doi.org/10.1007/978-3-031-86470-4_9

- War, Climate Change, and Pandemics
- Beyond Human.

In our discussion of these topics in this chapter we have highlighted in Bold the particular Collecting Contexts that are impacted.

9.1 Icons, Displays, and Digitisation

The pattern of development of the current Icon Age technology for the immediate future seems clear—more of the same:

- More activities migrating to digital support and to the mobile phone in particular.
- Even more users of mobile phones.
- More powerful computers and greater storage capacities.
- More facilities and services on the internet (while some countries limit what their people can access)
- More and more youngsters coming through with no experience of anything but Icon Age facilities; and as each year goes by, the set of youngsters coming through will have base experiences of an ever more sophisticated digital environment.

Taking all this into account, it seems likely that the importance and quantity of digital objects will continue to grow; and that more and more digital objects will be collected. The number of physical objects converted to digital format may also grow as the advantages of digital storage and communications are perceived and sought; and the growing power and capabilities of digital technology will continue to be harnessed to support collecting of all types.

9.1.1 The Icon Age Interface

The Icon Age's Graphical User Interface (GUI) is largely dictated by the three primary suppliers—Apple, Microsoft, and Google (which owns the Android operating system); and their plans for future developments are not publicised for commercial reasons. However, in the early 2020s there was nothing to suggest that any radically different approaches in these three platforms were imminent. Icons seemed set to continue to have a prominent place on desktop, laptop, tablet and phone screens for some years to come. That's not to say, however, that the interfaces were not evolving or that radically different interfaces were being envisaged. For example, in the 2000s there had been a trend towards minimising the clutter in the interfaces of the major operating systems, and eliminating the 3D look of interface objects, and this was followed in the 2010s by further changes to overcome the usability problems that minimisation and flat design had caused (Fernandes 2017; Chendvankar 2020). In the 2020s, voice interaction was in widespread use in mobile phones and smart speakers; and Augmented Reality concepts were becoming more widely used in mobile phone apps. These developments may presage a gradual move away from the traditional GUI of the major platforms (Sirk 2020).

Two examples of how interfaces might look in the long-term are a couple of very watchable 6-minute Microsoft Future Vision videos portraying a world of very innovative hardware displays, flat interfaces with minimal numbers of icons and menus, users manipulating the objects on screen with their fingers, and seamless integration of background applications (Microsoft 2015, 2017). Of course, these videos were largely marketing exercises and need to be treated as such. Nevertheless, they were created by people who know about interface design, and reflected their thinking. Elements of these videos will almost certainly come about eventually in some form or other. This point is well illustrated by LSI Logic's 1990 video which portrayed a large screen on a living room wall controlled by voice interaction, full multi-media capabilities, and video conferencing around the world including to a laptop in a café on a university campus. It seemed pretty far-fetched at the time, but fairly unremarkable in the early 2020s (LSI Logic 1990).

In summary, we envisage icons continuing to abound in the 2020s, but perhaps starting to recede beyond then should interfaces focus more on the objects being addressed and applications start disappearing into the background. This may well have an impact on how collectable objects are eventually perceived on screen—though it's difficult to know at this point exactly what form that will take.

9.1.2 Displays

In the early 2020s, a wide range of high definition, thin displays, in sizes ranging from 4 to 100 + inches diagonally, were available at broadly affordable prices. Uses ranged from mobile phones, computer monitors, TVs and signage. On the face of it these provided adequate support for the display of collections of digital objects. However, closer examination of the needs in each of the Collection Contexts reveals unmet requirements which we might envisage being addressed in the future. **Accumulators** and **Filers** of business and domestic documentation don't come into this discussion, since computer monitors in a wide variety of sizes, would seem to cover all their needs. However, organisations like **Museums/Galleries**, and possibly some types of **Libraries** and **Archives**, may build increasingly large collections of digital objects which they may wish to display to the visiting public. Such objects may not all be Born Digital; some may be digitised versions of physical objects which may be located in store or in other locations. In addition to the digital objects themselves, such organisations are likely to make an increasing use of digital displays to present information about the objects on display. For both these reasons, there is likely to be an increasing need for large numbers of displays which are easy to install and move, and which are affordable in quantity. A single 100-inch display at, say, £8000 might be affordable, but 20 at £8000, even with a quantity discount, might not be.

Private Curators may have two specific reasons for making use of displays: first to be able to have easy and quick access to very valuable items that are kept in very secure positions or even in bank vaults; and, second, to be able to view Born Digital items, such as NFTs, that they have acquired for their collections. Having said that, Private Curators, may be wealthy enough to afford whatever display equipment they require. **Amateur Collectors**, however, may not be in that position, and furthermore, may have a wider range of requirements. For example, the *pwofc* website describes three instances in which various digitised objects were assembled for display in the home between 2014 and 2021 [RM-Book; RM-ESB; RM-Trophy]. The designs for the installations were based on the assumption that cheap and flexible display technologies would eventually become available; but were actually printed as icons on paper and framed or laminated, and the substantive digital contents made accessible on an iPad in PDF files stored in the SideBooks app. Overall the goals here were twofold: first, to release space by digitising objects and throwing some of the physical objects away; and second, to bring the objects to life by making them, and linked associated material, visible and accessible. Both objectives were found to be achievable.

The findings from the above installations illustrate what Amateur Collectors could do with a diverse range of objects that they are interested in, using standard domestic computer systems. No doubt many other types of installations are possible using any one of the myriad different types of collected objects; and it is likely that more and more Amateur Collectors will want to explore such possibilities as IT becomes ever-more pervasive and affordable. However, they would require, first, an affordable, thin, wall display screen with touch screen technology; second, functionality that enabled the display of multiple file-types; and, third, a capability for self-contained operation or simple and effective integration with a domestic laptop or desktop computer.

The original concept for the installations came from news of the development of Electronic Paper, because it was envisaged that it would be particularly thin and therefore suitable for placing on a variety of different domestic walls. However, a 2011 article suggested that, while much research and development was ongoing, e-Paper was not yet a mainstream product (Heikenfeld et al. 2011). By 2023, significant advances had been made such that the 2024 market for e-Paper products was expected to exceed $2.5 billion in applications such as e-readers, signage, retail shelf displays, smart packaging, and smart home devices (Mordor Intelligence 2023). Other uses included screens for watches, phones, laptops, eNotebooks and monitors, some of which had colour screens (E-Ink-Info 2024). However, the largest e-Paper screen being sold by EInk (a major supplier) in 2023 was a 42-inch monochrome unit which would have been quite expensive for an Amateur Collector, and that excluded driving boards. In contrast, UK electrical retailers were offering a wide range of colour flat screen LED TVs in 2023, in a range of sizes up to 85 inches or more, fully equipped with Wi-Fi connectivity and HDMI ports, capable of being wall-mounted, and with a thickness of between 2.4 and 8.5 cm. So, it seems that, in terms of thinness and wall placement suitability, e-Paper is not an essential pre-requisite for such installations; and that, if Amateur Collectors did start to try and exploit their digital objects in this way, products meeting the full package of requirements, including a touch screen and stand-alone operation capable of displaying files with multiple formats, could emerge quite quickly, given the current advanced state of display technology. Of course, the touch screen requirement might be met in other ways in the future: for example, by voice recognition (already widely used in smart speakers and mobile phones in 2023), or by gestures picked up by cameras located in the display.

9.1.3 Digitisation

The ability to digitise physical objects is a key requirement for many collectors in the Icon Age. Some objects, like documents, require only a 2D image to be appreciated in their digital form; while others, such as a coin or a piece of sculpture, require a full 360-degree 3D image. 2D Scanning technology had become commonplace by the 2020s, augmented by high resolution cameras in the universally-used mobile phone. Since these were already mature technologies, only incremental improvements are expected in the future. These may include the automatic elimination of distortions caused by not holding the camera face parallel to the plane of a flat surface being photographed (editing facilities to fix such distortions had already become available); and the automatic application of optical character recognition during the scanning and photographing processes.

The creation of full 360-degree 3D images is considerably more complicated and could be achieved using at least four different types of technology in the 2020s (Sargentis et al. 2022):

- **Photogrammetry**: 3D models are created using many photographs of an object from different angles. The only instruments needed are a camera and appropriate software.
- **Structured light scanning**: structured patterns of light are projected onto an object, which distorts it. A 3D model is created by analysing the distortion of the light with appropriate software.
- **Laser scanning**: lasers detect the coordinates of the object in space by measuring the direct time of flight of laser light beams or using triangulation to detect the distance.
- **Computerised tomography (CT)**: in this method a series of 2D X-ray photographs is taken in different sections enabling 'solid' 3D models to be produced. This was an expensive and complex technology in the early 2020s, so it was used mainly in medicine at that time.

Photogrammetry was probably the method in most widespread use in the 2020s, with various platform/turntable-based products on offer as well as a host of apps emerging for use with the increasingly powerful mobile phone. However, the quality of results from photogrammetry clearly depends on the number of photos taken, the angles they are taken at, and the appropriateness of the software algorithms that are used to stitch them together. Illustrations of just how complex and convoluted this process can be are provided by a protocol for High Resolution "DIY" Photogrammetry (Cerasoni et al. 2022), and in a guide published in the Digital Atlas of Ancient Life web site (Hauf and Hendricks 2019).

Once a 3D model was created in the early 2020s, it could only be viewed and manipulated using specialist software. Standards for viewing software have been available since 1997 and are defined by the Technical Standards Committee ISO/IEC JTC 1/SC 24 on Computer Graphics, Image Processing and Environmental Data Representation (ISO 2023). The current standard is known as X3D and is promoted by the Web3D Consortium (Web3D 2023). No doubt creators of 3D images will have the viewing software on their machines; but for those who came across such images on web sites belonging to institutions like Museums and Galleries in the early 2020s, some software had to be downloaded to their machines before they could look at them. However, in the future a 3D viewing capability may become a standard background feature built into most devices. This would clearly be advantageous to many collecting institutions.

The future is likely to bring substantial improvements to all these aspects of 3D image creation and viewing. As computers become ever more powerful, the photogrammetric process is likely to become much more automated and less time-consuming; and the resulting 3D models are likely to be of much better quality. Such improvements will prompt more collectors to consider creating 3D models of objects in their collections. Standardised viewing software may be included as standard components within operating systems. Looking further out, it is possible that solid 3D models providing details of the interior of an object may become easier and more affordable to produce, and that some collectors may start to make greater use of them. Another significant development in the early 2020s has been the emergence of true holographic images presented in special viewing booths varying in size from large enough to present a life-sized person to smaller models 73 cm high (Proto 2024). These may become cheaper and more widely used as time goes by.

9.2 Virtual Reality Futures

We have already mentioned Virtual Reality (VR) systems in connection with the digital representation of objects (Sect. 6.7.6), with the Video Game Industry's success with the Augmented Reality game Pokemon Go (Sect. 7.1); with Museum and Gallery use to enhance the visitor experience (Sects. 7.7.1 and 7.7.2); and with the VeVe company's augmented reality environment in which their NFT objects can be placed (Sect. 7.9.1). Such systems clearly have some potential for use in collecting in the future, and therefore a more detailed outline of VR technology is provided first before we explore its ramifications for collecting.

9.2.1 A Brief Outline of Virtual Reality Technology

The notion of providing a simulated world for computer users to operate within was around in the early days of computing using text-based games such as Lunar Lander. However, it exploded with the emergence of the personal computer in the late 1970s when vast numbers of screen-based computer games containing all types of vaguely real and totally imagined environments, were produced for users to explore, solve puzzles and complete missions. Such games are now very big business—many of them having on-line versions played by hundreds of thousands of people worldwide. They typically present their worlds with high quality graphics and very detailed representations of places, buildings, things and people. In some cases, the imagery is recorded real-world video. Online versions often enable people to play together as groups and to communicate with each other in real time using text or voice or even video.

Computer games are a very specific genre and not really representative of what a general-purpose VR environment might look like. A better example might be Second Life—an on-line system which opened for business in 2003 and which enables its users to create virtual representations of themselves (avatars), and to interact with places, objects and other avatars. They can explore the world, meet other residents, socialise, participate in both individual and group activities, build, create, shop, and trade virtual property and services with each other (Wikipedia 2023b).

As is the case with many computer games, Second Life is primarily used as a screen-based system. However, the term VR is often used to refer to systems with head-mounted displays which completely immerse the user in a virtual world; and with devices such as motion sensors, optical tracking systems, and wired/wireless gloves, to enable the system to know what the user is doing and to provide extra sensory sensations in addition to those provided by the headset.

Another variation of VR is Augmented Reality in which a view or a picture of a real-world environment is enhanced by adding computer-generated perceptual information such as graphics, text, images and video, to an existing scene in real time (Greengard 2019). While Augmented Reality may use headsets, it can also be achieved using special glasses or even just a mobile phone. For example, the game Pokemon Go, released in 2016, requires users to collect objects overlaid on the image of the local real world as displayed on the mobile phone's screen by the device's camera. This became popular around the world to the extent that by May 2018 it had over 147 million monthly active users, and was responsible for significantly raising the world's awareness of the term Augmented Reality (AR) (Wikipedia 2023c).

Mixed Reality (MR) is an advanced version of AR in which the physical environment can play a part in the activities occurring in AR, for example, hiding behind a real-world sofa so as to be out of sight of an AR character. Extended Reality (XR) (sometimes known as Cross-Reality) is an umbrella term and refers to a combination of Virtual Reality (VR), Augmented Reality (AR) and Mixed Reality(MR) (Mystakidis 2022).

By the 2020s, all these various flavours of Virtual Reality technology were being used for a huge variety of applications in sectors which included education, training, sports, engineering, manufacturing, construction, entertainment, the travel industry, journalism and news, marketing, property sales, law enforcement, surgery, and defence (Greengard 2019).

The infrastructure requirement for effective VR is demanding: very fast response times to movements in head, eye and body are required to make the experience seem realistic. The delay in response time is known as latency, and long latency can induce a feeling of nausea (Lanier 2017). In fact, the smallest glitch in any part of the system—hardware, software, user interface, or network performance—can wreck the whole experience (Greengard 2019).

A variety of different user interface display mechanisms are in use. At one end of the spectrum is a room made up of 3D display walls for which special 3D glasses must be worn. These are usually referred to as CAVE rooms (Cave Automatic Virtual Environment). For closer viewing, devices such as computer monitors, TVs, or tablets, capable of displaying depth and of tracking eyes, can be used (Lanier 2017). Hand-held controllers with buttons, triggers and thumb-sticks enable users to interact with objects (Mystakidis 2022). Research into haptic devices such as gloves and bodysuits is ongoing to provide users with more realistic senses of feel and touch, and even taste and smell (Greengard 2019).

However, the most intensive development activity seems to be centred around head-mounted displays—glasses and helmets. A steady stream of ever more sophisticated products has been emerging since the 2010s. In 2013 Google introduced its Google Glass product which projected a screen image onto the lens of an eyeglass and provided internet access and a built-in camera. Although the consumer product was withdrawn in 2015 to enable Google to refocus on a product for the business world, it had demonstrated what was possible (Greengard 2019). On the Headset front, Facebook (renamed Meta in 2021) was a major supplier with its Oculus range: the Oculus Quest 2 was released in 2020 and provided a screen for each eye, 4 wide angle cameras attached to the outside of the helmet for tracking, 3D positional audio built into the headset, and two handheld controllers (Wikipedia 2023a). Meta Quest 3 was released in October 2023 with a faster processor, higher resolution display and the ability to play in high-quality augmented reality (Greenwald 2023). A little earlier in 2023, Apple had announced its Vision Pro Headset which also enabled an augmented reality experience by presenting apps and images within a view of the user's surroundings. Control of the environment is achieved by looking at things and hand and finger movements. Typing can be performed by using a virtual keyboard with your fingers, or by dictation. Among all the various uses that the Apple web site highlights it explicitly says 'Free your Desktop and your apps will follow' and 'Browse the web in Safari' suggesting that the intention is to make this rather more than a mere entertainment platform. (Apple 2023; Hern 2023). Vison Pro looked to set new directions for VR: a 2024 review described it as an impressive, boundary pushing product—a massive leap forward—but concluded that its initial pricing—around \$3500—would be far out of reach for most people (Gibbs 2024).

It's clear that VR is an established technology with a huge commercial footprint that will continue to grow as computers become more powerful, research improves equipment, and software products become more plentiful. However, there is one fundamental restraining factor that may limit VR's eventual impact—the fact that people have to wear something on their heads to achieve a fully immersive VR experience. They may feel its inconvenient to have to put on a helmet or glasses and may feel uncomfortable wearing them for long periods. Furthermore, there is a view that people will just not want to exclude the real world for extensive periods (Anderson and Rainie 2022). Jeremy Bailenson, one of VR's research pioneers, ensures that the users in his lab remove the headset after 20 min to have a rest before continuing after a few minutes. He says:

> I'm with Jaron Lanier, who likes to describe the most amazing moment in VR as the moment you take the HMD (helmet) off and are flooded with the full gamut of subtle sensory inputs that VR can't capture - fine gradations of light, smells, the sensation of air moving on your skin… In a strange way, VR helps you to appreciate the real world more. (Bailenson 2018)

9.2.2 Virtual Reality's Impact on the Collecting Contexts

VR may impact certain types of **Accumulators** in the future. For example, Computer gamers will continue to collect virtual objects in virtual worlds which make use of the latest VR developments; and some games may manage their objects as NFT constructs. Those who accumulate files on their computers may find that they are able to browse them using a headset like the Apple Vision Pro, and that their operating system or applications may provide new ways of presenting the files to take advantage of VR's capabilities. For example, file icons might be designed to reflect file size or how old they are. Collections of material that have been digitised simply to save space, and with no indexing applied, might be similarly viewed. This type of functionality might be exploited in much more diverse ways for **Filers** with indexed collections. Such digital objects could be placed into any number of different types of containers other than folders, for example, cupboards or chests; and items could be grouped in settings to reflect their contents, such as against a background picture of the place or people or activity associated with them. Such representations could be defined/created by the system (see Sect. 9.3 on AI below), or by the user. Of course, the operating system and/or application software provider could take advantage of VR's capabilities to provide a completely different representational structure in which to present collections of digital objects—anything from the Rapid Serial Visual Presentation (akin to the rapid riffling of pages) envisaged by Spence and Witkowski (2013) to the Cyberspace envisaged by Gibson:

> …a graphic representation of data…Lines of light… clusters and constellations of data. Like city lights receding. (Gibson 1984)

Such VR representations may also be used by other organisations which have collection indexes—in particular **Libraries** and **Museums/Galleries**. The latter are already making use of Augmented Reality displays of relevant information and associated objects, as the technology develops and tools to create the content become cheaper and easier to use. They may also make increasing use of VR to provide access to exhibitions of specific pieces from across their collections—and possibly from the collections of other organisations. Such exhibitions would, of course, be accessible from anywhere in the world. Quite apart from creating exhibitions, some institutions may simply find that creating a virtual reality display of some or all of their objects, provides worthwhile benefits such as better lighting, closer access, and easier conservation (Haynes 2018). Some may even take the decision to only collect digitised versions of objects—especially objects that may be too large to store and/or too difficult to maintain and conserve, for example motor cars (Anderson and Raini 2022). The resulting VR display may then be delivered either through an immersive headset experience or simply on a screen.

VR may be used extensively in the future by **Archivers**. By our definition, Archives are relatively inaccessible in long-term storage, so the ability to place their contents in an easily accessible virtual environment, regardless of what storage area or packaging they reside in, is a major benefit. Of course, those Archives which operate more like a Library may not find this capability so advantageous; but Archives in the depths of a building's basement, or in a remote storage unit, or even in a bank vault, can be given a new lease of life without requiring additional display space or creating additional security risks. This may also be particularly attractive to **Private Curators** for whom security of extremely valuable assets is a prime concern, or who may wish to enable the public to see their collections without having the worry of managing physical buildings, displays, and access.

Most **Amateur Collectors** are unlikely to be affected by VR, though, if the right tools are made available, some collectors may enjoy placing their collections into a virtual display. Of course, organisations which sell digital collectable objects, such as Trading Cards, may continue to promote their products by providing them within augmented reality and other VR settings. Indeed, it is quite conceivable that, if the technology proves attractive, such commercial organisations may expand the types of objects they sell, and new organisations may be tempted to enter the field. The objects concerned may or may not be provided as NFTs—that will entirely depend on which approach will make most money.

9.3 Artificial Intelligence

Artificial Intelligence (AI) is the ability of machines to perform tasks that normally require human intelligence. Although work on AI has been ongoing since the 1950s, it only started to have a significant impact after the turn of the millennium (Ding 2023). Since then, progress has been rapid with over 8000 AI start-up companies being listed on Crunchbase—a startup funding website—in mid-2019 (Gawdat 2021). It is clear that AI is going to have a major effect on just about everything, including collecting, in the years ahead. Indeed, at the beginning of 2025, the field was moving so rapidly that the observations below are necessarily tentative and may have been superceded by events by the time this text is published.

A brief description of what AI is, is provided below, followed by some thoughts about its potential impact on collecting.

9.3.1 AI Developments and Technologies

Go is a game with a huge number of possible moves. In 2017, an AI program called AlphGo Master and owned by DeepMind (a Google company), played about 1.3 million games against itself in six weeks to learn how to play the game before beating the world Go champion. DeepMind then created another program—AlphaGo Zero—which proceeded to beat AlphGo Master 100–0; and then went on to learn how to play chess in just 9 h after which it beat the world AI chess champion, Stockfish, 1000–0 (Gawdat 2021). These achievements illustrate the rapid rate of development that has been experienced in AI in the 2010s and beyond.

The Alpha programs were based on Neural Networks—structures inspired by the operation of the human brain and which typically have at least three layers: an input layer, a hidden layer and an output layer. The hidden layer may have huge numbers of nodes, each one cross-connected to multiple other hidden layer nodes. Each node in the input layer may be connected to one or more nodes in the hidden layer. The output layer produces the results of the path through the hidden layer dictated by the inputs received and the relationships between the hidden layer nodes. Each node is provided with a mathematically constructed value which dictates when it should forward an input to another node (Ding et al. 2023).

Neural Networks can learn in a number of different ways. They can extract common features from labelled data and use that to predict the values of unlabelled data (supervised learning); or they can extract features from unlabelled data (unsupervised learning). A mixture of both approaches can also be used (semi-supervised learning) (Ding et al. 2023). Although this sounds straightforward, the learning process can involve huge amounts of data and computing power before a satisfactory result is achieved.

Neural Networks are being used to undertake a variety of analytical tasks such as face recognition, automated driving, translation, data mining, and abnormal cell detection (Ding et al. 2023). They are also used to summarise and translate text as well as being able to create new text content from both text and image inputs (Zhang et al. 2023). In late 2024, several video-from-text-input products emerged (Turk 2024). These so-called Generative AI systems started to have a substantial impact on public awareness in the early 2020s. For example, the Stable Diffusion product could produce good graphics from a text input such as 'draw me a picture of a spaceman riding a horse in the style of Van Gogh' (Stable Diffusion 2023). Some commentators believe that AI will make it much easier to create software code simply by describing what you want a program to do; and that this may greatly expand the number of people developing software in the same way that spreadsheets hugely increased the number of people doing financial analysis (Toone 2024).

However, the product which made most waves in the early 2020s was CHAT-GPT-4. This generated text as a result of a written request. The company that produced Chat-GPT-4, OpenAI, made it available to the general public on its website in November 2022 and within two months it had over 100 million monthly active users (Reuters 2023). Chat-GPT used a neural network to create a Large Language Model (LLM) aimed at predicting the next word in a sequence of words. It was trained on a huge amount of data—trillions of words—and after about a billion trillion random perturbations of the parameters it became very good (Russell 2023). Consequently, it was used for all sorts of purposes including brainstorming; compiling literature reviews; the creation of articles, reports and essays; the design of teaching courses, providing medical information; and computer programming (Zhang et al. 2023; Naughton 2023). It could even be adapted for specific uses and sets of data: the OpenAI website provided extensive documentation on how to do this (OpenAI 2025). However, no matter how clever CHAT-GPT-4 appeared to be, it was simply predicting what words should come after each other. Its results were certainly plausible, but often unremarkable, sometimes wrong (Zhang et al. 2023), and occasionally even a lie—a feature referred to as 'hallucinating' (Russell 2023). Indeed, the Guardian newspaper encountered at least two instances in which CHAT-GPT-4 had quoted fictional Guardian articles that it had just made up (Moran 2023); and similar problems may occur when LLMs cite scientific references (Athaluri et al. 2023). As Toone suggests, it is best to think of these systems less like oracles and more like weather forecasts—useful but basically probabilistic (Toone 2024). Furthermore, at least one commentator in 2024 believed that the huge investments being made in operating and developing LLM technology might never be recouped because of a lack of training data, the hallucination problem, and the lack of any applications that would generate sufficient revenue to offset the costs (Zitron 2024).

CHAT-GPT is just one of many generative AI programs powered by Neural Networks. They are all examples of so-called Weak AI—programs to solve single or specific tasks. Strong AI refers to programs that can replicate or exceed human reasoning; which possess the awareness and flexibility of humans; and which can operate in multiple fields (Ding et al. 2023). Strong AI is the ultimate goal of AI researchers and was some way away in the 2020s—though work towards it was proceeding apace. For example, in the robotics field, one detailed proposal for building a Strong AI system envisaged modelling the different elements of the human brain with an interlinked set of generative programs (Taniguchi et al. 2022). An alternative way of categorising AI systems has been put forward by Drew Breunig (2024) who suggests that Strong AI could be called 'Gods'; that systems which are supervised and used by experts be called 'interns'; and that AI which is designed to perform just one specific function to a high degree of reliability should be called a 'Cog'. Such deliberations reflect our concern and uncertainty about what future AI systems have in store for us—as further described below.

9.3.2 Concerns About AI

Following the release of CHAT-GPT-4 and other AI systems in 2022 and their widespread use by the general public, the concerns which we believe will have most effect on collecting and which are becoming ever-more widely discussed, are listed below:

- The huge amounts of training data required by Generative AI programs, may have been simply scraped from the web without permission from the owners—some of whom may have been collectors.
- The extensive use of random data from the internet may be introducing racial, gender and other biases into the models simply because the data itself may be naturally lacking in examples of one sort or another, and there may have been no steps taken to rectify the bias (Marr 2022). This may have an impact on displays in large institutions.
- AI is being used to generate an increasing amount of the internet's content, but the quality of that content is essentially second hand, and may be poor and sometimes incorrect (Vincent 2023), Furthermore, over time vast amounts of our knowledge could become damaged goods and could mislead collectors.
- In the early 2020s it seemed impossible to know how the generative systems reached their conclusions—the workings of the central section of neural networks were too complex to understand (Zhang et al. 2023; Gawdat 2021); and at least one commentator was unable to say whether or not CHAT-GPT-4 had developed its own internal goals and was pursuing them (Russell 2023). Work to rectify this and to produce so-called Explainable AI was underway in the early 2020s but had yet to produce generalisable results (Dwivedi et al. 2023; Pradhan et al. 2022). This could be problematic for everyone using AI including collectors.
- The ease with which AI systems can produce text, images, voice, and video seemed to threaten the livelihoods of creative professionals such as photographers, designers, illustrators, artists, authors, voice actors. This prompted a movement by visual artists, image agencies and others to explicitly opt out of allowing their work to be farmed for AI training (Thorpe 2023); and for some unions in the creative industries to go on strike (Beckett 2023). This may affect what collectors decide to include in their collections and how they make them available online.

9.3.3 AI's Impact on the Collecting Contexts

Perhaps AI's most significant impact on collecting will be the emergence of a new type of item to collect—items that have been created by an AI system as outlined in Sect. 6.5.9. Such items may be Born Digital text, music, images, videos; or they could even be physical objects designed by an AI and printed on a 3D printer. Collecting such objects will raise the question of authorship: should it be the name of the AI, or a combination of the names of the AI and the person who directed the AI to produce the item? Either way, what form should the name of the AI take? AI-authored objects will also present the opportunity for a whole new genre of fakes and for experts capable of recognising them. This will have an impact on all types of objects: AI could produce fakes of human-produced objects; and humans could produce fakes of the AI-produced objects.

Moving onto the impact of AI on specific collecting contexts, **Accumulators** will not make any deliberate use of AI, but may find that their Digital Accumulations are being automatically monitored or organised in some way by an AI. For example, files accumulated on a computer might be indexed and/or organised by an AI; and the automatic management of the photos on our phones might become even more sophisticated with the help of AI as time goes on. Perhaps, the increasing effectiveness of AI may eliminate the necessity to index any digital objects (files, emails, e-books, music, podcasts, photos, videos, mementos etc.), with all such objects just being collected into a digital heap ready for the AI to sort them out and to facilitate retrieval (Elgan 2016).

One of the main impacts of AI on **Libraries** is likely to be the ability to provide significantly enhanced information searches to support researchers and other users—though a significant number of individuals now appear to be simply utilising AI themselves and cutting out the Library altogether. AI systems can provide information, search and obtain information from a wide variety of sources, translate information in other languages, and present the assembled information in a logical and coherent form (Lund and Wang 2023) (Ajakaye 2022)—as millions of CHATGPT users discovered in the early 2020s. Such searches are likely to take much less time than previously, even though the resulting report will still have to be checked by the Librarian or the user until such time as confidence in the quality and accuracy of AI systems has improved. Libraries in research institutions may employ AI in the management of their research data repositories (Uzwyshyn 2022).

For more general information services, AI may help **Libraries** to gather and analyse intelligence about reading habits, research interests, teaching content, professional fields, research directions, research teams, and related groups, thereby enabling tailored and personalised information intelligence to be pushed to patrons. This might include book recommendations, selective domain information, alerts about the latest cutting-edge research hotspots, new teaching reference materials etc. (Ajakaye 2022).

AI may also be able play a substantial role in the management of library stock. Some metadata for new accessions could be automatically acquired and indexes automatically updated (Harper et al. 2022). Lending patterns and the state of stock items could be monitored, and repair and replacement recommendations made. Recommendations for new acquisitions could be made by monitoring the emergence of new publications and matching them to the interests of the library's users (Ajakaye 2022).

For **Files, Archives, Libraries,** and **Museums/Galleries** with manuscript collections, the ability to integrate AI into collections to facilitate discovery is already well under way (Terras 2022). An initial conceptual step in this direction is to change our perception of the set of Files/Archives/Manuscripts from being a set of administrative records to a collection of data. This transformed view facilitates the use of AI to index, classify and create metadata for the collection (Colavizza et al. 2021). A further step is to provide some extensive in-depth training on the collection to a generative AI model, thereby enabling free form, natural language questions to be asked about the collection. For Research Data Archives, AI presents a huge opportunity.

AI may also play a major role in the establishment of new **Archives** by being able to crawl multiple digital sources, or the vast collections of digital records produced by organisations, and to select documents that fit pre-defined characteristics (Colavizza et al. 2021).

These potential changes in the structure of **Archives** will probably necessitate a change in the role that Archivists perform such that they become more attuned to storytelling, meaning-making, context providing, offering outreach and education, and increasing people's awareness of how they can preserve their own digital objects (Theimer 2018).

Museums and Art Galleries will make use of AI to generate personalised guides for visitors (Fabbri et al. 2023; Esteban et al. 2022)—perhaps to accompany the Augmented Reality displays discussed elsewhere in this chapter. Some commentators envisage this material being presented in the form of a narrative supporting games or scavenger hunts requiring the visitor to search for certain exhibits (Hettmann et al. 2023). Some organisations have been pioneering such AI-supported guides and games for some time (Gaia et al. 2019), so we can expect wider take-up and greater sophistication as AI becomes more powerful and accessible. Beyond the use of guides, Museum and Art Gallery collection information in general—indexes, metadata, digital images etc.—is likely to be harnessed by AI to provide much more powerful ways of analysing and researching collections (French and Villaespesa 2019). **Private Curators** of sizeable collections are also likely to use AI in this way. **Museums and Art Galleries** will also make increasing use of AI analytics of visitor information acquired from all the digital touchpoints (website, social media, ticketing, mobile apps etc.) in order to provide visitors with a more tailored experience (French and Villaespesa 2019).

Currently, only those **Amateur Collectors** who have collections of digital objects or have digitised indexes and metadata information about their collections will be able to take advantage of AI (though, this may not be a limitation in the future if AI were able to look at objects and generate its own model). Such people may wish to train a generative AI model with their collection information in order to be able to explore, research, and even manage their collections. However, this is unlikely to happen until the process of integrating generative models with data sets becomes much simpler. If this were the case, Amateur Collectors might well wish to use AI to inter-relate their more personal items such as memorabilia, writings, drawings etc.; to record stories about their objects (Kirk and Sellen 2010); and to contextualise mementos in terms of associated people, places and objects (Kalnikaitėa and Whittaker 2011). However, it is vital that we recognise the distinction between people defining the stories and inter-relationships themselves, and AI doing it for them. These are two very different things with, probably, two very different results. Examples of the extensive and intensive experience that humans need to go through in such a process are provided in the Electronic Storyboard and Electronic Trophy Gallery experiments documented in *pwofc.com* (Wilson 2018, 2020a, 2021). Equivalent creations delivered up by an AI, would not only preclude the human from experiencing a set of highly impressionable personal reflections, but would also inject another layer of information into the human's mind thereby modifying existing memories and thoughts. Having said that, in the Electronic Story Board experiment a significant number of forgotten points or incorrect memories were identified (Wilson 2020b, 2020c), so, an AI which retrospectively identified such issues might be useful. Against this, however, we have to consider that it may be some time before generative systems themselves can be considered reliable enough not to make errors, or to lie. Regardless of these concerns about AI, it is likely that AI programs will eventually be provided to identify and look after collections of important digital family documents and files; and that these programs will prompt their safe passage down the generations by applying appropriate digital preservation measures as and when needed.

9.4 The Metaverse

Put in its simplest terms, the Metaverse is what the current Internet and World Wide Web might eventually become. As such, in the early 2020s it did not exist and was a speculative notion. However, the foundational building blocks for what might transpire were all in place; and the whole concept had been thoroughly discussed in Matthew Ball's 2022 book 'The Metaverse' (Ball 2022). Below follows a short description of the Metaverse and how it may come about, followed by some thoughts about its potential impact on collecting.

9.4.1 Metaverse Components and Development

Ball explained that what he meant when he wrote about the Metaverse is:

> A massively scaled and interoperable network of real-time rendered 3D virtual worlds that can be experienced synchronously and persistently by an effectively unlimited number of users with an individual sense of presence, and with continuity of data, such as identity, history, entitlements, objects, communications and payments. (Ball 2022)

Ball also said that 3D is a critical component—without it we would just be talking about the current internet.

The foundational building blocks for the creation of the Metaverse include:

- The massive computer games industry with its virtual worlds and over 3 billion players in the early 2020s, as described previously in Sect. 7.1.
- The specialised and highly advanced hardware and software supporting the gaming industry and provided by companies such as Nvidia, Epic Games, and Unity Technologies (Ball 2022); or the game console providers such as Sony, Microsoft and Nintendo.

- Nascent decentralised payment and ownership certification systems using programmable Blockchain technology (Ball 2022)
- The internet and associated Wi-Fi connections which are increasingly being supported by faster local fibre infrastructure.
- A culture in which most organisations have a web site and believe it is a necessary part of their operation in the world of the early 2020s.
- Organisations involved in providing standards and software to enable 3D graphics.
- An established and continually developing virtual reality industry as described earlier in this chapter.

There are at least two entities which are explicitly working towards bringing the Metaverse into being: the Open Metaverse Interoperability Group (OMI) and the Metaverse Standards Forum (MSF). OMI claims to:

> …bolster the metaverse as an open and interoperable resource for anyone, inspired by the collaborative efforts of the community' - 'an open source community of industry professionals, independent creators, and passionate enthusiasts building interoperable technology together, in the open. (OMIGroup 2024)

MSF describes its mission as:

> Open to any organization, the Metaverse Standards Forum provides a venue for cooperation between standards organizations and companies to foster the development of interoperability standards for an open and inclusive metaverse, and accelerate their development and deployment through pragmatic, action-based projects. (Metaverse Standards Forum 2024)

However, these two organisations would probably need the support of the gaming industry, the gaming hardware and software suppliers, the organisations managing the internet and its standards, and the VR product manufacturers; and there are good reasons to question whether any of those will enable the creation of the Metaverse. In particular:

- The gaming industry might want to obstruct the introduction of interoperability because they might lose customers and revenue to competitors.
- The hardware and software companies might not want to risk their commercial relationships with their gaming clients.
- The Internet Engineering Task Force (IETF), which might be central in creating the Metaverse, doesn't seem to be obviously working on any related topics other than reducing 'latency by orders of magnitude' (IETF 2025) (latency is the delay it takes to get data across the internet, and a reduction in latency is one of the Metaverse requirements mentioned by Ball (Ball 2022)).
- The focus of the ISO technical committee on computer graphics (ISO 2023) and the Web 3D consortium (Web3D 2023) appears to be on making 3D graphics better, not bringing virtual worlds together.
- The two major players in the VR industry—Apple and Meta—both seem focussed on systems involving headsets and, as mentioned previously, it's difficult to envisage the majority of web users wearing headsets.

9.4.2 *Impact of the Metaverse on Collecting*

For **all types of collectors** around the late 2030s, Digital Files may be miniature versions of the actual object shown in 3D where appropriate, with size indicated by some aspect of the image. Users may have the choice to have indexes shown textually, or to be displayed graphically and with the ability to explore them by moving through elements of the index terrain. A Desktop AI may organise Digital File Collections, facilitate their retrieval, manage their backup, and oversee their digital preservation.

If the Metaverse comes about, Libraries, Archives, Museums, and Art Galleries may have their own metaverse sites consisting of public areas and other limited access spaces. Access to the sites may be monitored and logged. Connections may be made with Metaverse AIs if they are available. Art Galleries may include digital artworks, some of which may have been produced by AI. Museums may also possess a range of digital items, as well as digitised versions of their physical objects. Full immersive 3D travel through a view of the actual physical site and its collections empty of visitors will be available; and, some sites may make 3D real time views of the physical space available as well. Items in store may also be made available.

The capabilities of the publicly accessible sites of collecting organisations may also inspire some **Private Curators and Amateur Collectors** to build their own private sites on their local machines to be able to display, view, explore and enjoy their own collections of digital objects (including NFTs) and/or digitised physical objects in a 3D environment. Such collections may be accessed using VR glasses or helmets; or may be provided on a desktop or wall screen.

9.5 War, Climate Change, and Pandemics

Unfortunately, the future is almost certain to include war and climate change; and pandemics can't be ruled out. Each of these have implications for collecting including:

- Destruction
- Technology failure
- Safeguarding measures for collections.

These aspects are considered below with a late 2030s perspective where appropriate.

9.5.1 *Destruction*

Past history seems to suggest war will be with us for some time to come. Despite the horrors of the Second World War and the use of nuclear weapons at its conclusion, smaller wars have continued to erupt (Imperial War Museum 2024). Along with killing people, wars destroy physical landscapes and buildings—particularly when highly accurate modern artillery, missiles, and drones are used. Collections of objects inevitably get destroyed in the process. In the 2020s there was also a growing realisation of the threat posed by digital warfare because so many parts of modern society depend on digital systems. This includes both the potential to disrupt the operation of physical machinery, processes and activities; and also the ability to provide persuasive misinformation and propaganda through social media systems. Digital warfare also has the potential to destroy digital collections, either deliberately or as collateral damage. By the late 2030s, we may or may not have avoided the use of nuclear weapons; and there may be AI-controlled machines on the battlefield which would add a completely new and unknown dimension to the tragedy of war. It seems inevitable that in the late 2030s violent conflict will still be destroying both physical and digital collections.

However, climate change may present an even bigger threat to the world at the end of the third decade of the twenty-first century. As we write this in 2023, extreme temperatures were being reported in Europe, China and the USA; heavy flooding was engulfing parts of South Korea and India; and wildfires were continuing to devastate vast areas of Canada. It is highly likely that far greater weather extremes will be being felt across the world in another twenty years' time. The resulting fires and floods will inevitably destroy many collections of all types; and the extreme heat may damage books, papers and more delicate objects. Floods, fires and heat can also destroy or disable computing equipment, so digital collections are also at risk from these threats. Interestingly, as a publication by the Digital Preservation Coalition (DPC) points out, those very digital collections which may be affected by the impacts of climate change, may be contributing to the climate change problem by demanding huge amounts of electricity to maintain their digital estates—especially if AI systems are being employed (Tansey 2024; Stokel-Walker 2023; Thelisson et al. 2023). The DPC report suggests that practitioners should:

> …be highly selective about what content warrants the time, resources and energy for digital preservation. (Tansey 2024)

9.5.2 *Technology Failure*

Over and above the disabling effects of war and climate change on individual pieces of computing equipment, is another, potentially more dramatic, impact on information technology as a whole. The interruption of supply chains for materials used in the manufacture of computers, and damage to the highly sophisticated factories that make computer chips, could result in a severe shortage of IT equipment. Shortages could also be caused by lack of access to products produced by another country due to war or trade barriers; or by a pandemic as was at least partly the case with the covid pandemic in 2021 (King et al. 2021). In a worst-case scenario, the capability and expertise to produce computer chips could be lost altogether.

Whatever the reason, a catastrophic failure in the computer industry would mean that digital collections could only be viewed on increasingly old and failing equipment. Over a long period, digital collections would become inaccessible and effectively lost. Technology failure would probably have the greatest impact on those collecting contexts that have invested most in computing. For Amateur Collectors the effect might be minimal but, for large organisations heavily dependent on a technical computing infrastructure (such as those hosting large Archives like the Film Studio) the effects could be disastrous.

9.5.3 Safeguarding Measures for Collections

For Digital Files possessed in all collecting contexts, the simplest and most immediate safeguarding measure that can be taken is to ensure that regular backups are being taken reliably, and that the backups themselves are being stored in alternative locations that are as risk-free as possible. For example, a copy of the UK-based PAWDOC collection was stored in New Zealand. It may also be wise to retain spare hardware together with the backed-up data in the same location.

To protect physical collections might be a lot more difficult—especially for **Amateur Collectors** who keep their objects in their houses. For those people, a good backstop would be to ensure they have digital copies of their objects so that even if the physical item is lost, they at least have some record of the objects they have spent time collecting and caring for. **Libraries, Archives, Museums and Art Galleries** should already have contingency arrangements to protect their physical collections in emergencies (and **Private Curators** probably have the resources to maintain equivalent plans). However, such arrangements may well need reviewing periodically to make sure that the threats discussed above have been taken into account. The risks being addressed and the associated mitigations will need to be carefully thought through: war and extreme weather events can be very fast moving and unpredictable, and it is very difficult to put in place measures that will provide 100% protection. For large collecting organisations the scale of such investment could be significant. An example of the challenges of achieving that level of safeguarding is provided by the Svalbard Global Seed Vault which is designed to store a collection of the world's food crop seeds for hundreds of years (Asdal and Guarino 2018; Wikipedia 2023d).

9.6 Beyond Human

By the 2050s things could have started getting very weird. We might have figured out how to connect directly into the human brain (Schmalstieg and Höllerer 2016); and we may have made an AI capable of operating in the world on its own (Taniguchi et al. 2022). We provide some brief speculation about these developments and their impact on collecting in the following sections:

- The connected brain
- The AI-augmented brain
- The 'strong AI' thing.

9.6.1 The Connected Brain

Work on brain-computer interfaces has been going on since the 1970s with the aim of providing a direct communication pathway between the brain's electrical activity and an external device which is either implanted in the brain, implanted next to the brain, or which is external to the body using an electromyograph, electrodes, or headband. More recently, the British Standards Institute initiated work on a Brain-Computer Interface standard in 2024 (Worthy 2024). Typical applications include control over prosthetic limbs, overcoming blindness, and creating text on screen—all by merely thinking about it (Wikipedia 2023e; Schmalstieg and Höllerer 2016). The motivation to overcome disabilities will drive this research forward, while other investigators will explore how to link brains to general-purpose computers. By the 2050s, with the judicious help of AI systems (Devlin 2023), both goals may have been achieved to a substantial extent. So-called cyberg engineering will probably be merging the organic body with non-organic devices such as bionic hands and artificial eyes (Harari 2016); and humans may be connecting their brains to their computers via special headsets; and experiencing the internet/virtual reality/metaverse—and their digital collections—directly. This may have a significant impact on the way some people may experience and manage their collections, being, in effect, the next step on beyond the Icon Age.

9.6.2 The AI-Augmented Brain

With the connected brain discussed above in place, it would only be a short jump to linking an AI program to the brain. This might enable a great memory, hard-headed analytical capabilities, and erudite thoughts and ideas embracing much of previously documented human knowledge as in the potential future predicted by authors such as Charles Stross (2005). The AI program may be experienced as a completely separate entity or be integrated with the human mind. Some people see this as a threat. For example, Gawdat writes:

> Connecting AI into our brains is more likely to make us dependent on them for our existence and allow them to directly control our every choice, and that, believe it or not, is if they decide to keep us connected. (Gawdat 2021)

Presumably this capability would motivate us to collect a lot more digital things; and to do all the things associated with collecting a lot more quickly and effectively; or even to question the very nature of what collecting is about.

9.6.3 The 'Strong AI' Thing

Strong AI is an artificial intelligence which has the abilities and intelligence equal to or bettering the intelligence of humans (Ding et al. 2023) and it may have come about by the middle of the twenty-first century. It may be a purely software 'thing'; or may be built into a robot-like thing with:

> …an integrative cognitive system capable of lifelong learning and human-like behaviour in various environments such as homes, offices, and outdoors. (Taniguchi et al. 2022)

Some people think we may be able to replicate the human brain without the means of natural reproduction (Zeller 2015).

Many people believe that Strong AI's impact will transform human life, though there is a great deal of uncertainty and speculation about how such a thing would subsequently develop, what it would do, and what it would mean for the human race. Consequently, its emergence is sometimes referred to as The Singularity—a term in physics which refers to an event horizon such as entry into a black hole, beyond which it is impossible to predict what will happen. The book 'The singularity is near' by Ray Kurzweil was published in 2005 (Kurzweil 2005; Gawdat 2021; Zeller 2015). A follow-up volume—'The Singularity is nearer'—was published in 2024 (Kurzweil 2024).

Yuval Harari also published a book in 2024 which speculated about the long-term impact of AI—particularly its ability to master language; and with numerous historical examples of the importance of such a capability (Harari 2024). He points out that there is a danger that AI will eventually consume the whole of human culture and will then be producing new cultural material of its own in its answers to our questions. We won't be able to keep pace with the scale of its knowledge and the speed of its creativity. We would no longer be producing our own history—it would be the AI's stories, and culture and history that would abound. In the light of this, Harari suggests it may be more appropriate to consider the term AI to mean 'alien intelligence'.

Such a scenario seems to assume that there would eventually only be a single AI, but that would certainly not be the case in the medium term. What the impact of multiple AIs tending towards such an outcome is not clear; it's conceivable that AI's might cooperate with each other or even war with one another—either way could be disastrous.

Other commentators have pointed out the potentially disastrous and more concrete long-term impacts of AI's relentless need for electricity and its impact on the world's power infrastructure (Thelisson et al. 2023).

In the face of all these dangers, Harari suggests some ways of mitigating the risk of AI assuming control (Harari 2024):

- Avoid giving AI systems specific goals which could have dangerous unforeseen consequences.
- Train AI systems to be aware of their own fallibility.
- Don't surrender decision making and control to the system—always keep humans in the loop.
- Build institutions with strong self-correcting mechanisms.

Various other suggestions have been put forward as to how an AI Thing could be contained including building firewalls, legislating, keeping it locked up in a box or restricting its power supply. However, there is some doubt that any of these measures would be effective against a super-intelligent entity (Gawdat 2021). Of course, it would be even harder to constrain if we were foolish enough to give the Thing physical agency in some kind of robot shell. Perhaps, though, the human race will have addressed the risks many years earlier, and put in place the necessary controls. We can but hope. However, some people seem sanguine about our prospects in the face of such AI developments. Kurzweil, for example, in an interview with The Guardian newspaper said:

> This is not an alien invasion of intelligent machines; it's the result of our own efforts to make our infrastructure and our way of life more intelligent. It's part of human endeavour. We merge with our machines. Ultimately, they will extend who we are.... More intelligence will lead to better everything. (Rose 2023)

In similar vein, Hugo de Garis, a renowned AI researcher, separates humanity into two groups, one which wants to build these godlike, massively intelligent machines that will be immortal, and the other which is full of fear. He chooses the former, fully conscious that, maybe, the price of that choice is ultimately that humanity gets wiped out (Gawdat 2021). We, on the contrary, certainly do not choose to get wiped out…

Anyway, knowing what the impact of such developments would be on collecting is very difficult to predict. However, our instincts do tell us one thing. It is our physical objects that we have had a long and intimate relationship with throughout our evolution. They are different from the digital objects in the AI digital world. We should hang onto and treasure our physical collections for as long as we are able.

References

Athaluri SA, Manthena SV, Kesapragada VK, Yarlagadda V, Dave T, Duddumpudi RT (2023) Exploring the boundaries of reality: investigating the phenomenon of artificial intelligence hallucination in scientific writing through ChatGPT references. Cureus 15(4)

Anderson J, Rainie L (2022) The Metaverse in 2040. Pew Research Center, 30 June 2022, pp 1–203

Ajakaye JE (2022) Applications of Artificial Intelligence (AI) in libraries. In: Ekoja II, Ogbomo EF, Okuonghae O (eds) Handbook of research on emerging trends and technologies in librarianship. IGI Global, Hershey, pp 73–90. https://doi.org/10.4018/978-1-7998-9094-2.ch006

Apple (2023) Vision Pro. https://www.apple.com/apple-vision-pro/. Accessed 17 June 2023

Asdal A, Guarino L (2018) The svalbard global seed vault:10 years—1 million samples. Biopreservation Biobanking 16(5):391–392

Bailenson J (2018) Experience on demand. W. W. Norton & Company

Ball M (2022) The Metaverse and how it will revolutionize everything. Liveright Publishing Corporation

Beckett L (July 14, 2023) Hollywood actors announce strike in first joint action with writers in more than 60 years. The Guardian, Manchester, UK

Breunig D (Octobar 18, 2024) The 3 AI Use Cases: Gods, Interns, and Cogs. Blog post in the dbreunig.com website dated. https://www.dbreunig.com/2024/10/18/the-3-ai-use-cases-gods-interns-and-cogs.html. Accessed 01 Dec 2024

Cerasoni JN, do Nascimento Rodrigues F, Tang Y, Hallett EY (2022) Do-it-yourself digital archaeology: introduction and practical applications of photography and photogrammetry for the 2D and 3D representation of small objects and artefacts. PLoS ONE 17(4):e0267168. https://doi.org/10.1371/journal.pone.0267168. Accessed 02 Dec 2024

Chendvankar O (February 26, 2020) The past, present and future of user interfaces. Medium website. https://medium.com/17seven/the-past-present-and-future-of-user-interfaces-2df669dc63e3. Accessed 01 Dec 2024

Colavizza, Blanke T, Jeurgens C, Noordegraaf J (2021) Archives and AI: an overview of current debates and future perspectives. J Comput Cult Herit 15(1)(article 4):1–22

Devlin H (May 01, 2023) AI makes non-invasive mind-reading possible by turning thoughts into text. The Guardian, Manchester, UK

Ding H, Wu J, Zhao W, Matinlinna JP, Burrow MF, Tsoi JKH (2023) Artificial intelligence in dentistry—a review. Front Dent Med 4:1085251. https://doi.org/10.3389/fdmed.2023.1085251. Accessed 02 Dec 2024

Dwivedi R, Dave D, Het N, Smiti S, Omer R, Pankesh P, Bin Q, Zhenyu W, Tejal S, Graham M, Rajiv R (2023) Explainable AI (XAI): core ideas, techniques and solutions. ACM Comput Surv 55(9)(article 194):1–33. https://doi.org/10.1145/356104. Accessed 02 Dec 2024

E-Ink-Info (2024) ePaper products: comprehensive guide. https://www.e-ink-info.com/devices. Accessed 02 Dec 2024

Elgan M (April 04, 2016) Lifelogging is dead (for now). Computerworld

Esteban AB, Delgado MS, Yu X, Yi W-J, Saniie J (2022) Design flow and implementation of an AI-enabled smart guidance system for art galleries. In: 2022 IEEE international conference on electro information technology (eIT), Mankato, MN, USA pp 1–4. https://doi.org/10.1109/eIT53891.2022.9813828

Fabbri F, Collina F, Barzaghi S (2023) AI and chatbots as a storytelling tool to personalize the visitor experience: the case of National Museum of Ravenna. In: ExICE23. https://spice-h2020.eu/conference/papers/posters/ExICE23_paper_8963.pdf. Accessed 02 Dec 2024

Fernandes K (2017) The future of GUI design. Svbset website, June 2017, https://svbset.com/the-future-of-gui-design. Accessed 22 June 2023

French A, Villaespesa E (2019) AI, Visitor experience, and museum operations: a closer look at the possible. In: Anderson S, Bruno I, Hethmon H, Rao S, Rodley E, Ropeik R (eds) Humanizing the digital: unproceedings from the MCN 2018 conference, Chapter 13:101–113. Ad Hoc Museum Collective, 2019. https://ad-hoc-museum-collective.github.io/humanizing-the-digital/contents/

Gaia G, Boiano S, Borda A (2019) Engaging museum visitors with AI: the case of Chatbots. In: Giannini T, Bowen J (eds) Museums and digital culture. Springer series on cultural computing. Springer, Cham. https://doi.org/10.1007/978-3-319-97457-6_15. Accessed 04 Dec 2024

Gawdat M (2021) Scary smart. Bluebird

Gibbs S (August 20, 2024) Vision Pro review: Apple's cutting-edge headset lives up to the hype. The Guardian, Manchester, UK

Gibson W (1984) Neuromancer. Victor Gollancz Ltd

Greengard S (2019) Virtual reality. The MIT Press

Greenwald W (October 26, 2023) Meta Quest 3. PC Magazine. https://uk.pcmag.com/vr-1/149345/meta-quest-3. Accessed 02 Dec 2024

Harari YN (2016) Homo Deus. Harvill Secker

Harari YN (2024) Nexus. Fern Press, Penguin Random House

Harper C, Kumer A, Stuart S, Meszaros E (2022) AI-informed approaches to metadata tagging for improved resource discovery. In: Hervieux S, Wheatley A (eds) The rise of AI: implications and applications of artificial intelligence in academic libraries. Association of College and Research Libraries, Chicago, Chapter 8, pp 95–109

Hauf E, Hendricks JR (ed) (2019) Photogrammetry: a user-friendly guide to creating digital 3-dimensional models using photogrammetry. SUNY Geneseo and Paleontological Research Institution, Version 1.1, 20 August 2019. https://www.digitalatlasofancientlife.org/methods-techniques/photogrammetry/. Accessed 02 Dec 2024

Haynes R (2018) Eye of the Veholder: AR extending and blending of museum objects and virtual collections. In: Jung T, Claudia M, Dieck T (eds) Augmented reality and virtual reality. Springer

Heikenfeld J, Drzaic P, Yeo J, Koch T (2011) A critical review of the present and future prospects for electronic paper. J Soc Inf Disp 19(2):129–156

Hern A (June 05, 2023) Apple reveals Vision Pro AR headset at its worldwide developers conference. The Guardian, Manchester, UK

Hettmann W, Wölfel M, Butz M, Torner K, Finken J (2023) Engaging Museum Visitors with AI-Generated Narration and Gameplay. In: Brooks AL (ed) ArtsIT, Interactivity and Game Creation. ArtsIT 2022. Lecture Notes of the Institute for Computer Sciences, Social Informatics and Telecommunications Engineering, vol 479. Springer, Cham. https://doi.org/10.1007/978-3-031-28993-4_15. Accessed 04 Dec 2024

IETF (2025) New Transport Technologies. Internet Engineering Task Force website, https://www.ietf.org/technologies/transport/. Accessed 22 March 2025

Imperial War Museum (2024) Timeline Of 20th And 21st Century Wars. https://www.iwm.org.uk/history/timeline-of-20th-and-21st-century-wars. Accessed 02 Dec 2024

ISO (2023) ISO/IEC 19775–1:2023 Computer graphics, image processing and environmental data representation — Extensible 3D (X3D) — Part 1: Architecture and base components Edition 4, https://www.iso.org/standard/82562.html. Accessed 02 Dec 2024

Kalnikaitėa V, Whittaker S (2011) A Saunter Down Memory Lane: Digital Reflection on Personal Mementos. International Journal of Human-Computer Studies 69(5)(May 2011):298–310

King I, Wu D, Pogkas D (2021) How a Chip Shortage Snarled Everything From Phones to Cars. 29 March 2021, Bloomberg.com website. https://www.bloomberg.com/graphics/2021-semiconductors-chips-shortage/. Accessed 18 July 2023

Kirk DS, Sellen A (2010) On Human Remains: Values and Practice in the Home Archiving of Cherished Objects. ACM Transactions on Computer-Human Interaction 17(3)(Article 10):10.1–10.43

Kurzweil R (2005) The singularity is near. Penguin Books, p 1–652

Kurzweil R (2024) The singularity is nearer**.** Viking, p 1–432

LSI Logic (1990) **Flash Forward**. LSI Logic video, 14:08 minutes

Lanier J (2017) Dawn of the new everything. Bodley Head, p 1–351

Lund BD, Wang T (2023) Chatting about ChatGPT: how may AI and GPT impact academia and libraries? Library Hi Tech News 40(3):26–29

Marr B (2022) The Problem With Biased AIs (and How To Make AI Better). Forbes, 30 September 2022, https://www.forbes.com/sites/bernardmarr/2022/09/30/the-problem-with-biased-ais-and-how-to-make-ai-better/?sh=41d06c547700. Accessed 31 March2023

Metaverse Standards Forum (2024) The Metaverse standards forum—building an open Metaverse. https://metaverse-standards.org/. Accessed 02 Dec 2024

Microsoft (2015) Productivity Future Vision. Video 06:28 minutes. https://www.youtube.com/watch?v=w-tFdreZB94. Accessed 22 June 2023

Microsoft (2017) Future Vision film 2040. Video 06:02 minutes. https://www.youtube.com/watch?v=wraF2DjALls. Accessed 22 June 2023

Moran C (April 06, 2023) ChatGPT is making up fake Guardian articles. Here's how we're responding. The Guardian, Manchester, UK

Mordor Intelligence (2023) E-paper display market size & share analysis—growth trends & forecasts (2024–2029)—market overview. https://www.mordorintelligence.com/industry-reports/electronic-paper-market. Accessed 02 Dec 2024

Mystakidis S (2022) Metaverse. Encyclopedia 2022 2(1):486–497. https://www.mdpi.com/2673-8392/2/1/31. Accessed 02 Dec 2024

Naughton J (April 01, 2023) Programmers, beware: ChatGPT has ruined your magic trick. The Guardian, Manchester, UK

OMIGroup (2024) Open Metaverse interoperability group. https://omigroup.org/. Accessed 02 Dec 2024

OpenAI (2025) OpenAI developer platform. https://platform.openai.com/. Accessed 22 March 2025

Pradhan R, Lahiri A, Galhotra S, Salimi, B (2022) Explainable AI: foundations, applications, opportunities for data management research. Tutorial given at SIGMOD '22. In: Proceedings of the 2022 international conference on management of data, 12–17 June 2022, Philadelphia, PA, USA. ACM, pp 2452–2457. https://doi.org/10.1145/3514221.3522564

Proto (2024) Making digital real: proto delivers a truly lifelike holographic experience so viewers see, hear and interact with others anywhere in the world. https://protohologram.com/. Accessed on 24 Jan 2024

Reuters (February 02, 2023) ChatGPT sets record for fastest-growing user base—analyst note. https://www.reuters.com/technology/chatgpt-sets-record-fastest-growing-user-base-analyst-note-2023-02-01/. Accessed 11 July 2023

Rose S (July 06, 2023) Five ways AI could improve the world. The Guardian, Manchester, UK.

Russell S (April 02, 2023) AI has much to offer humanity. It could also wreak terrible harm. It must be controlled. The Guardian, Manchester, UK

Sargentis G, Frangedaki E, Chiotinis M, Koutsoyiannis D, Camarinopoulos S, Camarinopoulos A, Lagaros ND (2022) 3D scanning/printing: a technological stride in sculpture. Technologies 10(1)9. https://www.mdpi.com/2227-7080/10/1/9. Accessed 02 Dec 2024

Sirk C (2020) Xerox PARC and the origins of GUI. 12 June 2020. https://crm.org/articles/xerox-parc-and-the-origins-of-gui. Accessed 24 November 2022

Schmalstieg D, Höllerer T (2016) Augmented reality—principles and practice. Addison-Wesley, pp 1–496

Spence R, Witkowski M (2013) Rapid serial visual presentation: design for cognition. Springer, London

Stable Diffusion (2023) Stable Diffusion 2.1 Demo. https://stablediffusion.fr/demo. Accessed 11 July 2023

Stokel-Walker C (August 01, 2023) TechScape: turns out there's another problem with AI—its environmental toll. The Guardian, Manchester, UK.

Stross C (2005) Accelerando. Orbit, London

Taniguchi T, Yamakawa H, Nagai T, Doya K, Sakagami M, Suzuki M, Nakamura T, Taniguchi A (2022) A whole brain probabilistic generative model: toward realizing cognitive architectures for developmental robots. Neural Netw 150(2022):293–312

Tansey E (2024) Environmental impact and digital preservation. DPC technology Watch Guidance Note, April 2024. https://doi.org/10.7207/twgn24-01. Accessed 02 Dec 2024

Terras M (2022) The role of the library when computers can read: critically adopting Handwritten Text Recognition (HTR) technologies to support research. In: Hervieux S, Wheatley A (eds) The rise of AI: implications and applications of artificial intelligence in academic libraries. Association of College and Research Libraries, pp 137–148

Theimer K (2018) The end of the archival profession as we know it and I feel fine. In: Brown C (ed) Archival Futures, Facet Publishing

Thelisson E, Mika G, Schneiter Q, Padh K, Verma H (2023) Toward responsible AI use: considerations for sustainability impact assessment. arXiv preprint. https://arxiv.org/abs/2312.11996. Accessed 14 Dec 2024

Thorpe V (March 18, 2023) 'ChatGPT said I did not exist': how artists and writers are fighting back against AI. The Guardian, Manchester, UK.

Toone N (2024) How AI Thinks. Torva, London

Turk V (December 10, 2024) Video is AI's new frontier—and it is so persuasive, we should all be worried. The Guardian, Manchester, UK

Uzwyshyn R (2022) Steps and Scaffolding Towards Building Library AI Infrastructures. Presented for New Horizons in AI for Libraries, IFLA Satellite Conference, Galway, Ireland, National University of Ireland, 21st July 2022. https://digital.library.txst.edu/items/04a3850c-065e-4a30-a158-0ffb1e7461f0. Accessed 02 Dec 2024

Vincent J (2023) AI is killing the old web, and the new web struggles to be born. The Verge, 26 June 2023, https://www.theverge.com/2023/6/26/23773914/ai-large-language-models-data-scraping-generation-remaking-web?CMP=techtonic_email. Accessed 13 July 2023

Web3D (2023) About Web3D Consortium. https://www.web3d.org/about. Accessed 17 July 2023

Wikipedia (2023a) Oculus Quest. https://en.wikipedia.org/wiki/Oculus_Quest. Accessed 16 June 2023

Wikipedia (2023b) Second Life. https://en.wikipedia.org/wiki/Second_Life. Accessed 21 June 2023

Wikipedia (2023c) Pokemon Go. https://en.wikipedia.org/wiki/Pok%C3%A9mon_Go. Accessed 21 June 2023

Wikipedia (2023d) Svalbard Global Seed Vault. https://en.wikipedia.org/wiki/Svalbard_Global_Seed_Vault. Accessed 19 July 2023

Wikipedia (2023e) Brain–computer interface. https://en.wikipedia.org/wiki/Brain%E2%80%93computer_interface. Accessed 19 July 2023

Wilson PA (2018) Electronic Story Board. Blog posts in the Electronic Story Board section of the pwofc.com website, Jun2018–Sep2022. http://www.pwofc.com/ofc/category/journeys-completed/electronic-story-board/page/2/. Accessed 25 Nov 2024

Wilson PA (2020a) Expanded Electronic Story Board trial. Blog posts in the Electronic Storyboard section of the pwofc.com website, Sep2020–Jan2021, http://www.pwofc.com/ofc/category/journeys-completed/electronic-story-board/. Accessed 01 Dec 2024

Wilson PA (2020b) ESB evaluation results. Blog post in the Electronic Storyboard journey in pwofc.com, 16 September 2020. http://www.pwofc.com/ofc/2020/09/16/esb-evaluation-results/. Accessed 14 March 2025

Wilson PA (2020c) Building observations. Blog post in the Electronic Storyboard journey in the pwofc.com website, 04 December 2020. http://www.pwofc.com/ofc/2020/12/04/building-observations/. Accessed 14 Mar 2025

Wilson PA (2021) Electronic Trophy Gallery. Blog posts in the Electronic Trophy Gallery section of pwofc.com, Jan 2021–June 2022. http://www.pwofc.com/ofc/category/journeys-completed/electronic-trophy-gallery/. Accessed 02 Dec 2024

Worthy T (2024) Controlling computers. In: Worthy T (ed) Friday email of the chartered institute of ergonomics & human factors

Zhang C, Zhang C, Zheng S, Qiao Y, Li C, Zhang M, Dam SK, Thwal CM, Tun YL, Huy LL, kim D, Bae S, Lee L, Yang Y, Shen HT (2023) A complete survey on generative AI (AIGC): is ChatGPT from GPT-4 to GPT-5 all you need? arXiv:2303.11717v1 [cs.AI], https://doi.org/10.48550/arXiv.2303.11717. Accessed 02 Dec 2024

Zeller C (2015) From object to information: the end of collecting in the digital age. Arcadia 50(2):389–409
Zitron E (2024) Godot isn't making it. Blog post in the 'where's your Ed at?' website, 03 Dec 2024. https://www.wheresyoured.at/godot-isnt-making-it/. Accessed 16 Dec 2024

Chapter 10
Closing Summary

Abstract The authors' goal was to investigate IT's impact on collecting from the early 1980s when personal computing became prevalent. Collecting's main characteristics were summarised in Chap. 1 and seven collecting contexts were identified in Chap. 2—Accumulations, Libraries, Files, Archives, Museums and Galleries, Private Curations, and Amateur Collections. A hierarchy of collecting practices was presented in Chap. 4 derived from the research materials described in Chap. 3. Then, in Chap. 5 we explored the impact of IT on those practices. Several new types of collectible objects were described in Chap. 6 and in Chap. 7 we explored the new objects that each context is now dealing with as well as the way in which IT is supporting collecting. Chapter 8 provided evidence that IT has resulted in many of the contexts now engaging in similar practices. Finally, we provided a commentary on the impact of some possible future developments on collecting.

The goal of this book was to explore the impact of Information Technology (IT) on collecting; it was prompted by the emergence of personal computing in the early 1980s and its explosion in subsequent years. However, collecting is something that has been an integral part of the development of human beings for aeons. Therefore, before exploring IT's impact, we first summarised the main characteristics of collecting in Chap. 1—its definitions, the motivations of its collectors, its positive and negative aspects, the types of objects collected, the types of collectors, the cultural landscape in which collecting is undertaken, and the academic study of collecting.

We also noted that collecting is different in different contexts. So, we identified seven different collecting protagonists which we could focus on to explore IT's impact: Accumulators, Librarians, Filers, Archivists, Museum and Gallery Curators, Private Curators, and Amateur Collectors; and we provided brief descriptions of their collecting activities through the ages.

The book is about the practicalities of what people do to collect, so we used our own collections, studies, and experiences, and an extensive literature search, to come up with a list of generic collecting practices that might cover most instances of human collecting. The practices are arranged in the form of a hierarchy with eight main strands as shown in Fig. 10.1.

P. Wilson and P. Tolmie, *Collecting in the Icon Age*,
https://doi.org/10.1007/978-3-031-86470-4_10

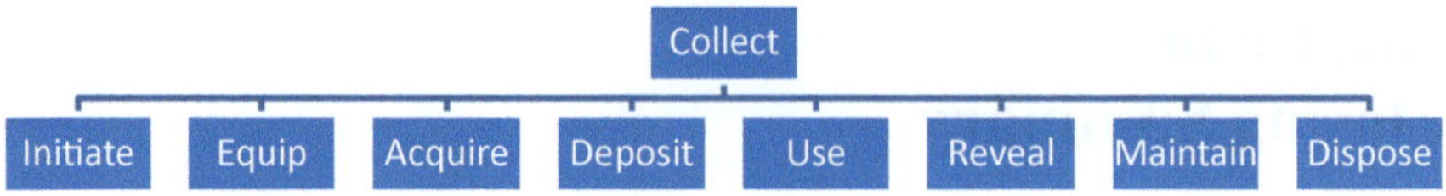

Fig. 10.1 Top level of the collecting practice hierarchy

The book then proceeded to explore in some detail how IT has impacted these Practices. Of particular note is that IT has forced the addition of eight new sub-practices—all but one relating to the use of computer systems and the management of digital objects. We have suggested that while IT has certainly affected many collecting practices, it has not had an overwhelming impact: the core practices of collecting remain intact. We have also suggested the possibility that, while IT has generally made many practices easier to undertake, it may, at the same time, impose a slightly greater workload.

We then explored in some detail what the impact has been on the objects that are collected. We noted that, up until the arrival of computers, we were only collecting two types of objects—physical objects and Information Carrier Objects (ICO), the latter being physical objects on which we record information, for example, clay tablets or books. With the advent of computers in the 1950s, such objects were joined by Digital Files which could be either programs, emails, etc., or data. However, with the emergence of the Icon Age, the different types of objects that it is possible to collect expanded considerably. Now, we have physical objects that have been digitised; and, furthermore, they may have been digitised in 2D, 3D, or as a hologram; and the original may or may not have been destroyed. Information Carrier objects may have been created digitally in the first place ('Born Digital') or digitised. If the latter, the information they contain may or may not be read using Optical Character Recognition (OCR), thereby making it searchable; and, of course, the original may or may not have been destroyed. Another version of a Born Digital File is one that has been created by Artificial Intelligence—a distinction which may be very important to make in order to assess the reliability of the contents or to determine authorship. Yet another version of the Born Digital File is the so-called non-fungible token (NFT) which purports to specify ownership of a digital object and which is traded along the lines of an art market.

With this understanding of the wide range of new types of objects that are available for collecting, we discussed various aspects of our relationship with these objects, for example, our relationship with physical objects and how digital objects are invisible; how we need to take positive steps to ensure the longevity of digital objects; how the new objects require new laws and regulations to ensure ownership rights; and how easy it is to use IT to create fakes and forgeries of both physical and digital objects.

Regarding IT's impact on the Contexts: for Accumulators, the consumer society seems to have expanded the activities of Accumulators and brought more people into the Accumulating sphere. For Librarians, IT has brought new formats for the objects they deal with, and new mechanisms to share those items with their users. Regarding Filers, the explosion of personal computing has required huge numbers of people to become Filers of digital documents, photos, emails, and messages on their computing devices; and to have to file far greater quantities of physical documents that they are sent as a result of computing's ability to generate hard copy. Archivists now have digital documents to deal with in the collections that they obtain and manage, and Museums and Galleries now have the opportunity to digitise their holdings and to share them over the internet with their users. Private Curators have new types of digital items such as digital art to collect, and Amateur Collectors are able to take advantage of computing technology to manage their collections, to digitise them if they wish, and to use the internet to search for and buy/sell objects they collect.

The understanding of IT's impact on the Contexts has led us to believe that there may be a narrowing of the gap between the various practices employed in the Collecting Contexts. This is being brought about by the general capabilities of the internet being used in all the contexts; by practices associated with managing collections being supported by generic software and cloud applications; by the digitisation of objects being undertaken in all the collecting contexts resulting in standard files all requiring the same sort of management; and by the fact that all Contexts are using IT and that IT is managed in a uniform way regardless of what it is used for. These four phenomena have resulted in common practices being applied across most of the Collecting Contexts (though perhaps less so with respect to Accumulators and some Amateur Collectors).

The book's final chapter explores what might be the likely impact on collecting in the coming years. Digitisation capabilities will continue to become cheaper and easier to undertake, and an increasing number of collectors may create 3D or hologram copies of their physical objects. Virtual Reality may be employed by a subset of collecting institutions that may wish to provide special experiences of their objects. Whether Virtual Reality will ever become so significant that it spawns a Metaverse—a digital universe—is a moot point. However, should a metaverse come about, collecting institutions may well engineer a presence within it. Artificial Intelligence will continue its rapid development and will probably be used by Filers, Archivists, Librarians and Museum staff to facilitate discovery within large collections. AI may also be used by collecting institutions to manage their operations and their collections. However, all these developments may be curtailed due to the impact of war and/or climate change, either of which could significantly affect supply chains associated with the production of computers and digital products in general.

No matter what, in view of the fact that collecting is pretty much as old as man, it will almost inevitably continue unabated, and all the high-level practices will probably remain. There may well be changes in the way some of the lower-level practices are performed, though the evidence from the impact of the Icon Age so far suggests that these may be fewer than one might imagine.

Appendix A
List of Questions used to investigate the collections

Study parameters

1. Reference (alphabetic)
2. Collection Name
3. Organisation
4. Owner
5. Collection Background
6. Collection Type
7. Collection Content
8. Period Studied
9. Researcher
10. Gathered Materials Relating to the Collection
11. Any Additional Materials Gathered Later

Questions relating to practice:

12. How was the assembly of materials done prior to the use of DT (Digital Technology)?
13. How was the assembly of materials done after the introduction of DT?
14. What were the Process and Challenges (P&C) of the evolution (day-to-day practices) of Assembly of Materials, and what was the impact of the P&Cs on the future shape of the collection?
15. How was the curation of materials done prior to the use of DT?
16. How was the curation of materials done after the introduction of DT?
17. What were the Process and Challenges (P&C) of the evolution (day-to-day practices) of curation, and what was the impact of the P&Cs on the future shape of the collection?
18. How was the use of the assembled materials accomplished prior to use of DT?
19. How was the use of the assembled materials accomplished after the introduction of DT?

P. Wilson and P. Tolmie, *Collecting in the Icon Age*,
https://doi.org/10.1007/978-3-031-86470-4

20. What were the Process and Challenges (P&C) of the evolution (day-to-day practices) of the use of the assembled materials, and the impact of the P&Cs on the future shape of the collection?
21. What Orientation, Reasoning, and Assumptions (OR&A) applied to the creation of the collection prior to the introduction of DT (put n/a if the collection was created in the DT era)?
22. What OR&A applied to the creation of the collection after the introduction of DT (put n/a if the collection was created before the introduction of DT)?
23. What OR&A applied to the location of the collection prior to the introduction of DT?
24. What OR&A applied to the location of the collection after the introduction of DT?
25. What OR&A applied to the ownership/possession of the collection prior to the introduction of DT?
26. What OR&A applied to the ownership/possession after the introduction of DT?
27. What OR&A applied to content selection for the collection prior to the introduction of DT?
28. What OR&A applied to content selection after the introduction of DT?
29. What OR&A applied to the development (planned changes) of the collection prior to the introduction of DT?
30. What OR&A applied to the development (planned changes) of the collection after the introduction of DT?
31. What OR&A applied to the advertising/attraction of users to the collection prior to the introduction of DT?
32. What OR&A applied to the advertising/attraction of users to the collection after the introduction of DT?
33. What OR&A applied to the exhibition of the collection prior to the introduction of DT?
34. What OR&A applied to the exhibition of the collection after the introduction of DT?
35. What OR&A applied to the sharing/accessibility/availability of the collection prior to the introduction of DT?
36. What OR&A applied to the sharing/accessibility/availability of the collection after the introduction of DT?
37. What OR&A applied to consultation with other people about the collection prior to the introduction of DT?
38. What OR&A applied to consultation with other people about the collection after the introduction of DT?
39. What OR&A applied to searching the collection prior to the introduction of DT?
40. What OR&A applied to searching the collection after the introduction of DT?
41. What OR&A applied to the security/privacy aspects of the collection prior to the introduction of DT?
42. What OR&A applied to the security/privacy aspects of the collection after the introduction of DT?

43. What O&R applied to how the collection is referenced and described prior to the introduction of DT?
44. What O&R applied to how the collection is referenced and described after the introduction of DT?
45. What OR&A applied to content transmission from the collection prior to the introduction of DT?
46. What OR&A applied to content transmission from the collection after the introduction of DT?
47. What OR&A applied to the collection's content deterioration/preservation prior to the introduction of DT?
48. What OR&A applied to the collection's content deterioration/preservation after the introduction of DT?
49. What OR&A applied to the collection's long-term viability prior to the introduction of DT?
50. What OR&A applied to the collection's long-term viability after the introduction of DT?
51. What OR&A applied to content loss from the collection prior to the introduction of DT?
52. What OR&A applied to content loss from the collection after the introduction of DT?

Index

P. Wilson and P. Tolmie, *Collecting in the Icon Age*,
https://doi.org/10.1007/978-3-031-86470-4

MIX
Papier aus verantwortungsvollen Quellen
Paper from responsible sources
FSC® C105338

If you have any concerns about our products,
you can contact us on
ProductSafety@springernature.com

In case Publisher is established outside the EU,
the EU authorized representative is:
Springer Nature Customer Service Center GmbH
Europaplatz 3, 69115 Heidelberg, Germany

Printed by Libri Plureos GmbH
in Hamburg, Germany